PERSEPOLIS 2

PERSEPOLIS 2

MARJANE SATRAPI

PANTHEON

To my parents

L'Association

Pantheon Books and colophon are registered trademarks of Random House, Inc.

Library of Congress Cataloging-in-Publication Data
Satrapi, Marjane, [date]
[Persepolis 2. English]
Persepolis 2 : the story of a return / Marjane Satrapi.
    p.   cm.
Sequel to Persepolis.
ISBN 0-375-42288-9
1. Satrapi, Marjane, 1969–Comic books, strips, etc. I. Title:
Persepolis two. II. Title.
PN6747.S245P4913 2004   741.5'944–dc22   2003070699

www.pantheonbooks.com
Printed in the United States of America
First American Edition
2 4 6 8 9 7 5 3 1

NOVEMBER 1984. I AM IN AUSTRIA. I HAD COME HERE WITH THE IDEA OF LEAVING A RELIGIOUS IRAN FOR AN OPEN AND SECULAR EUROPE AND THAT ZOZO, MY MOTHER'S BEST FRIEND, WOULD LOVE ME LIKE HER OWN DAUGHTER.

ONLY HERE I AM! SHE LEFT ME AT A BOARDING HOUSE RUN BY NUNS.

MY ROOM WAS SMALL, AND FOR THE FIRST TIME IN MY LIFE I HAD TO SHARE MY SPACE WITH ANOTHER PERSON.

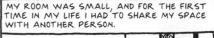

I HADN'T MET HER YET. I ONLY KNEW THAT HER NAME WAS LUCIA.

I WONDERED WHAT SHE WOULD LOOK LIKE.

EUROPE, THE ALPS, SWITZERLAND, AUSTRIA... FROM THIS I DEDUCED THAT SHE WOULD BE LIKE HEIDI.

THIS WAS OKAY WITH ME. I REALLY LIKED HEIDI.

1

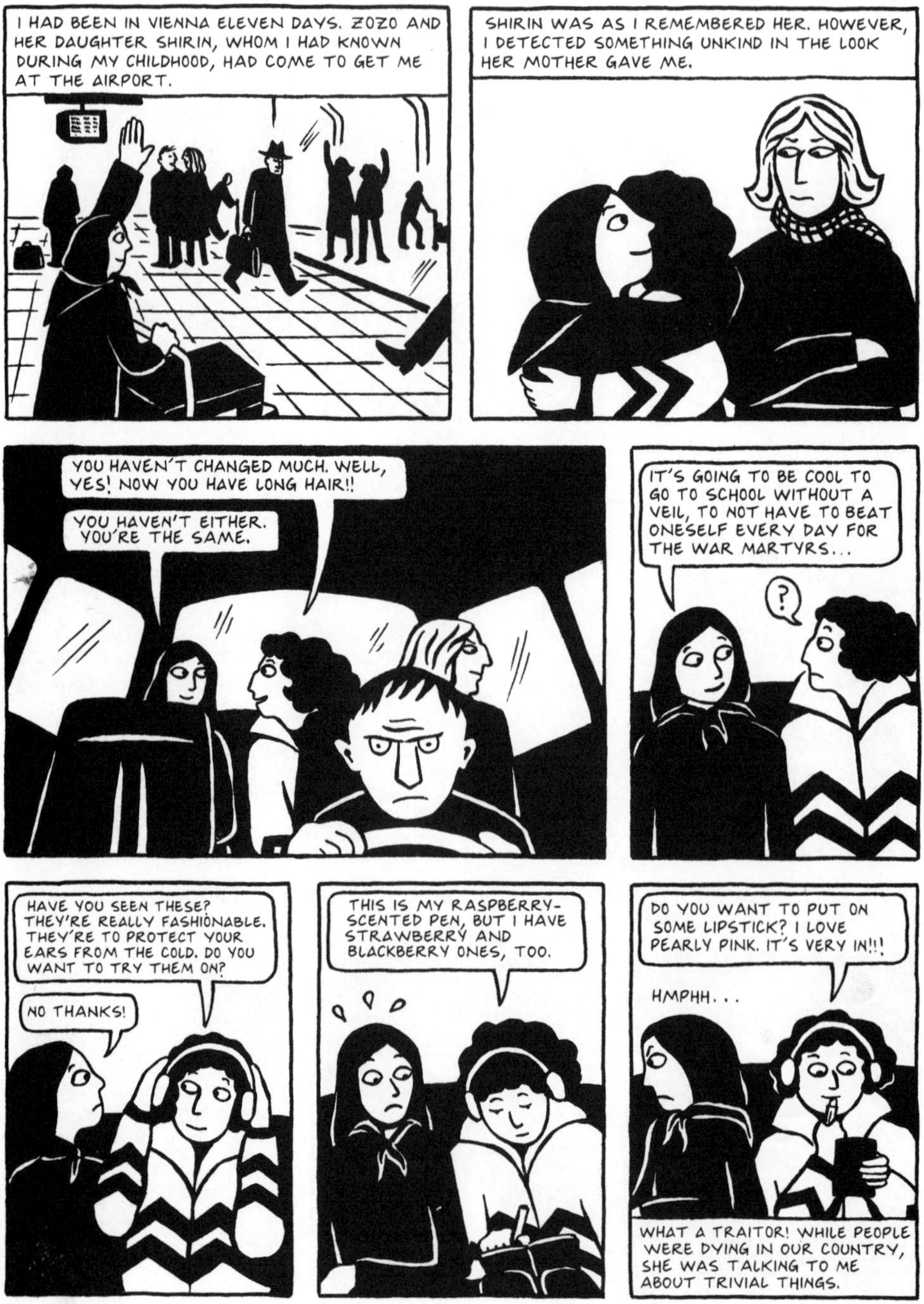
I HAD BEEN IN VIENNA ELEVEN DAYS. ZOZO AND HER DAUGHTER SHIRIN, WHOM I HAD KNOWN DURING MY CHILDHOOD, HAD COME TO GET ME AT THE AIRPORT.
SHIRIN WAS AS I REMEMBERED HER. HOWEVER, I DETECTED SOMETHING UNKIND IN THE LOOK HER MOTHER GAVE ME.
YOU HAVEN'T CHANGED MUCH. WELL, YES! NOW YOU HAVE LONG HAIR!!
YOU HAVEN'T EITHER. YOU'RE THE SAME.
IT'S GOING TO BE COOL TO GO TO SCHOOL WITHOUT A VEIL, TO NOT HAVE TO BEAT ONESELF EVERY DAY FOR THE WAR MARTYRS...
?
HAVE YOU SEEN THESE? THEY'RE REALLY FASHIONABLE. THEY'RE TO PROTECT YOUR EARS FROM THE COLD. DO YOU WANT TO TRY THEM ON?
NO THANKS!
THIS IS MY RASPBERRY-SCENTED PEN, BUT I HAVE STRAWBERRY AND BLACKBERRY ONES, TOO.
DO YOU WANT TO PUT ON SOME LIPSTICK? I LOVE PEARLY PINK. IT'S VERY IN!!!
HMPHH...
WHAT A TRAITOR! WHILE PEOPLE WERE DYING IN OUR COUNTRY, SHE WAS TALKING TO ME ABOUT TRIVIAL THINGS.

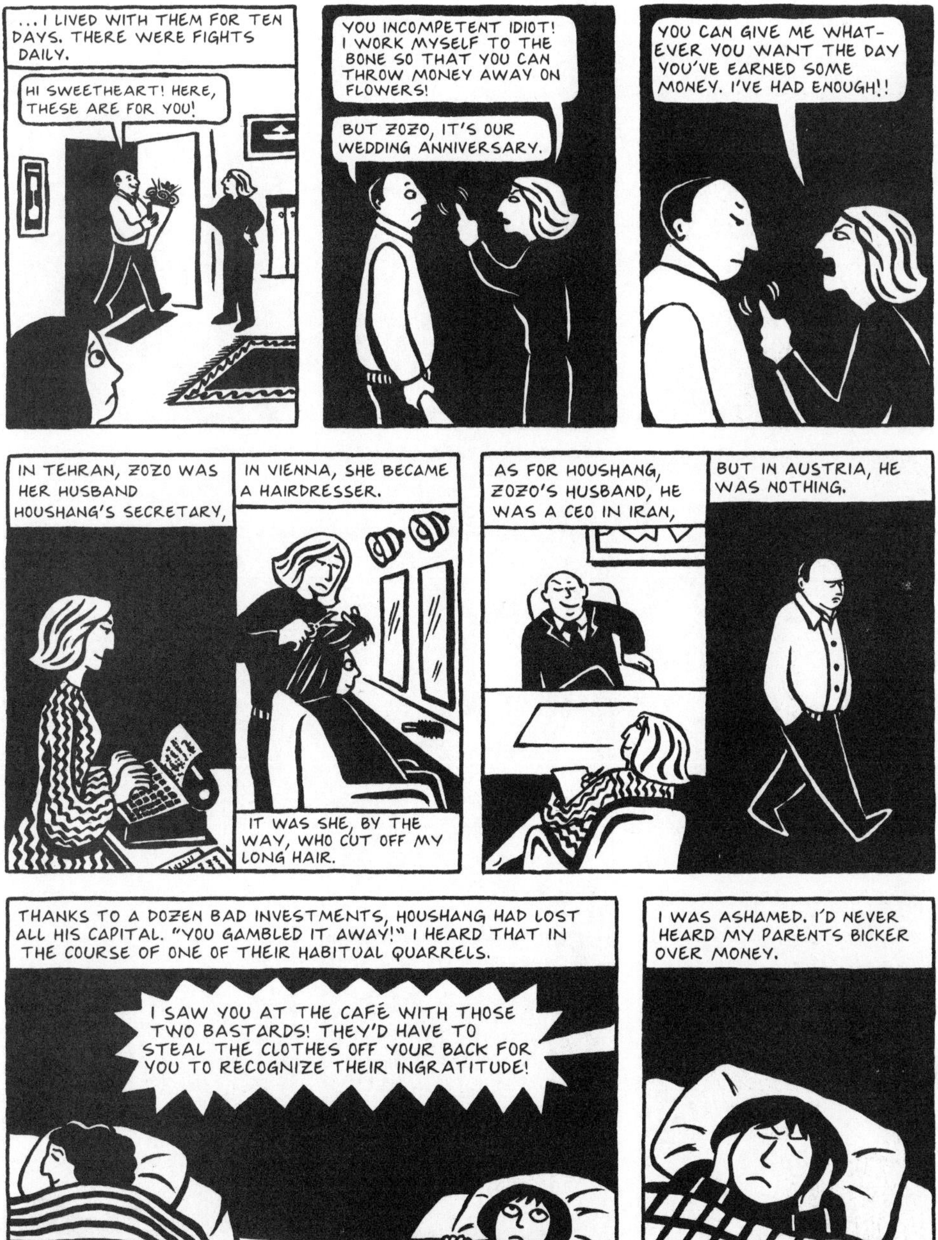
...I LIVED WITH THEM FOR TEN DAYS. THERE WERE FIGHTS DAILY.
HI SWEETHEART! HERE, THESE ARE FOR YOU!
YOU INCOMPETENT IDIOT! I WORK MYSELF TO THE BONE SO THAT YOU CAN THROW MONEY AWAY ON FLOWERS!
BUT ZOZO, IT'S OUR WEDDING ANNIVERSARY.
YOU CAN GIVE ME WHATEVER YOU WANT THE DAY YOU'VE EARNED SOME MONEY. I'VE HAD ENOUGH!!
IN TEHRAN, ZOZO WAS HER HUSBAND HOUSHANG'S SECRETARY,
IN VIENNA, SHE BECAME A HAIRDRESSER.
IT WAS SHE, BY THE WAY, WHO CUT OFF MY LONG HAIR.
AS FOR HOUSHANG, ZOZO'S HUSBAND, HE WAS A CEO IN IRAN,
BUT IN AUSTRIA, HE WAS NOTHING.
THANKS TO A DOZEN BAD INVESTMENTS, HOUSHANG HAD LOST ALL HIS CAPITAL. "YOU GAMBLED IT AWAY!" I HEARD THAT IN THE COURSE OF ONE OF THEIR HABITUAL QUARRELS.
I SAW YOU AT THE CAFÉ WITH THOSE TWO BASTARDS! THEY'D HAVE TO STEAL THE CLOTHES OFF YOUR BACK FOR YOU TO RECOGNIZE THEIR INGRATITUDE!
I WAS ASHAMED. I'D NEVER HEARD MY PARENTS BICKER OVER MONEY.
PROBABLY BECAUSE MY FATHER WASN'T INCOMPETENT...

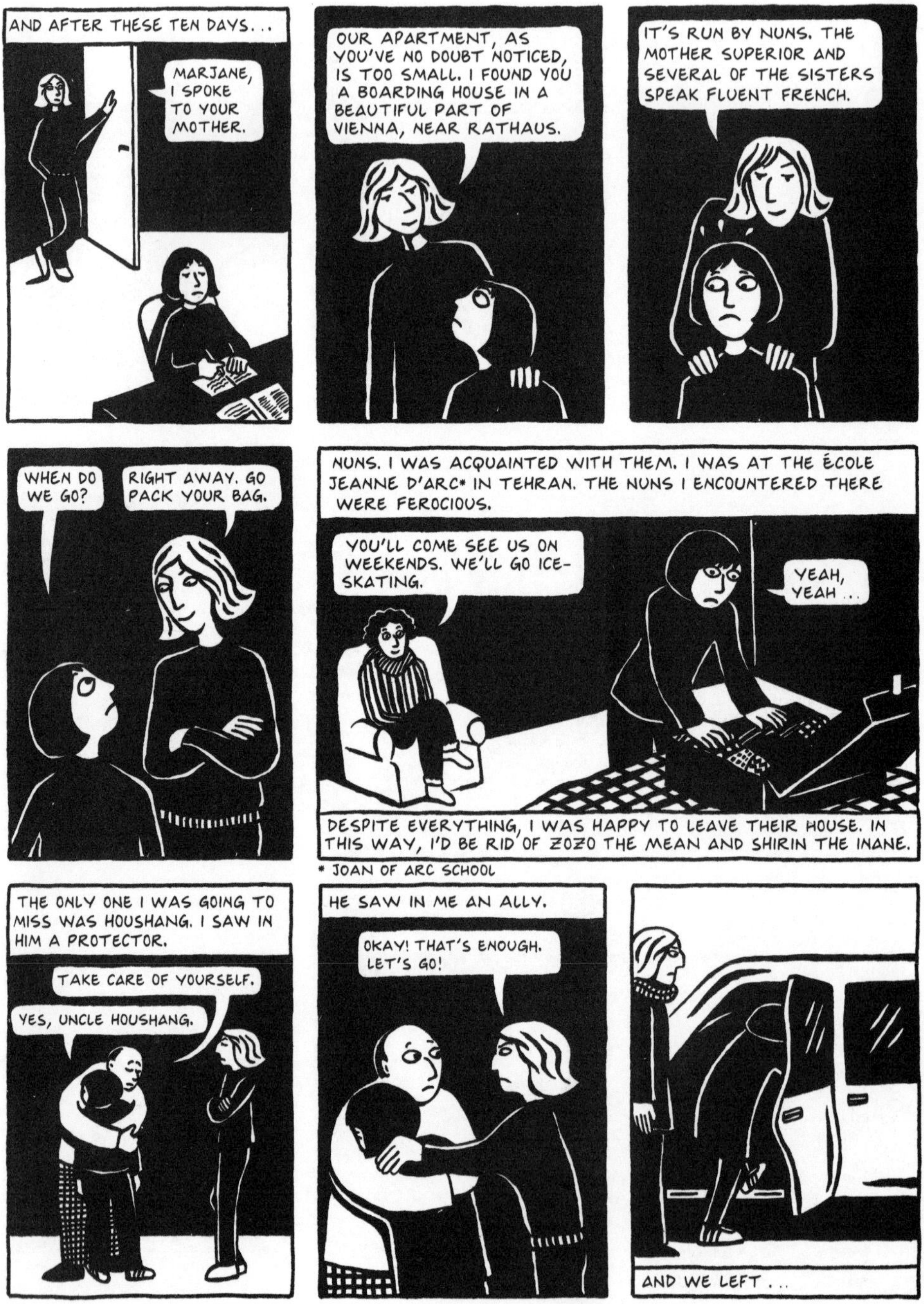
AND AFTER THESE TEN DAYS...
MARJANE, I SPOKE TO YOUR MOTHER.
OUR APARTMENT, AS YOU'VE NO DOUBT NOTICED, IS TOO SMALL. I FOUND YOU A BOARDING HOUSE IN A BEAUTIFUL PART OF VIENNA, NEAR RATHAUS.
IT'S RUN BY NUNS. THE MOTHER SUPERIOR AND SEVERAL OF THE SISTERS SPEAK FLUENT FRENCH.
WHEN DO WE GO?
RIGHT AWAY. GO PACK YOUR BAG.
NUNS. I WAS ACQUAINTED WITH THEM. I WAS AT THE ÉCOLE JEANNE D'ARC* IN TEHRAN. THE NUNS I ENCOUNTERED THERE WERE FEROCIOUS.
YOU'LL COME SEE US ON WEEKENDS. WE'LL GO ICE-SKATING.
YEAH, YEAH...
DESPITE EVERYTHING, I WAS HAPPY TO LEAVE THEIR HOUSE. IN THIS WAY, I'D BE RID OF ZOZO THE MEAN AND SHIRIN THE INANE.
* JOAN OF ARC SCHOOL
THE ONLY ONE I WAS GOING TO MISS WAS HOUSHANG. I SAW IN HIM A PROTECTOR.
TAKE CARE OF YOURSELF.
YES, UNCLE HOUSHANG.
HE SAW IN ME AN ALLY.
OKAY! THAT'S ENOUGH. LET'S GO!
AND WE LEFT...

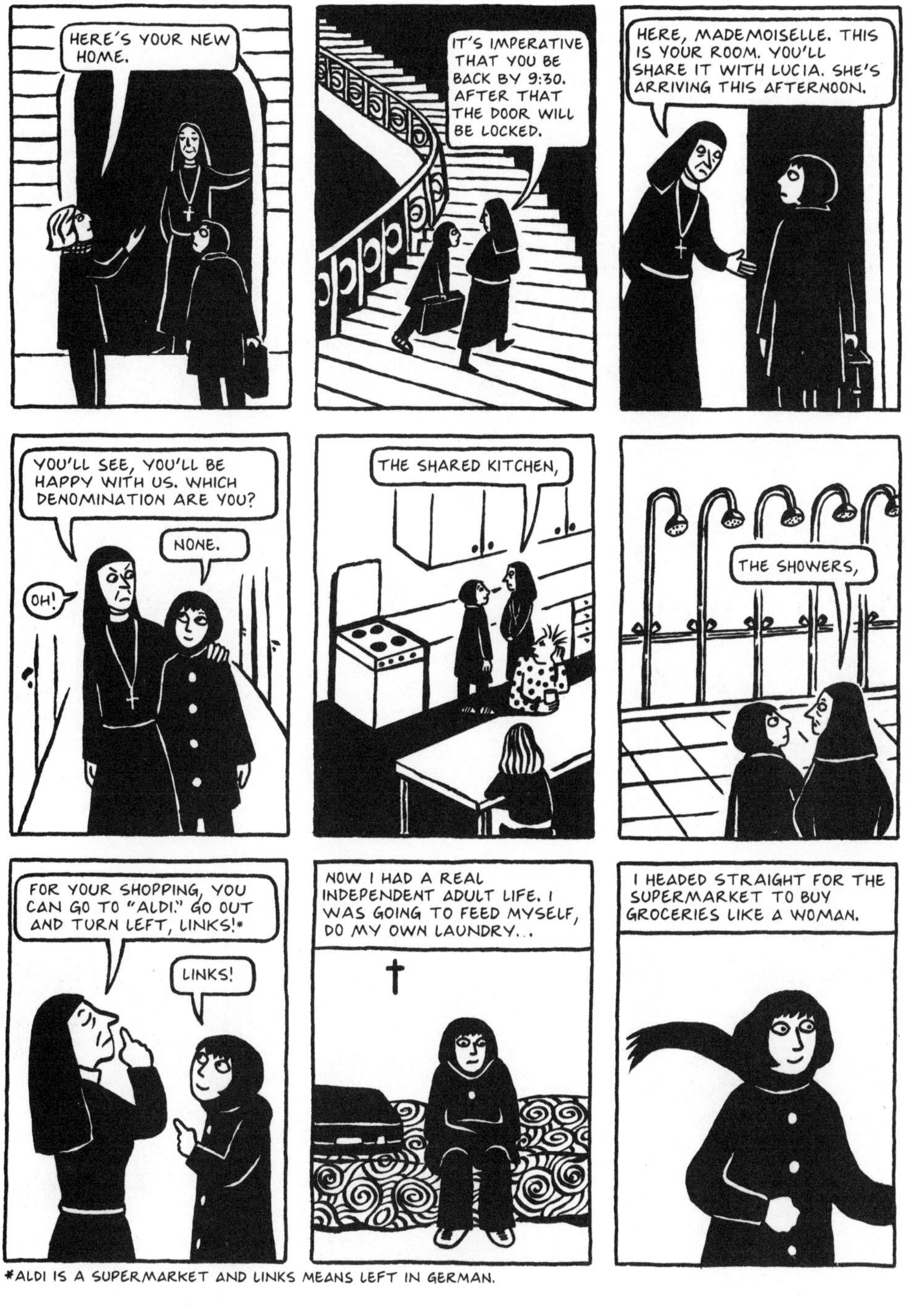
HERE'S YOUR NEW HOME.
IT'S IMPERATIVE THAT YOU BE BACK BY 9:30. AFTER THAT THE DOOR WILL BE LOCKED.
HERE, MADEMOISELLE. THIS IS YOUR ROOM. YOU'LL SHARE IT WITH LUCIA. SHE'S ARRIVING THIS AFTERNOON.
YOU'LL SEE, YOU'LL BE HAPPY WITH US. WHICH DENOMINATION ARE YOU?
NONE.
OH!
THE SHARED KITCHEN,
THE SHOWERS,
FOR YOUR SHOPPING, YOU CAN GO TO "ALDI." GO OUT AND TURN LEFT, LINKS!*
LINKS!
NOW I HAD A REAL INDEPENDENT ADULT LIFE. I WAS GOING TO FEED MYSELF, DO MY OWN LAUNDRY...
I HEADED STRAIGHT FOR THE SUPERMARKET TO BUY GROCERIES LIKE A WOMAN.

*ALDI IS A SUPERMARKET AND LINKS MEANS LEFT IN GERMAN.

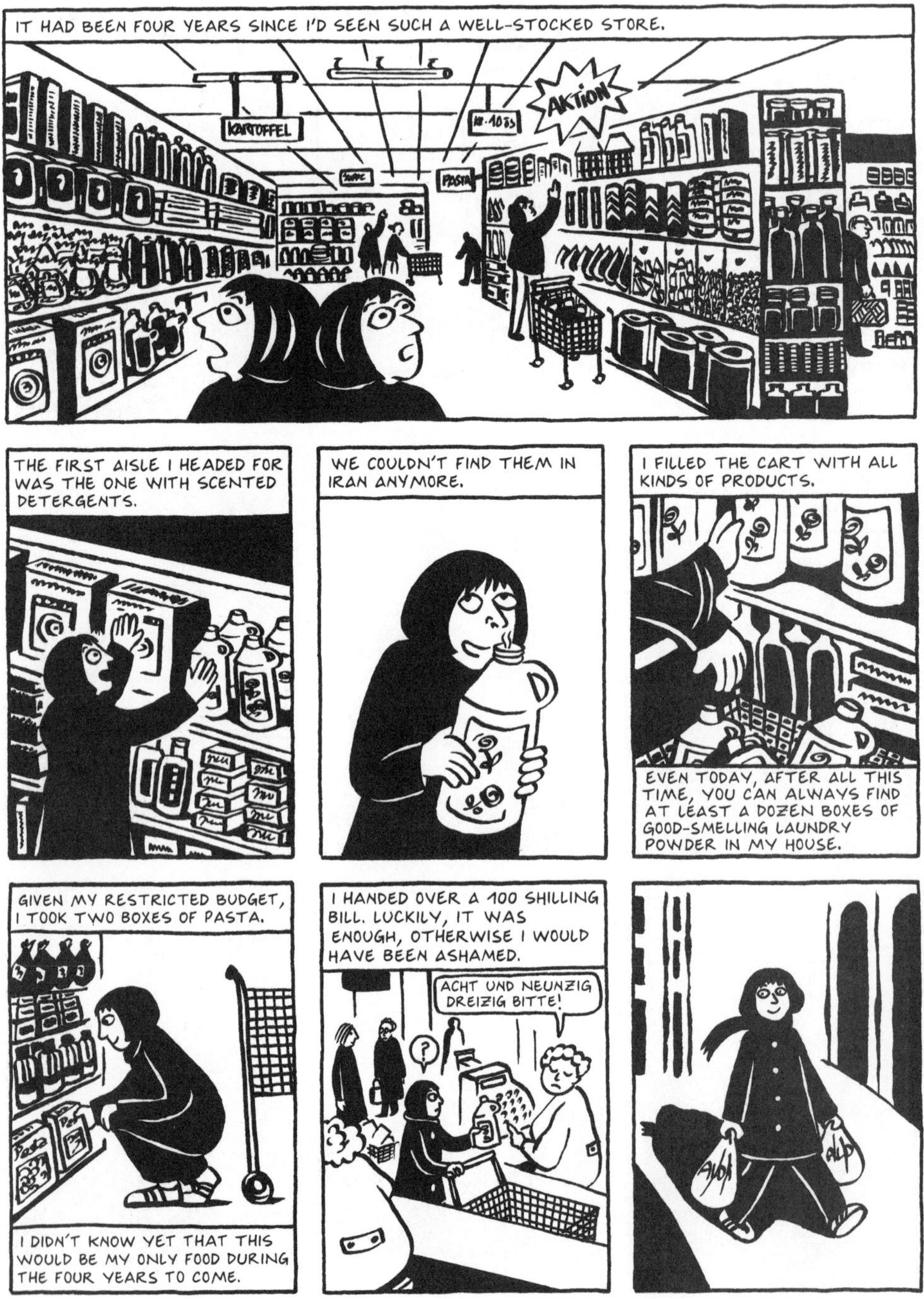
IT HAD BEEN FOUR YEARS SINCE I'D SEEN SUCH A WELL-STOCKED STORE.
KARTOFFEL
AKTION
PASTA
THE FIRST AISLE I HEADED FOR WAS THE ONE WITH SCENTED DETERGENTS.
WE COULDN'T FIND THEM IN IRAN ANYMORE.
I FILLED THE CART WITH ALL KINDS OF PRODUCTS.
EVEN TODAY, AFTER ALL THIS TIME, YOU CAN ALWAYS FIND AT LEAST A DOZEN BOXES OF GOOD-SMELLING LAUNDRY POWDER IN MY HOUSE.
GIVEN MY RESTRICTED BUDGET, I TOOK TWO BOXES OF PASTA.
I DIDN'T KNOW YET THAT THIS WOULD BE MY ONLY FOOD DURING THE FOUR YEARS TO COME.
I HANDED OVER A 100 SHILLING BILL. LUCKILY, IT WAS ENOUGH, OTHERWISE I WOULD HAVE BEEN ASHAMED.
ACHT UND NEUNZIG DREIZIG BITTE!
?

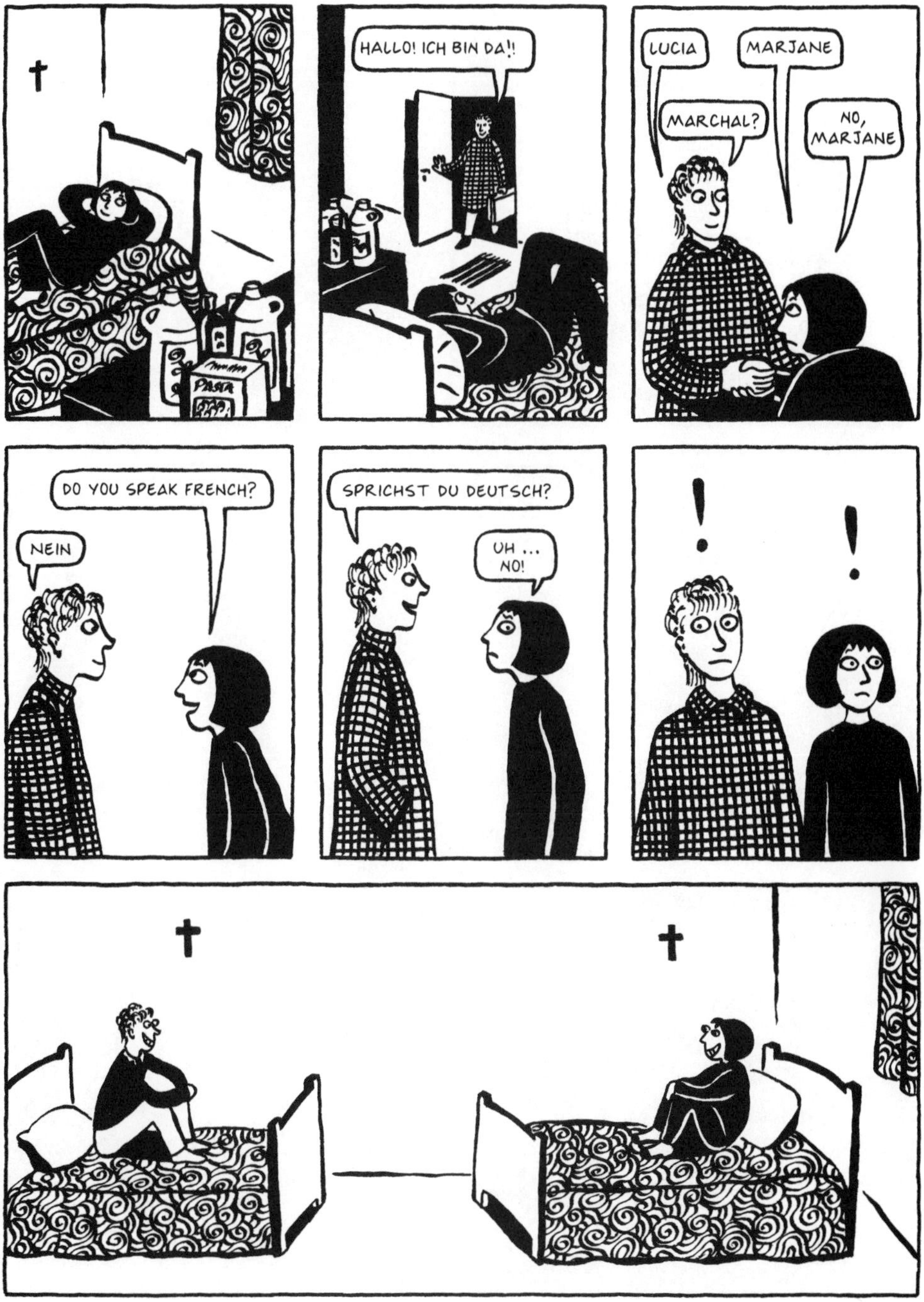
HALLO! ICH BIN DA!!
LUCIA
MARJANE
MARCHAL?
NO, MARJANE
DO YOU SPEAK FRENCH?
NEIN
SPRICHST DU DEUTSCH?
UH ... NO!
!
!

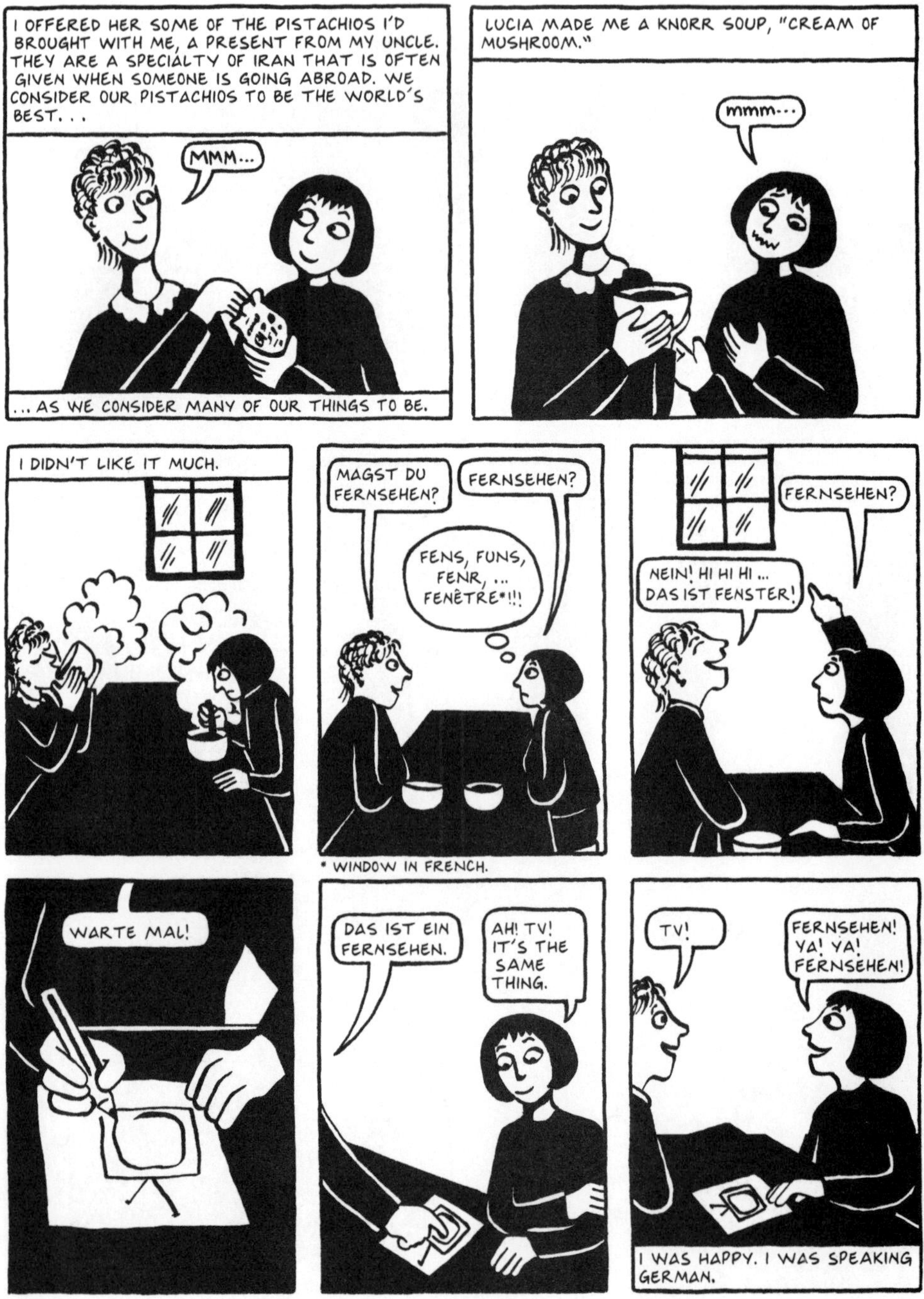
I OFFERED HER SOME OF THE PISTACHIOS I'D BROUGHT WITH ME, A PRESENT FROM MY UNCLE. THEY ARE A SPECIALTY OF IRAN THAT IS OFTEN GIVEN WHEN SOMEONE IS GOING ABROAD. WE CONSIDER OUR PISTACHIOS TO BE THE WORLD'S BEST. . .
MMM...
... AS WE CONSIDER MANY OF OUR THINGS TO BE.
LUCIA MADE ME A KNORR SOUP, "CREAM OF MUSHROOM."
mmm...
I DIDN'T LIKE IT MUCH.
MAGST DU FERNSEHEN?
FERNSEHEN?
FENS, FUNS, FENR, ... FENÊTRE*!!!
FERNSEHEN?
NEIN! HI HI HI ... DAS IST FENSTER!
WARTE MAL!
DAS IST EIN FERNSEHEN.
AH! TV! IT'S THE SAME THING.
TV!
FERNSEHEN! YA! YA! FERNSEHEN!
I WAS HAPPY. I WAS SPEAKING GERMAN.

* WINDOW IN FRENCH.

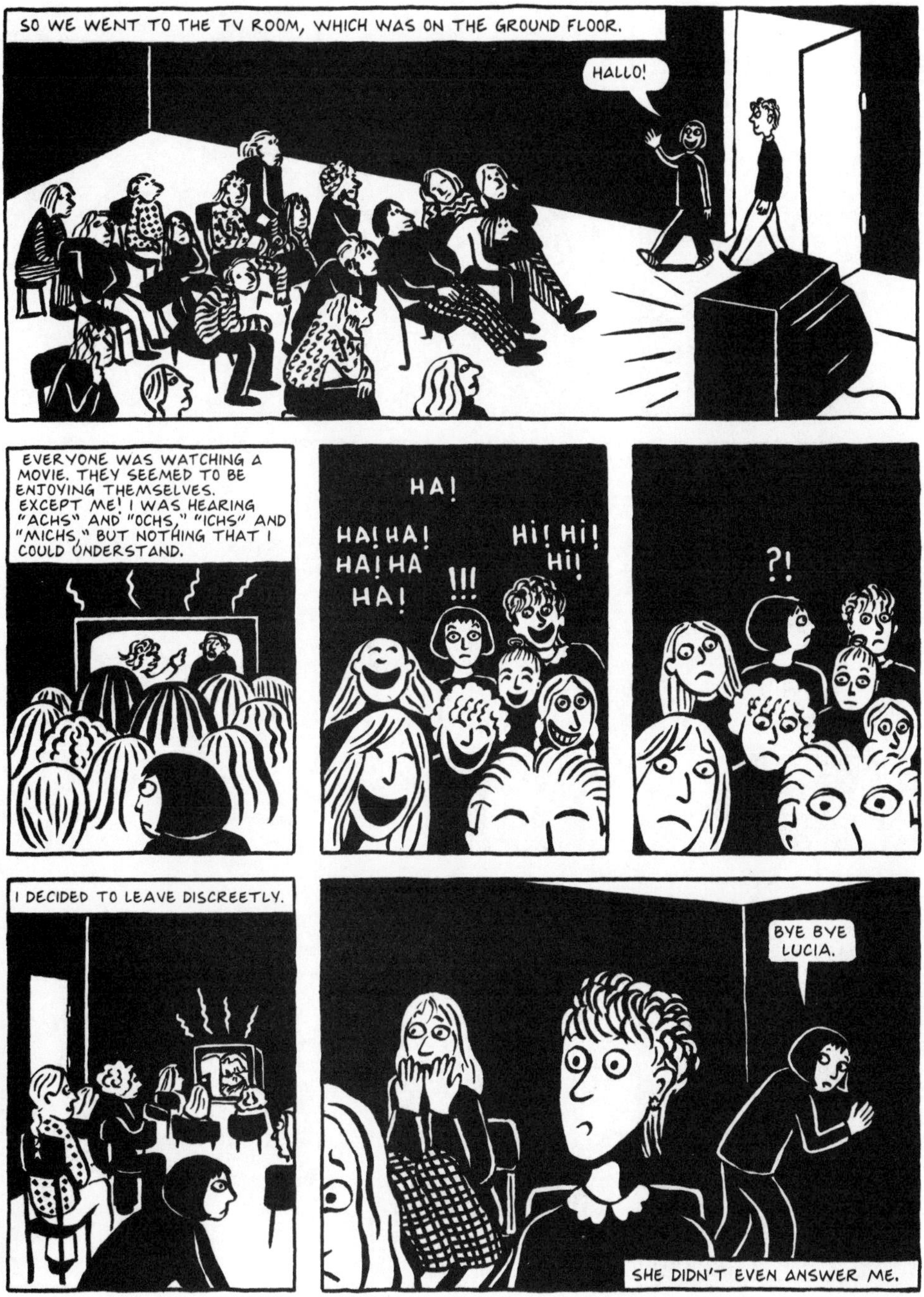
SO WE WENT TO THE TV ROOM, WHICH WAS ON THE GROUND FLOOR.
HALLO!
EVERYONE WAS WATCHING A MOVIE. THEY SEEMED TO BE ENJOYING THEMSELVES. EXCEPT ME! I WAS HEARING "ACHS" AND "OCHS," "ICHS" AND "MICHS," BUT NOTHING THAT I COULD UNDERSTAND.
HA!
HA! HA! HA! HA HA!
!!!
HI! HI! HI!
?!
I DECIDED TO LEAVE DISCREETLY.
BYE BYE LUCIA.
SHE DIDN'T EVEN ANSWER ME.

TYROL

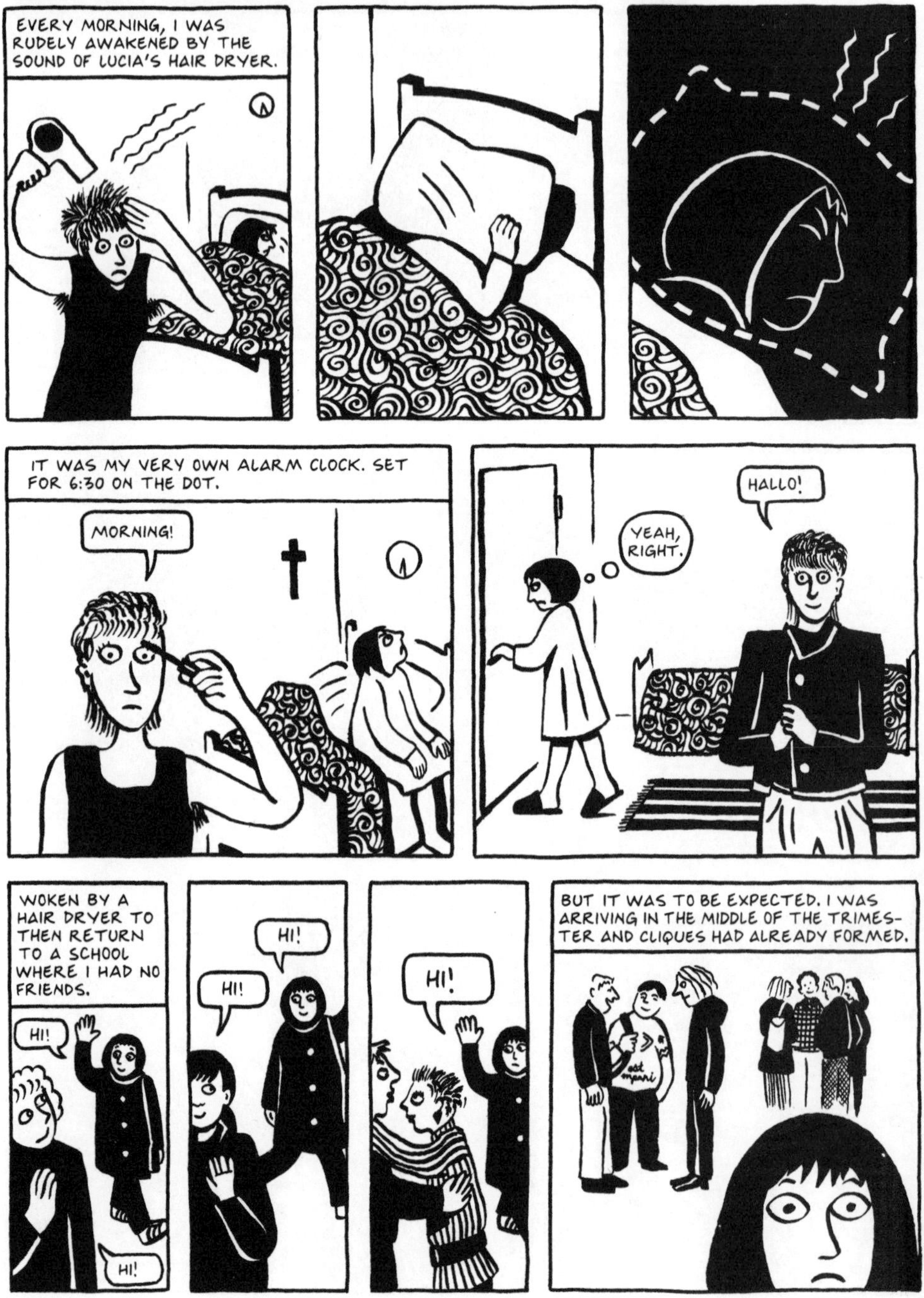

EVERY MORNING, I WAS RUDELY AWAKENED BY THE SOUND OF LUCIA'S HAIR DRYER.
IT WAS MY VERY OWN ALARM CLOCK. SET FOR 6:30 ON THE DOT.
MORNING!
HALLO!
YEAH, RIGHT.
WOKEN BY A HAIR DRYER TO THEN RETURN TO A SCHOOL WHERE I HAD NO FRIENDS.
HI!
HI!
HI!
HI!
HI!
BUT IT WAS TO BE EXPECTED. I WAS ARRIVING IN THE MIDDLE OF THE TRIMESTER AND CLIQUES HAD ALREADY FORMED.

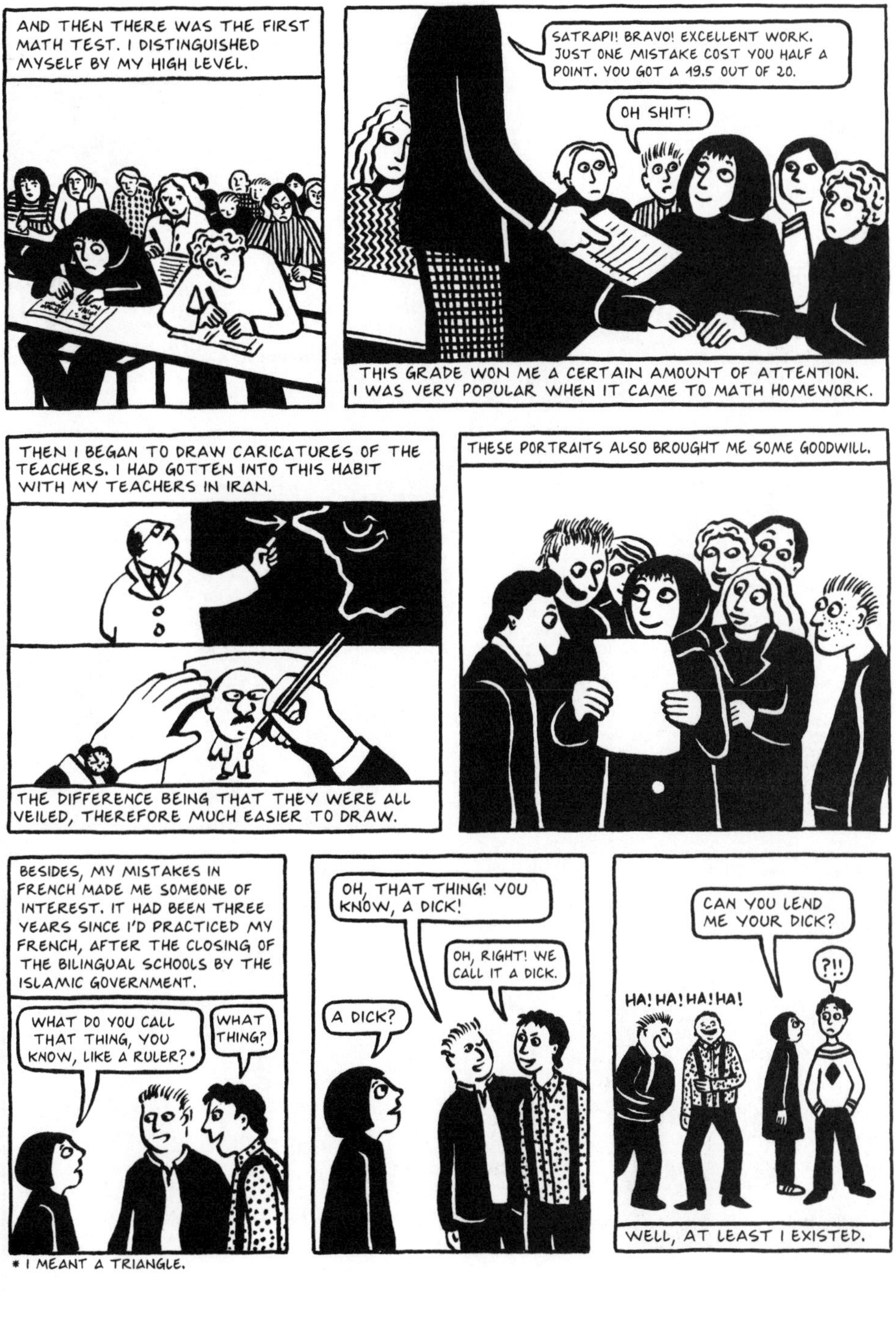
AND THEN THERE WAS THE FIRST MATH TEST. I DISTINGUISHED MYSELF BY MY HIGH LEVEL.
SATRAPI! BRAVO! EXCELLENT WORK. JUST ONE MISTAKE COST YOU HALF A POINT. YOU GOT A 19.5 OUT OF 20.
OH SHIT!
THIS GRADE WON ME A CERTAIN AMOUNT OF ATTENTION. I WAS VERY POPULAR WHEN IT CAME TO MATH HOMEWORK.
THEN I BEGAN TO DRAW CARICATURES OF THE TEACHERS. I HAD GOTTEN INTO THIS HABIT WITH MY TEACHERS IN IRAN.
THE DIFFERENCE BEING THAT THEY WERE ALL VEILED, THEREFORE MUCH EASIER TO DRAW.
THESE PORTRAITS ALSO BROUGHT ME SOME GOODWILL.
BESIDES, MY MISTAKES IN FRENCH MADE ME SOMEONE OF INTEREST. IT HAD BEEN THREE YEARS SINCE I'D PRACTICED MY FRENCH, AFTER THE CLOSING OF THE BILINGUAL SCHOOLS BY THE ISLAMIC GOVERNMENT.
WHAT DO YOU CALL THAT THING, YOU KNOW, LIKE A RULER?*
WHAT THING?
A DICK?
OH, THAT THING! YOU KNOW, A DICK!
OH, RIGHT! WE CALL IT A DICK.
CAN YOU LEND ME YOUR DICK?
HA! HA! HA! HA!
?!!
WELL, AT LEAST I EXISTED.

* I MEANT A TRIANGLE.

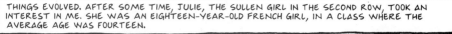

THINGS EVOLVED. AFTER SOME TIME, JULIE, THE SULLEN GIRL IN THE SECOND ROW, TOOK AN INTEREST IN ME. SHE WAS AN EIGHTEEN-YEAR-OLD FRENCH GIRL, IN A CLASS WHERE THE AVERAGE AGE WAS FOURTEEN.

I UNDERSTOOD LATER THAT HER RESERVE CAME FROM THE FACT THAT SHE CONSIDERED THE OTHERS TO BE SPOILED CHILDREN. BUT I WAS DIFFERENT. I HAD KNOWN WAR.

SHE INTRODUCED ME TO MOMO. HE WAS TWO YEARS OLDER.

THIS IS MARJANE. SHE'S IRANIAN. SHE'S KNOWN WAR.

WAR?

DELIGHTED!

YOU'VE ALREADY SEEN LOTS OF DEAD PEOPLE?

UM... A FEW.

COOL!

MOMO GREETED PEOPLE IN HIS OWN WAY.

MMM...

...MMM

SO IT WAS HE WHO KISSED ME ON THE MOUTH FOR THE FIRST TIME.

...THROUGH MOMO, I GOT TO KNOW THIERRY AND OLIVIER, TWO SWISS ORPHANS WHO WERE LIVING IN AUSTRIA WITH THEIR UNCLE, A DIPLOMAT.

I'M ALSO A BIT OF AN ORPHAN.

YOUR PARENTS ARE DEAD?

NO, THEY'RE IN IRAN.

THE FACT THAT I WAS LIVING WITHOUT MY PARENTS ALSO SUITED JULIE.

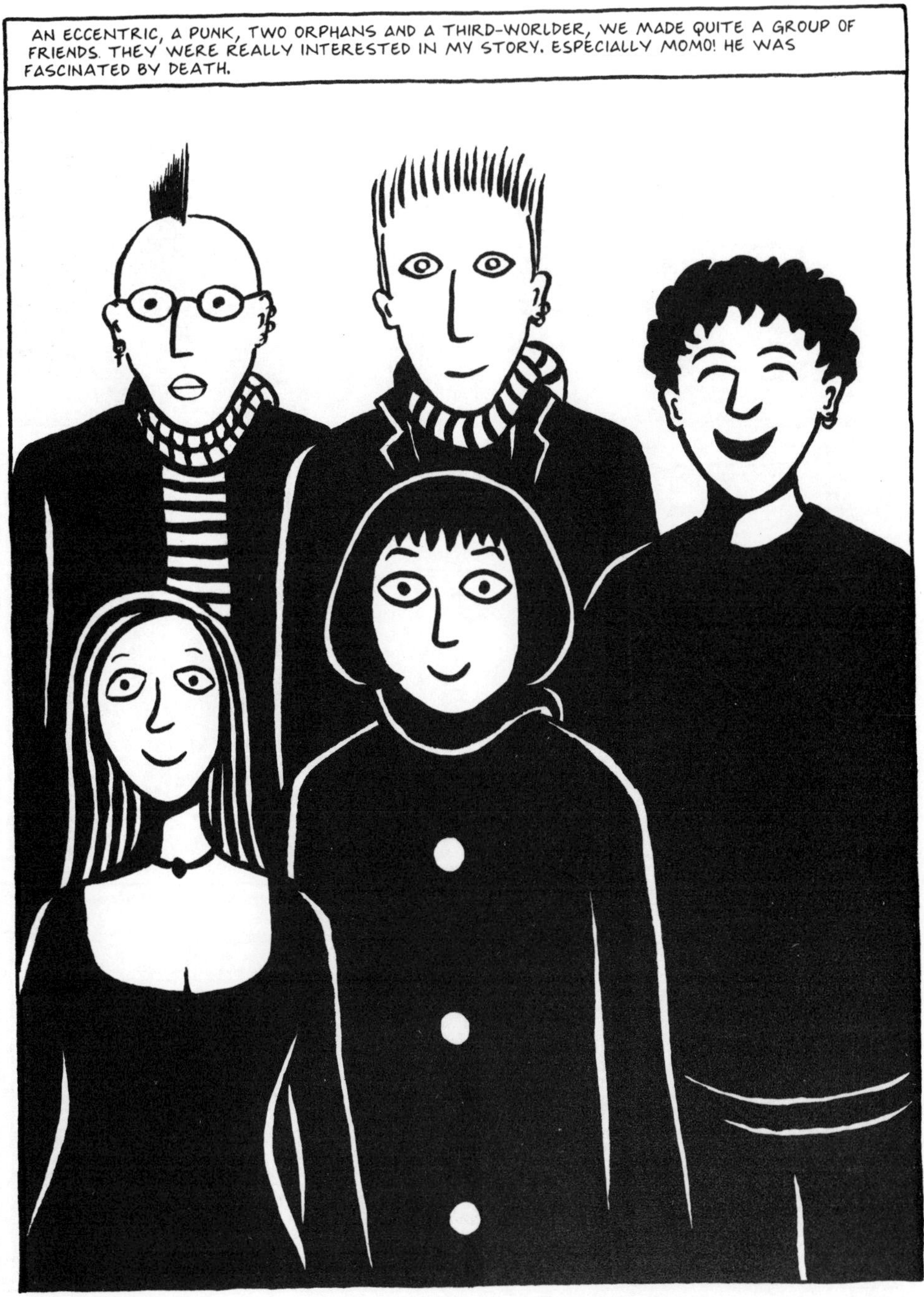
AN ECCENTRIC, A PUNK, TWO ORPHANS AND A THIRD-WORLDER, WE MADE QUITE A GROUP OF FRIENDS. THEY WERE REALLY INTERESTED IN MY STORY. ESPECIALLY MOMO! HE WAS FASCINATED BY DEATH.

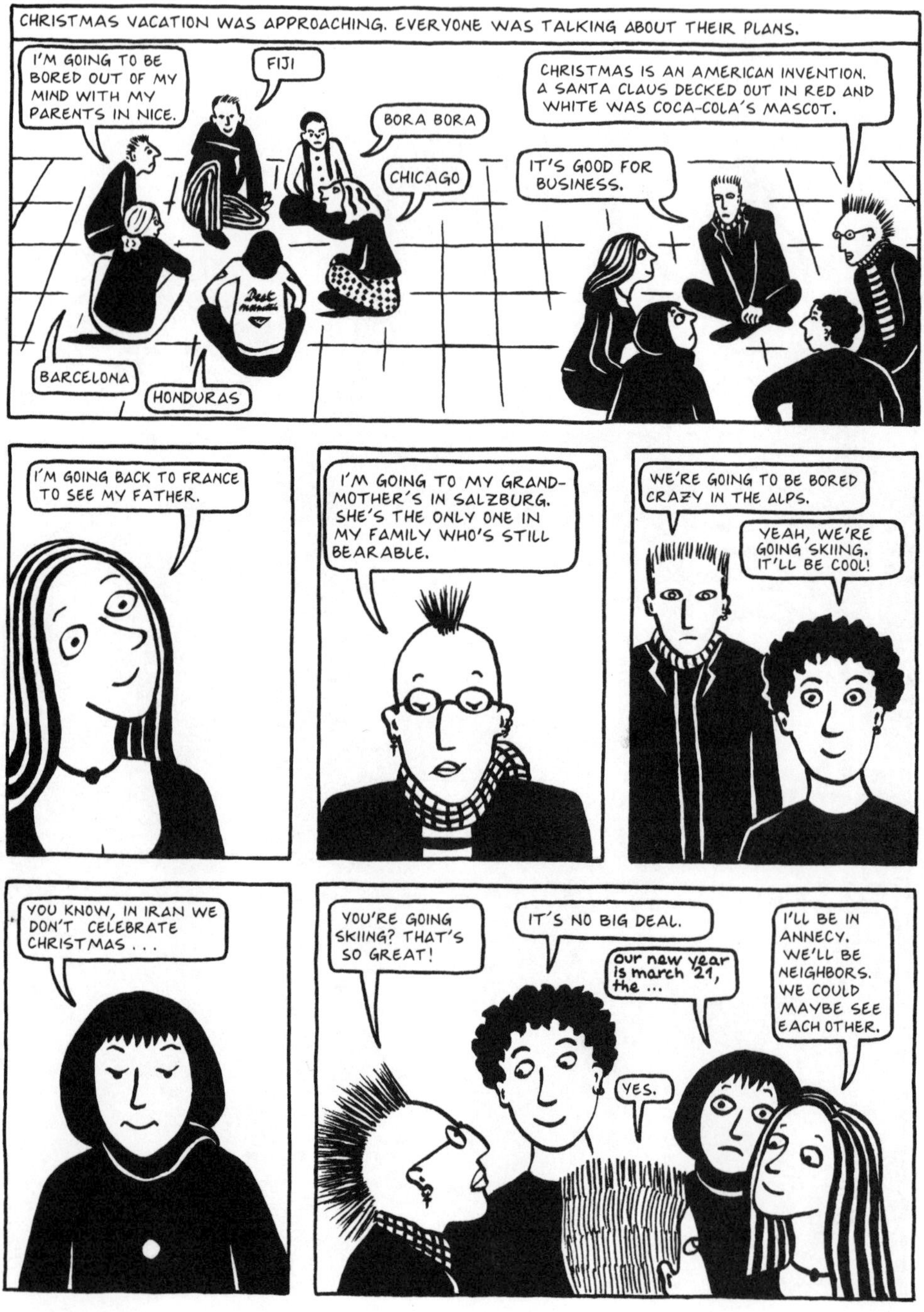
CHRISTMAS VACATION WAS APPROACHING. EVERYONE WAS TALKING ABOUT THEIR PLANS.
I'M GOING TO BE BORED OUT OF MY MIND WITH MY PARENTS IN NICE.
FIJI
BORA BORA
CHICAGO
BARCELONA
HONDURAS
CHRISTMAS IS AN AMERICAN INVENTION. A SANTA CLAUS DECKED OUT IN RED AND WHITE WAS COCA-COLA'S MASCOT.
IT'S GOOD FOR BUSINESS.
I'M GOING BACK TO FRANCE TO SEE MY FATHER.
I'M GOING TO MY GRANDMOTHER'S IN SALZBURG. SHE'S THE ONLY ONE IN MY FAMILY WHO'S STILL BEARABLE.
WE'RE GOING TO BE BORED CRAZY IN THE ALPS.
YEAH, WE'RE GOING SKIING. IT'LL BE COOL!
YOU KNOW, IN IRAN WE DON'T CELEBRATE CHRISTMAS . . .
YOU'RE GOING SKIING? THAT'S SO GREAT!
IT'S NO BIG DEAL.
our new year is march 21, the ...
YES.
I'LL BE IN ANNECY. WE'LL BE NEIGHBORS. WE COULD MAYBE SEE EACH OTHER.

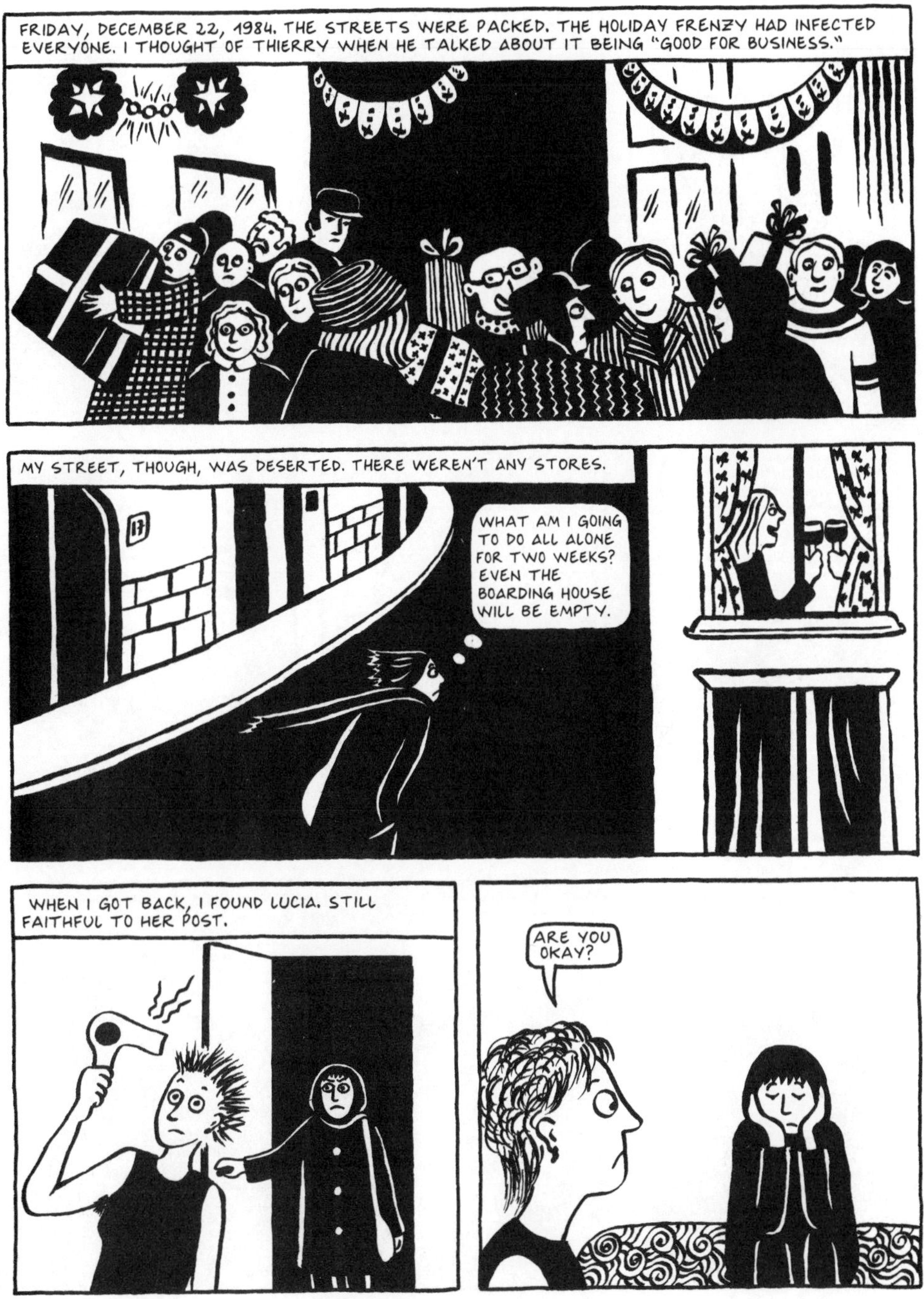
FRIDAY, DECEMBER 22, 1984. THE STREETS WERE PACKED. THE HOLIDAY FRENZY HAD INFECTED EVERYONE. I THOUGHT OF THIERRY WHEN HE TALKED ABOUT IT BEING "GOOD FOR BUSINESS."
MY STREET, THOUGH, WAS DESERTED. THERE WEREN'T ANY STORES.
17
WHAT AM I GOING TO DO ALL ALONE FOR TWO WEEKS? EVEN THE BOARDING HOUSE WILL BE EMPTY.
WHEN I GOT BACK, I FOUND LUCIA. STILL FAITHFUL TO HER POST.
ARE YOU OKAY?

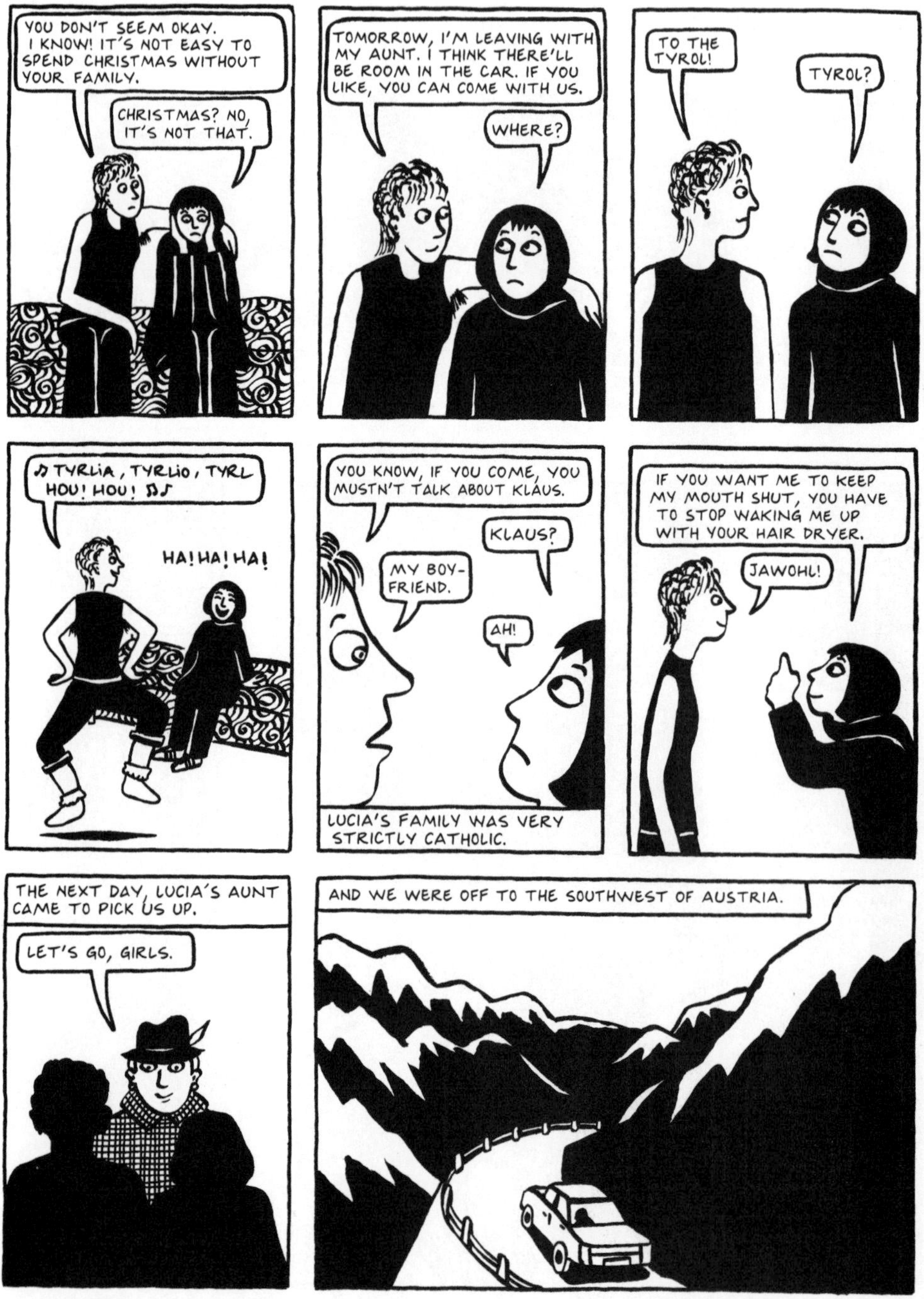
YOU DON'T SEEM OKAY. I KNOW! IT'S NOT EASY TO SPEND CHRISTMAS WITHOUT YOUR FAMILY.
CHRISTMAS? NO, IT'S NOT THAT.
TOMORROW, I'M LEAVING WITH MY AUNT. I THINK THERE'LL BE ROOM IN THE CAR. IF YOU LIKE, YOU CAN COME WITH US.
WHERE?
TO THE TYROL!
TYROL?
♫ TYRLiA, TYRLiO, TYRL HOU! HOU! ♫♪
HA! HA! HA!
YOU KNOW, IF YOU COME, YOU MUSTN'T TALK ABOUT KLAUS.
KLAUS?
MY BOY-FRIEND.
AH!
LUCIA'S FAMILY WAS VERY STRICTLY CATHOLIC.
IF YOU WANT ME TO KEEP MY MOUTH SHUT, YOU HAVE TO STOP WAKING ME UP WITH YOUR HAIR DRYER.
JAWOHL!
THE NEXT DAY, LUCIA'S AUNT CAME TO PICK US UP.
LET'S GO, GIRLS.
AND WE WERE OFF TO THE SOUTHWEST OF AUSTRIA.

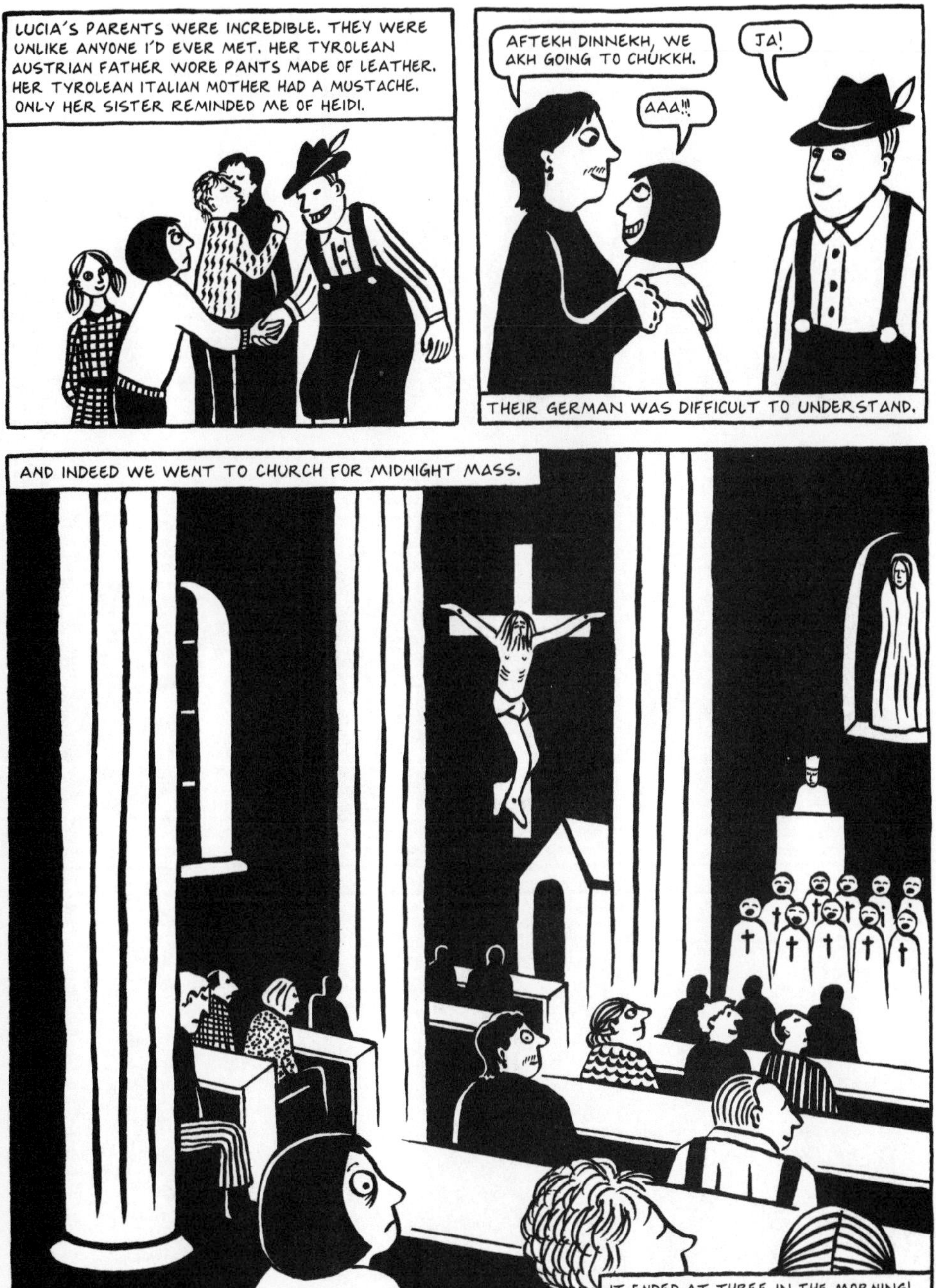
LUCIA'S PARENTS WERE INCREDIBLE. THEY WERE UNLIKE ANYONE I'D EVER MET. HER TYROLEAN AUSTRIAN FATHER WORE PANTS MADE OF LEATHER. HER TYROLEAN ITALIAN MOTHER HAD A MUSTACHE. ONLY HER SISTER REMINDED ME OF HEIDI.
AFTEKH DINNEKH, WE AKH GOING TO CHUKKH.
AAA!!
JA!
THEIR GERMAN WAS DIFFICULT TO UNDERSTAND.
AND INDEED WE WENT TO CHURCH FOR MIDNIGHT MASS.
IT ENDED AT THREE IN THE MORNING!

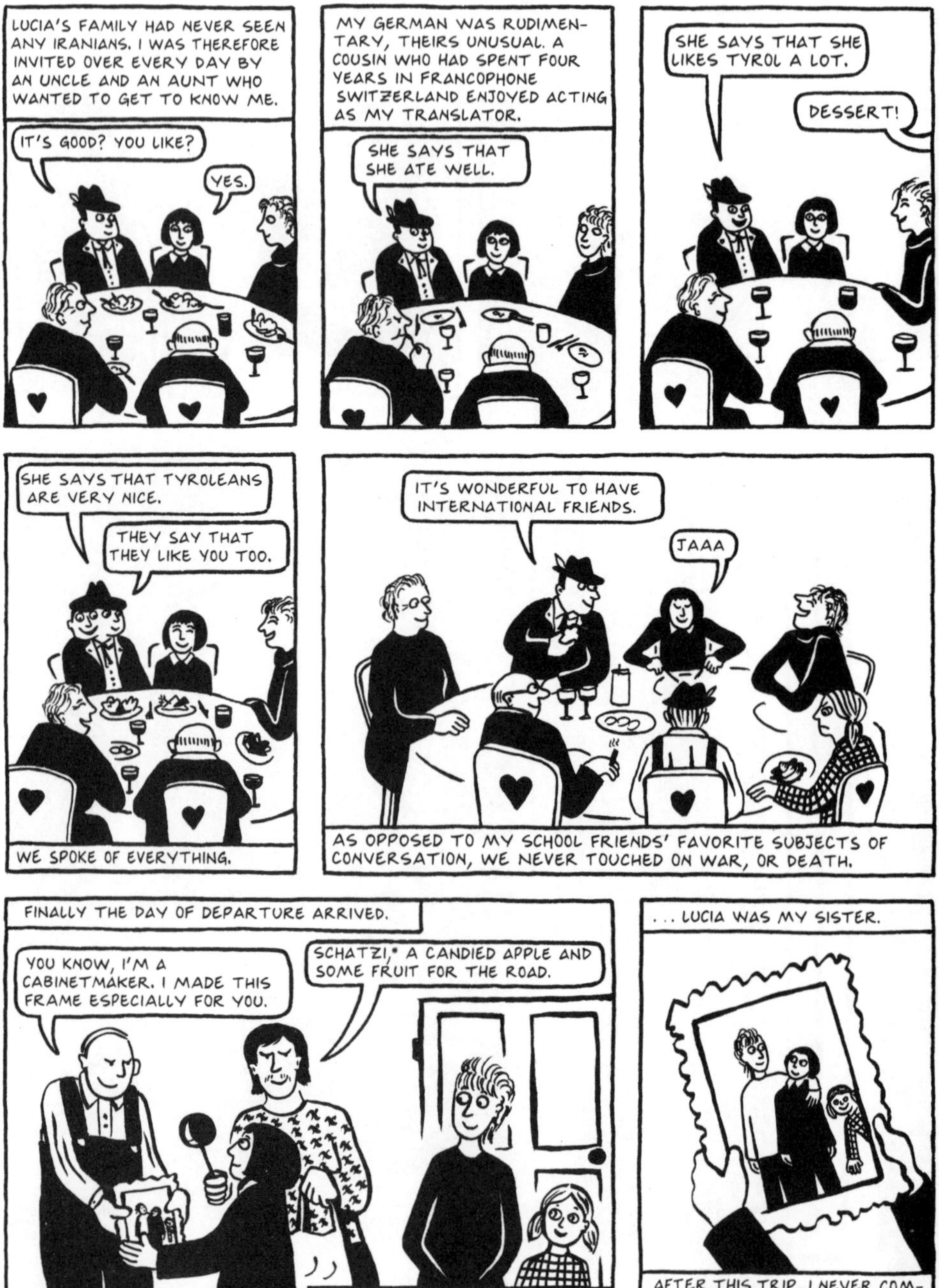
LUCIA'S FAMILY HAD NEVER SEEN ANY IRANIANS. I WAS THEREFORE INVITED OVER EVERY DAY BY AN UNCLE AND AN AUNT WHO WANTED TO GET TO KNOW ME.
IT'S GOOD? YOU LIKE?
YES.
MY GERMAN WAS RUDIMENTARY, THEIRS UNUSUAL. A COUSIN WHO HAD SPENT FOUR YEARS IN FRANCOPHONE SWITZERLAND ENJOYED ACTING AS MY TRANSLATOR.
SHE SAYS THAT SHE ATE WELL.
SHE SAYS THAT SHE LIKES TYROL A LOT.
DESSERT!
SHE SAYS THAT TYROLEANS ARE VERY NICE.
THEY SAY THAT THEY LIKE YOU TOO.
WE SPOKE OF EVERYTHING.
IT'S WONDERFUL TO HAVE INTERNATIONAL FRIENDS.
JAAA
AS OPPOSED TO MY SCHOOL FRIENDS' FAVORITE SUBJECTS OF CONVERSATION, WE NEVER TOUCHED ON WAR, OR DEATH.
FINALLY THE DAY OF DEPARTURE ARRIVED.
YOU KNOW, I'M A CABINETMAKER. I MADE THIS FRAME ESPECIALLY FOR YOU.
SCHATZI,* A CANDIED APPLE AND SOME FRUIT FOR THE ROAD.
I HAD A NEW SET OF PARENTS ...
... LUCIA WAS MY SISTER.
AFTER THIS TRIP, I NEVER COMPLAINED ABOUT HER HAIR DRYER.

* DEAR

PASTA

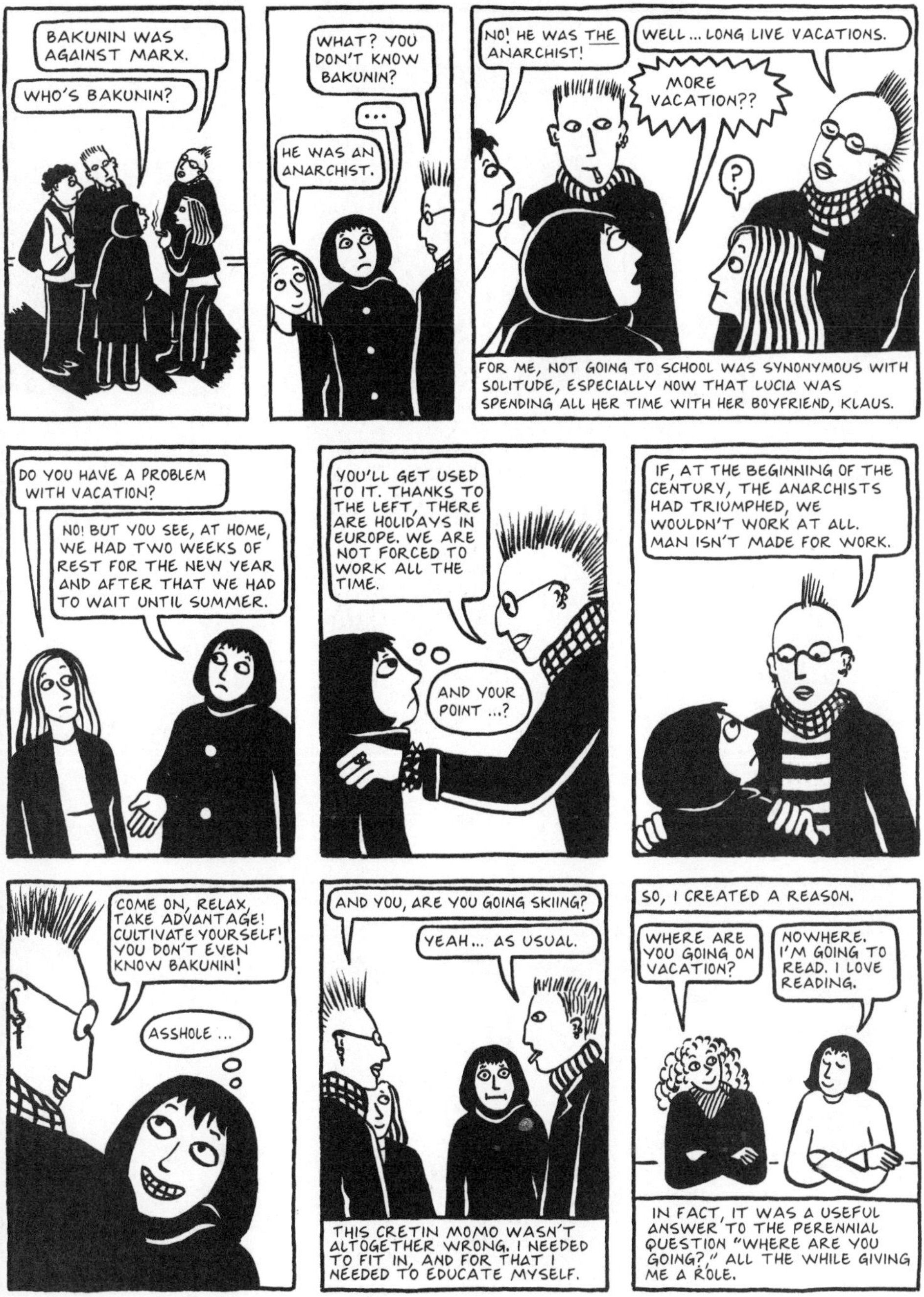

BAKUNIN WAS AGAINST MARX.
WHO'S BAKUNIN?
WHAT? YOU DON'T KNOW BAKUNIN?
...
HE WAS AN ANARCHIST.
NO! HE WAS THE ANARCHIST!
WELL ... LONG LIVE VACATIONS.
MORE VACATION??
?
FOR ME, NOT GOING TO SCHOOL WAS SYNONYMOUS WITH SOLITUDE, ESPECIALLY NOW THAT LUCIA WAS SPENDING ALL HER TIME WITH HER BOYFRIEND, KLAUS.
DO YOU HAVE A PROBLEM WITH VACATION?
NO! BUT YOU SEE, AT HOME, WE HAD TWO WEEKS OF REST FOR THE NEW YEAR AND AFTER THAT WE HAD TO WAIT UNTIL SUMMER.
YOU'LL GET USED TO IT. THANKS TO THE LEFT, THERE ARE HOLIDAYS IN EUROPE. WE ARE NOT FORCED TO WORK ALL THE TIME.
AND YOUR POINT ...?
IF, AT THE BEGINNING OF THE CENTURY, THE ANARCHISTS HAD TRIUMPHED, WE WOULDN'T WORK AT ALL. MAN ISN'T MADE FOR WORK.
COME ON, RELAX, TAKE ADVANTAGE! CULTIVATE YOURSELF! YOU DON'T EVEN KNOW BAKUNIN!
ASSHOLE ...
AND YOU, ARE YOU GOING SKIING?
YEAH ... AS USUAL.
THIS CRETIN MOMO WASN'T ALTOGETHER WRONG. I NEEDED TO FIT IN, AND FOR THAT I NEEDED TO EDUCATE MYSELF.
SO, I CREATED A REASON.
WHERE ARE YOU GOING ON VACATION?
NOWHERE. I'M GOING TO READ. I LOVE READING.
IN FACT, IT WAS A USEFUL ANSWER TO THE PERENNIAL QUESTION "WHERE ARE YOU GOING?," ALL THE WHILE GIVING ME A ROLE.

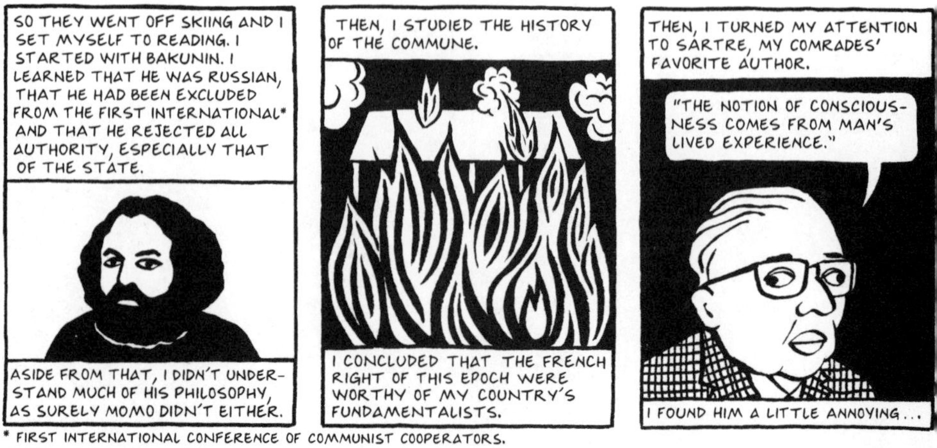
SO THEY WENT OFF SKIING AND I SET MYSELF TO READING. I STARTED WITH BAKUNIN. I LEARNED THAT HE WAS RUSSIAN, THAT HE HAD BEEN EXCLUDED FROM THE FIRST INTERNATIONAL* AND THAT HE REJECTED ALL AUTHORITY, ESPECIALLY THAT OF THE STATE.
ASIDE FROM THAT, I DIDN'T UNDERSTAND MUCH OF HIS PHILOSOPHY, AS SURELY MOMO DIDN'T EITHER.
THEN, I STUDIED THE HISTORY OF THE COMMUNE.
I CONCLUDED THAT THE FRENCH RIGHT OF THIS EPOCH WERE WORTHY OF MY COUNTRY'S FUNDAMENTALISTS.
THEN, I TURNED MY ATTENTION TO SARTRE, MY COMRADES' FAVORITE AUTHOR.
"THE NOTION OF CONSCIOUSNESS COMES FROM MAN'S LIVED EXPERIENCE."
I FOUND HIM A LITTLE ANNOYING...

* FIRST INTERNATIONAL CONFERENCE OF COMMUNIST COOPERATORS.

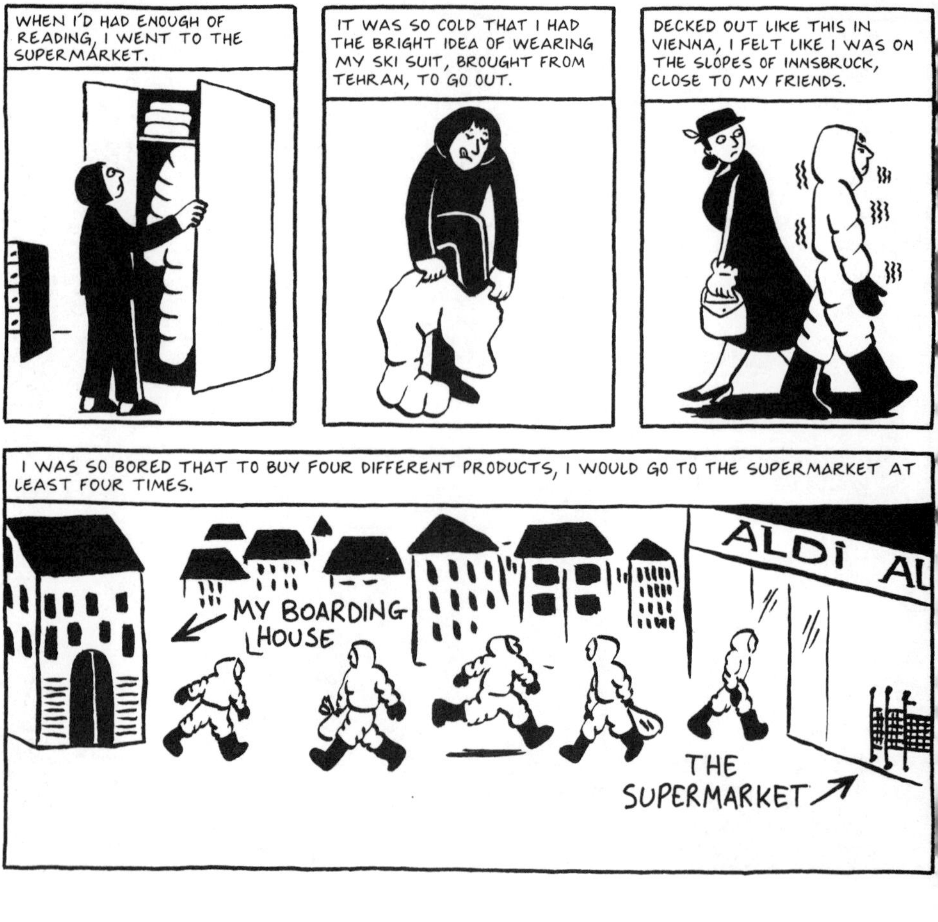
WHEN I'D HAD ENOUGH OF READING, I WENT TO THE SUPERMARKET.
IT WAS SO COLD THAT I HAD THE BRIGHT IDEA OF WEARING MY SKI SUIT, BROUGHT FROM TEHRAN, TO GO OUT.
DECKED OUT LIKE THIS IN VIENNA, I FELT LIKE I WAS ON THE SLOPES OF INNSBRUCK, CLOSE TO MY FRIENDS.
I WAS SO BORED THAT TO BUY FOUR DIFFERENT PRODUCTS, I WOULD GO TO THE SUPERMARKET AT LEAST FOUR TIMES.
MY BOARDING HOUSE
ALDI
AL
THE SUPERMARKET

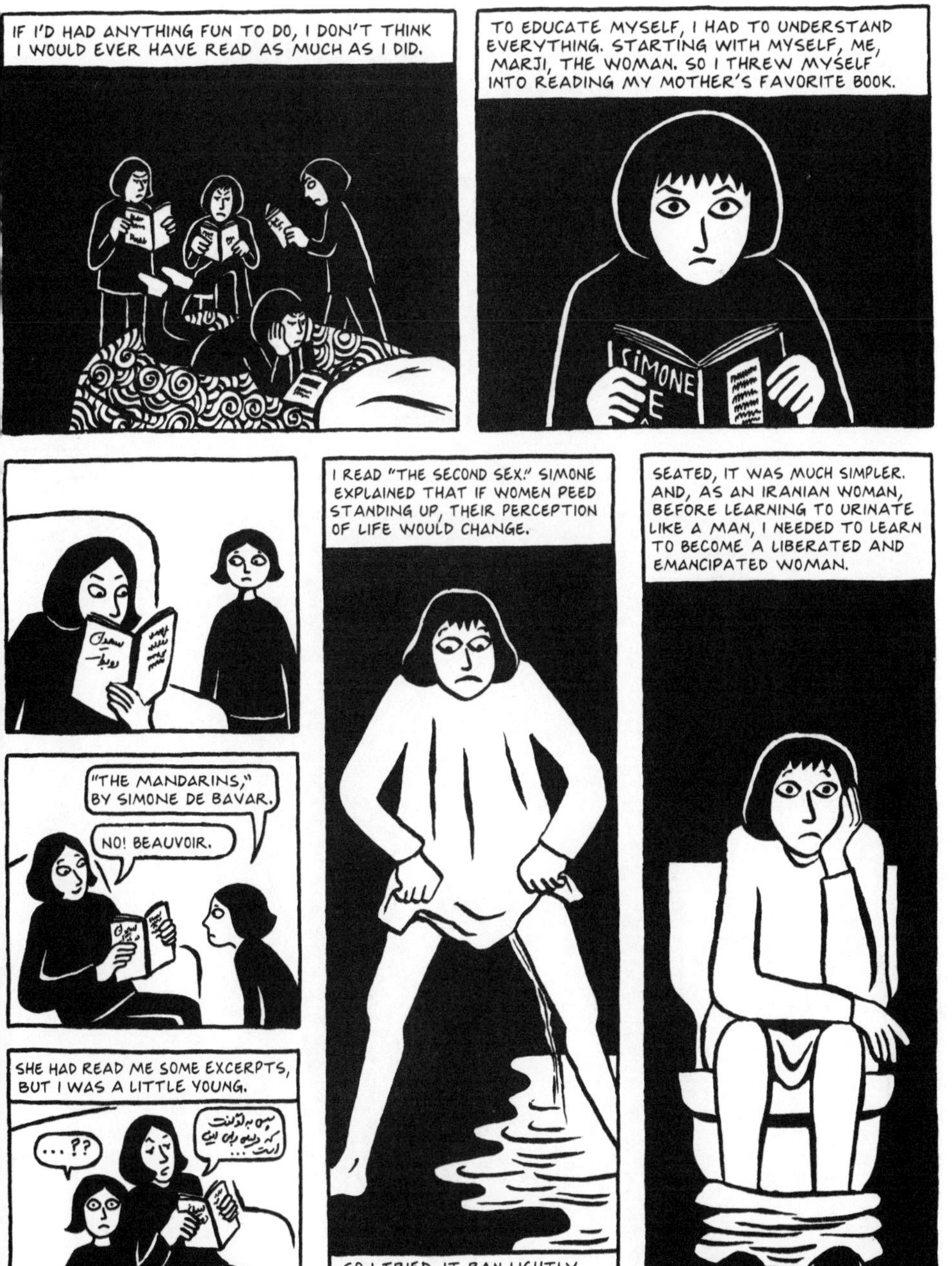

IF I'D HAD ANYTHING FUN TO DO, I DON'T THINK I WOULD EVER HAVE READ AS MUCH AS I DID.
TO EDUCATE MYSELF, I HAD TO UNDERSTAND EVERYTHING. STARTING WITH MYSELF, ME, MARJI, THE WOMAN. SO I THREW MYSELF INTO READING MY MOTHER'S FAVORITE BOOK.
SIMONE
"THE MANDARINS," BY SIMONE DE BAVAR.
NO! BEAUVOIR.
SHE HAD READ ME SOME EXCERPTS, BUT I WAS A LITTLE YOUNG.
...??
I READ "THE SECOND SEX." SIMONE EXPLAINED THAT IF WOMEN PEED STANDING UP, THEIR PERCEPTION OF LIFE WOULD CHANGE.
SO I TRIED. IT RAN LIGHTLY DOWN MY LEFT LEG. IT WAS A LITTLE DISGUSTING.
SEATED, IT WAS MUCH SIMPLER. AND, AS AN IRANIAN WOMAN, BEFORE LEARNING TO URINATE LIKE A MAN, I NEEDED TO LEARN TO BECOME A LIBERATED AND EMANCIPATED WOMAN.

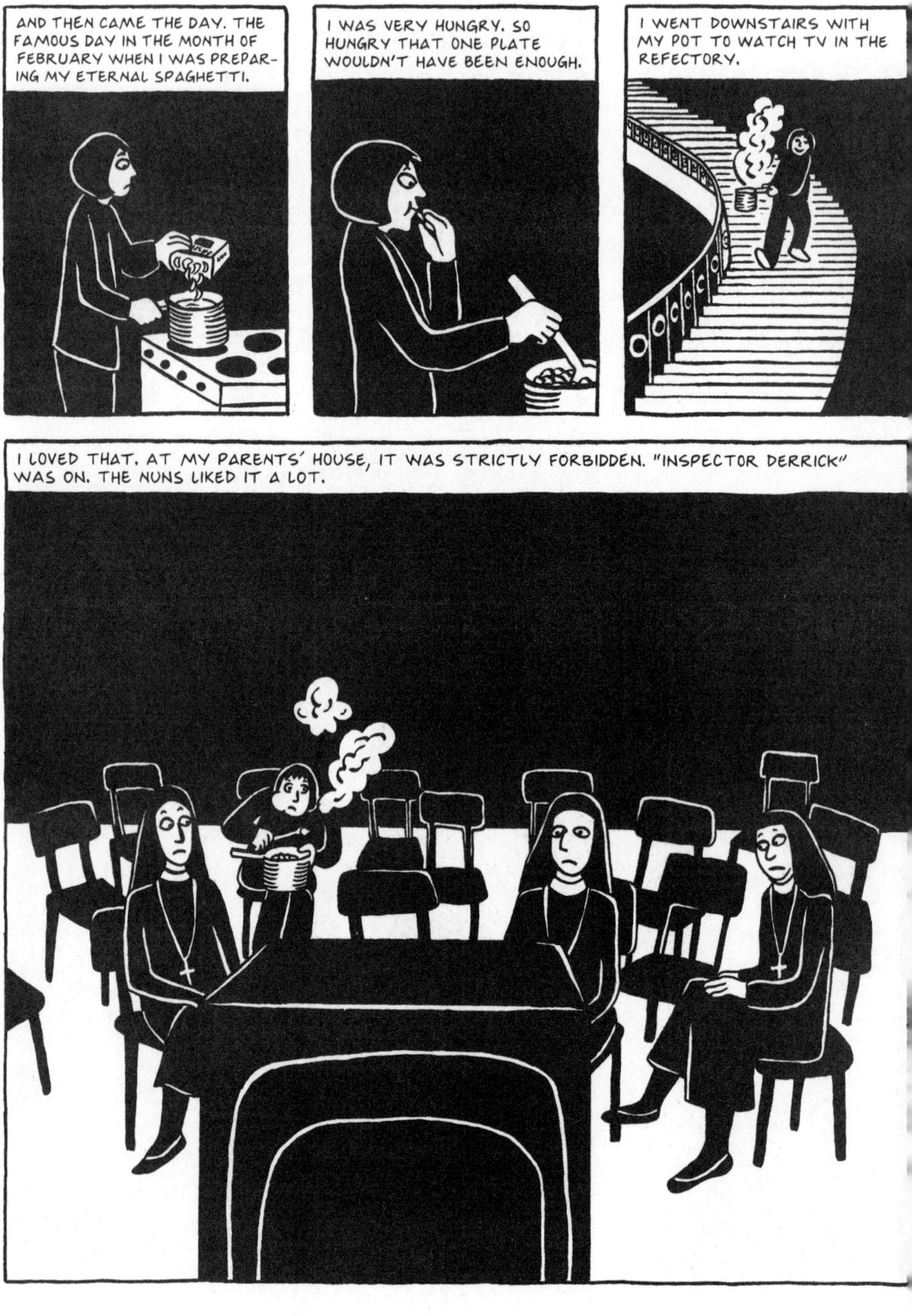
AND THEN CAME THE DAY. THE FAMOUS DAY IN THE MONTH OF FEBRUARY WHEN I WAS PREPARING MY ETERNAL SPAGHETTI.
I WAS VERY HUNGRY. SO HUNGRY THAT ONE PLATE WOULDN'T HAVE BEEN ENOUGH.
I WENT DOWNSTAIRS WITH MY POT TO WATCH TV IN THE REFECTORY.
I LOVED THAT. AT MY PARENTS' HOUSE, IT WAS STRICTLY FORBIDDEN. "INSPECTOR DERRICK" WAS ON. THE NUNS LIKED IT A LOT.

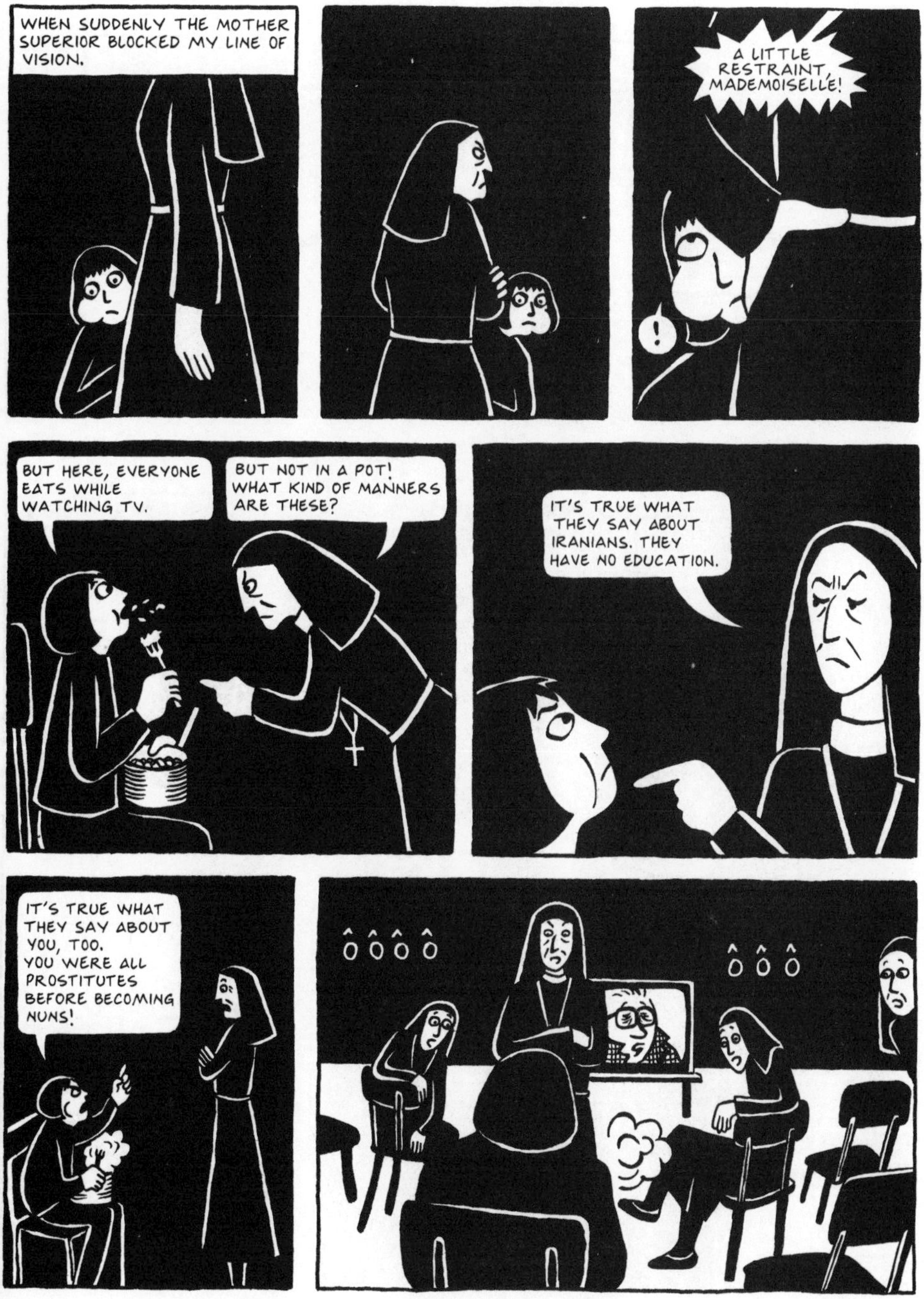
WHEN SUDDENLY THE MOTHER SUPERIOR BLOCKED MY LINE OF VISION.
A LITTLE RESTRAINT, MADEMOISELLE!
!
BUT HERE, EVERYONE EATS WHILE WATCHING TV.
BUT NOT IN A POT! WHAT KIND OF MANNERS ARE THESE?
IT'S TRUE WHAT THEY SAY ABOUT IRANIANS. THEY HAVE NO EDUCATION.
IT'S TRUE WHAT THEY SAY ABOUT YOU, TOO. YOU WERE ALL PROSTITUTES BEFORE BECOMING NUNS!

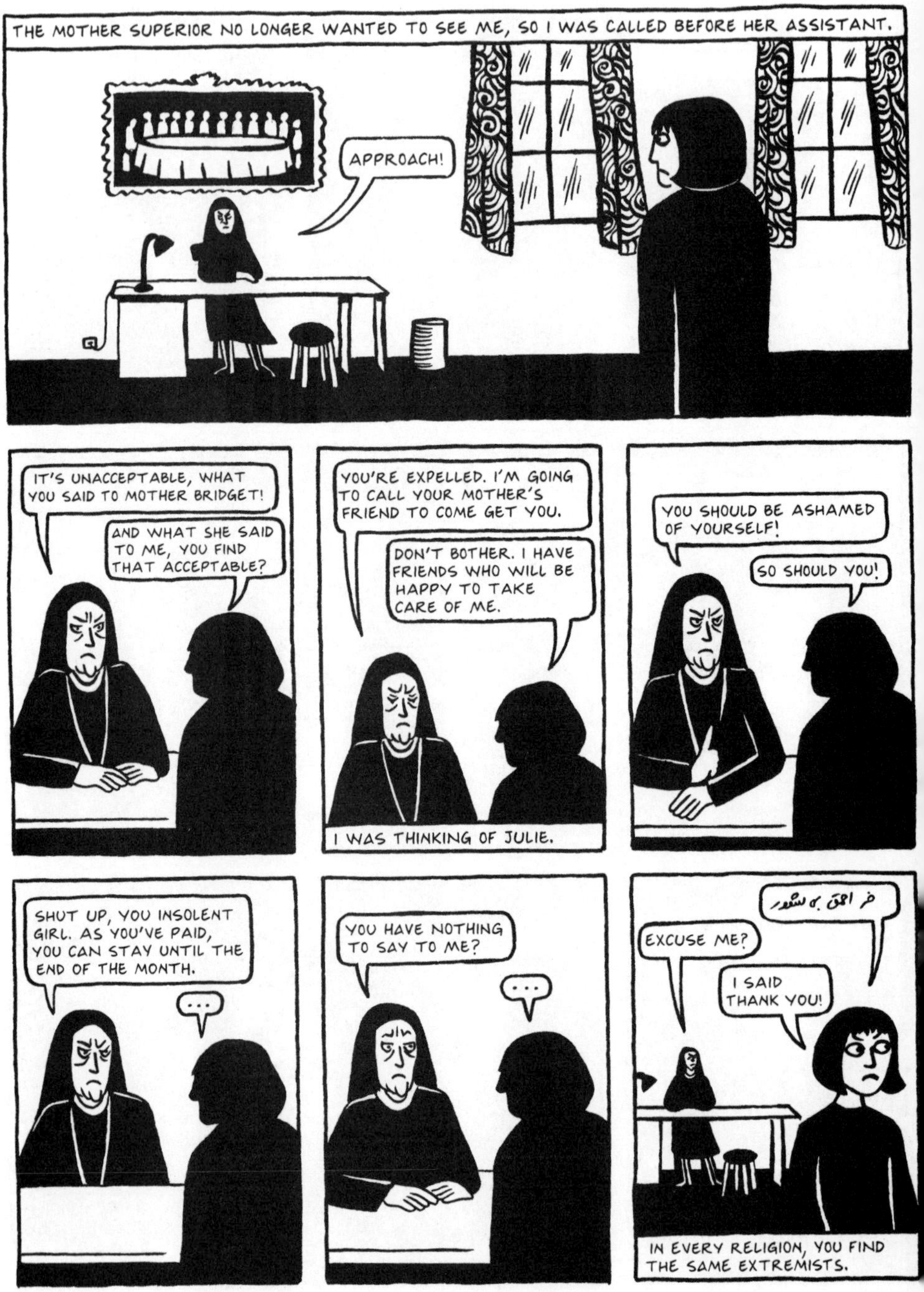
THE MOTHER SUPERIOR NO LONGER WANTED TO SEE ME, SO I WAS CALLED BEFORE HER ASSISTANT.
APPROACH!
IT'S UNACCEPTABLE, WHAT YOU SAID TO MOTHER BRIDGET!
AND WHAT SHE SAID TO ME, YOU FIND THAT ACCEPTABLE?
YOU'RE EXPELLED. I'M GOING TO CALL YOUR MOTHER'S FRIEND TO COME GET YOU.
DON'T BOTHER. I HAVE FRIENDS WHO WILL BE HAPPY TO TAKE CARE OF ME.
I WAS THINKING OF JULIE.
YOU SHOULD BE ASHAMED OF YOURSELF!
SO SHOULD YOU!
SHUT UP, YOU INSOLENT GIRL. AS YOU'VE PAID, YOU CAN STAY UNTIL THE END OF THE MONTH.
...
YOU HAVE NOTHING TO SAY TO ME?
...
خر احمق بی شعور
EXCUSE ME?
I SAID THANK YOU!
IN EVERY RELIGION, YOU FIND THE SAME EXTREMISTS.

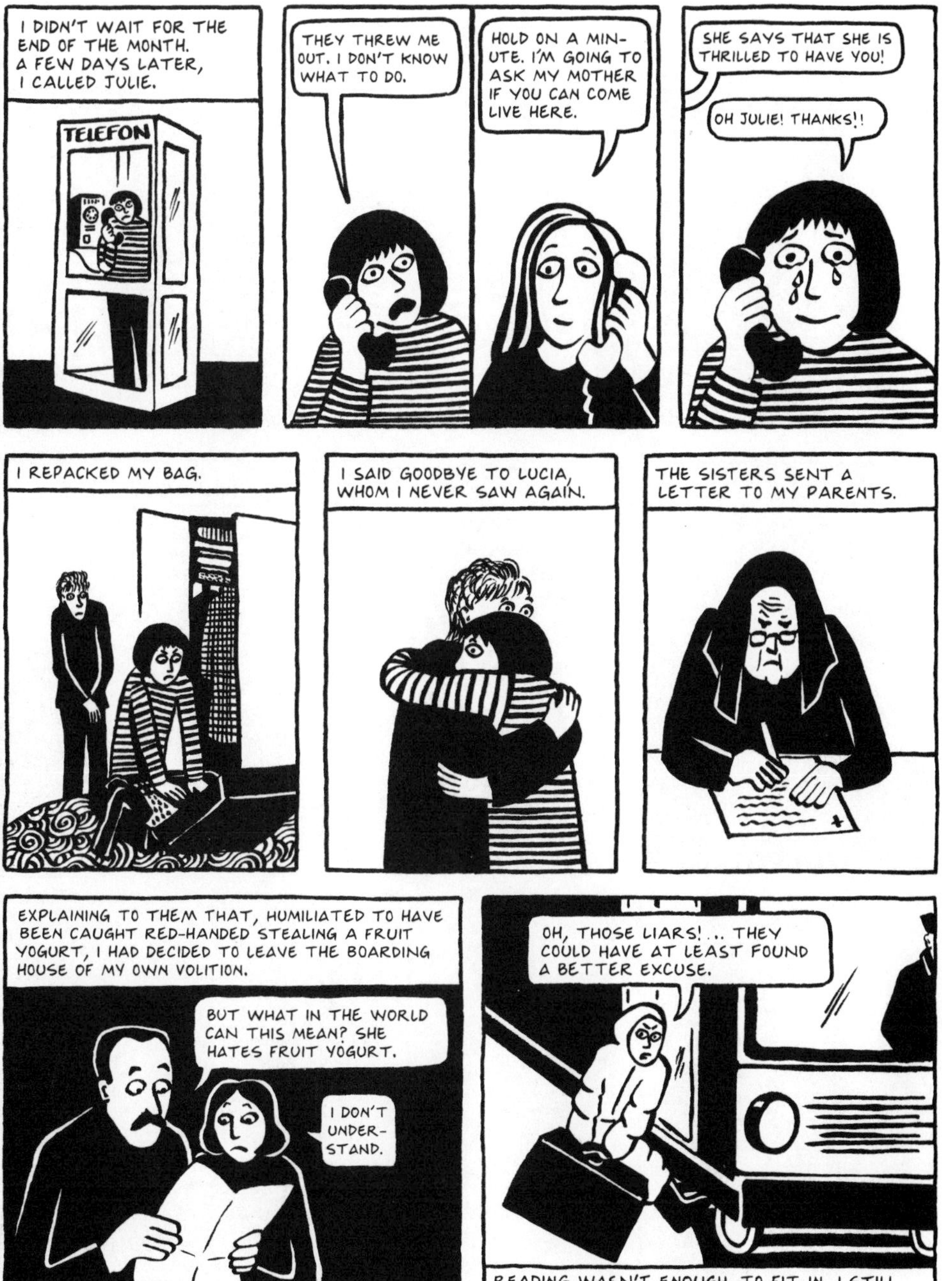

I DIDN'T WAIT FOR THE END OF THE MONTH. A FEW DAYS LATER, I CALLED JULIE.
TELEFON
THEY THREW ME OUT. I DON'T KNOW WHAT TO DO.
HOLD ON A MIN-UTE. I'M GOING TO ASK MY MOTHER IF YOU CAN COME LIVE HERE.
SHE SAYS THAT SHE IS THRILLED TO HAVE YOU!
OH JULIE! THANKS!!
I REPACKED MY BAG.
I SAID GOODBYE TO LUCIA, WHOM I NEVER SAW AGAIN.
THE SISTERS SENT A LETTER TO MY PARENTS.
EXPLAINING TO THEM THAT, HUMILIATED TO HAVE BEEN CAUGHT RED-HANDED STEALING A FRUIT YOGURT, I HAD DECIDED TO LEAVE THE BOARDING HOUSE OF MY OWN VOLITION.
BUT WHAT IN THE WORLD CAN THIS MEAN? SHE HATES FRUIT YOGURT.
I DON'T UNDER-STAND.
HAPPILY, MY PARENTS KNEW MY TASTES.
OH, THOSE LIARS! ... THEY COULD HAVE AT LEAST FOUND A BETTER EXCUSE.
READING WASN'T ENOUGH. TO FIT IN, I STILL HAD A LONG WAY TO GO.

THE PILL

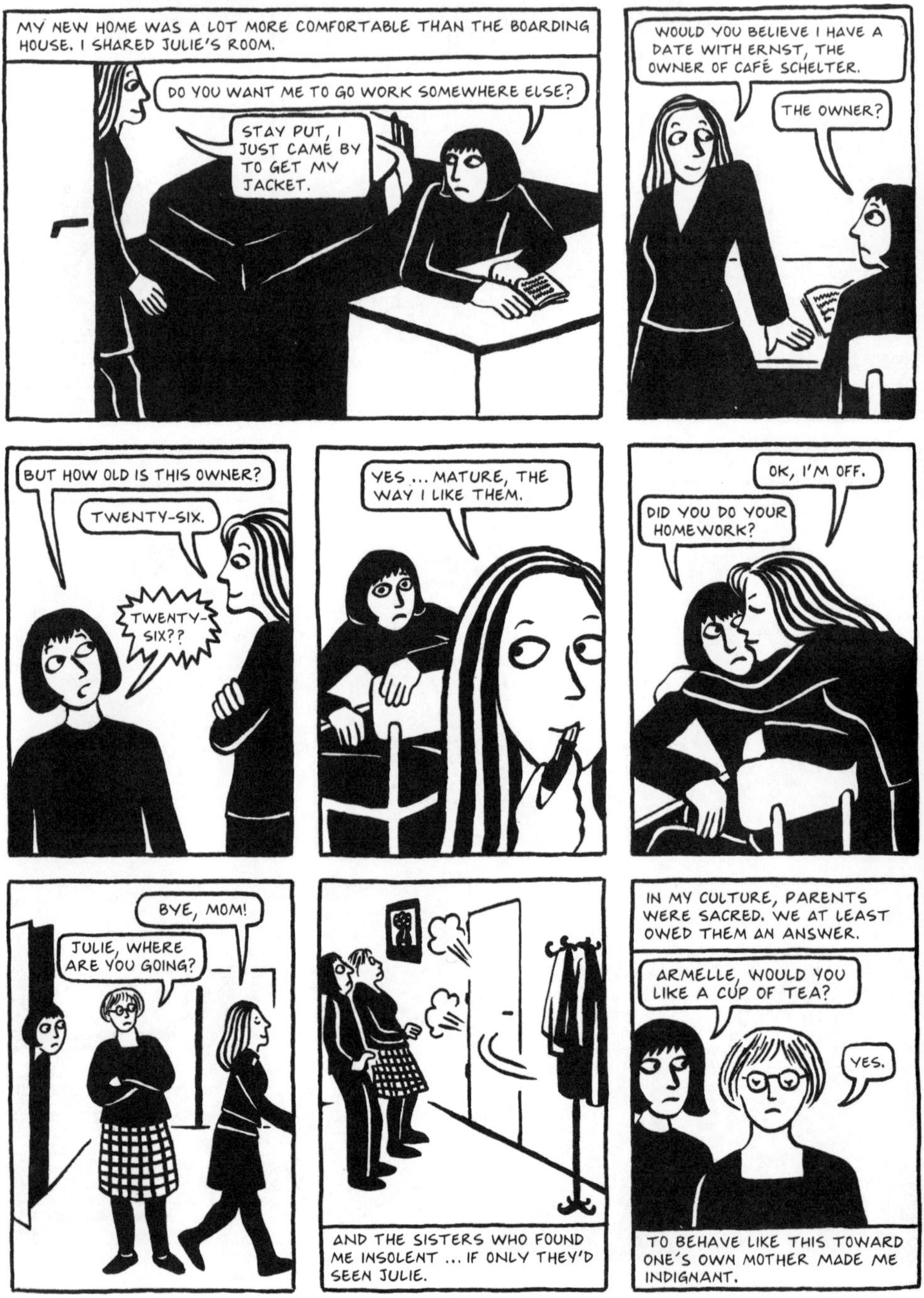

MY NEW HOME WAS A LOT MORE COMFORTABLE THAN THE BOARDING HOUSE. I SHARED JULIE'S ROOM.
DO YOU WANT ME TO GO WORK SOMEWHERE ELSE?
STAY PUT, I JUST CAME BY TO GET MY JACKET.
WOULD YOU BELIEVE I HAVE A DATE WITH ERNST, THE OWNER OF CAFÉ SCHELTER.
THE OWNER?
BUT HOW OLD IS THIS OWNER?
TWENTY-SIX.
TWENTY-SIX??
YES ... MATURE, THE WAY I LIKE THEM.
OK, I'M OFF.
DID YOU DO YOUR HOMEWORK?
BYE, MOM!
JULIE, WHERE ARE YOU GOING?
AND THE SISTERS WHO FOUND ME INSOLENT ... IF ONLY THEY'D SEEN JULIE.
IN MY CULTURE, PARENTS WERE SACRED. WE AT LEAST OWED THEM AN ANSWER.
ARMELLE, WOULD YOU LIKE A CUP OF TEA?
YES.
TO BEHAVE LIKE THIS TOWARD ONE'S OWN MOTHER MADE ME INDIGNANT.

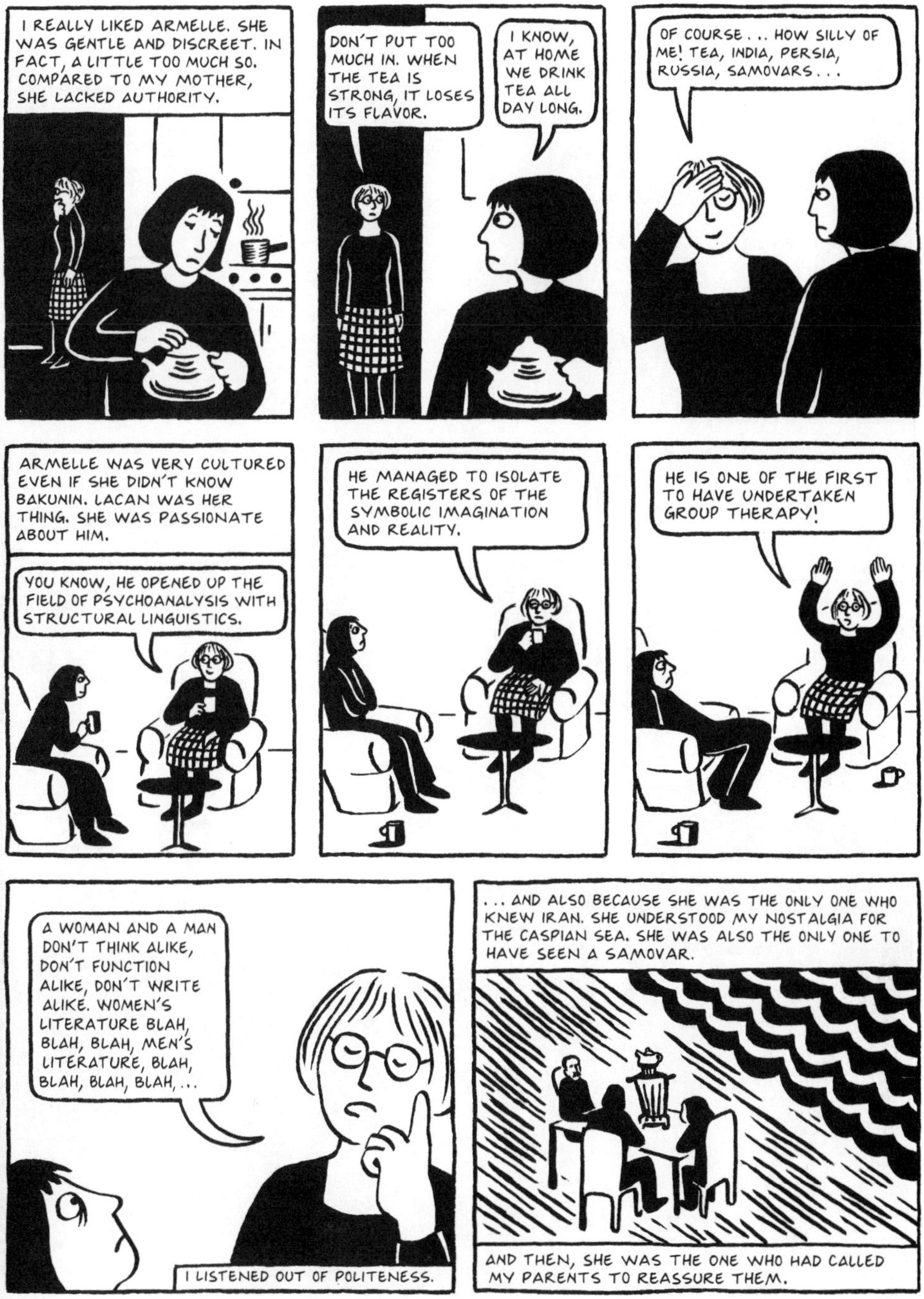

I REALLY LIKED ARMELLE. SHE WAS GENTLE AND DISCREET. IN FACT, A LITTLE TOO MUCH SO. COMPARED TO MY MOTHER, SHE LACKED AUTHORITY.
DON'T PUT TOO MUCH IN. WHEN THE TEA IS STRONG, IT LOSES ITS FLAVOR.
I KNOW, AT HOME WE DRINK TEA ALL DAY LONG.
OF COURSE... HOW SILLY OF ME! TEA, INDIA, PERSIA, RUSSIA, SAMOVARS...
ARMELLE WAS VERY CULTURED EVEN IF SHE DIDN'T KNOW BAKUNIN. LACAN WAS HER THING. SHE WAS PASSIONATE ABOUT HIM.
YOU KNOW, HE OPENED UP THE FIELD OF PSYCHOANALYSIS WITH STRUCTURAL LINGUISTICS.
HE MANAGED TO ISOLATE THE REGISTERS OF THE SYMBOLIC IMAGINATION AND REALITY.
HE IS ONE OF THE FIRST TO HAVE UNDERTAKEN GROUP THERAPY!
A WOMAN AND A MAN DON'T THINK ALIKE, DON'T FUNCTION ALIKE, DON'T WRITE ALIKE. WOMEN'S LITERATURE BLAH, BLAH, BLAH, MEN'S LITERATURE, BLAH, BLAH, BLAH, BLAH, ...
I LISTENED OUT OF POLITENESS.
... AND ALSO BECAUSE SHE WAS THE ONLY ONE WHO KNEW IRAN. SHE UNDERSTOOD MY NOSTALGIA FOR THE CASPIAN SEA. SHE WAS ALSO THE ONLY ONE TO HAVE SEEN A SAMOVAR.
AND THEN, SHE WAS THE ONE WHO HAD CALLED MY PARENTS TO REASSURE THEM.

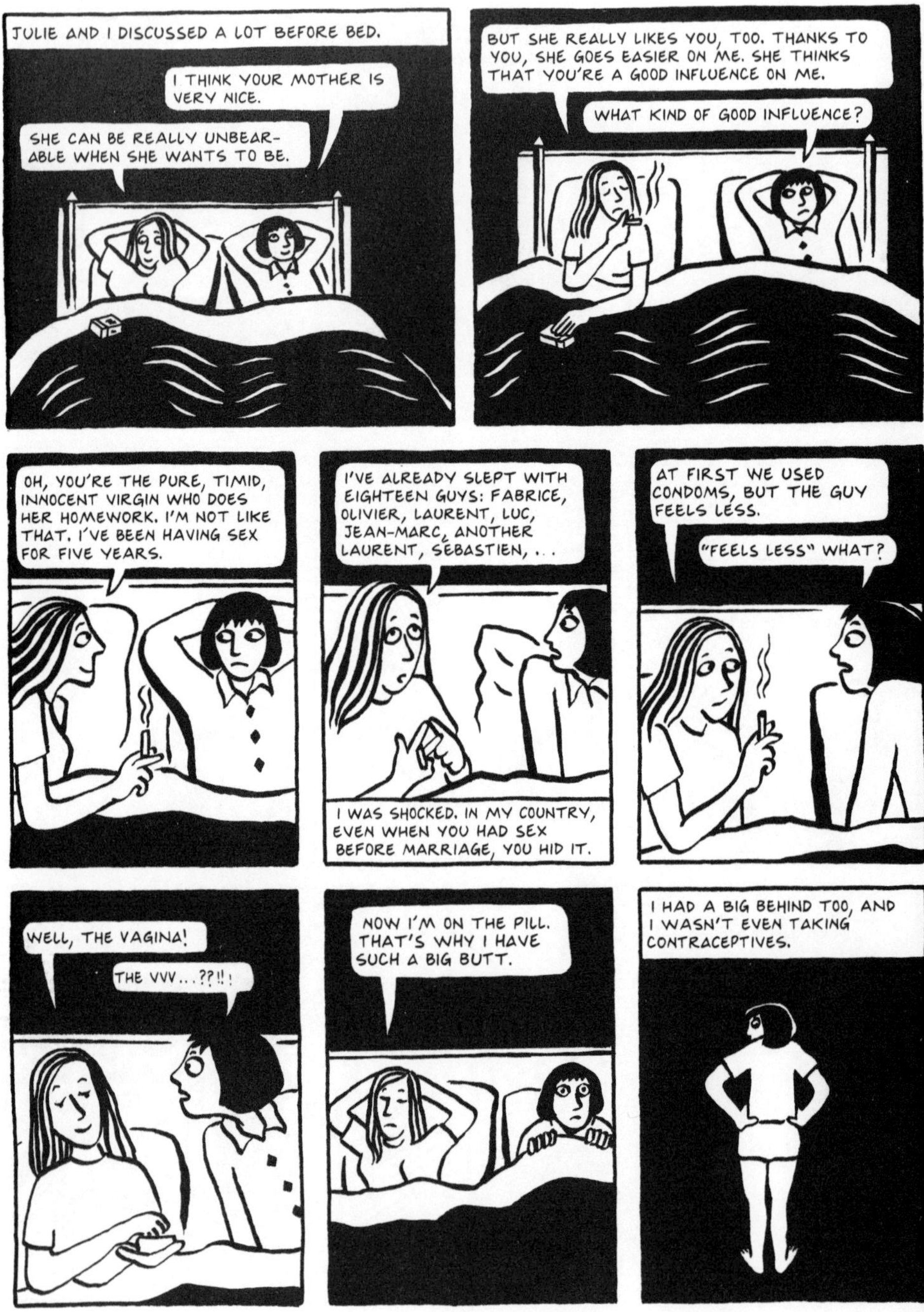
JULIE AND I DISCUSSED A LOT BEFORE BED.
I THINK YOUR MOTHER IS VERY NICE.
SHE CAN BE REALLY UNBEARABLE WHEN SHE WANTS TO BE.
BUT SHE REALLY LIKES YOU, TOO. THANKS TO YOU, SHE GOES EASIER ON ME. SHE THINKS THAT YOU'RE A GOOD INFLUENCE ON ME.
WHAT KIND OF GOOD INFLUENCE?
OH, YOU'RE THE PURE, TIMID, INNOCENT VIRGIN WHO DOES HER HOMEWORK. I'M NOT LIKE THAT. I'VE BEEN HAVING SEX FOR FIVE YEARS.
I'VE ALREADY SLEPT WITH EIGHTEEN GUYS: FABRICE, OLIVIER, LAURENT, LUC, JEAN-MARC, ANOTHER LAURENT, SÉBASTIEN, . . .
I WAS SHOCKED. IN MY COUNTRY, EVEN WHEN YOU HAD SEX BEFORE MARRIAGE, YOU HID IT.
AT FIRST WE USED CONDOMS, BUT THE GUY FEELS LESS.
"FEELS LESS" WHAT?
WELL, THE VAGINA!
THE VVV...??!!!
NOW I'M ON THE PILL. THAT'S WHY I HAVE SUCH A BIG BUTT.
I HAD A BIG BEHIND TOO, AND I WASN'T EVEN TAKING CONTRACEPTIVES.

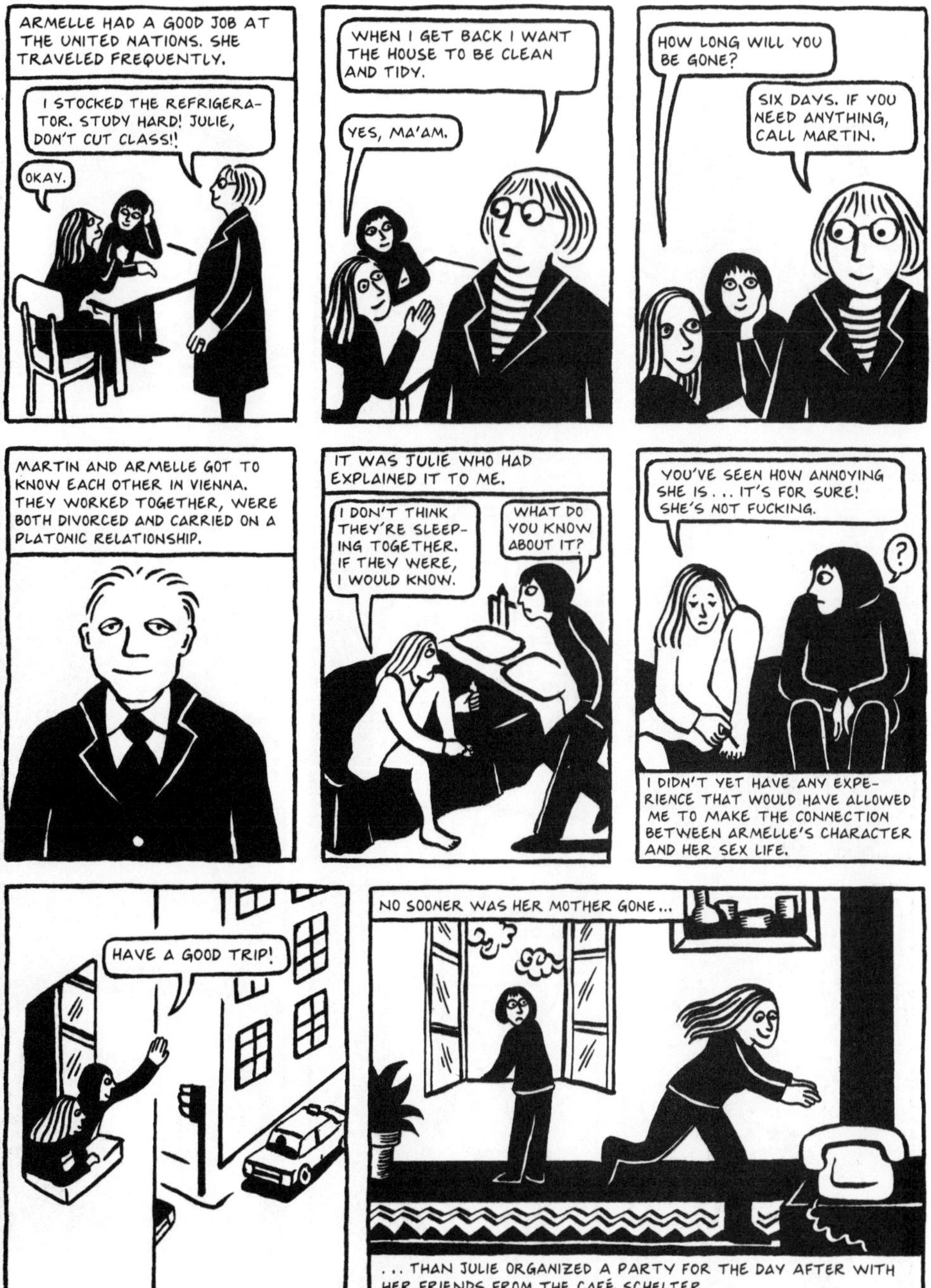
ARMELLE HAD A GOOD JOB AT THE UNITED NATIONS. SHE TRAVELED FREQUENTLY.
I STOCKED THE REFRIGERATOR. STUDY HARD! JULIE, DON'T CUT CLASS!!
OKAY.
WHEN I GET BACK I WANT THE HOUSE TO BE CLEAN AND TIDY.
YES, MA'AM.
HOW LONG WILL YOU BE GONE?
SIX DAYS. IF YOU NEED ANYTHING, CALL MARTIN.
MARTIN AND ARMELLE GOT TO KNOW EACH OTHER IN VIENNA. THEY WORKED TOGETHER, WERE BOTH DIVORCED AND CARRIED ON A PLATONIC RELATIONSHIP.
IT WAS JULIE WHO HAD EXPLAINED IT TO ME.
I DON'T THINK THEY'RE SLEEPING TOGETHER. IF THEY WERE, I WOULD KNOW.
WHAT DO YOU KNOW ABOUT IT?
YOU'VE SEEN HOW ANNOYING SHE IS . . . IT'S FOR SURE! SHE'S NOT FUCKING.
?
I DIDN'T YET HAVE ANY EXPERIENCE THAT WOULD HAVE ALLOWED ME TO MAKE THE CONNECTION BETWEEN ARMELLE'S CHARACTER AND HER SEX LIFE.
HAVE A GOOD TRIP!
NO SOONER WAS HER MOTHER GONE...
. . . THAN JULIE ORGANIZED A PARTY FOR THE DAY AFTER WITH HER FRIENDS FROM THE CAFÉ SCHELTER.

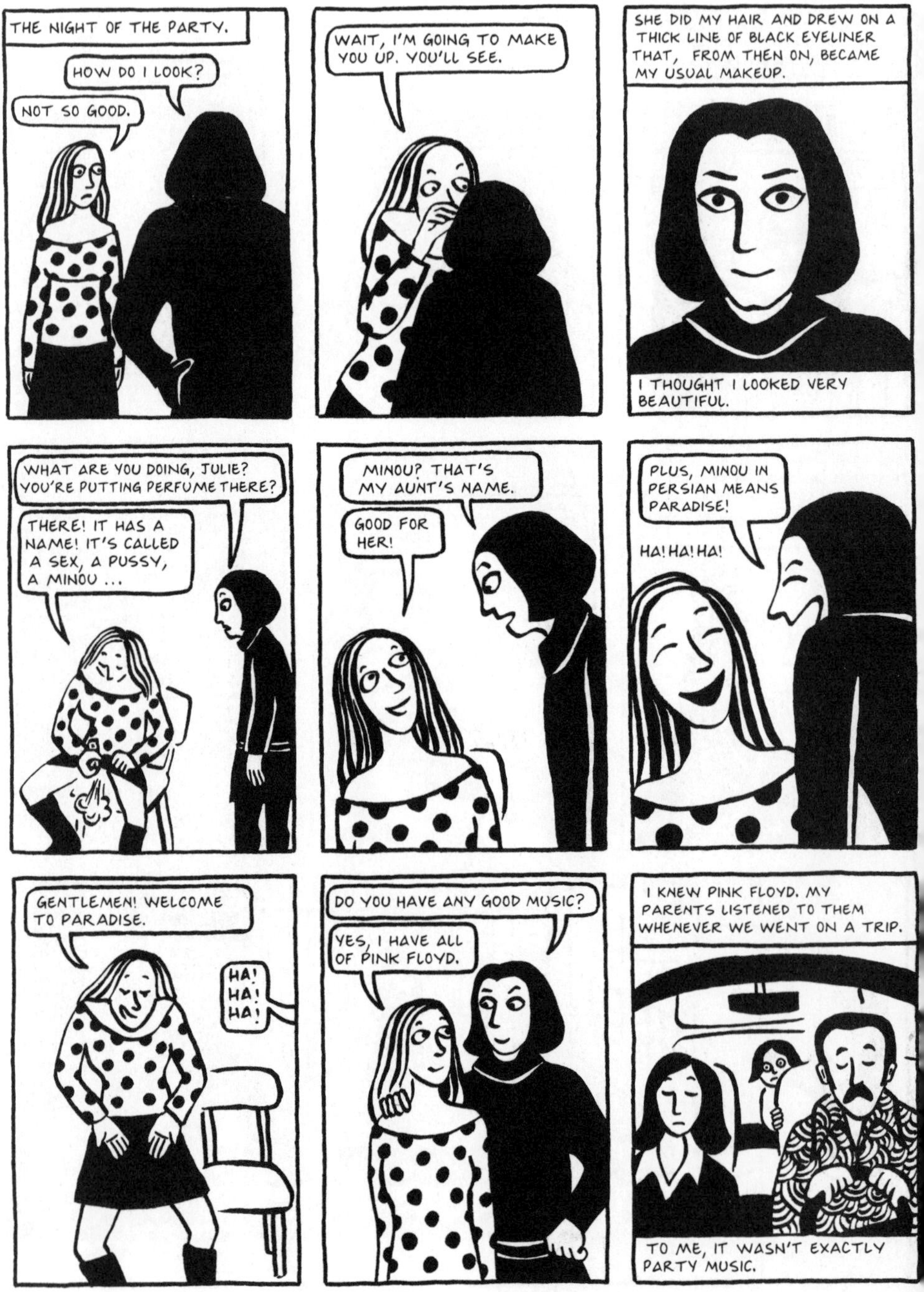
THE NIGHT OF THE PARTY.
HOW DO I LOOK?
NOT SO GOOD.
WAIT, I'M GOING TO MAKE YOU UP. YOU'LL SEE.
SHE DID MY HAIR AND DREW ON A THICK LINE OF BLACK EYELINER THAT, FROM THEN ON, BECAME MY USUAL MAKEUP.
I THOUGHT I LOOKED VERY BEAUTIFUL.
WHAT ARE YOU DOING, JULIE? YOU'RE PUTTING PERFUME THERE?
THERE! IT HAS A NAME! IT'S CALLED A SEX, A PUSSY, A MINOU ...
MINOU? THAT'S MY AUNT'S NAME.
GOOD FOR HER!
PLUS, MINOU IN PERSIAN MEANS PARADISE!
HA! HA! HA!
GENTLEMEN! WELCOME TO PARADISE.
HA! HA! HA!
DO YOU HAVE ANY GOOD MUSIC?
YES, I HAVE ALL OF PINK FLOYD.
I KNEW PINK FLOYD. MY PARENTS LISTENED TO THEM WHENEVER WE WENT ON A TRIP.
TO ME, IT WASN'T EXACTLY PARTY MUSIC.

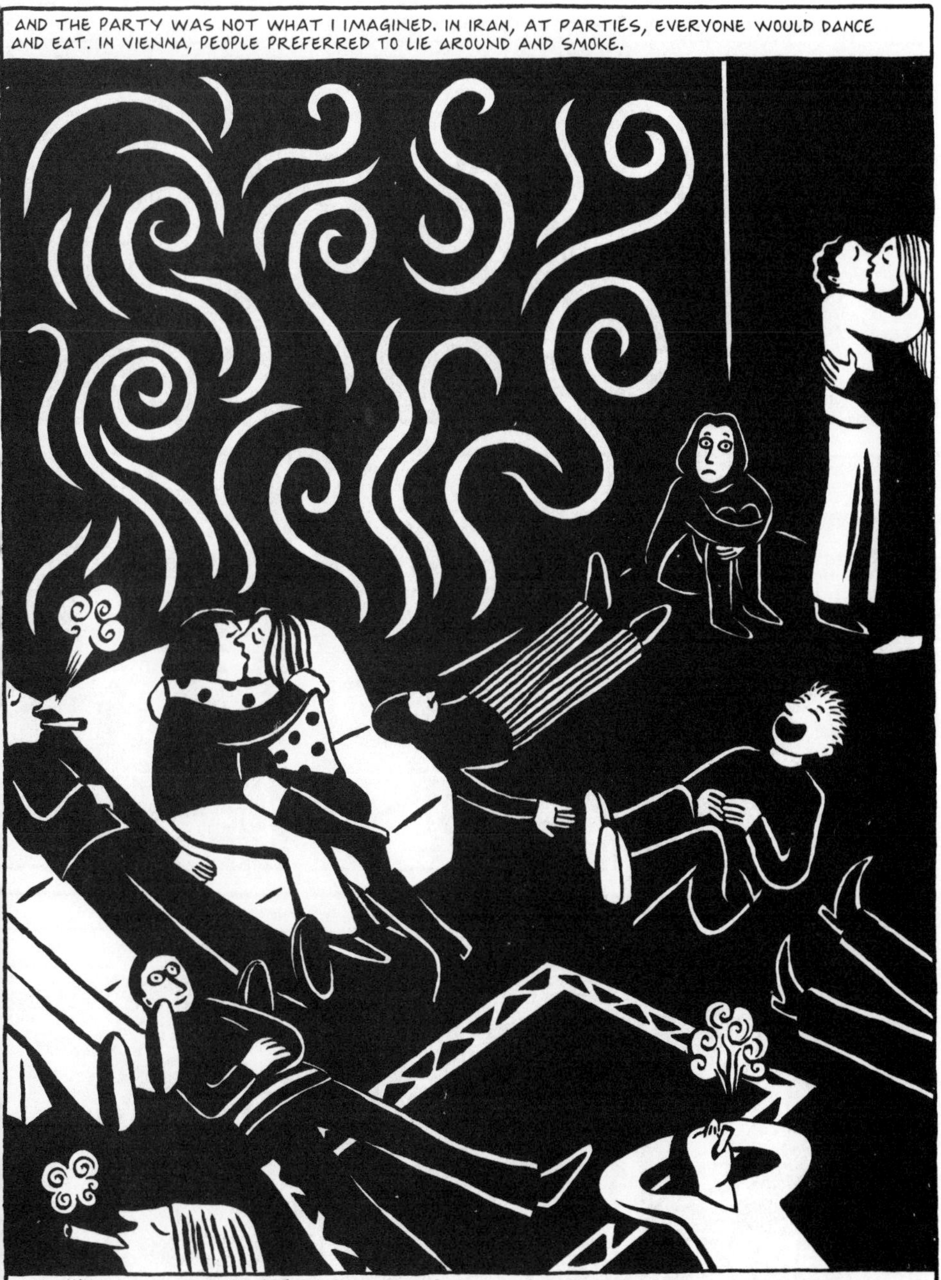

AND THE PARTY WAS NOT WHAT I IMAGINED. IN IRAN, AT PARTIES, EVERYONE WOULD DANCE AND EAT. IN VIENNA, PEOPLE PREFERRED TO LIE AROUND AND SMOKE.
AND THEN, I WAS TURNED OFF BY ALL THESE PUBLIC DISPLAYS OF AFFECTION. WHAT DO YOU EXPECT, I CAME FROM A TRADITIONALIST COUNTRY.

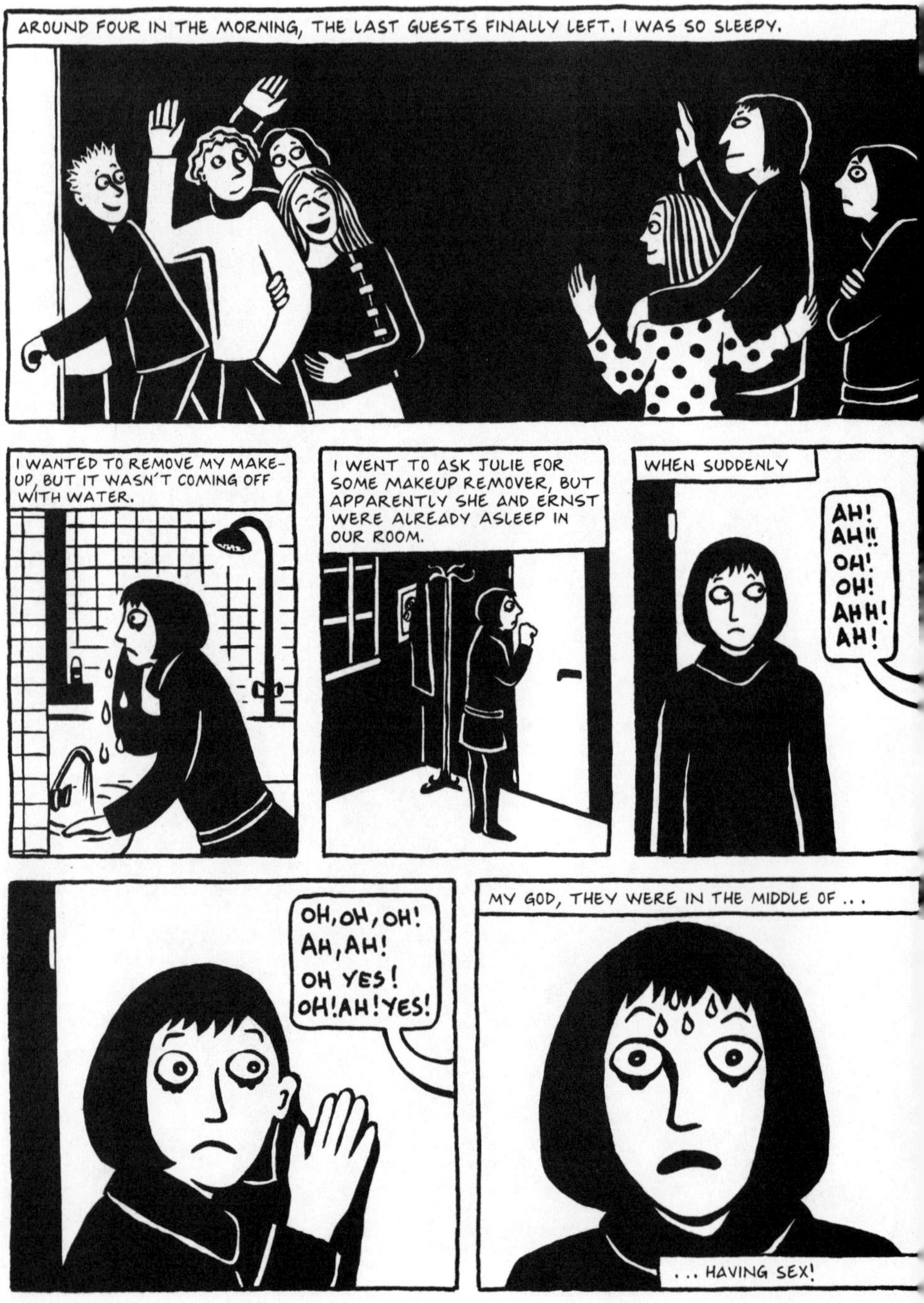
AROUND FOUR IN THE MORNING, THE LAST GUESTS FINALLY LEFT. I WAS SO SLEEPY.
I WANTED TO REMOVE MY MAKE-UP, BUT IT WASN'T COMING OFF WITH WATER.
I WENT TO ASK JULIE FOR SOME MAKEUP REMOVER, BUT APPARENTLY SHE AND ERNST WERE ALREADY ASLEEP IN OUR ROOM.
WHEN SUDDENLY
AH! AH!! OH! OH! AHH! AH!
OH, OH, OH! AH, AH! OH YES! OH! AH! YES!
MY GOD, THEY WERE IN THE MIDDLE OF . . .
. . . HAVING SEX!

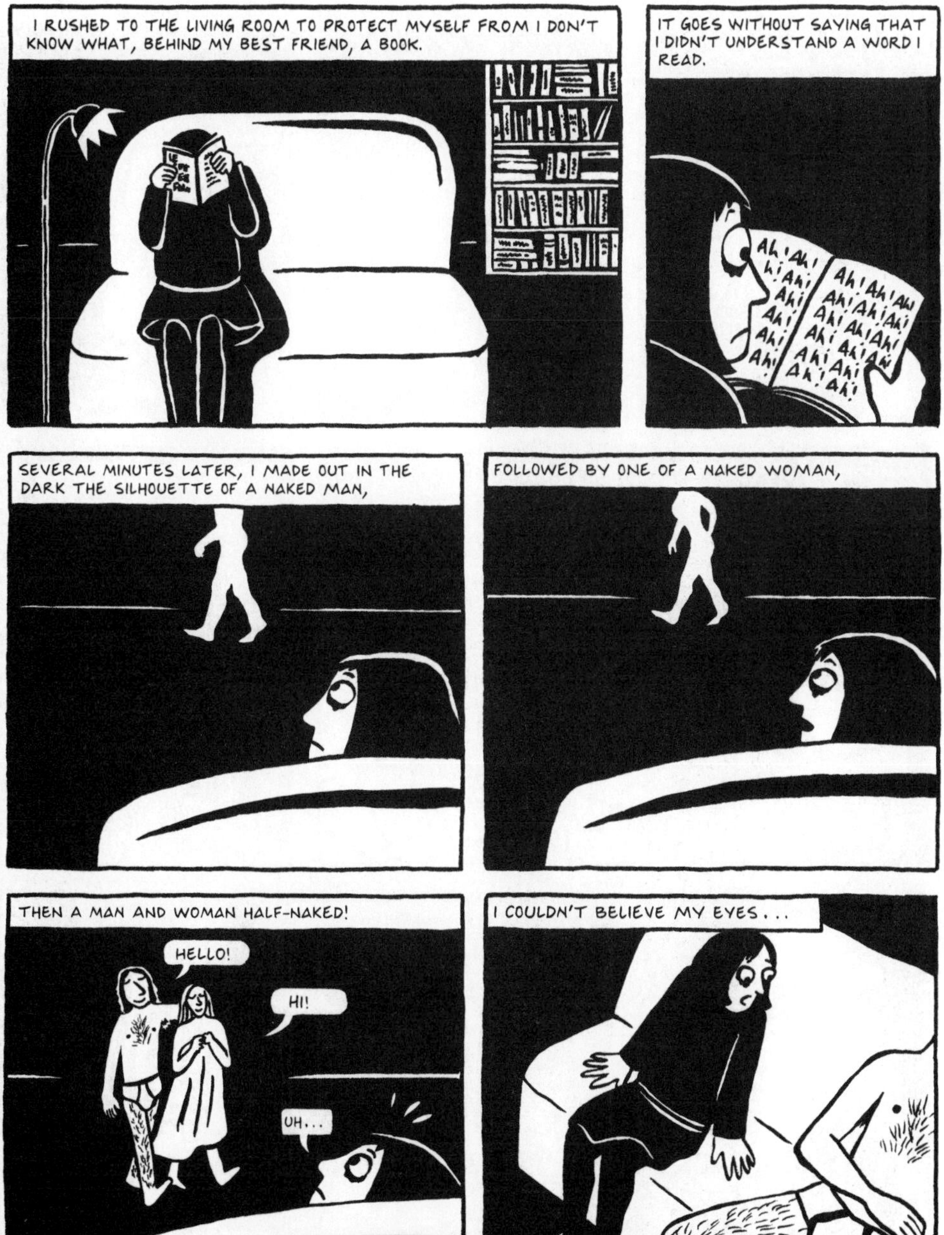
I RUSHED TO THE LIVING ROOM TO PROTECT MYSELF FROM I DON'T KNOW WHAT, BEHIND MY BEST FRIEND, A BOOK.
IT GOES WITHOUT SAYING THAT I DIDN'T UNDERSTAND A WORD I READ.
SEVERAL MINUTES LATER, I MADE OUT IN THE DARK THE SILHOUETTE OF A NAKED MAN,
FOLLOWED BY ONE OF A NAKED WOMAN,
THEN A MAN AND WOMAN HALF-NAKED!
HELLO!
HI!
UH...
I COULDN'T BELIEVE MY EYES...
... I'D NEVER SEEN THAT!

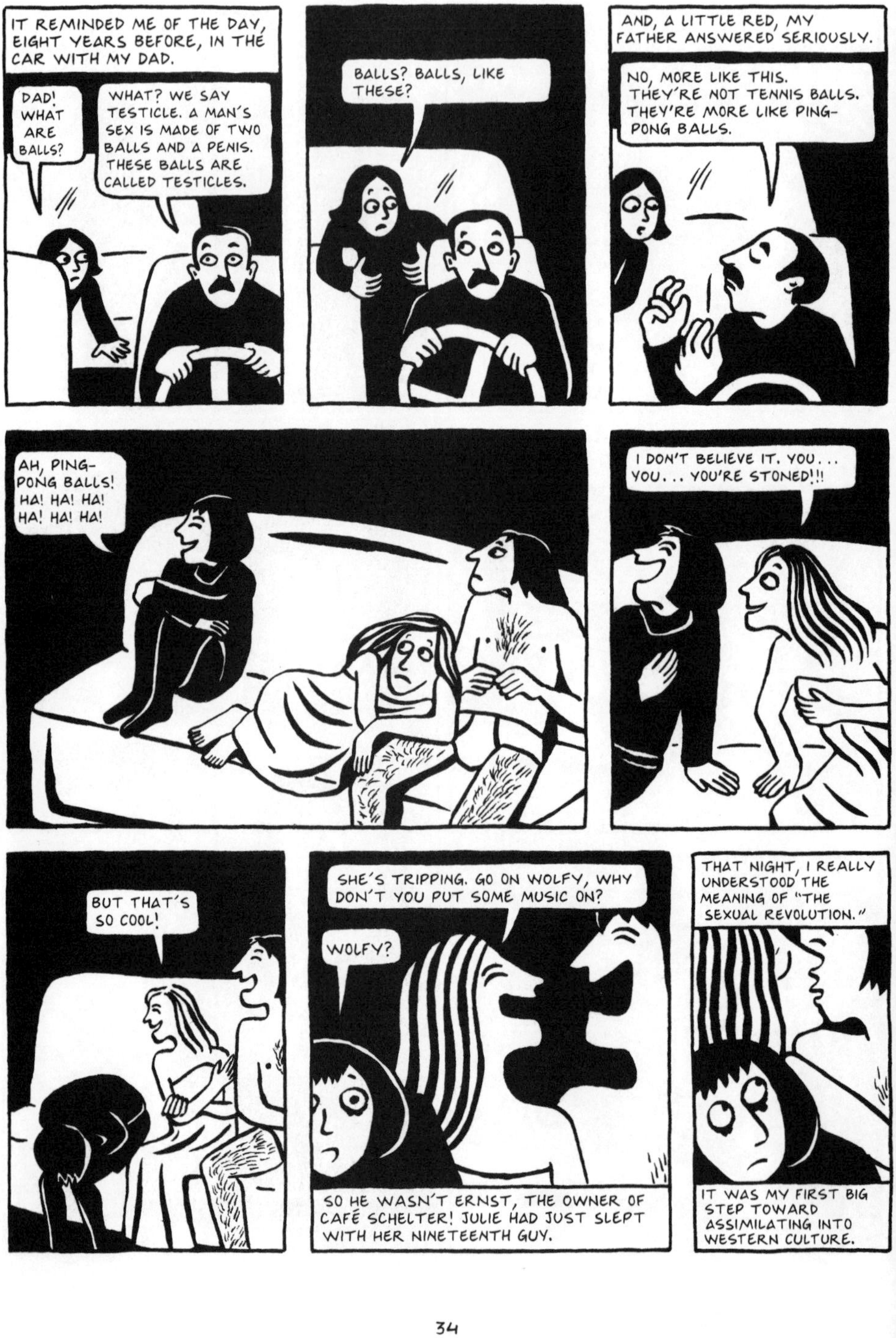
IT REMINDED ME OF THE DAY, EIGHT YEARS BEFORE, IN THE CAR WITH MY DAD.
DAD! WHAT ARE BALLS?
WHAT? WE SAY TESTICLE. A MAN'S SEX IS MADE OF TWO BALLS AND A PENIS. THESE BALLS ARE CALLED TESTICLES.
BALLS? BALLS, LIKE THESE?
AND, A LITTLE RED, MY FATHER ANSWERED SERIOUSLY.
NO, MORE LIKE THIS. THEY'RE NOT TENNIS BALLS. THEY'RE MORE LIKE PING-PONG BALLS.
AH, PING-PONG BALLS! HA! HA! HA! HA! HA! HA!
I DON'T BELIEVE IT. YOU... YOU... YOU'RE STONED!!!
BUT THAT'S SO COOL!
SHE'S TRIPPING. GO ON WOLFY, WHY DON'T YOU PUT SOME MUSIC ON?
WOLFY?
SO HE WASN'T ERNST, THE OWNER OF CAFÉ SCHELTER! JULIE HAD JUST SLEPT WITH HER NINETEENTH GUY.
THAT NIGHT, I REALLY UNDERSTOOD THE MEANING OF "THE SEXUAL REVOLUTION."
IT WAS MY FIRST BIG STEP TOWARD ASSIMILATING INTO WESTERN CULTURE.

THE VEGETABLE

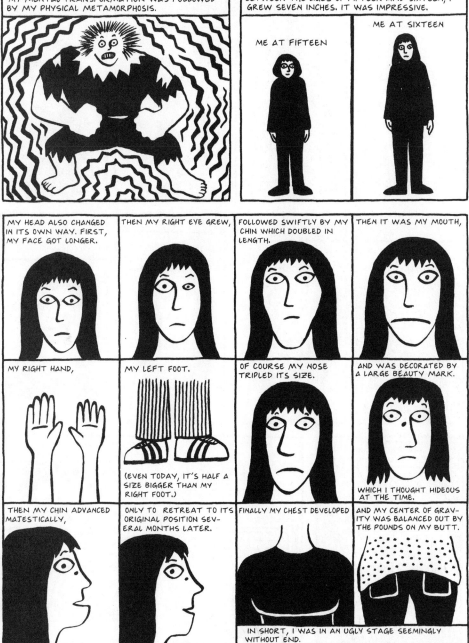

MY MENTAL TRANSFORMATION WAS FOLLOWED BY MY PHYSICAL METAMORPHOSIS.

BETWEEN THE AGES OF FIFTEEN AND SIXTEEN, I GREW SEVEN INCHES. IT WAS IMPRESSIVE.

ME AT FIFTEEN

ME AT SIXTEEN

MY HEAD ALSO CHANGED IN ITS OWN WAY. FIRST, MY FACE GOT LONGER.

THEN MY RIGHT EYE GREW,

FOLLOWED SWIFTLY BY MY CHIN WHICH DOUBLED IN LENGTH.

THEN IT WAS MY MOUTH,

MY RIGHT HAND,

MY LEFT FOOT.

(EVEN TODAY, IT'S HALF A SIZE BIGGER THAN MY RIGHT FOOT.)

OF COURSE MY NOSE TRIPLED ITS SIZE.

AND WAS DECORATED BY A LARGE BEAUTY MARK.

WHICH I THOUGHT HIDEOUS AT THE TIME.

THEN MY CHIN ADVANCED MAJESTICALLY,

ONLY TO RETREAT TO ITS ORIGINAL POSITION SEVERAL MONTHS LATER.

FINALLY MY CHEST DEVELOPED

AND MY CENTER OF GRAVITY WAS BALANCED OUT BY THE POUNDS ON MY BUTT.

IN SHORT, I WAS IN AN UGLY STAGE SEEMINGLY WITHOUT END.

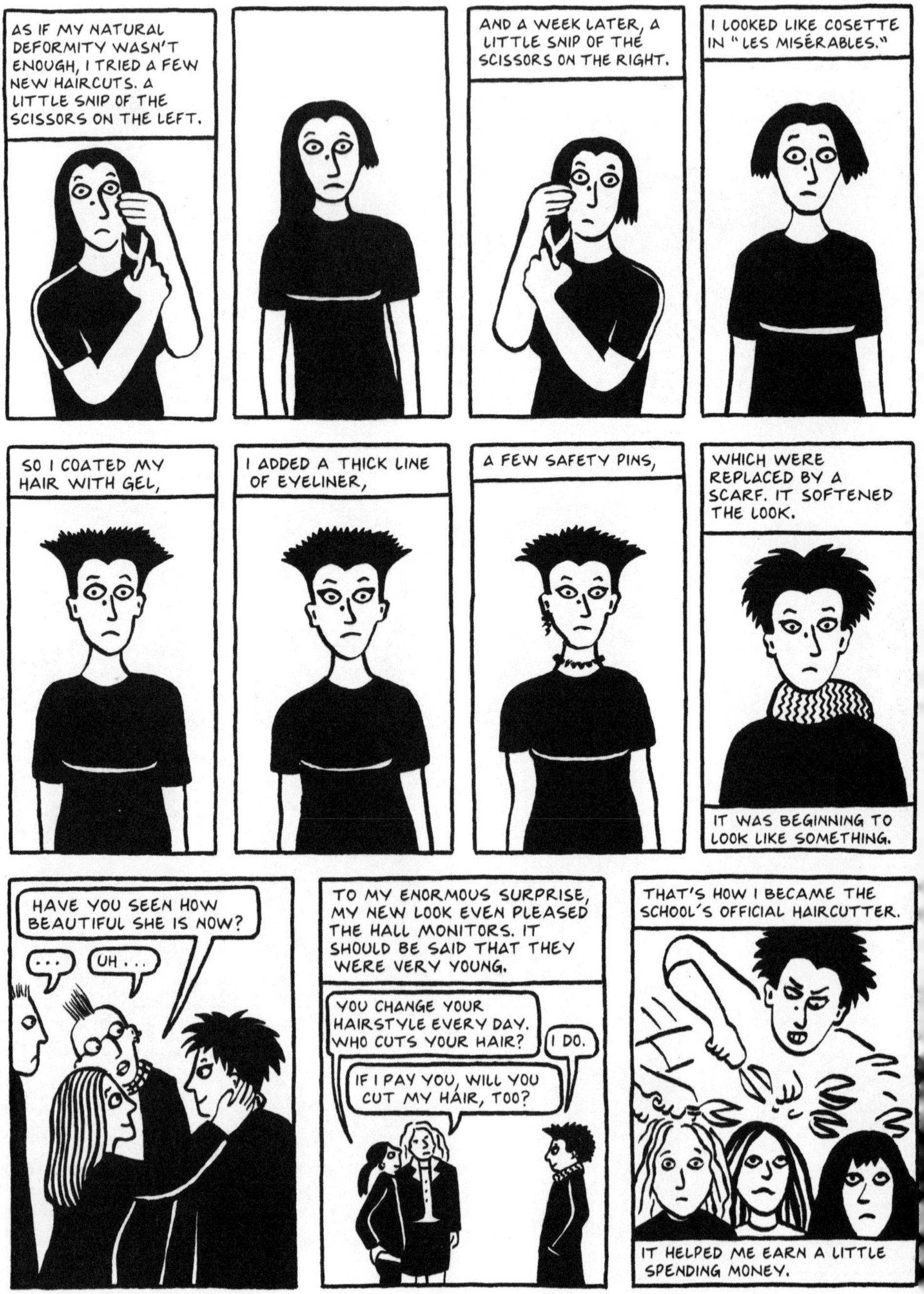
AS IF MY NATURAL DEFORMITY WASN'T ENOUGH, I TRIED A FEW NEW HAIRCUTS. A LITTLE SNIP OF THE SCISSORS ON THE LEFT.
AND A WEEK LATER, A LITTLE SNIP OF THE SCISSORS ON THE RIGHT.
I LOOKED LIKE COSETTE IN "LES MISÉRABLES."
SO I COATED MY HAIR WITH GEL,
I ADDED A THICK LINE OF EYELINER,
A FEW SAFETY PINS,
WHICH WERE REPLACED BY A SCARF. IT SOFTENED THE LOOK.
IT WAS BEGINNING TO LOOK LIKE SOMETHING.
HAVE YOU SEEN HOW BEAUTIFUL SHE IS NOW?
...
UH...
TO MY ENORMOUS SURPRISE, MY NEW LOOK EVEN PLEASED THE HALL MONITORS. IT SHOULD BE SAID THAT THEY WERE VERY YOUNG.
YOU CHANGE YOUR HAIRSTYLE EVERY DAY. WHO CUTS YOUR HAIR?
I DO.
IF I PAY YOU, WILL YOU CUT MY HAIR, TOO?
THAT'S HOW I BECAME THE SCHOOL'S OFFICIAL HAIRCUTTER.
IT HELPED ME EARN A LITTLE SPENDING MONEY.

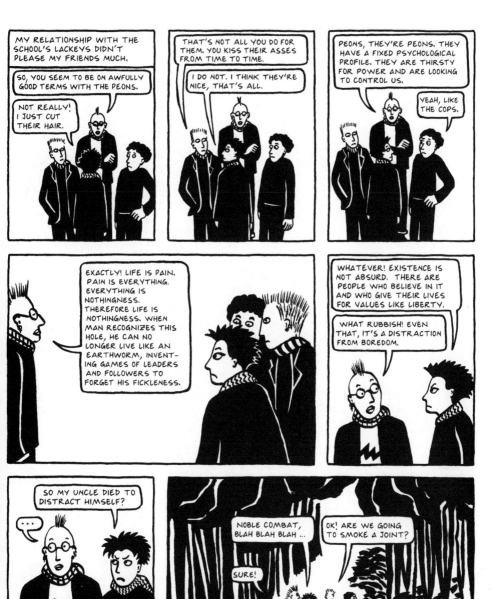

MY RELATIONSHIP WITH THE SCHOOL'S LACKEYS DIDN'T PLEASE MY FRIENDS MUCH.

SO, YOU SEEM TO BE ON AWFULLY GOOD TERMS WITH THE PEONS.

NOT REALLY! I JUST CUT THEIR HAIR.

THAT'S NOT ALL YOU DO FOR THEM. YOU KISS THEIR ASSES FROM TIME TO TIME.

I DO NOT. I THINK THEY'RE NICE, THAT'S ALL.

PEONS, THEY'RE PEONS. THEY HAVE A FIXED PSYCHOLOGICAL PROFILE. THEY ARE THIRSTY FOR POWER AND ARE LOOKING TO CONTROL US.

YEAH, LIKE THE COPS.

EXACTLY! LIFE IS PAIN. PAIN IS EVERYTHING. EVERYTHING IS NOTHINGNESS. THEREFORE LIFE IS NOTHINGNESS. WHEN MAN RECOGNIZES THIS HOLE, HE CAN NO LONGER LIVE LIKE AN EARTHWORM, INVENT-ING GAMES OF LEADERS AND FOLLOWERS TO FORGET HIS FICKLENESS.

WHATEVER! EXISTENCE IS NOT ABSURD. THERE ARE PEOPLE WHO BELIEVE IN IT AND WHO GIVE THEIR LIVES FOR VALUES LIKE LIBERTY.

WHAT RUBBISH! EVEN THAT, IT'S A DISTRACTION FROM BOREDOM.

SO MY UNCLE DIED TO DISTRACT HIMSELF?

...

FOR MOMO, DEATH WAS THE ONLY DOMAIN WHERE MY KNOWLEDGE EXCEEDED HIS. ON THIS SUBJECT, I ALWAYS HAD THE LAST WORD.

NOBLE COMBAT, BLAH BLAH BLAH ...

SURE!

OK! ARE WE GOING TO SMOKE A JOINT?

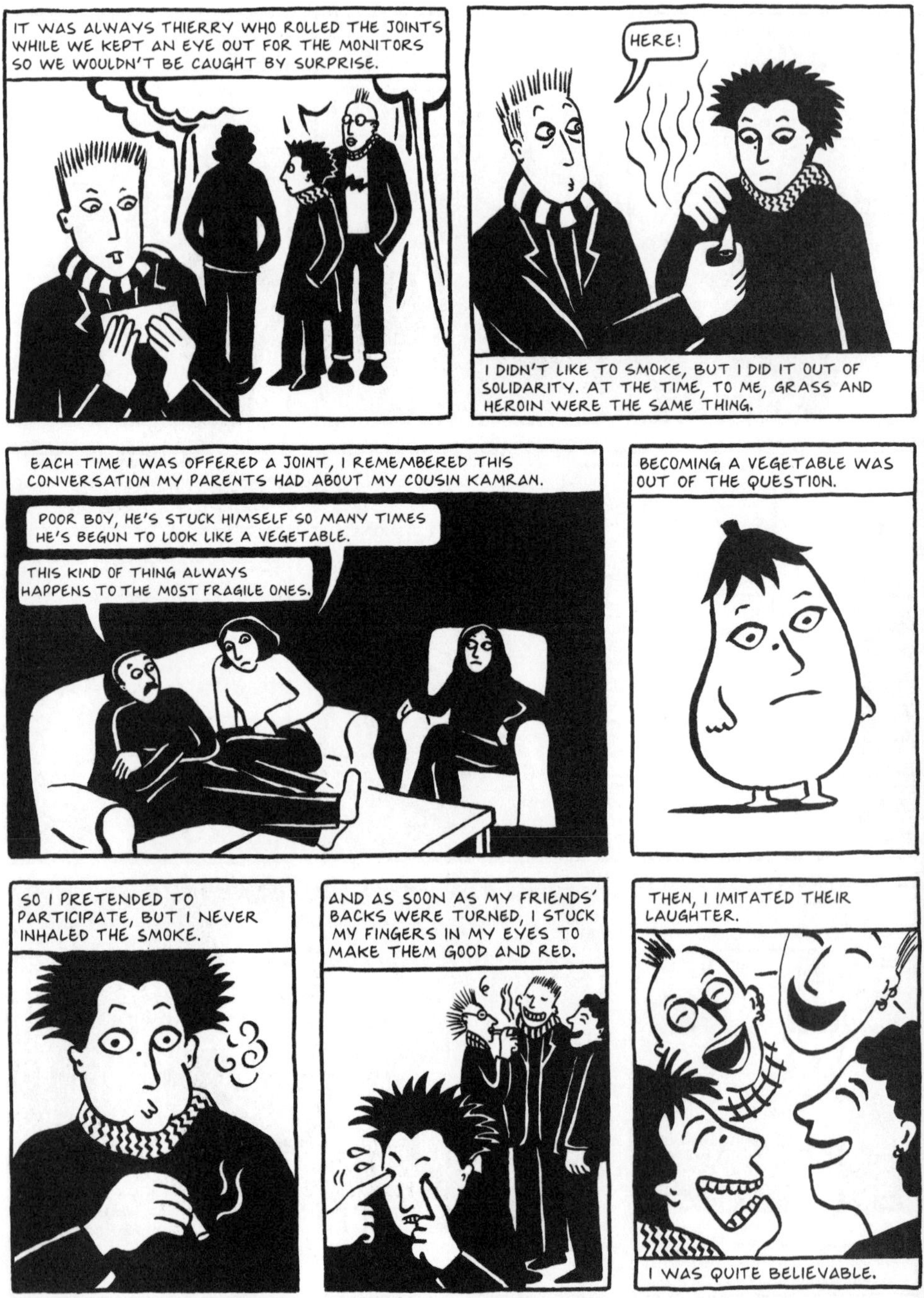
IT WAS ALWAYS THIERRY WHO ROLLED THE JOINTS WHILE WE KEPT AN EYE OUT FOR THE MONITORS SO WE WOULDN'T BE CAUGHT BY SURPRISE.
HERE!
I DIDN'T LIKE TO SMOKE, BUT I DID IT OUT OF SOLIDARITY. AT THE TIME, TO ME, GRASS AND HEROIN WERE THE SAME THING.
EACH TIME I WAS OFFERED A JOINT, I REMEMBERED THIS CONVERSATION MY PARENTS HAD ABOUT MY COUSIN KAMRAN.
POOR BOY, HE'S STUCK HIMSELF SO MANY TIMES HE'S BEGUN TO LOOK LIKE A VEGETABLE.
THIS KIND OF THING ALWAYS HAPPENS TO THE MOST FRAGILE ONES.
BECOMING A VEGETABLE WAS OUT OF THE QUESTION.
SO I PRETENDED TO PARTICIPATE, BUT I NEVER INHALED THE SMOKE.
AND AS SOON AS MY FRIENDS' BACKS WERE TURNED, I STUCK MY FINGERS IN MY EYES TO MAKE THEM GOOD AND RED.
THEN, I IMITATED THEIR LAUGHTER.
I WAS QUITE BELIEVABLE.

THE HARDER I TRIED TO ASSIMILATE, THE MORE I HAD THE FEELING THAT I WAS DISTANCING MYSELF FROM MY CULTURE, BETRAYING MY PARENTS AND MY ORIGINS, THAT I WAS PLAYING A GAME BY SOMEBODY ELSE'S RULES.

EACH TELEPHONE CALL FROM MY PARENTS REMINDED ME OF MY COWARDICE AND MY BETRAYAL. I WAS AT ONCE HAPPY TO HEAR THEIR VOICES AND ASHAMED TO TALK TO THEM.

- YES, I'M DOING FINE. I'M GETTING GOOD GRADES.

- FRIENDS? OF COURSE, LOTS!

- DAD ...

- DAD, I LOVE YOU!

- YOU HAVE SOME GOOD FRIENDS?

- THAT DOESN'T SURPRISE ME, YOU ALWAYS HAD A TALENT FOR COMMUNICATING WITH PEOPLE!

- EAT ORANGES. THEY'RE FULL OF VITAMIN C.

- US TOO, WE ADORE YOU. YOU'RE THE CHILD ALL PARENTS DREAM OF HAVING!

IF ONLY THEY KNEW ... IF THEY KNEW THAT THEIR DAUGHTER WAS MADE UP LIKE A PUNK, THAT SHE SMOKED JOINTS TO MAKE A GOOD IMPRESSION, THAT SHE HAD SEEN MEN IN THEIR UNDERWEAR WHILE THEY WERE BEING BOMBED EVERY DAY, THEY WOULDN'T CALL ME THEIR DREAM CHILD.

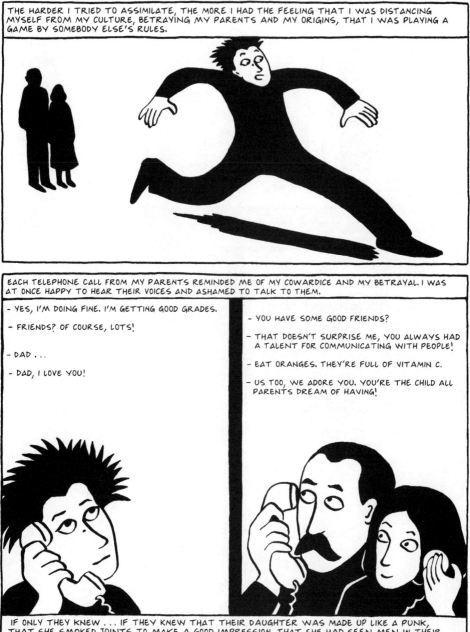

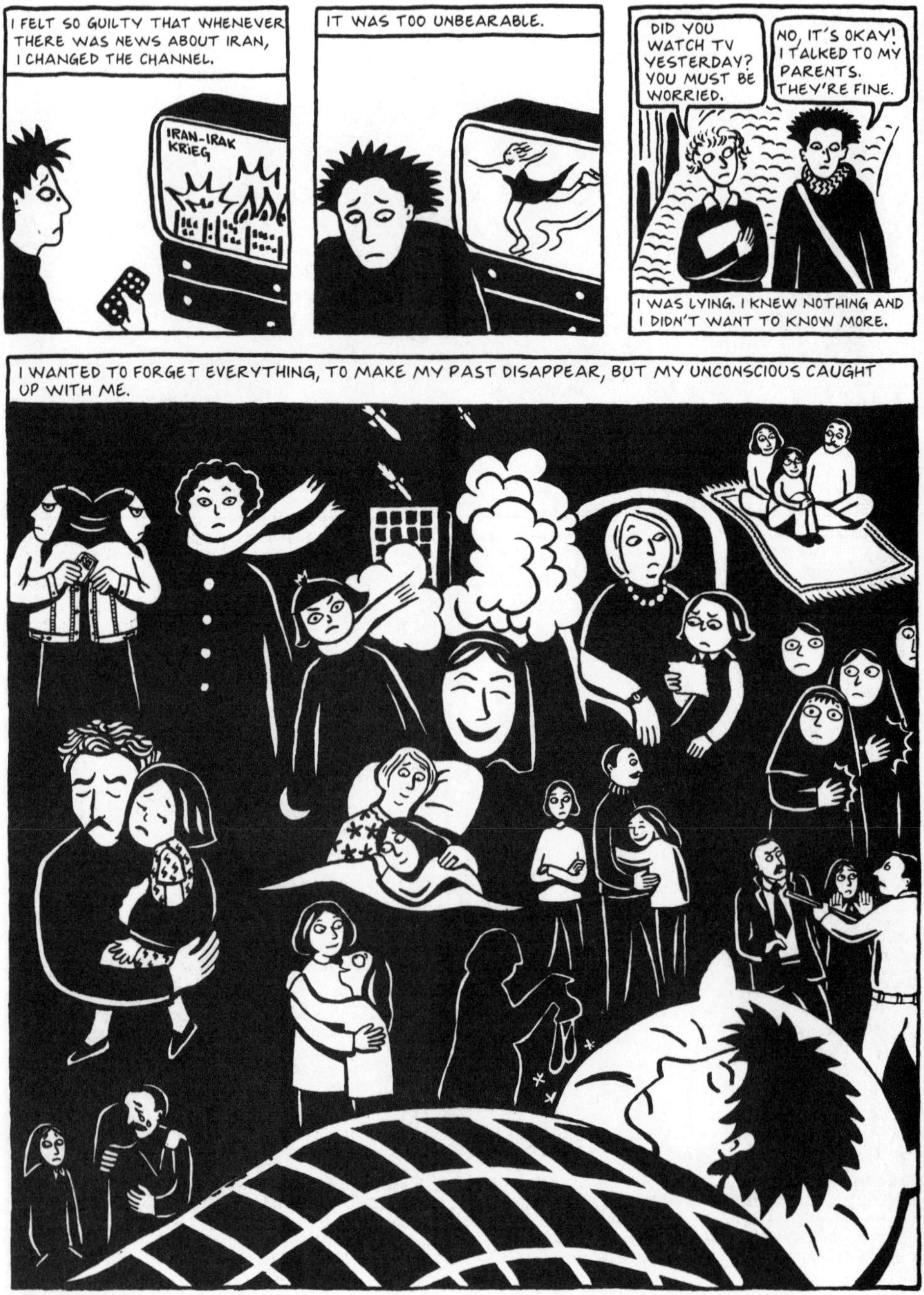
I FELT SO GUILTY THAT WHENEVER THERE WAS NEWS ABOUT IRAN, I CHANGED THE CHANNEL.
IRAN-IRAK KRIEG
IT WAS TOO UNBEARABLE.
DID YOU WATCH TV YESTERDAY? YOU MUST BE WORRIED.
NO, IT'S OKAY! I TALKED TO MY PARENTS. THEY'RE FINE.
I WAS LYING. I KNEW NOTHING AND I DIDN'T WANT TO KNOW MORE.
I WANTED TO FORGET EVERYTHING, TO MAKE MY PAST DISAPPEAR, BUT MY UNCONSCIOUS CAUGHT UP WITH ME.

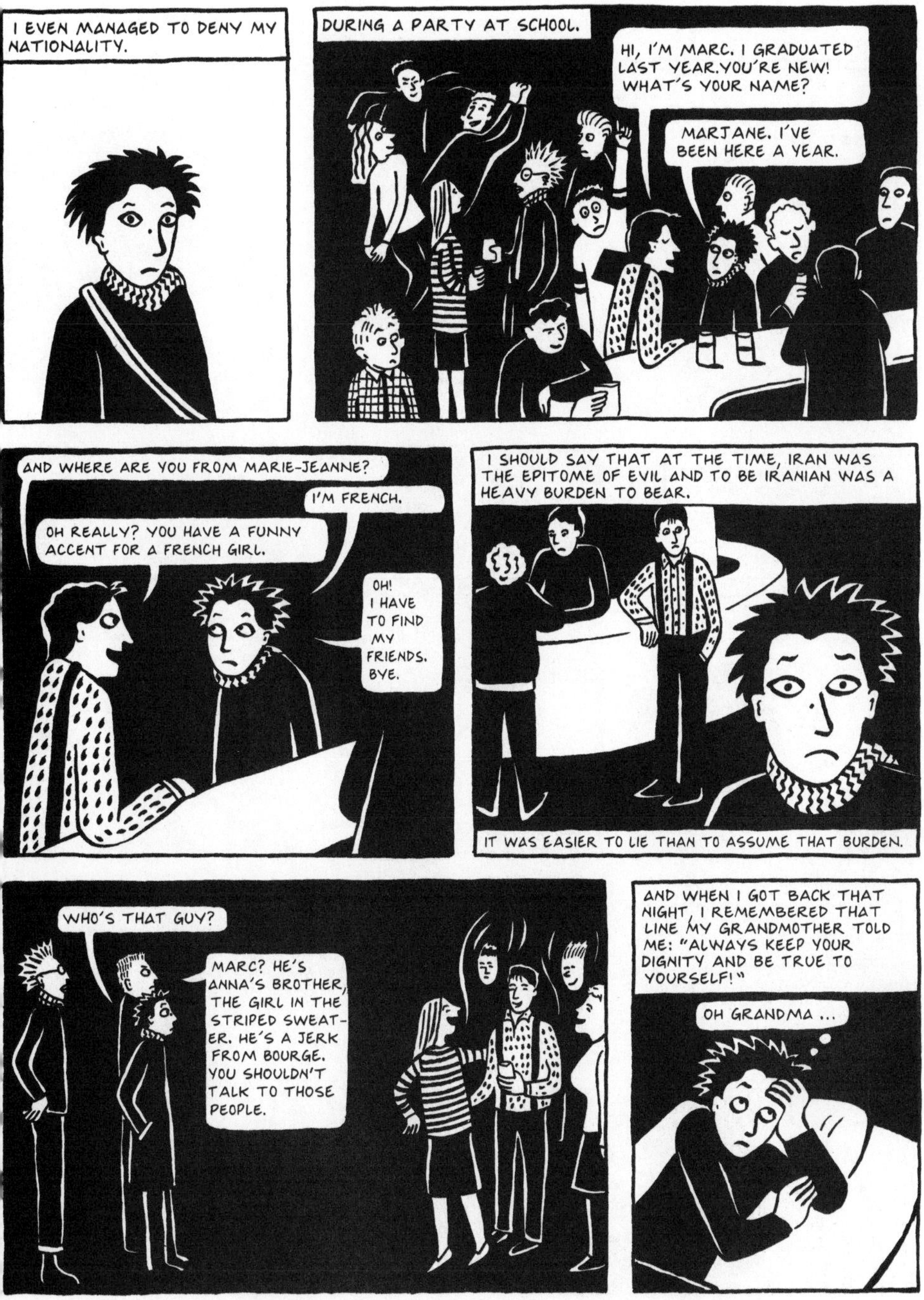

I EVEN MANAGED TO DENY MY NATIONALITY.
DURING A PARTY AT SCHOOL.
HI, I'M MARC. I GRADUATED LAST YEAR. YOU'RE NEW! WHAT'S YOUR NAME?
MARJANE. I'VE BEEN HERE A YEAR.
AND WHERE ARE YOU FROM MARIE-JEANNE?
I'M FRENCH.
OH REALLY? YOU HAVE A FUNNY ACCENT FOR A FRENCH GIRL.
OH! I HAVE TO FIND MY FRIENDS. BYE.
I SHOULD SAY THAT AT THE TIME, IRAN WAS THE EPITOME OF EVIL AND TO BE IRANIAN WAS A HEAVY BURDEN TO BEAR.
IT WAS EASIER TO LIE THAN TO ASSUME THAT BURDEN.
WHO'S THAT GUY?
MARC? HE'S ANNA'S BROTHER, THE GIRL IN THE STRIPED SWEATER. HE'S A JERK FROM BOURGE. YOU SHOULDN'T TALK TO THOSE PEOPLE.
AND WHEN I GOT BACK THAT NIGHT, I REMEMBERED THAT LINE MY GRANDMOTHER TOLD ME: "ALWAYS KEEP YOUR DIGNITY AND BE TRUE TO YOURSELF!"
OH GRANDMA ...

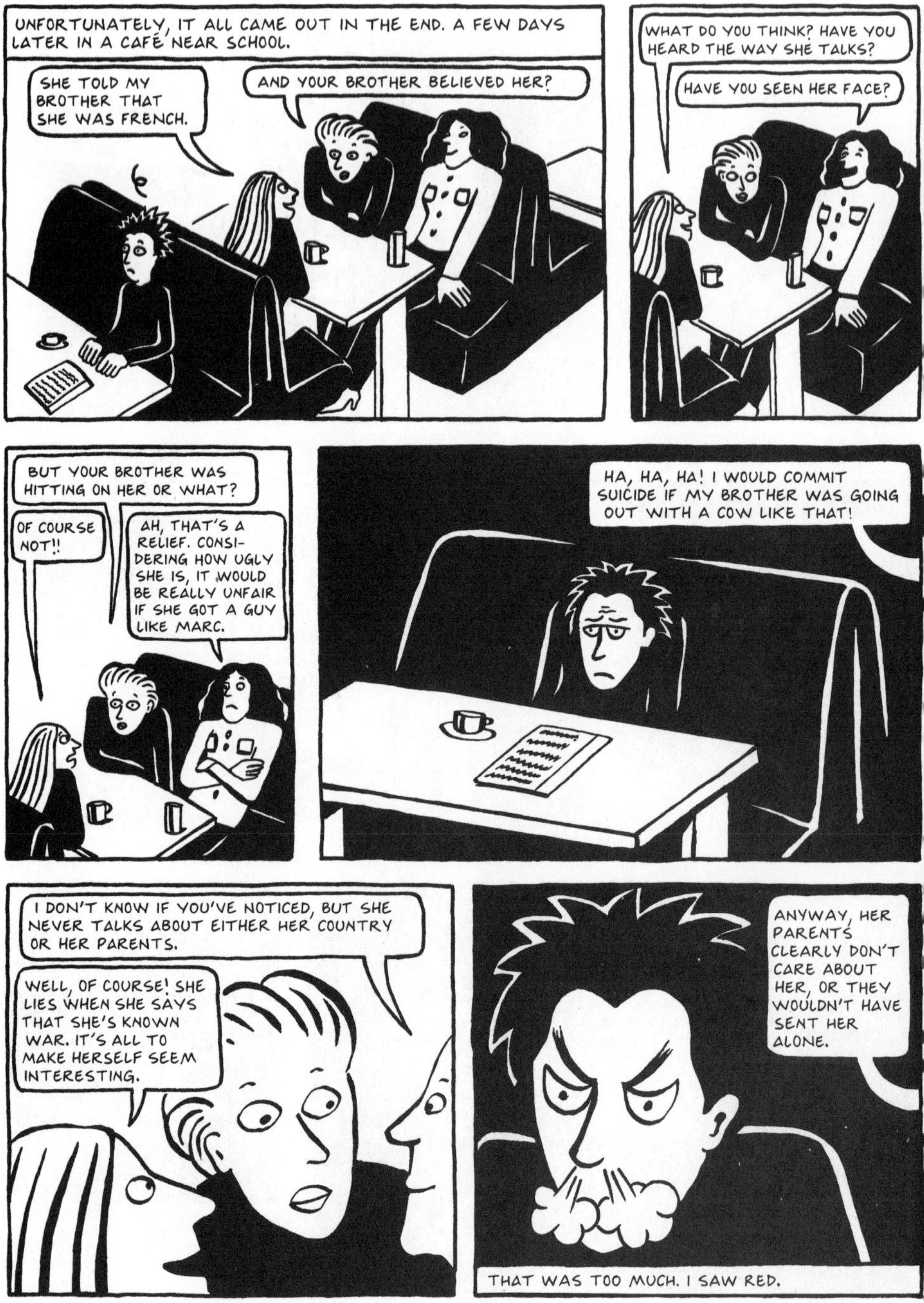
UNFORTUNATELY, IT ALL CAME OUT IN THE END. A FEW DAYS LATER IN A CAFÉ NEAR SCHOOL.
SHE TOLD MY BROTHER THAT SHE WAS FRENCH.
AND YOUR BROTHER BELIEVED HER?
WHAT DO YOU THINK? HAVE YOU HEARD THE WAY SHE TALKS?
HAVE YOU SEEN HER FACE?
BUT YOUR BROTHER WAS HITTING ON HER OR WHAT?
OF COURSE NOT!!
AH, THAT'S A RELIEF. CONSIDERING HOW UGLY SHE IS, IT WOULD BE REALLY UNFAIR IF SHE GOT A GUY LIKE MARC.
HA, HA, HA! I WOULD COMMIT SUICIDE IF MY BROTHER WAS GOING OUT WITH A COW LIKE THAT!
I DON'T KNOW IF YOU'VE NOTICED, BUT SHE NEVER TALKS ABOUT EITHER HER COUNTRY OR HER PARENTS.
WELL, OF COURSE! SHE LIES WHEN SHE SAYS THAT SHE'S KNOWN WAR. IT'S ALL TO MAKE HERSELF SEEM INTERESTING.
ANYWAY, HER PARENTS CLEARLY DON'T CARE ABOUT HER, OR THEY WOULDN'T HAVE SENT HER ALONE.
THAT WAS TOO MUCH. I SAW RED.

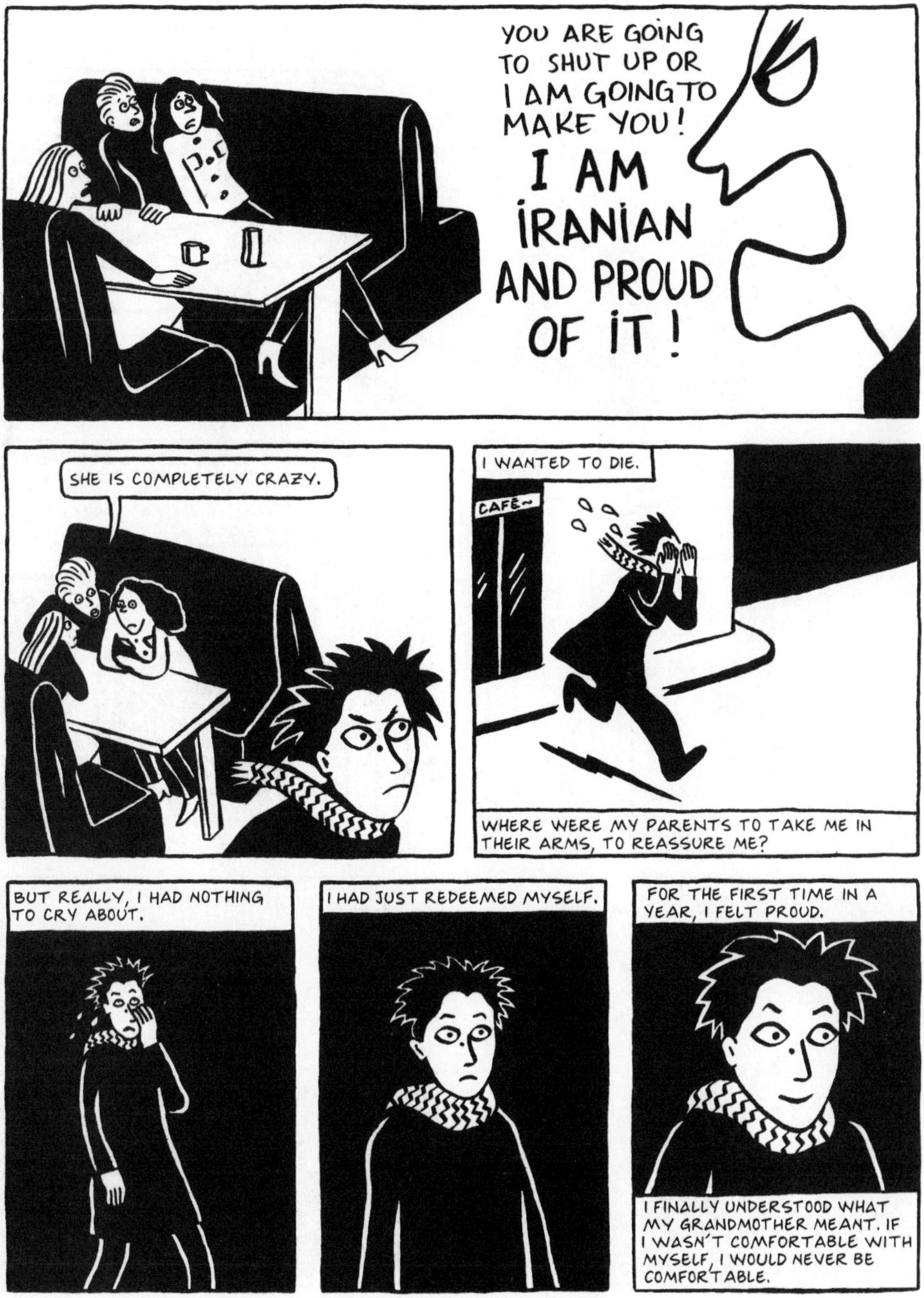
YOU ARE GOING TO SHUT UP OR I AM GOING TO MAKE YOU!
I AM IRANIAN AND PROUD OF IT!
SHE IS COMPLETELY CRAZY.
I WANTED TO DIE.
CAFÉ
WHERE WERE MY PARENTS TO TAKE ME IN THEIR ARMS, TO REASSURE ME?
BUT REALLY, I HAD NOTHING TO CRY ABOUT.
I HAD JUST REDEEMED MYSELF.
FOR THE FIRST TIME IN A YEAR, I FELT PROUD.
I FINALLY UNDERSTOOD WHAT MY GRANDMOTHER MEANT. IF I WASN'T COMFORTABLE WITH MYSELF, I WOULD NEVER BE COMFORTABLE.

THE HORSE

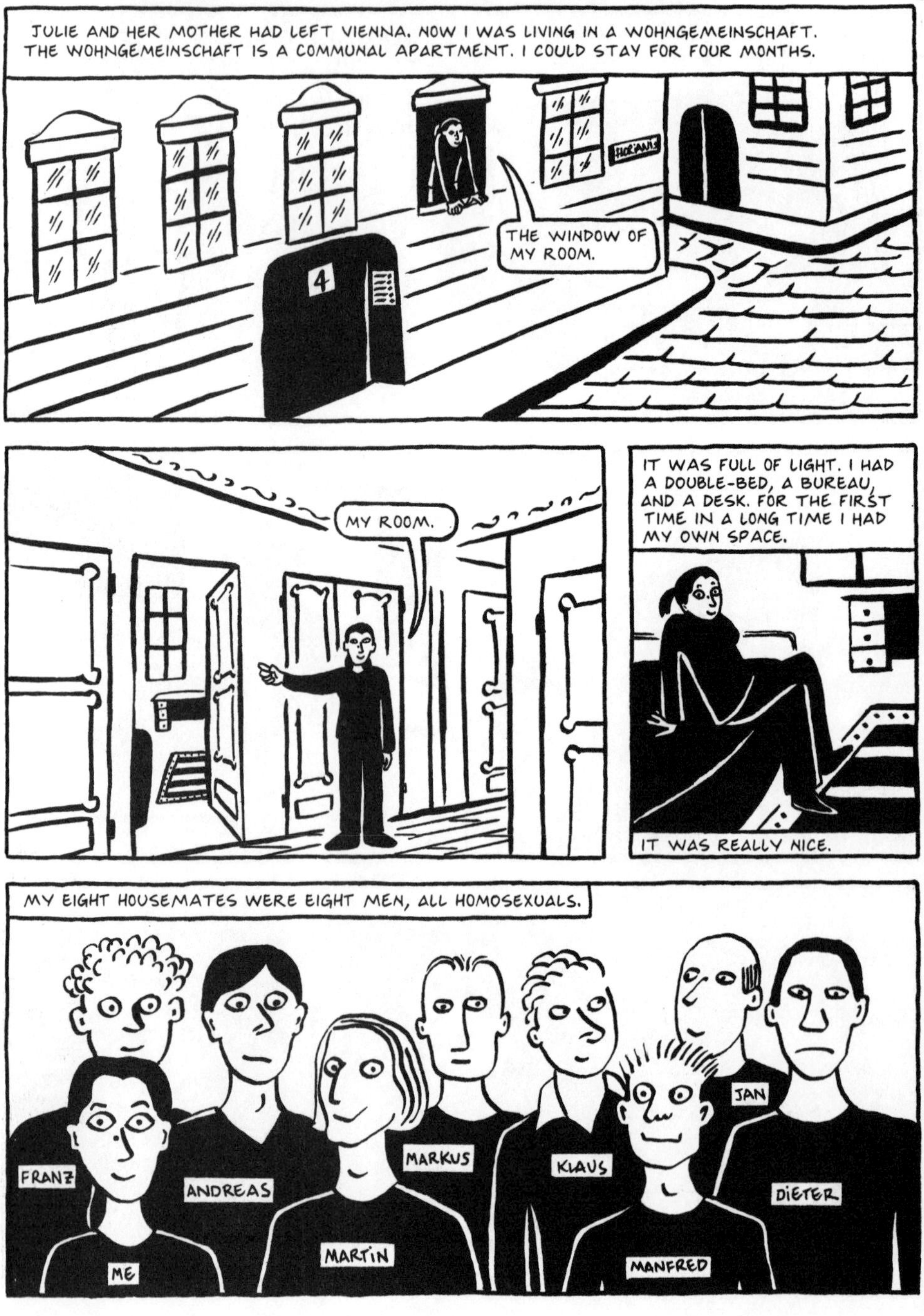
JULIE AND HER MOTHER HAD LEFT VIENNA. NOW I WAS LIVING IN A WOHNGEMEINSCHAFT. THE WOHNGEMEINSCHAFT IS A COMMUNAL APARTMENT. I COULD STAY FOR FOUR MONTHS.
4
THE WINDOW OF MY ROOM.
MY ROOM.
IT WAS FULL OF LIGHT. I HAD A DOUBLE-BED, A BUREAU, AND A DESK. FOR THE FIRST TIME IN A LONG TIME I HAD MY OWN SPACE.
IT WAS REALLY NICE.
MY EIGHT HOUSEMATES WERE EIGHT MEN, ALL HOMOSEXUALS.
FRANZ
ANDREAS
MARKUS
KLAUS
JAN
DIETER
ME
MARTIN
MANFRED

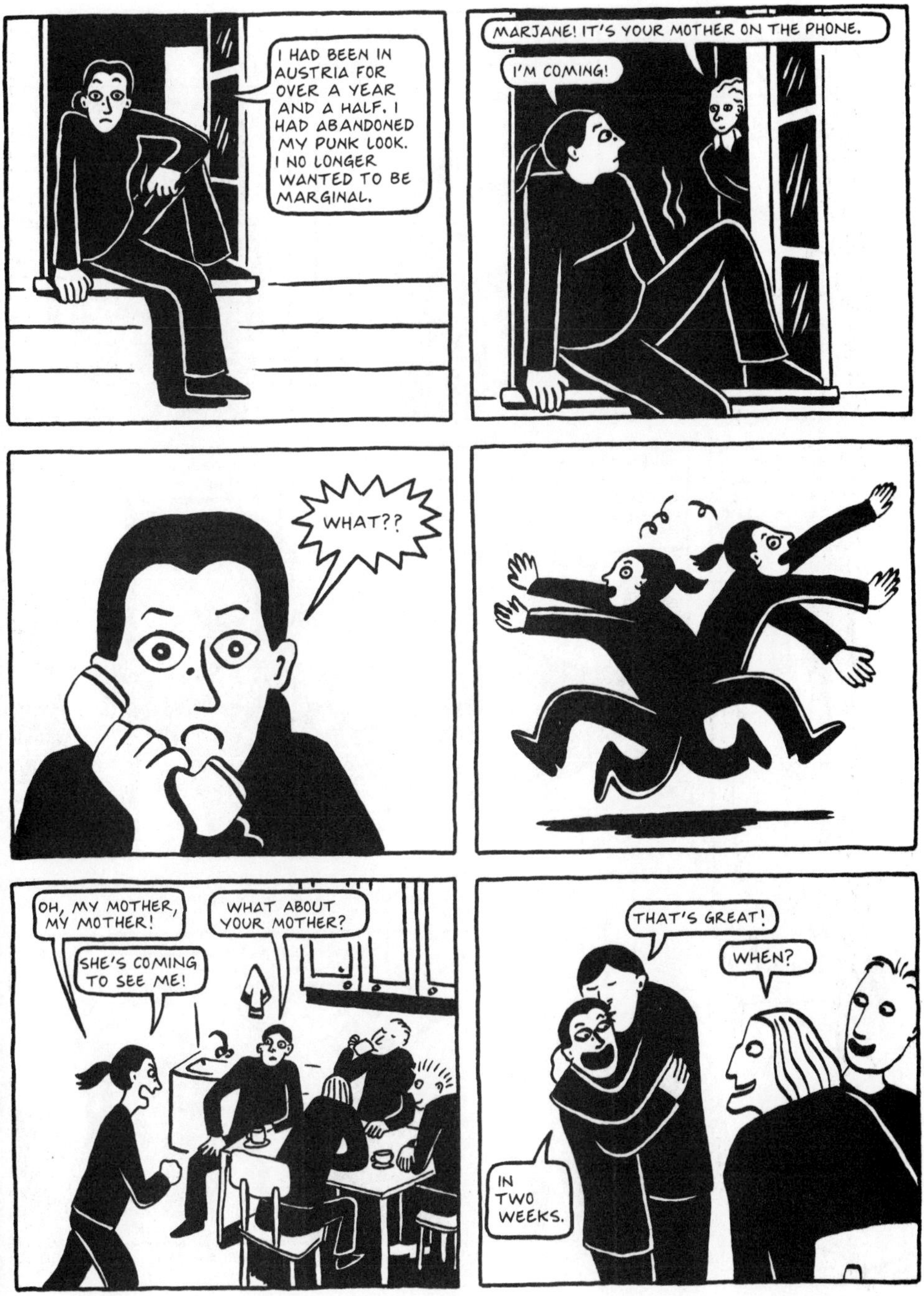
I HAD BEEN IN AUSTRIA FOR OVER A YEAR AND A HALF. I HAD ABANDONED MY PUNK LOOK. I NO LONGER WANTED TO BE MARGINAL.
MARJANE! IT'S YOUR MOTHER ON THE PHONE.
I'M COMING!
WHAT??
OH, MY MOTHER, MY MOTHER!
WHAT ABOUT YOUR MOTHER?
SHE'S COMING TO SEE ME!
THAT'S GREAT!
WHEN?
IN TWO WEEKS.

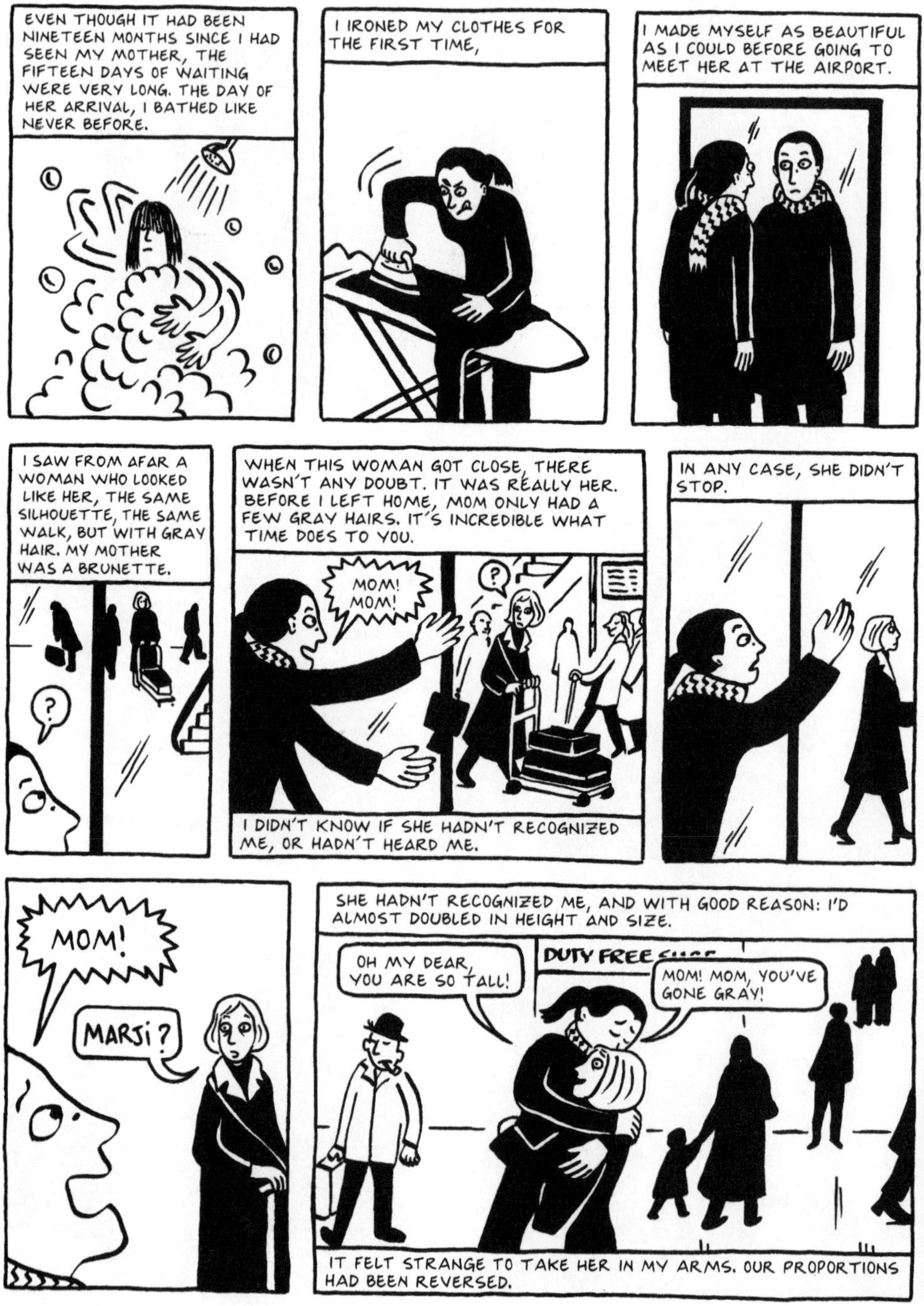
EVEN THOUGH IT HAD BEEN NINETEEN MONTHS SINCE I HAD SEEN MY MOTHER, THE FIFTEEN DAYS OF WAITING WERE VERY LONG. THE DAY OF HER ARRIVAL, I BATHED LIKE NEVER BEFORE.
I IRONED MY CLOTHES FOR THE FIRST TIME,
I MADE MYSELF AS BEAUTIFUL AS I COULD BEFORE GOING TO MEET HER AT THE AIRPORT.
I SAW FROM AFAR A WOMAN WHO LOOKED LIKE HER, THE SAME SILHOUETTE, THE SAME WALK, BUT WITH GRAY HAIR. MY MOTHER WAS A BRUNETTE.
?
WHEN THIS WOMAN GOT CLOSE, THERE WASN'T ANY DOUBT. IT WAS REALLY HER. BEFORE I LEFT HOME, MOM ONLY HAD A FEW GRAY HAIRS. IT'S INCREDIBLE WHAT TIME DOES TO YOU.
MOM! MOM!
?
I DIDN'T KNOW IF SHE HADN'T RECOGNIZED ME, OR HADN'T HEARD ME.
IN ANY CASE, SHE DIDN'T STOP.
MOM!
MARJI?
SHE HADN'T RECOGNIZED ME, AND WITH GOOD REASON: I'D ALMOST DOUBLED IN HEIGHT AND SIZE.
OH MY DEAR, YOU ARE SO TALL!
DUTY FREE
MOM! MOM, YOU'VE GONE GRAY!
IT FELT STRANGE TO TAKE HER IN MY ARMS. OUR PROPORTIONS HAD BEEN REVERSED.

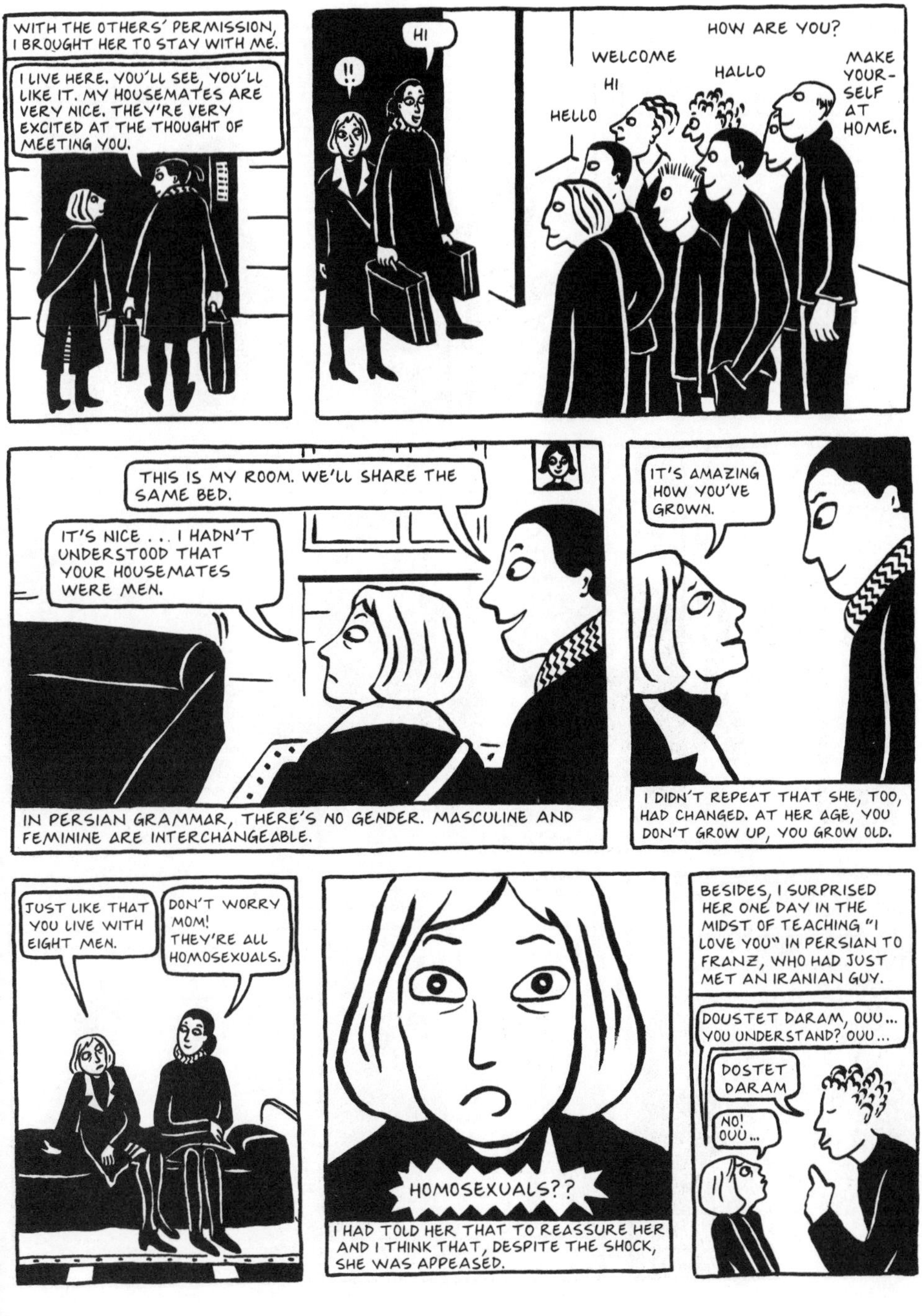

WITH THE OTHERS' PERMISSION, I BROUGHT HER TO STAY WITH ME.
I LIVE HERE. YOU'LL SEE, YOU'LL LIKE IT. MY HOUSEMATES ARE VERY NICE. THEY'RE VERY EXCITED AT THE THOUGHT OF MEETING YOU.
!!
HI
HOW ARE YOU?
WELCOME
HI
HALLO
MAKE YOURSELF AT HOME.
HELLO
THIS IS MY ROOM. WE'LL SHARE THE SAME BED.
IT'S NICE . . . I HADN'T UNDERSTOOD THAT YOUR HOUSEMATES WERE MEN.
IN PERSIAN GRAMMAR, THERE'S NO GENDER. MASCULINE AND FEMININE ARE INTERCHANGEABLE.
IT'S AMAZING HOW YOU'VE GROWN.
I DIDN'T REPEAT THAT SHE, TOO, HAD CHANGED. AT HER AGE, YOU DON'T GROW UP, YOU GROW OLD.
JUST LIKE THAT YOU LIVE WITH EIGHT MEN.
DON'T WORRY MOM! THEY'RE ALL HOMOSEXUALS.
HOMOSEXUALS??
I HAD TOLD HER THAT TO REASSURE HER AND I THINK THAT, DESPITE THE SHOCK, SHE WAS APPEASED.
BESIDES, I SURPRISED HER ONE DAY IN THE MIDST OF TEACHING "I LOVE YOU" IN PERSIAN TO FRANZ, WHO HAD JUST MET AN IRANIAN GUY.
DOUSTET DARAM, OUU... YOU UNDERSTAND? OUU...
DOSTET DARAM
NO! OUU...

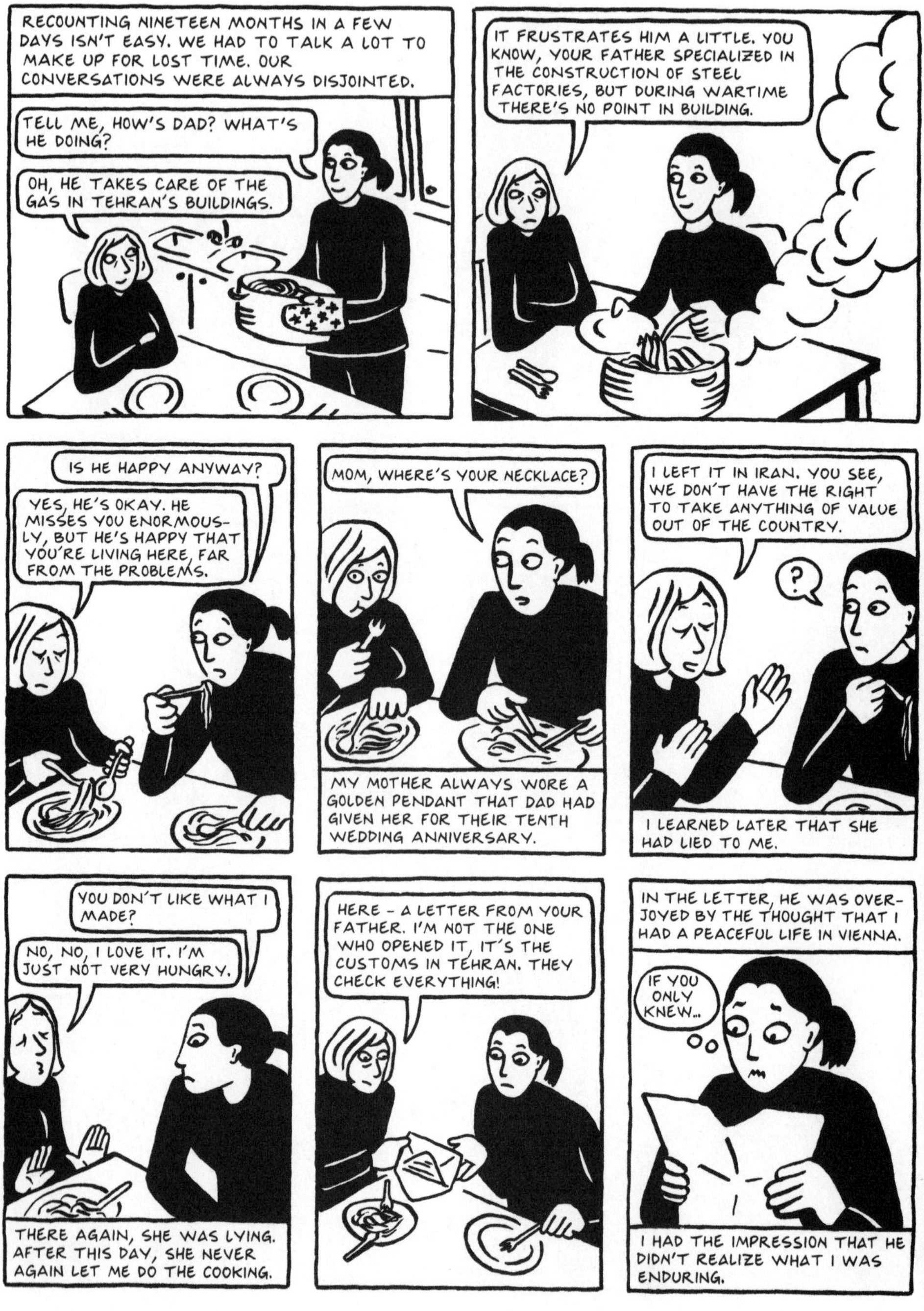
RECOUNTING NINETEEN MONTHS IN A FEW DAYS ISN'T EASY. WE HAD TO TALK A LOT TO MAKE UP FOR LOST TIME. OUR CONVERSATIONS WERE ALWAYS DISJOINTED.
TELL ME, HOW'S DAD? WHAT'S HE DOING?
OH, HE TAKES CARE OF THE GAS IN TEHRAN'S BUILDINGS.
IT FRUSTRATES HIM A LITTLE. YOU KNOW, YOUR FATHER SPECIALIZED IN THE CONSTRUCTION OF STEEL FACTORIES, BUT DURING WARTIME THERE'S NO POINT IN BUILDING.
IS HE HAPPY ANYWAY?
YES, HE'S OKAY. HE MISSES YOU ENORMOUSLY, BUT HE'S HAPPY THAT YOU'RE LIVING HERE, FAR FROM THE PROBLEMS.
MOM, WHERE'S YOUR NECKLACE?
MY MOTHER ALWAYS WORE A GOLDEN PENDANT THAT DAD HAD GIVEN HER FOR THEIR TENTH WEDDING ANNIVERSARY.
I LEFT IT IN IRAN. YOU SEE, WE DON'T HAVE THE RIGHT TO TAKE ANYTHING OF VALUE OUT OF THE COUNTRY.
?
I LEARNED LATER THAT SHE HAD LIED TO ME.
YOU DON'T LIKE WHAT I MADE?
NO, NO, I LOVE IT. I'M JUST NOT VERY HUNGRY.
THERE AGAIN, SHE WAS LYING. AFTER THIS DAY, SHE NEVER AGAIN LET ME DO THE COOKING.
HERE - A LETTER FROM YOUR FATHER. I'M NOT THE ONE WHO OPENED IT, IT'S THE CUSTOMS IN TEHRAN. THEY CHECK EVERYTHING!
IN THE LETTER, HE WAS OVERJOYED BY THE THOUGHT THAT I HAD A PEACEFUL LIFE IN VIENNA.
IF YOU ONLY KNEW...
I HAD THE IMPRESSION THAT HE DIDN'T REALIZE WHAT I WAS ENDURING.

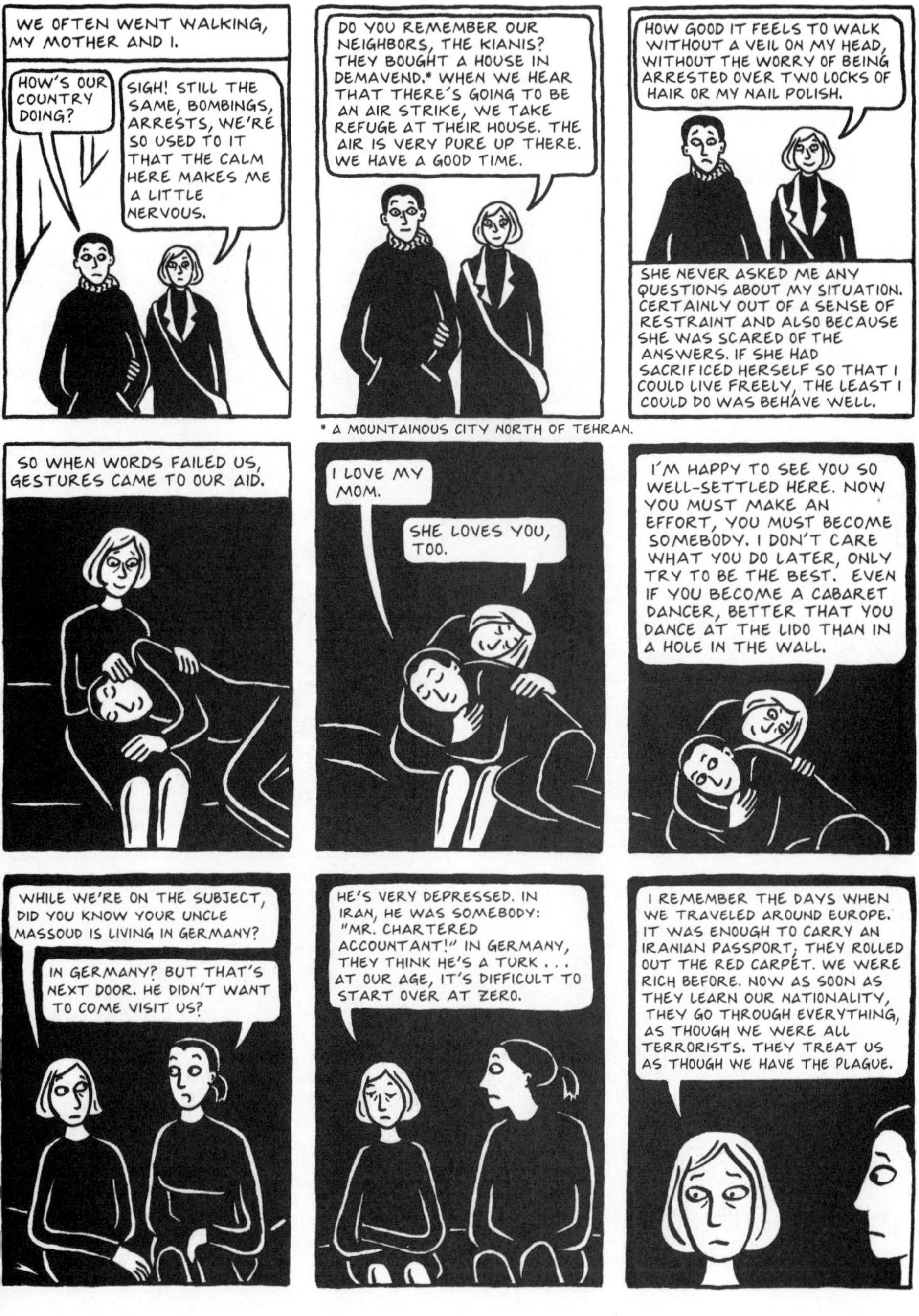
WE OFTEN WENT WALKING, MY MOTHER AND I.
HOW'S OUR COUNTRY DOING?
SIGH! STILL THE SAME, BOMBINGS, ARRESTS, WE'RE SO USED TO IT THAT THE CALM HERE MAKES ME A LITTLE NERVOUS.
DO YOU REMEMBER OUR NEIGHBORS, THE KIANIS? THEY BOUGHT A HOUSE IN DEMAVEND.* WHEN WE HEAR THAT THERE'S GOING TO BE AN AIR STRIKE, WE TAKE REFUGE AT THEIR HOUSE. THE AIR IS VERY PURE UP THERE. WE HAVE A GOOD TIME.
HOW GOOD IT FEELS TO WALK WITHOUT A VEIL ON MY HEAD, WITHOUT THE WORRY OF BEING ARRESTED OVER TWO LOCKS OF HAIR OR MY NAIL POLISH.
SHE NEVER ASKED ME ANY QUESTIONS ABOUT MY SITUATION. CERTAINLY OUT OF A SENSE OF RESTRAINT AND ALSO BECAUSE SHE WAS SCARED OF THE ANSWERS. IF SHE HAD SACRIFICED HERSELF SO THAT I COULD LIVE FREELY, THE LEAST I COULD DO WAS BEHAVE WELL.
* A MOUNTAINOUS CITY NORTH OF TEHRAN.
SO WHEN WORDS FAILED US, GESTURES CAME TO OUR AID.
I LOVE MY MOM.
SHE LOVES YOU, TOO.
I'M HAPPY TO SEE YOU SO WELL-SETTLED HERE. NOW YOU MUST MAKE AN EFFORT, YOU MUST BECOME SOMEBODY. I DON'T CARE WHAT YOU DO LATER, ONLY TRY TO BE THE BEST. EVEN IF YOU BECOME A CABARET DANCER, BETTER THAT YOU DANCE AT THE LIDO THAN IN A HOLE IN THE WALL.
WHILE WE'RE ON THE SUBJECT, DID YOU KNOW YOUR UNCLE MASSOUD IS LIVING IN GERMANY?
IN GERMANY? BUT THAT'S NEXT DOOR. HE DIDN'T WANT TO COME VISIT US?
HE'S VERY DEPRESSED. IN IRAN, HE WAS SOMEBODY: "MR. CHARTERED ACCOUNTANT!" IN GERMANY, THEY THINK HE'S A TURK . . . AT OUR AGE, IT'S DIFFICULT TO START OVER AT ZERO.
I REMEMBER THE DAYS WHEN WE TRAVELED AROUND EUROPE. IT WAS ENOUGH TO CARRY AN IRANIAN PASSPORT; THEY ROLLED OUT THE RED CARPET. WE WERE RICH BEFORE. NOW AS SOON AS THEY LEARN OUR NATIONALITY, THEY GO THROUGH EVERYTHING, AS THOUGH WE WERE ALL TERRORISTS. THEY TREAT US AS THOUGH WE HAVE THE PLAGUE.

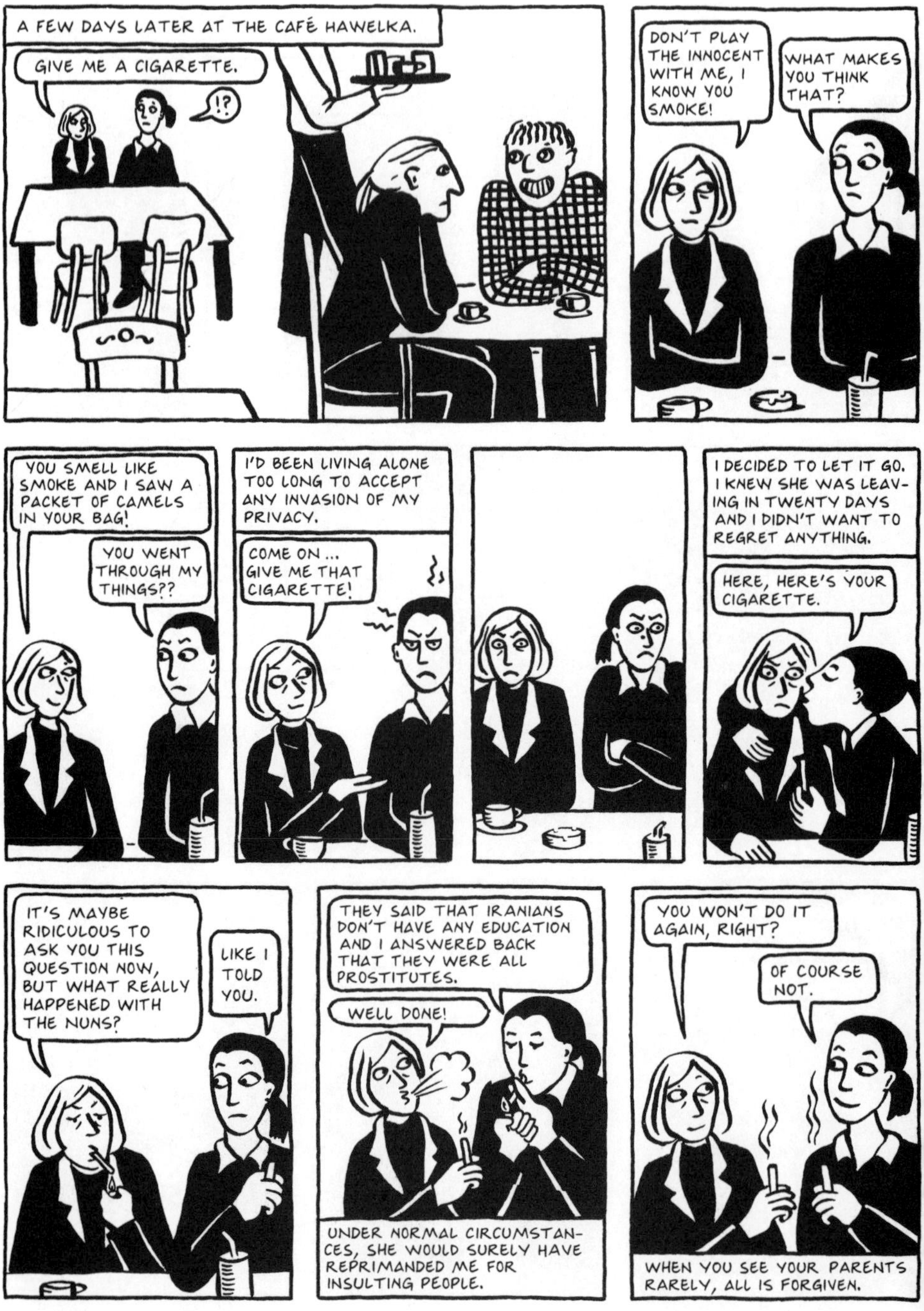
A FEW DAYS LATER AT THE CAFÉ HAWELKA.
GIVE ME A CIGARETTE.
!?
DON'T PLAY THE INNOCENT WITH ME, I KNOW YOU SMOKE!
WHAT MAKES YOU THINK THAT?
YOU SMELL LIKE SMOKE AND I SAW A PACKET OF CAMELS IN YOUR BAG!
YOU WENT THROUGH MY THINGS??
I'D BEEN LIVING ALONE TOO LONG TO ACCEPT ANY INVASION OF MY PRIVACY.
COME ON ... GIVE ME THAT CIGARETTE!
I DECIDED TO LET IT GO. I KNEW SHE WAS LEAVING IN TWENTY DAYS AND I DIDN'T WANT TO REGRET ANYTHING.
HERE, HERE'S YOUR CIGARETTE.
IT'S MAYBE RIDICULOUS TO ASK YOU THIS QUESTION NOW, BUT WHAT REALLY HAPPENED WITH THE NUNS?
LIKE I TOLD YOU.
THEY SAID THAT IRANIANS DON'T HAVE ANY EDUCATION AND I ANSWERED BACK THAT THEY WERE ALL PROSTITUTES.
WELL DONE!
UNDER NORMAL CIRCUMSTANCES, SHE WOULD SURELY HAVE REPRIMANDED ME FOR INSULTING PEOPLE.
YOU WON'T DO IT AGAIN, RIGHT?
OF COURSE NOT.
WHEN YOU SEE YOUR PARENTS RARELY, ALL IS FORGIVEN.

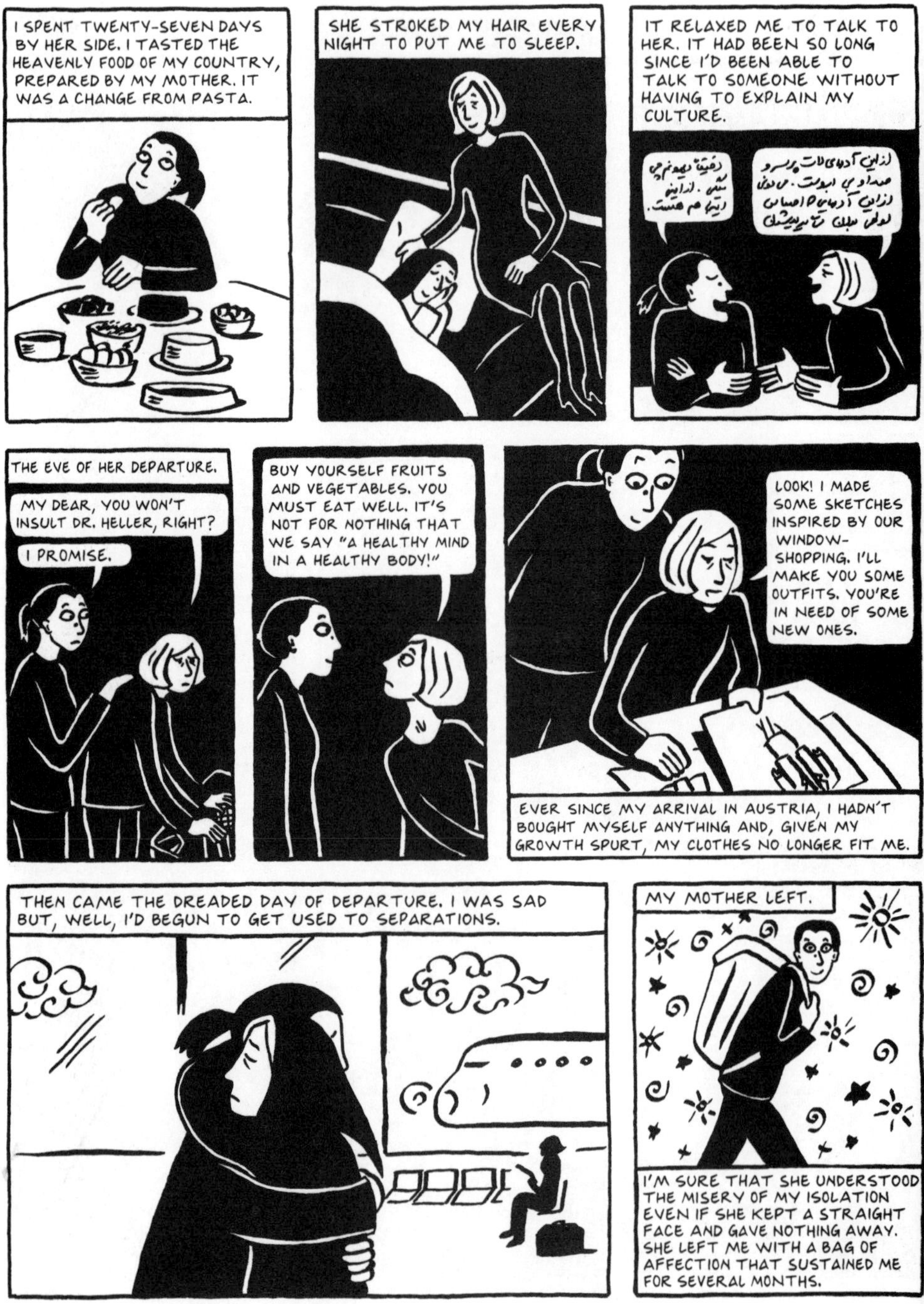

I SPENT TWENTY-SEVEN DAYS BY HER SIDE. I TASTED THE HEAVENLY FOOD OF MY COUNTRY, PREPARED BY MY MOTHER. IT WAS A CHANGE FROM PASTA.
SHE STROKED MY HAIR EVERY NIGHT TO PUT ME TO SLEEP.
IT RELAXED ME TO TALK TO HER. IT HAD BEEN SO LONG SINCE I'D BEEN ABLE TO TALK TO SOMEONE WITHOUT HAVING TO EXPLAIN MY CULTURE.
THE EVE OF HER DEPARTURE.
MY DEAR, YOU WON'T INSULT DR. HELLER, RIGHT?
I PROMISE.
BUY YOURSELF FRUITS AND VEGETABLES. YOU MUST EAT WELL. IT'S NOT FOR NOTHING THAT WE SAY "A HEALTHY MIND IN A HEALTHY BODY!"
LOOK! I MADE SOME SKETCHES INSPIRED BY OUR WINDOW-SHOPPING. I'LL MAKE YOU SOME OUTFITS. YOU'RE IN NEED OF SOME NEW ONES.
EVER SINCE MY ARRIVAL IN AUSTRIA, I HADN'T BOUGHT MYSELF ANYTHING AND, GIVEN MY GROWTH SPURT, MY CLOTHES NO LONGER FIT ME.
THEN CAME THE DREADED DAY OF DEPARTURE. I WAS SAD BUT, WELL, I'D BEGUN TO GET USED TO SEPARATIONS.
MY MOTHER LEFT.
I'M SURE THAT SHE UNDERSTOOD THE MISERY OF MY ISOLATION EVEN IF SHE KEPT A STRAIGHT FACE AND GAVE NOTHING AWAY. SHE LEFT ME WITH A BAG OF AFFECTION THAT SUSTAINED ME FOR SEVERAL MONTHS.

HIDE AND SEEK

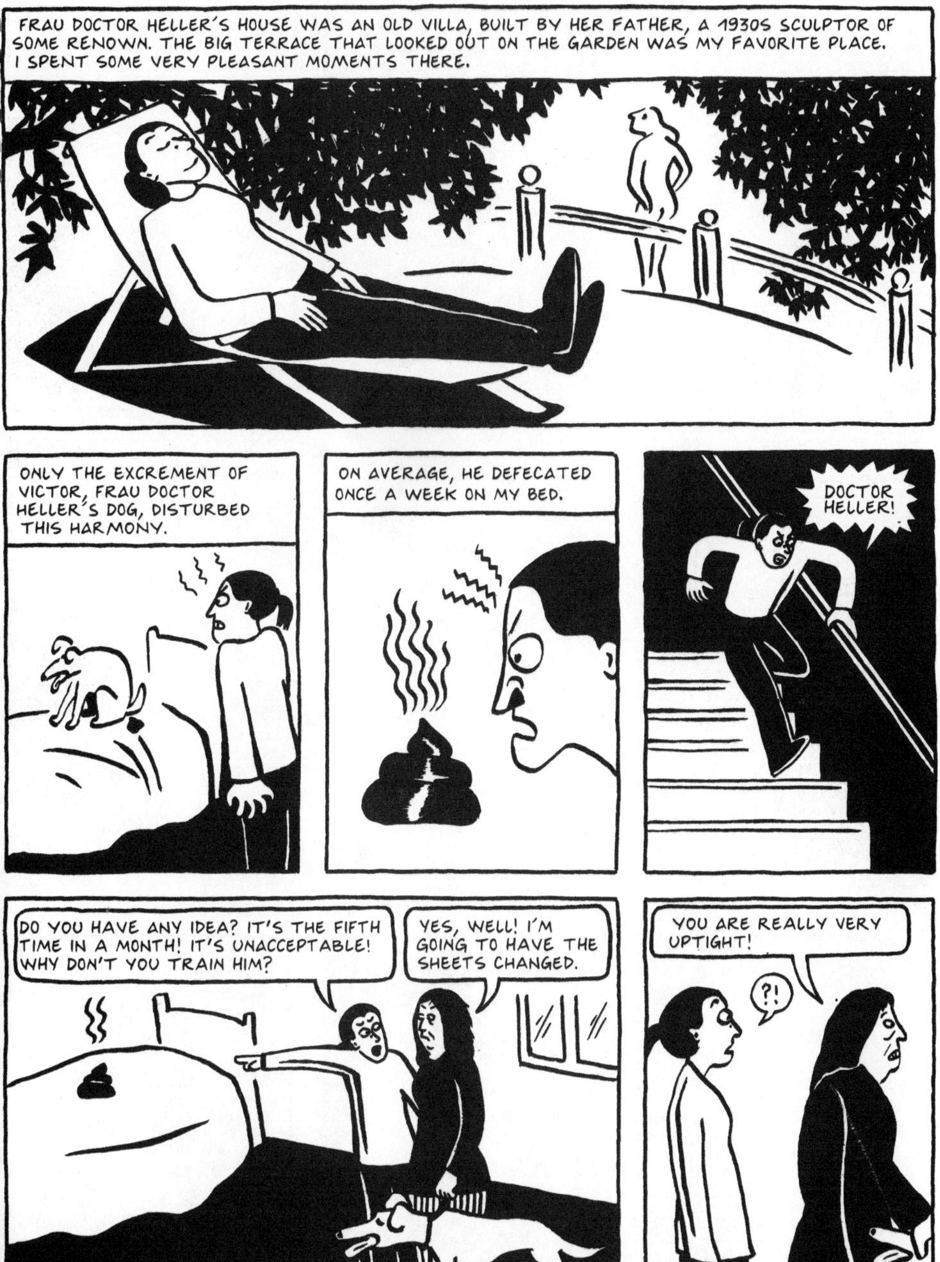

FRAU DOCTOR HELLER'S HOUSE WAS AN OLD VILLA, BUILT BY HER FATHER, A 1930S SCULPTOR OF SOME RENOWN. THE BIG TERRACE THAT LOOKED OUT ON THE GARDEN WAS MY FAVORITE PLACE. I SPENT SOME VERY PLEASANT MOMENTS THERE.
ONLY THE EXCREMENT OF VICTOR, FRAU DOCTOR HELLER'S DOG, DISTURBED THIS HARMONY.
ON AVERAGE, HE DEFECATED ONCE A WEEK ON MY BED.
DOCTOR HELLER!
DO YOU HAVE ANY IDEA? IT'S THE FIFTH TIME IN A MONTH! IT'S UNACCEPTABLE! WHY DON'T YOU TRAIN HIM?
YES, WELL! I'M GOING TO HAVE THE SHEETS CHANGED.
I OFTEN FORGOT THAT HE WAS TOO OLD TO LEARN ANYTHING.
YOU ARE REALLY VERY UPTIGHT!
?!

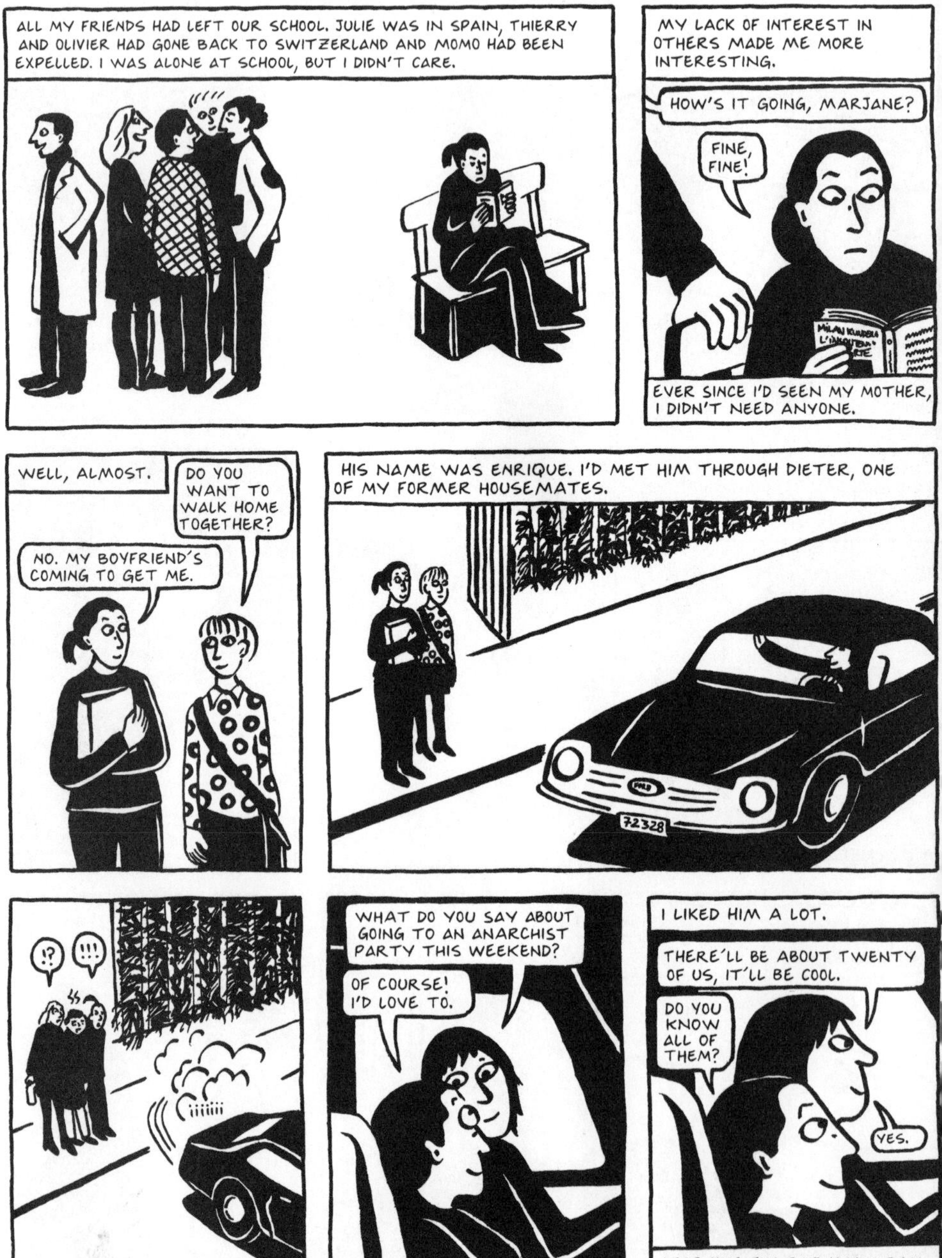
ALL MY FRIENDS HAD LEFT OUR SCHOOL. JULIE WAS IN SPAIN, THIERRY AND OLIVIER HAD GONE BACK TO SWITZERLAND AND MOMO HAD BEEN EXPELLED. I WAS ALONE AT SCHOOL, BUT I DIDN'T CARE.
MY LACK OF INTEREST IN OTHERS MADE ME MORE INTERESTING.
HOW'S IT GOING, MARJANE?
FINE, FINE!
EVER SINCE I'D SEEN MY MOTHER, I DIDN'T NEED ANYONE.
WELL, ALMOST.
DO YOU WANT TO WALK HOME TOGETHER?
NO. MY BOYFRIEND'S COMING TO GET ME.
HIS NAME WAS ENRIQUE. I'D MET HIM THROUGH DIETER, ONE OF MY FORMER HOUSEMATES.
72328
!?
!!!
ENRIQUE WAS HALF-AUSTRIAN, HALF-SPANISH.
WHAT DO YOU SAY ABOUT GOING TO AN ANARCHIST PARTY THIS WEEKEND?
OF COURSE! I'D LOVE TO.
ENRIQUE WAS TWENTY AND PLAYED THE PIANO.
I LIKED HIM A LOT.
THERE'LL BE ABOUT TWENTY OF US, IT'LL BE COOL.
DO YOU KNOW ALL OF THEM?
YES.
LEARNING THAT HE KNEW REAL ANARCHISTS ONLY INTENSIFIED MY FEELINGS FOR HIM.

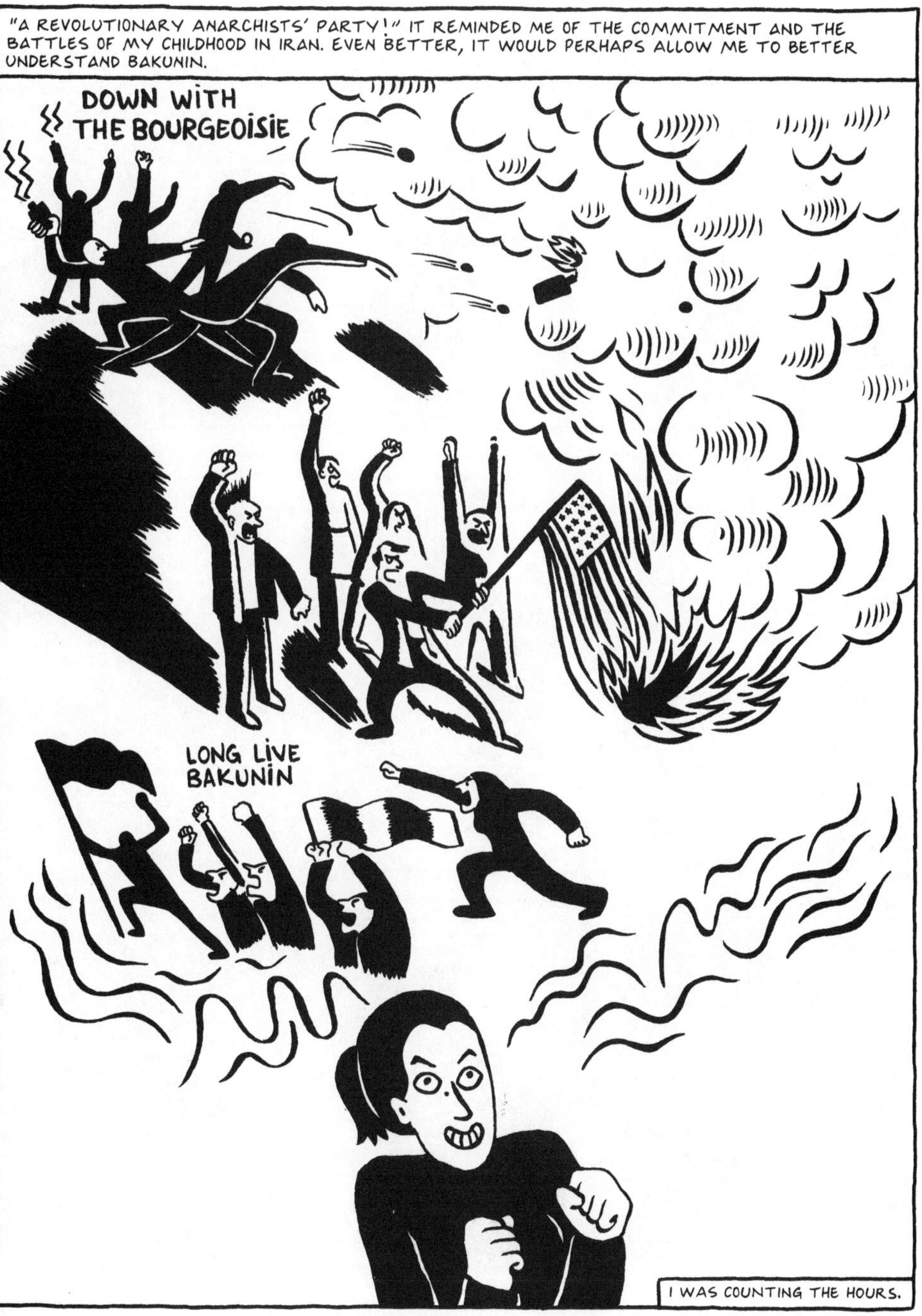
"A REVOLUTIONARY ANARCHISTS' PARTY!" IT REMINDED ME OF THE COMMITMENT AND THE BATTLES OF MY CHILDHOOD IN IRAN. EVEN BETTER, IT WOULD PERHAPS ALLOW ME TO BETTER UNDERSTAND BAKUNIN.
DOWN WITH THE BOURGEOISIE
LONG LIVE BAKUNIN
I WAS COUNTING THE HOURS.

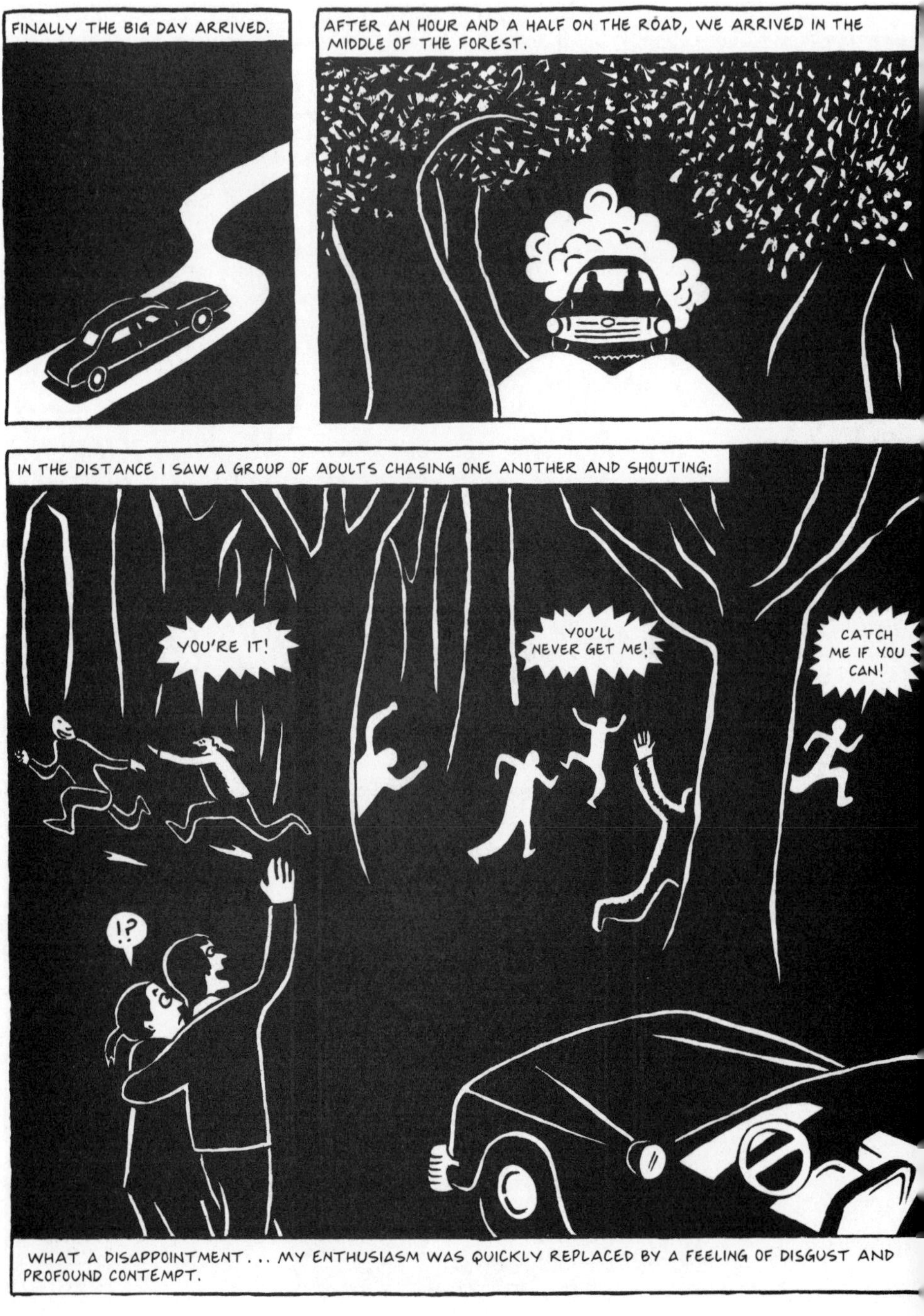
FINALLY THE BIG DAY ARRIVED.
AFTER AN HOUR AND A HALF ON THE ROAD, WE ARRIVED IN THE MIDDLE OF THE FOREST.
IN THE DISTANCE I SAW A GROUP OF ADULTS CHASING ONE ANOTHER AND SHOUTING:
YOU'RE IT!
YOU'LL NEVER GET ME!
CATCH ME IF YOU CAN!
!?
WHAT A DISAPPOINTMENT... MY ENTHUSIASM WAS QUICKLY REPLACED BY A FEELING OF DISGUST AND PROFOUND CONTEMPT.

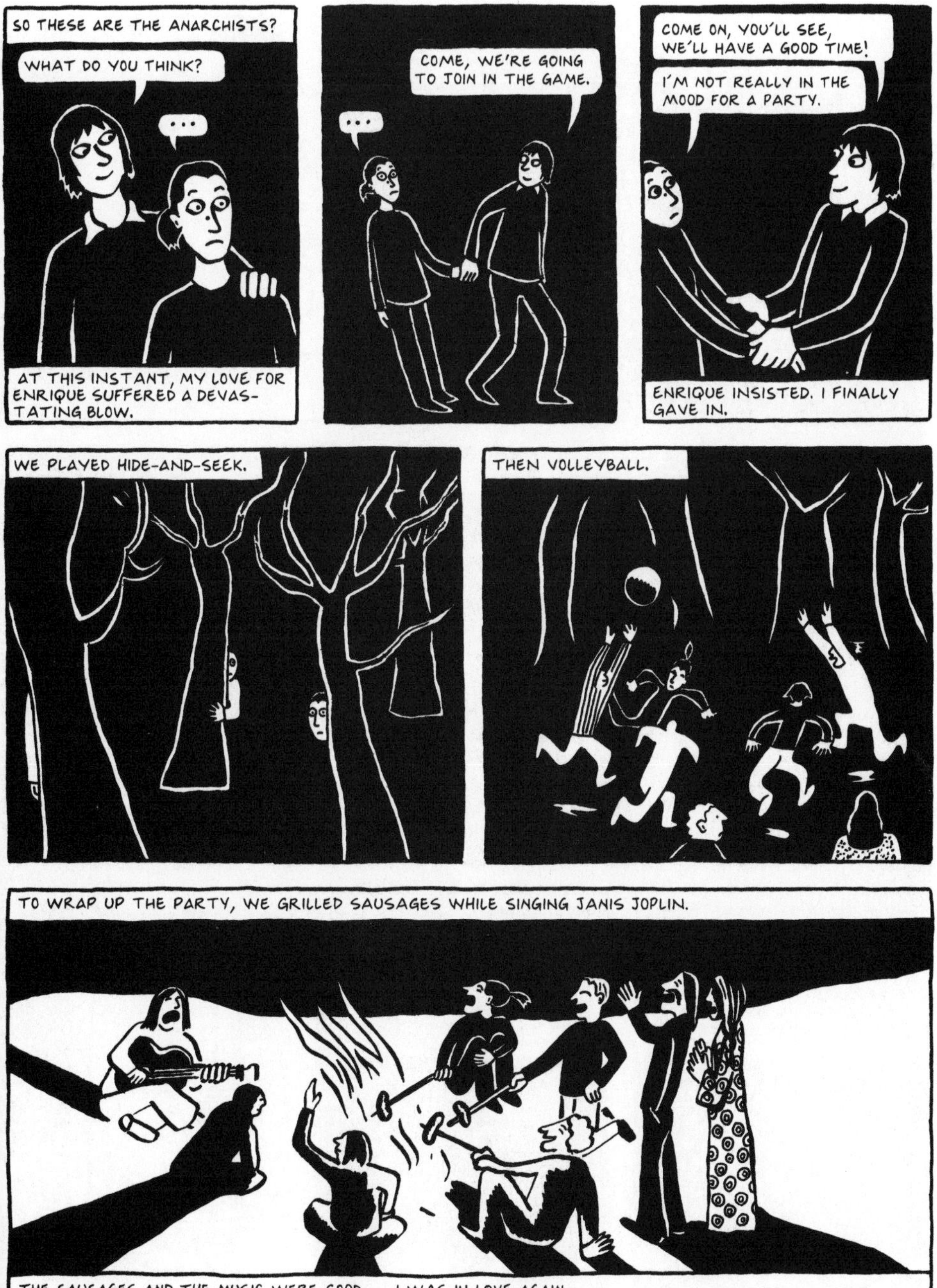
SO THESE ARE THE ANARCHISTS?
WHAT DO YOU THINK?
...
AT THIS INSTANT, MY LOVE FOR ENRIQUE SUFFERED A DEVAS-TATING BLOW.
COME, WE'RE GOING TO JOIN IN THE GAME.
...
COME ON, YOU'LL SEE, WE'LL HAVE A GOOD TIME!
I'M NOT REALLY IN THE MOOD FOR A PARTY.
ENRIQUE INSISTED. I FINALLY GAVE IN.
WE PLAYED HIDE-AND-SEEK.
THEN VOLLEYBALL.
TO WRAP UP THE PARTY, WE GRILLED SAUSAGES WHILE SINGING JANIS JOPLIN.
THE SAUSAGES AND THE MUSIC WERE GOOD... I WAS IN LOVE AGAIN.

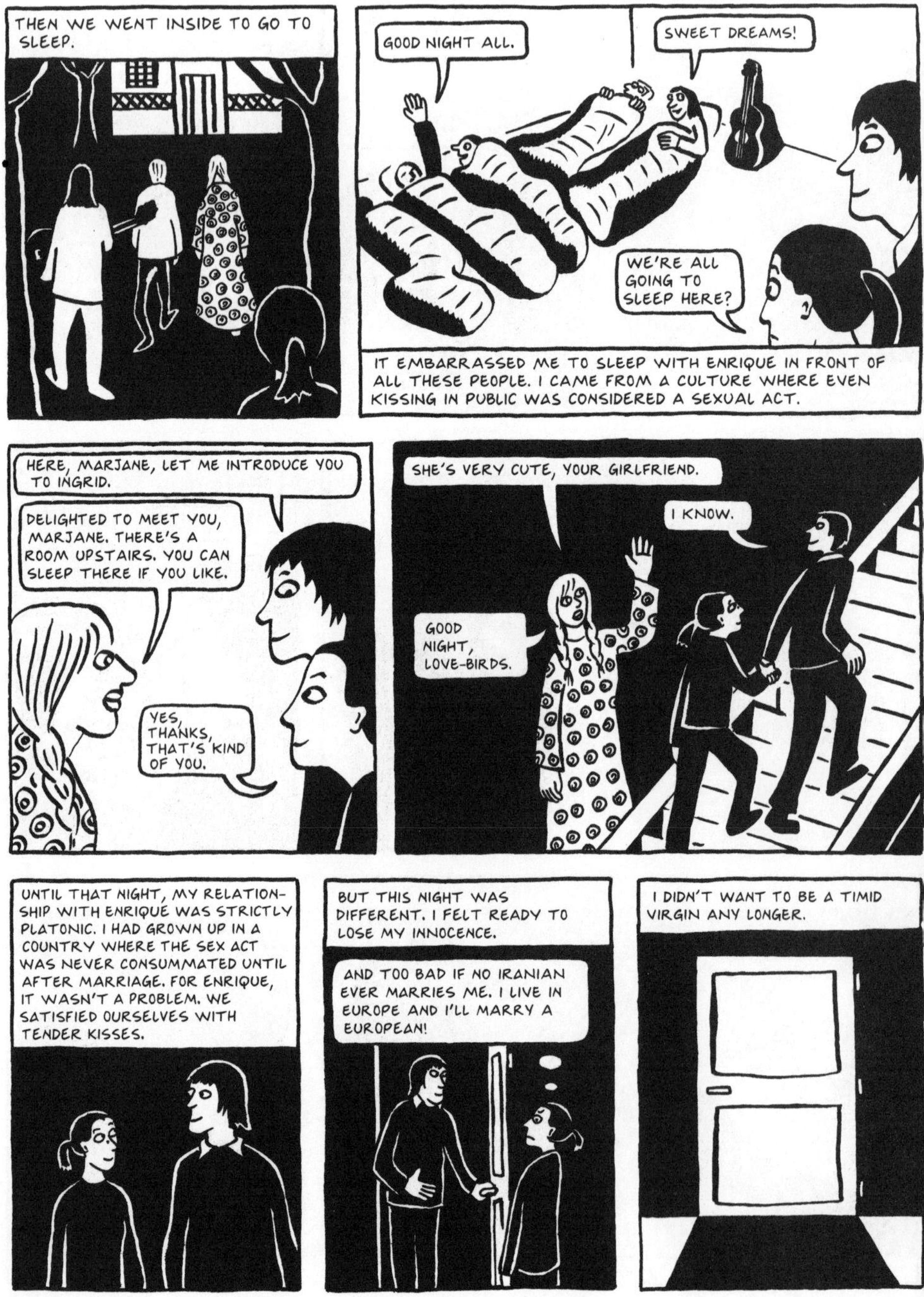
THEN WE WENT INSIDE TO GO TO SLEEP.
GOOD NIGHT ALL.
SWEET DREAMS!
WE'RE ALL GOING TO SLEEP HERE?
IT EMBARRASSED ME TO SLEEP WITH ENRIQUE IN FRONT OF ALL THESE PEOPLE. I CAME FROM A CULTURE WHERE EVEN KISSING IN PUBLIC WAS CONSIDERED A SEXUAL ACT.
HERE, MARJANE, LET ME INTRODUCE YOU TO INGRID.
DELIGHTED TO MEET YOU, MARJANE. THERE'S A ROOM UPSTAIRS. YOU CAN SLEEP THERE IF YOU LIKE.
YES, THANKS, THAT'S KIND OF YOU.
SHE'S VERY CUTE, YOUR GIRLFRIEND.
I KNOW.
GOOD NIGHT, LOVE-BIRDS.
UNTIL THAT NIGHT, MY RELATIONSHIP WITH ENRIQUE WAS STRICTLY PLATONIC. I HAD GROWN UP IN A COUNTRY WHERE THE SEX ACT WAS NEVER CONSUMMATED UNTIL AFTER MARRIAGE. FOR ENRIQUE, IT WASN'T A PROBLEM. WE SATISFIED OURSELVES WITH TENDER KISSES.
BUT THIS NIGHT WAS DIFFERENT. I FELT READY TO LOSE MY INNOCENCE.
AND TOO BAD IF NO IRANIAN EVER MARRIES ME. I LIVE IN EUROPE AND I'LL MARRY A EUROPEAN!
I DIDN'T WANT TO BE A TIMID VIRGIN ANY LONGER.

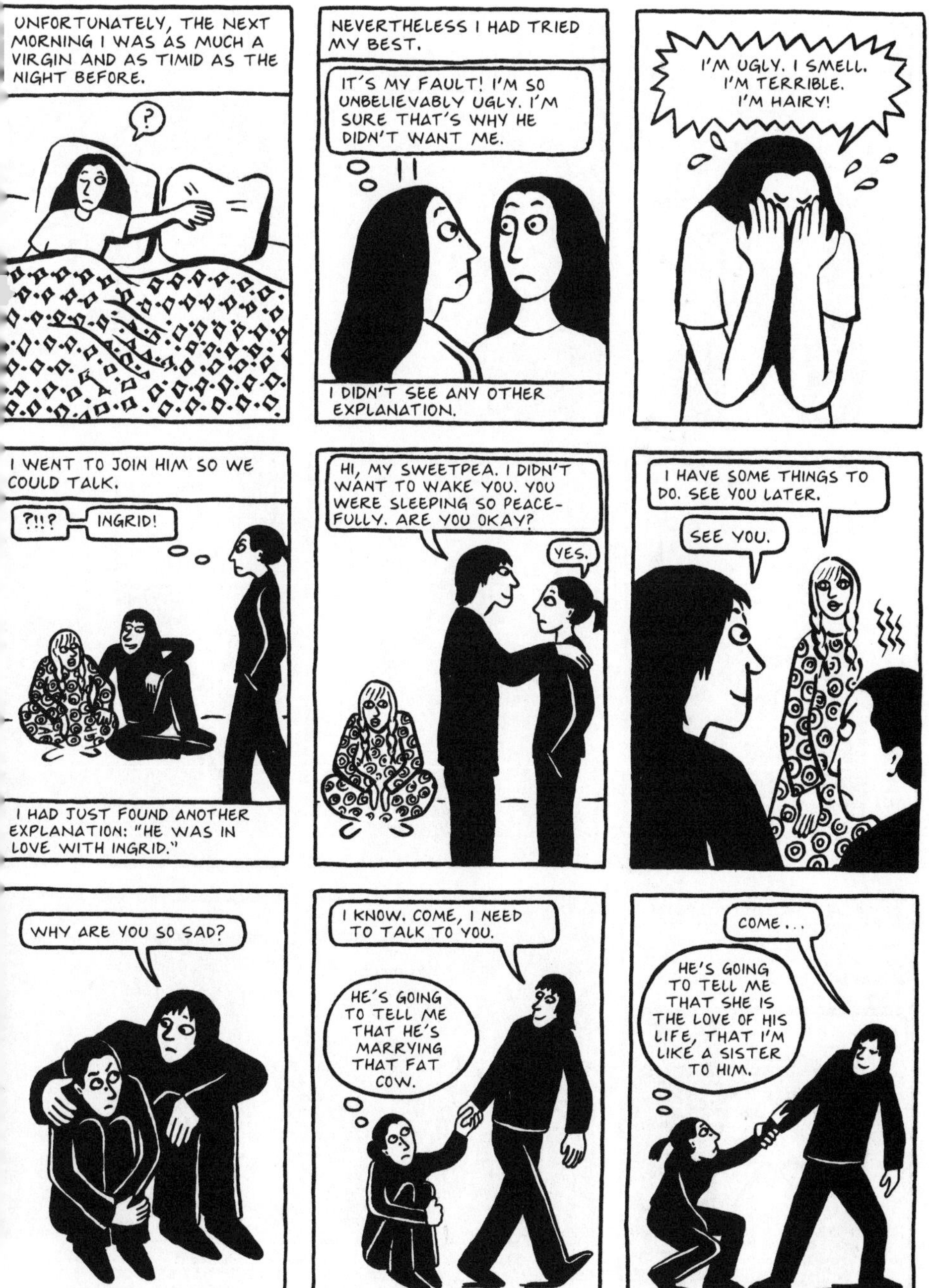
UNFORTUNATELY, THE NEXT MORNING I WAS AS MUCH A VIRGIN AND AS TIMID AS THE NIGHT BEFORE.
?
NEVERTHELESS I HAD TRIED MY BEST.
IT'S MY FAULT! I'M SO UNBELIEVABLY UGLY. I'M SURE THAT'S WHY HE DIDN'T WANT ME.
I DIDN'T SEE ANY OTHER EXPLANATION.
I'M UGLY. I SMELL. I'M TERRIBLE. I'M HAIRY!
I WENT TO JOIN HIM SO WE COULD TALK.
?!!?
INGRID!
I HAD JUST FOUND ANOTHER EXPLANATION: "HE WAS IN LOVE WITH INGRID."
HI, MY SWEETPEA. I DIDN'T WANT TO WAKE YOU. YOU WERE SLEEPING SO PEACEFULLY. ARE YOU OKAY?
YES.
I HAVE SOME THINGS TO DO. SEE YOU LATER.
SEE YOU.
WHY ARE YOU SO SAD?
I KNOW. COME, I NEED TO TALK TO YOU.
HE'S GOING TO TELL ME THAT HE'S MARRYING THAT FAT COW.
COME...
HE'S GOING TO TELL ME THAT SHE IS THE LOVE OF HIS LIFE, THAT I'M LIKE A SISTER TO HIM.

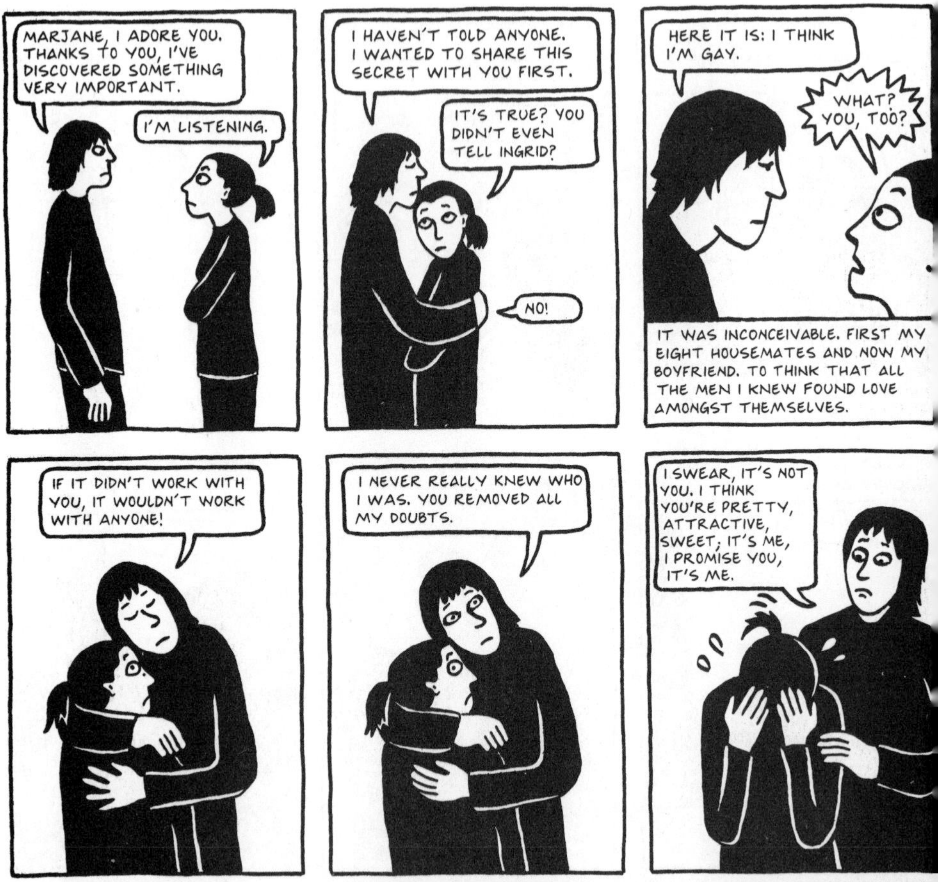
MARJANE, I ADORE YOU. THANKS TO YOU, I'VE DISCOVERED SOMETHING VERY IMPORTANT.
I'M LISTENING.
I HAVEN'T TOLD ANYONE. I WANTED TO SHARE THIS SECRET WITH YOU FIRST.
IT'S TRUE? YOU DIDN'T EVEN TELL INGRID?
NO!
HERE IT IS: I THINK I'M GAY.
WHAT? YOU, TOO?
IT WAS INCONCEIVABLE. FIRST MY EIGHT HOUSEMATES AND NOW MY BOYFRIEND. TO THINK THAT ALL THE MEN I KNEW FOUND LOVE AMONGST THEMSELVES.
IF IT DIDN'T WORK WITH YOU, IT WOULDN'T WORK WITH ANYONE!
I NEVER REALLY KNEW WHO I WAS. YOU REMOVED ALL MY DOUBTS.
I SWEAR, IT'S NOT YOU. I THINK YOU'RE PRETTY, ATTRACTIVE, SWEET; IT'S ME, I PROMISE YOU, IT'S ME.
NEVERTHELESS, SOMEWHERE INSIDE, I WAS REASSURED. IT WAS EASIER TO ACCEPT THAT HE WAS GAY THAN THAT HE HAD A PREFERENCE FOR INGRID OR HE FOUND ME UGLY.
I'M HAPPY FOR YOU.
WHAT ELSE COULD I SAY?
PROMISE ME THAT WE'LL ALWAYS BE FRIENDS.
I PROMISE.
I GAVE MY WORD, BUT I WAS TOO YOUNG TO KEEP IT. THIS CHASTE LOVE AFFAIR FRUSTRATED ME MORE THAN IT SATISFIED ME. I WANTED TO LOVE AND BE LOVED FOR REAL.

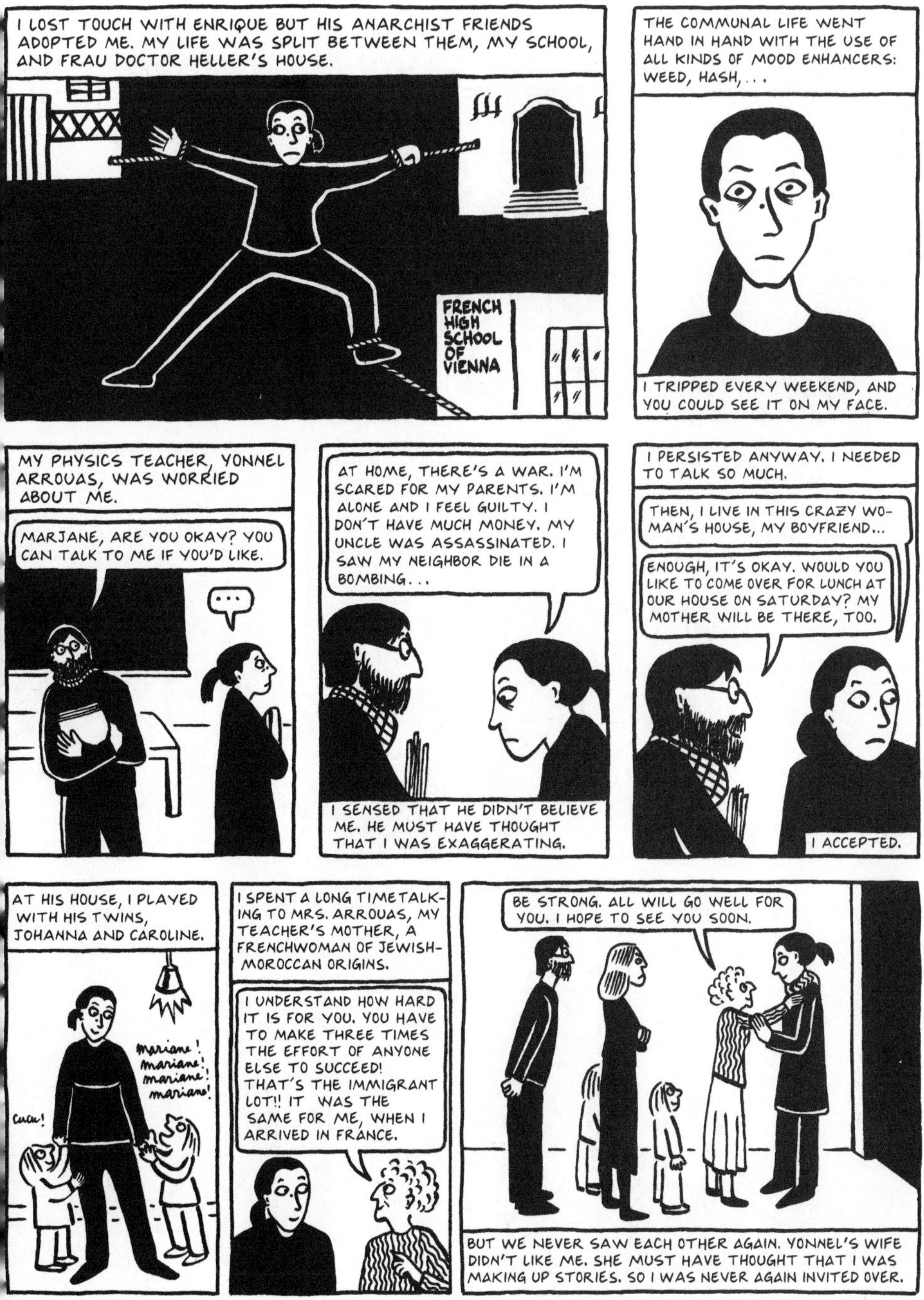

I LOST TOUCH WITH ENRIQUE BUT HIS ANARCHIST FRIENDS ADOPTED ME. MY LIFE WAS SPLIT BETWEEN THEM, MY SCHOOL, AND FRAU DOCTOR HELLER'S HOUSE.
FRENCH HIGH SCHOOL OF VIENNA
THE COMMUNAL LIFE WENT HAND IN HAND WITH THE USE OF ALL KINDS OF MOOD ENHANCERS: WEED, HASH, . . .
I TRIPPED EVERY WEEKEND, AND YOU COULD SEE IT ON MY FACE.
MY PHYSICS TEACHER, YONNEL ARROUAS, WAS WORRIED ABOUT ME.
MARJANE, ARE YOU OKAY? YOU CAN TALK TO ME IF YOU'D LIKE.
...
AT HOME, THERE'S A WAR. I'M SCARED FOR MY PARENTS. I'M ALONE AND I FEEL GUILTY. I DON'T HAVE MUCH MONEY. MY UNCLE WAS ASSASSINATED. I SAW MY NEIGHBOR DIE IN A BOMBING. . .
I SENSED THAT HE DIDN'T BELIEVE ME. HE MUST HAVE THOUGHT THAT I WAS EXAGGERATING.
I PERSISTED ANYWAY. I NEEDED TO TALK SO MUCH.
THEN, I LIVE IN THIS CRAZY WOMAN'S HOUSE, MY BOYFRIEND...
ENOUGH, IT'S OKAY. WOULD YOU LIKE TO COME OVER FOR LUNCH AT OUR HOUSE ON SATURDAY? MY MOTHER WILL BE THERE, TOO.
I ACCEPTED.
AT HIS HOUSE, I PLAYED WITH HIS TWINS, JOHANNA AND CAROLINE.
mariane! mariane! mariane! mariane!
cucu!
I SPENT A LONG TIME TALKING TO MRS. ARROUAS, MY TEACHER'S MOTHER, A FRENCHWOMAN OF JEWISH-MOROCCAN ORIGINS.
I UNDERSTAND HOW HARD IT IS FOR YOU. YOU HAVE TO MAKE THREE TIMES THE EFFORT OF ANYONE ELSE TO SUCCEED! THAT'S THE IMMIGRANT LOT!! IT WAS THE SAME FOR ME, WHEN I ARRIVED IN FRANCE.
BE STRONG. ALL WILL GO WELL FOR YOU. I HOPE TO SEE YOU SOON.
BUT WE NEVER SAW EACH OTHER AGAIN. YONNEL'S WIFE DIDN'T LIKE ME. SHE MUST HAVE THOUGHT THAT I WAS MAKING UP STORIES. SO I WAS NEVER AGAIN INVITED OVER.

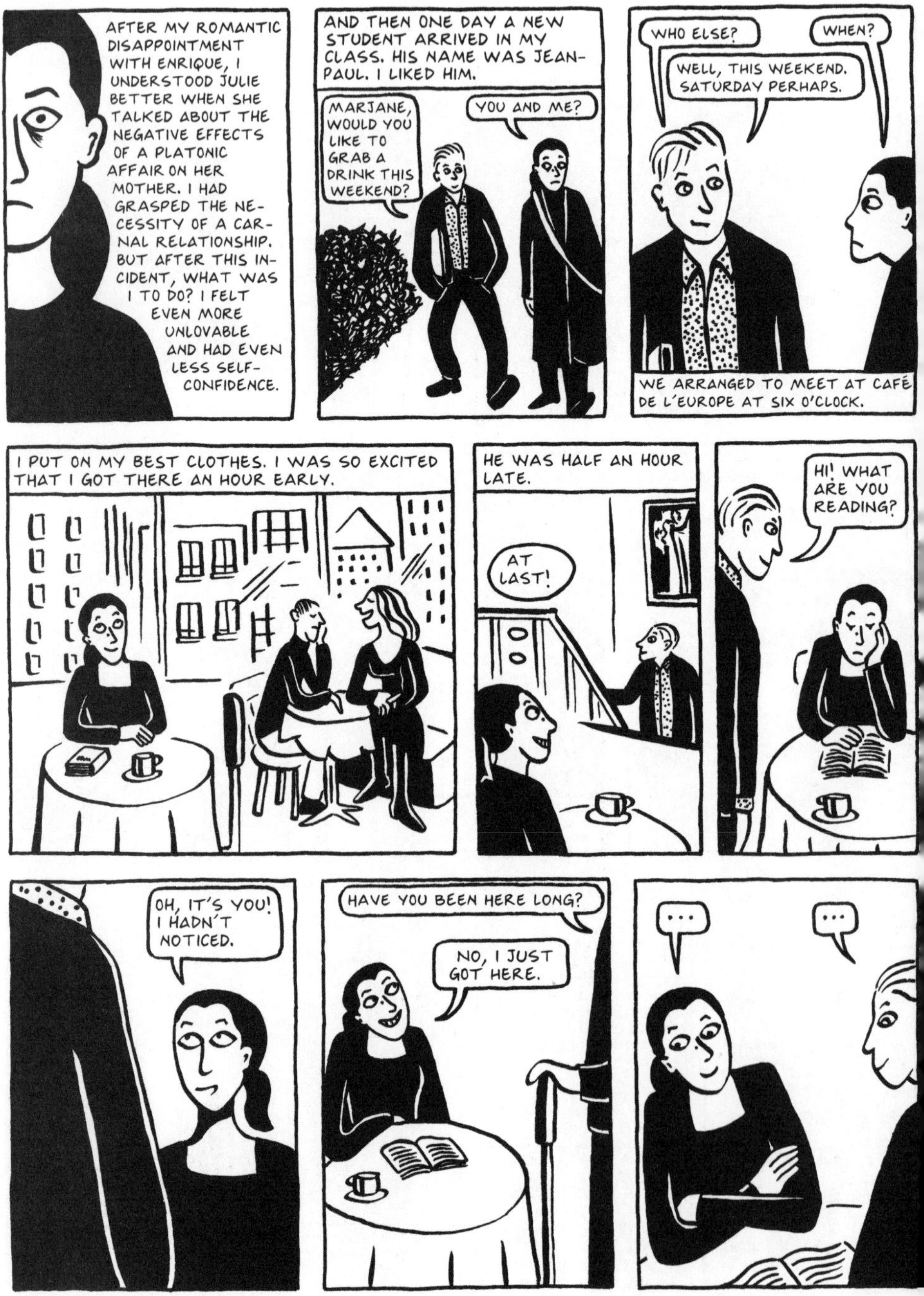
AFTER MY ROMANTIC DISAPPOINTMENT WITH ENRIQUE, I UNDERSTOOD JULIE BETTER WHEN SHE TALKED ABOUT THE NEGATIVE EFFECTS OF A PLATONIC AFFAIR ON HER MOTHER. I HAD GRASPED THE NECESSITY OF A CARNAL RELATIONSHIP. BUT AFTER THIS INCIDENT, WHAT WAS I TO DO? I FELT EVEN MORE UNLOVABLE AND HAD EVEN LESS SELF-CONFIDENCE.
AND THEN ONE DAY A NEW STUDENT ARRIVED IN MY CLASS. HIS NAME WAS JEAN-PAUL. I LIKED HIM.
MARJANE, WOULD YOU LIKE TO GRAB A DRINK THIS WEEKEND?
YOU AND ME?
WHO ELSE?
WHEN?
WELL, THIS WEEKEND. SATURDAY PERHAPS.
WE ARRANGED TO MEET AT CAFÉ DE L'EUROPE AT SIX O'CLOCK.
I PUT ON MY BEST CLOTHES. I WAS SO EXCITED THAT I GOT THERE AN HOUR EARLY.
HE WAS HALF AN HOUR LATE.
AT LAST!
HI! WHAT ARE YOU READING?
OH, IT'S YOU! I HADN'T NOTICED.
HAVE YOU BEEN HERE LONG?
NO, I JUST GOT HERE.
...
...

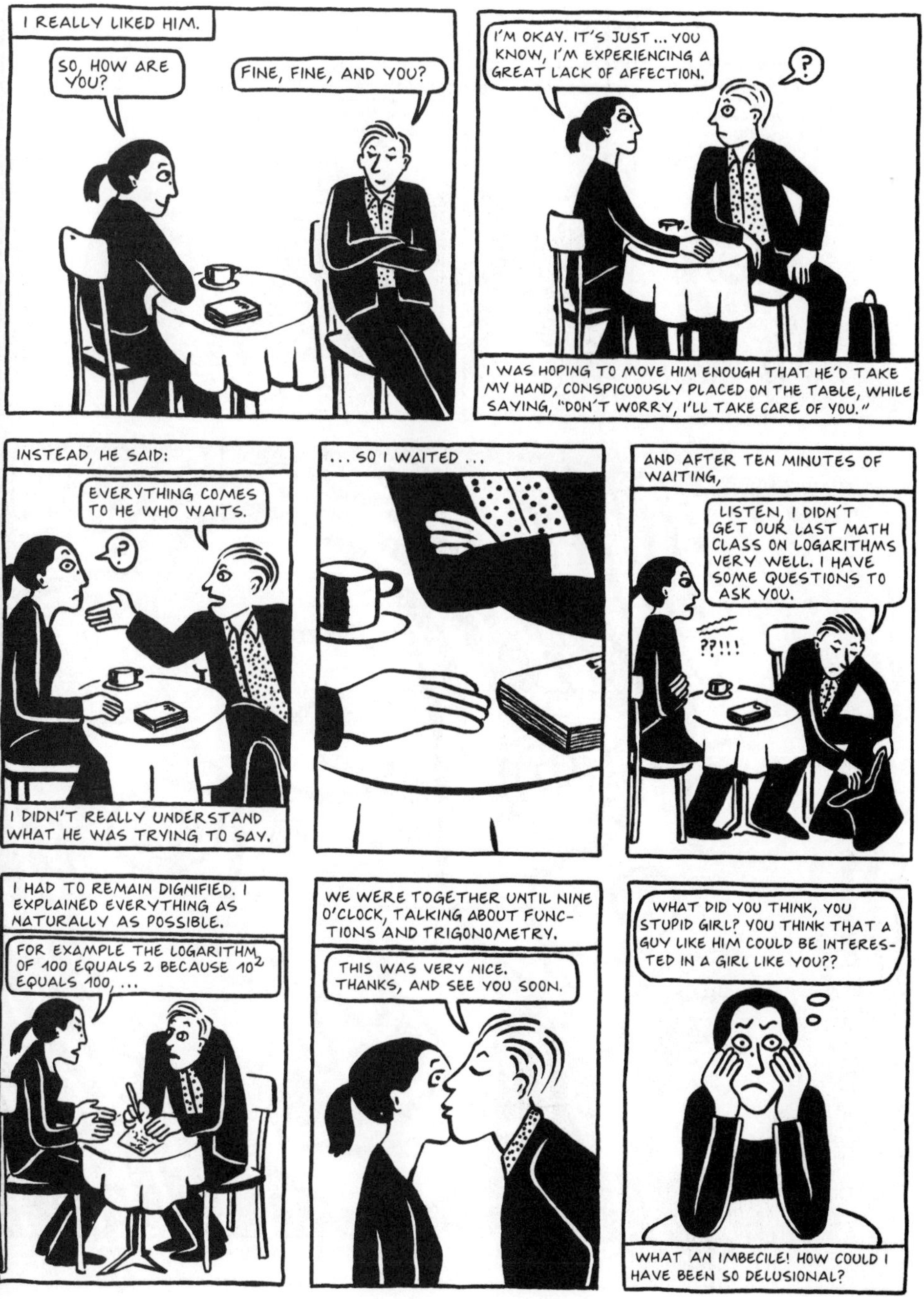

I REALLY LIKED HIM.
SO, HOW ARE YOU?
FINE, FINE, AND YOU?
I'M OKAY. IT'S JUST... YOU KNOW, I'M EXPERIENCING A GREAT LACK OF AFFECTION.
?
I WAS HOPING TO MOVE HIM ENOUGH THAT HE'D TAKE MY HAND, CONSPICUOUSLY PLACED ON THE TABLE, WHILE SAYING, "DON'T WORRY, I'LL TAKE CARE OF YOU."
INSTEAD, HE SAID:
EVERYTHING COMES TO HE WHO WAITS.
?
I DIDN'T REALLY UNDERSTAND WHAT HE WAS TRYING TO SAY.
... SO I WAITED ...
AND AFTER TEN MINUTES OF WAITING,
LISTEN, I DIDN'T GET OUR LAST MATH CLASS ON LOGARITHMS VERY WELL. I HAVE SOME QUESTIONS TO ASK YOU.
??!!!
I HAD TO REMAIN DIGNIFIED. I EXPLAINED EVERYTHING AS NATURALLY AS POSSIBLE.
FOR EXAMPLE THE LOGARITHM OF 100 EQUALS 2 BECAUSE 10² EQUALS 100, ...
WE WERE TOGETHER UNTIL NINE O'CLOCK, TALKING ABOUT FUNCTIONS AND TRIGONOMETRY.
THIS WAS VERY NICE. THANKS, AND SEE YOU SOON.
WHAT DID YOU THINK, YOU STUPID GIRL? YOU THINK THAT A GUY LIKE HIM COULD BE INTERESTED IN A GIRL LIKE YOU??
WHAT AN IMBECILE! HOW COULD I HAVE BEEN SO DELUSIONAL?

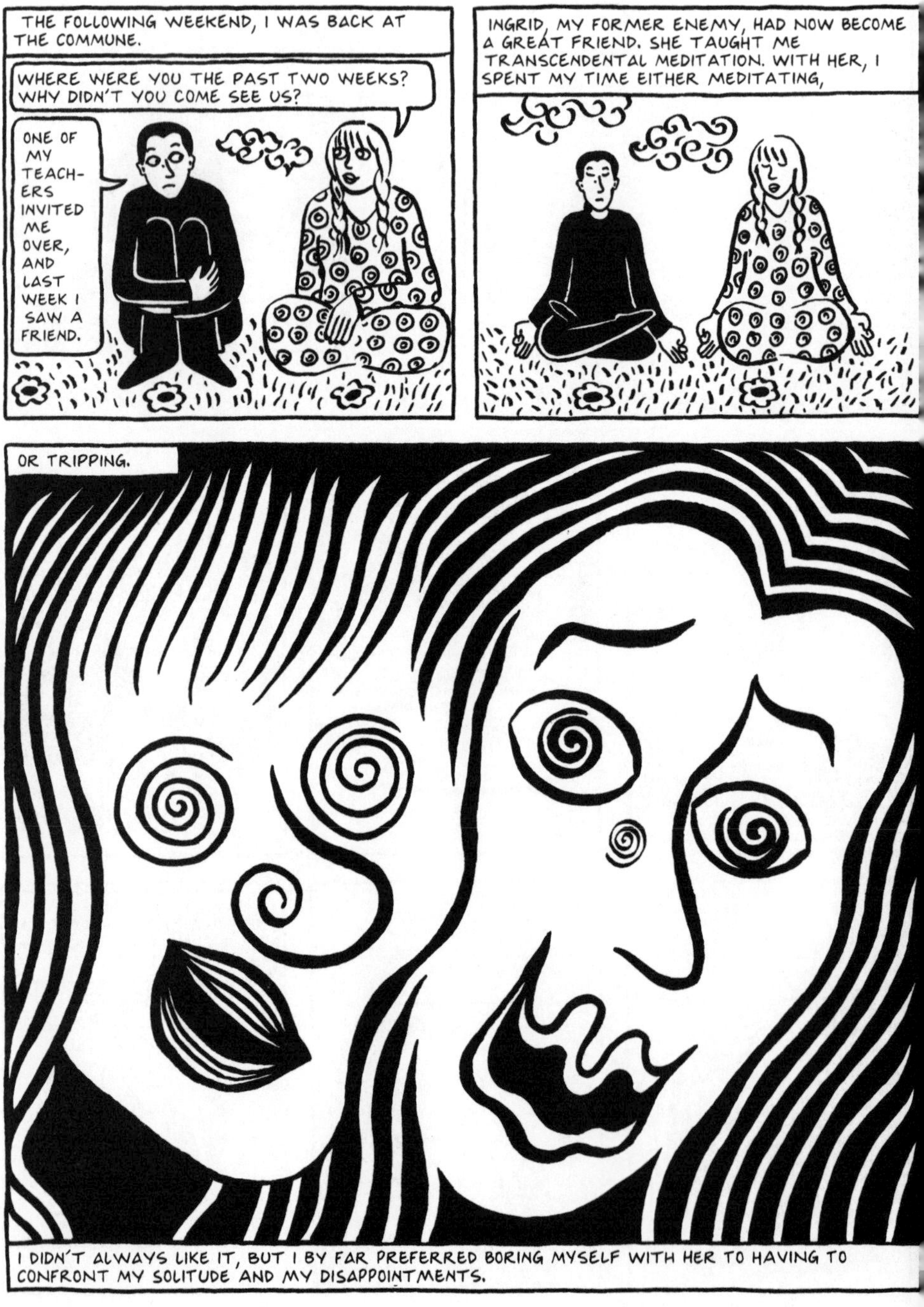
THE FOLLOWING WEEKEND, I WAS BACK AT THE COMMUNE.
WHERE WERE YOU THE PAST TWO WEEKS? WHY DIDN'T YOU COME SEE US?
ONE OF MY TEACHERS INVITED ME OVER, AND LAST WEEK I SAW A FRIEND.
INGRID, MY FORMER ENEMY, HAD NOW BECOME A GREAT FRIEND. SHE TAUGHT ME TRANSCENDENTAL MEDITATION. WITH HER, I SPENT MY TIME EITHER MEDITATING,
OR TRIPPING.
I DIDN'T ALWAYS LIKE IT, BUT I BY FAR PREFERRED BORING MYSELF WITH HER TO HAVING TO CONFRONT MY SOLITUDE AND MY DISAPPOINTMENTS.

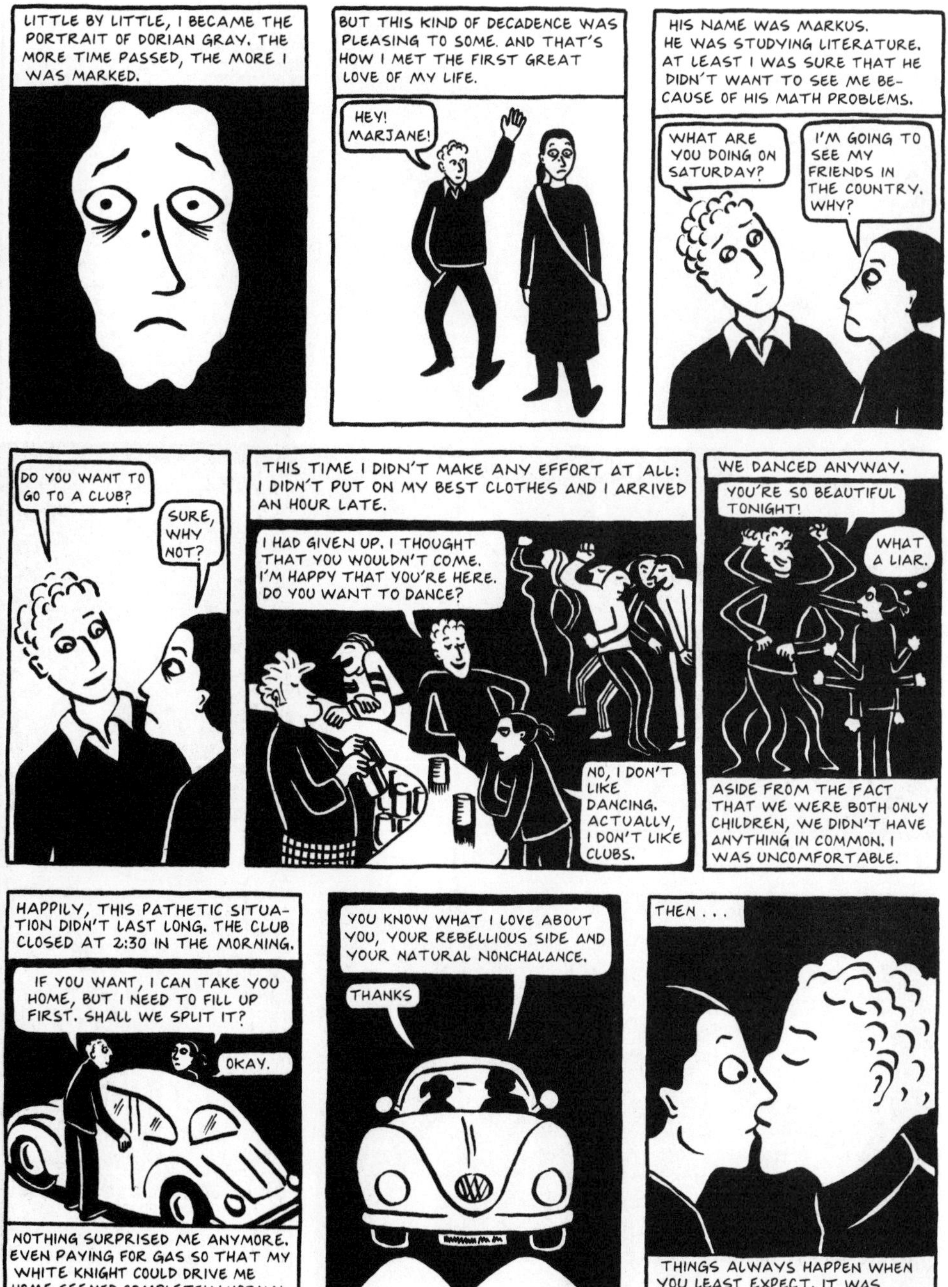
LITTLE BY LITTLE, I BECAME THE PORTRAIT OF DORIAN GRAY. THE MORE TIME PASSED, THE MORE I WAS MARKED.
BUT THIS KIND OF DECADENCE WAS PLEASING TO SOME. AND THAT'S HOW I MET THE FIRST GREAT LOVE OF MY LIFE.
HEY! MARJANE!
HIS NAME WAS MARKUS. HE WAS STUDYING LITERATURE. AT LEAST I WAS SURE THAT HE DIDN'T WANT TO SEE ME BECAUSE OF HIS MATH PROBLEMS.
WHAT ARE YOU DOING ON SATURDAY?
I'M GOING TO SEE MY FRIENDS IN THE COUNTRY. WHY?
DO YOU WANT TO GO TO A CLUB?
SURE, WHY NOT?
THIS TIME I DIDN'T MAKE ANY EFFORT AT ALL: I DIDN'T PUT ON MY BEST CLOTHES AND I ARRIVED AN HOUR LATE.
I HAD GIVEN UP. I THOUGHT THAT YOU WOULDN'T COME. I'M HAPPY THAT YOU'RE HERE. DO YOU WANT TO DANCE?
NO, I DON'T LIKE DANCING. ACTUALLY, I DON'T LIKE CLUBS.
WE DANCED ANYWAY.
YOU'RE SO BEAUTIFUL TONIGHT!
WHAT A LIAR.
ASIDE FROM THE FACT THAT WE WERE BOTH ONLY CHILDREN, WE DIDN'T HAVE ANYTHING IN COMMON. I WAS UNCOMFORTABLE.
HAPPILY, THIS PATHETIC SITUATION DIDN'T LAST LONG. THE CLUB CLOSED AT 2:30 IN THE MORNING.
IF YOU WANT, I CAN TAKE YOU HOME, BUT I NEED TO FILL UP FIRST. SHALL WE SPLIT IT?
OKAY.
NOTHING SURPRISED ME ANYMORE. EVEN PAYING FOR GAS SO THAT MY WHITE KNIGHT COULD DRIVE ME HOME SEEMED COMPLETELY NORMAL.
YOU KNOW WHAT I LOVE ABOUT YOU, YOUR REBELLIOUS SIDE AND YOUR NATURAL NONCHALANCE.
THANKS
THEN . . .
THINGS ALWAYS HAPPEN WHEN YOU LEAST EXPECT. IT WAS HAPPINESS.

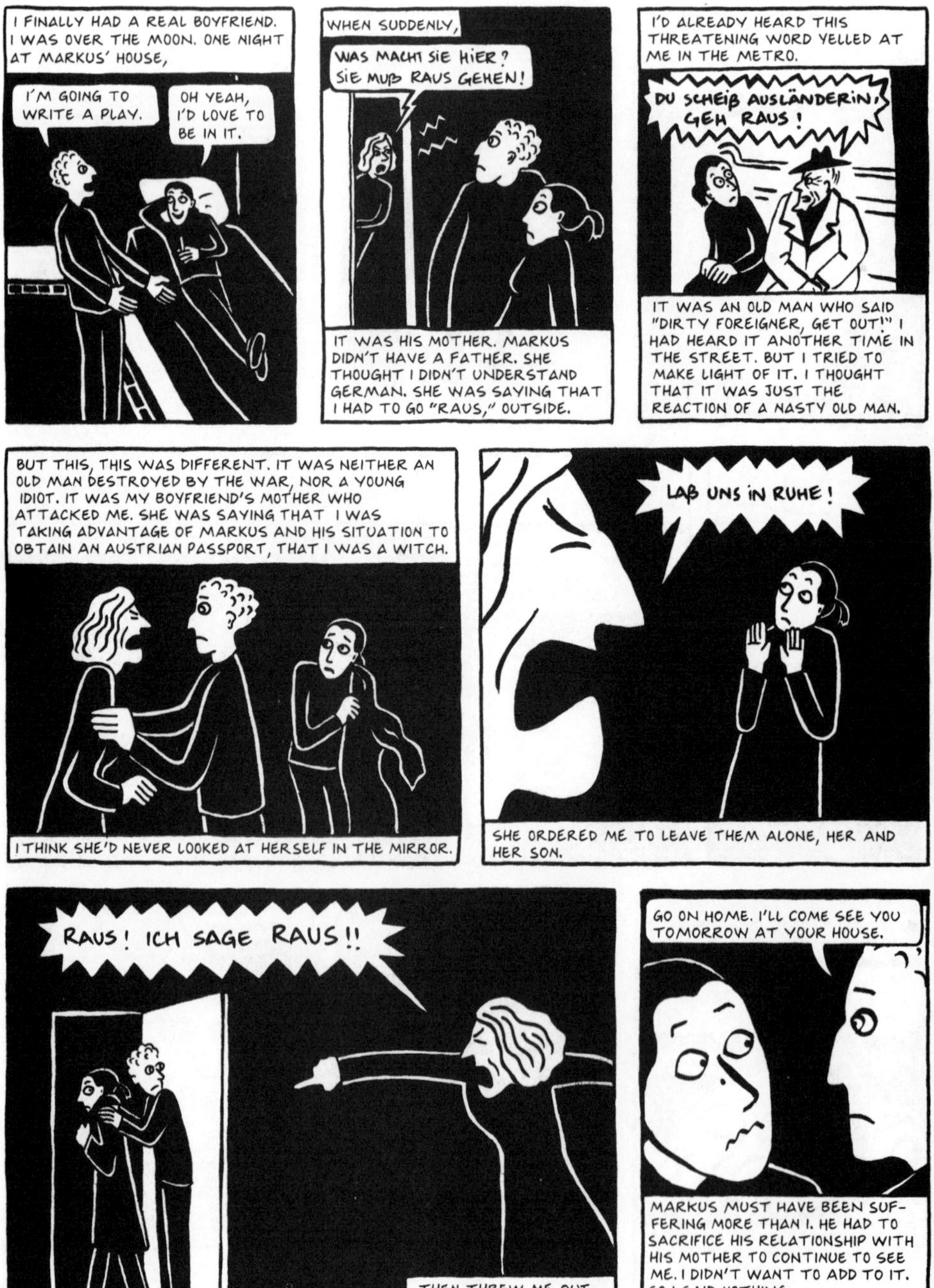
I FINALLY HAD A REAL BOYFRIEND. I WAS OVER THE MOON. ONE NIGHT AT MARKUS' HOUSE,
I'M GOING TO WRITE A PLAY.
OH YEAH, I'D LOVE TO BE IN IT.
WHEN SUDDENLY,
WAS MACHT SIE HIER? SIE MUß RAUS GEHEN!
IT WAS HIS MOTHER. MARKUS DIDN'T HAVE A FATHER. SHE THOUGHT I DIDN'T UNDERSTAND GERMAN. SHE WAS SAYING THAT I HAD TO GO "RAUS," OUTSIDE.
I'D ALREADY HEARD THIS THREATENING WORD YELLED AT ME IN THE METRO.
DU SCHEIß AUSLÄNDERIN, GEH RAUS!
IT WAS AN OLD MAN WHO SAID "DIRTY FOREIGNER, GET OUT!" I HAD HEARD IT ANOTHER TIME IN THE STREET. BUT I TRIED TO MAKE LIGHT OF IT. I THOUGHT THAT IT WAS JUST THE REACTION OF A NASTY OLD MAN.
BUT THIS, THIS WAS DIFFERENT. IT WAS NEITHER AN OLD MAN DESTROYED BY THE WAR, NOR A YOUNG IDIOT. IT WAS MY BOYFRIEND'S MOTHER WHO ATTACKED ME. SHE WAS SAYING THAT I WAS TAKING ADVANTAGE OF MARKUS AND HIS SITUATION TO OBTAIN AN AUSTRIAN PASSPORT, THAT I WAS A WITCH.
I THINK SHE'D NEVER LOOKED AT HERSELF IN THE MIRROR.
LAß UNS IN RUHE!
SHE ORDERED ME TO LEAVE THEM ALONE, HER AND HER SON.
RAUS! ICH SAGE RAUS!!
THEN THREW ME OUT.
GO ON HOME. I'LL COME SEE YOU TOMORROW AT YOUR HOUSE.
MARKUS MUST HAVE BEEN SUFFERING MORE THAN I. HE HAD TO SACRIFICE HIS RELATIONSHIP WITH HIS MOTHER TO CONTINUE TO SEE ME. I DIDN'T WANT TO ADD TO IT. SO I SAID NOTHING ...

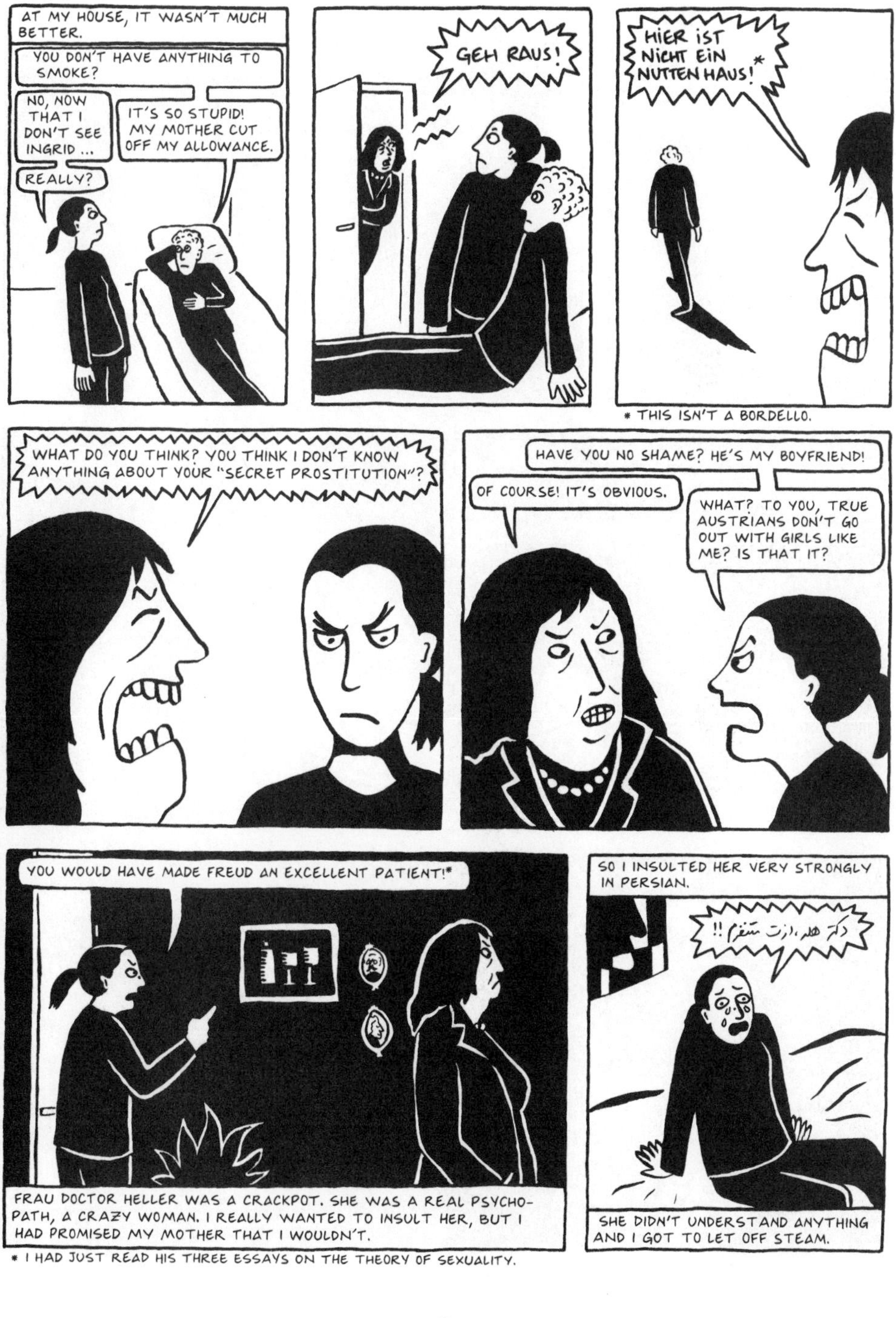
AT MY HOUSE, IT WASN'T MUCH BETTER.
YOU DON'T HAVE ANYTHING TO SMOKE?
NO, NOW THAT I DON'T SEE INGRID ...
IT'S SO STUPID! MY MOTHER CUT OFF MY ALLOWANCE.
REALLY?
GEH RAUS!
HIER IST NICHT EIN NUTTEN HAUS!*
* THIS ISN'T A BORDELLO.
WHAT DO YOU THINK? YOU THINK I DON'T KNOW ANYTHING ABOUT YOUR "SECRET PROSTITUTION"?
HAVE YOU NO SHAME? HE'S MY BOYFRIEND!
OF COURSE! IT'S OBVIOUS.
WHAT? TO YOU, TRUE AUSTRIANS DON'T GO OUT WITH GIRLS LIKE ME? IS THAT IT?
YOU WOULD HAVE MADE FREUD AN EXCELLENT PATIENT!*
FRAU DOCTOR HELLER WAS A CRACKPOT. SHE WAS A REAL PSYCHOPATH, A CRAZY WOMAN. I REALLY WANTED TO INSULT HER, BUT I HAD PROMISED MY MOTHER THAT I WOULDN'T.
SO I INSULTED HER VERY STRONGLY IN PERSIAN.
SHE DIDN'T UNDERSTAND ANYTHING AND I GOT TO LET OFF STEAM.

* I HAD JUST READ HIS THREE ESSAYS ON THE THEORY OF SEXUALITY.

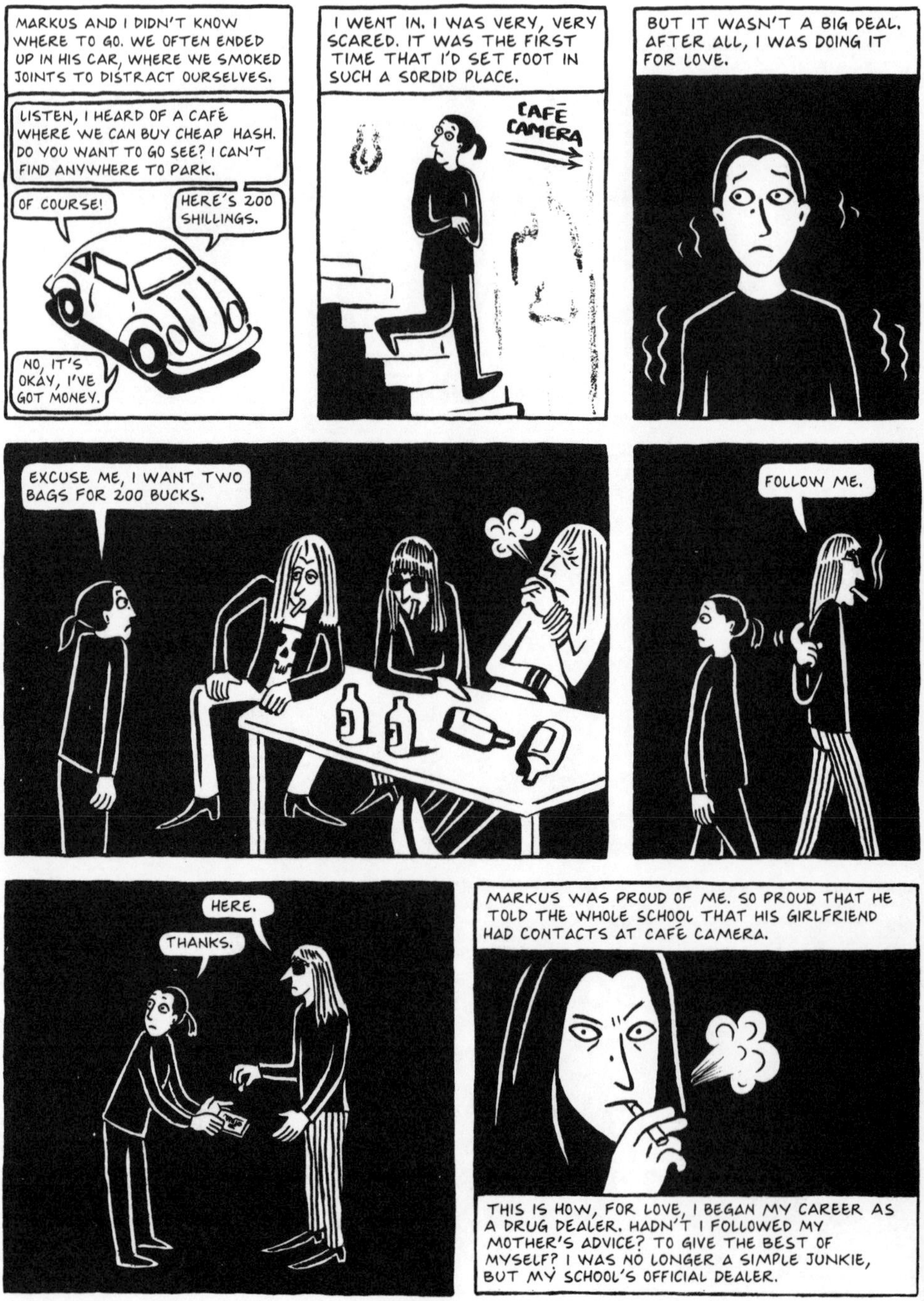
MARKUS AND I DIDN'T KNOW WHERE TO GO. WE OFTEN ENDED UP IN HIS CAR, WHERE WE SMOKED JOINTS TO DISTRACT OURSELVES.
LISTEN, I HEARD OF A CAFÉ WHERE WE CAN BUY CHEAP HASH. DO YOU WANT TO GO SEE? I CAN'T FIND ANYWHERE TO PARK.
OF COURSE!
HERE'S 200 SHILLINGS.
NO, IT'S OKAY, I'VE GOT MONEY.
I WENT IN. I WAS VERY, VERY SCARED. IT WAS THE FIRST TIME THAT I'D SET FOOT IN SUCH A SORDID PLACE.
CAFÉ CAMERA
BUT IT WASN'T A BIG DEAL. AFTER ALL, I WAS DOING IT FOR LOVE.
EXCUSE ME, I WANT TWO BAGS FOR 200 BUCKS.
FOLLOW ME.
HERE.
THANKS.
MARKUS WAS PROUD OF ME. SO PROUD THAT HE TOLD THE WHOLE SCHOOL THAT HIS GIRLFRIEND HAD CONTACTS AT CAFÉ CAMERA.
THIS IS HOW, FOR LOVE, I BEGAN MY CAREER AS A DRUG DEALER. HADN'T I FOLLOWED MY MOTHER'S ADVICE? TO GIVE THE BEST OF MYSELF? I WAS NO LONGER A SIMPLE JUNKIE, BUT MY SCHOOL'S OFFICIAL DEALER.

THE CROISSANT

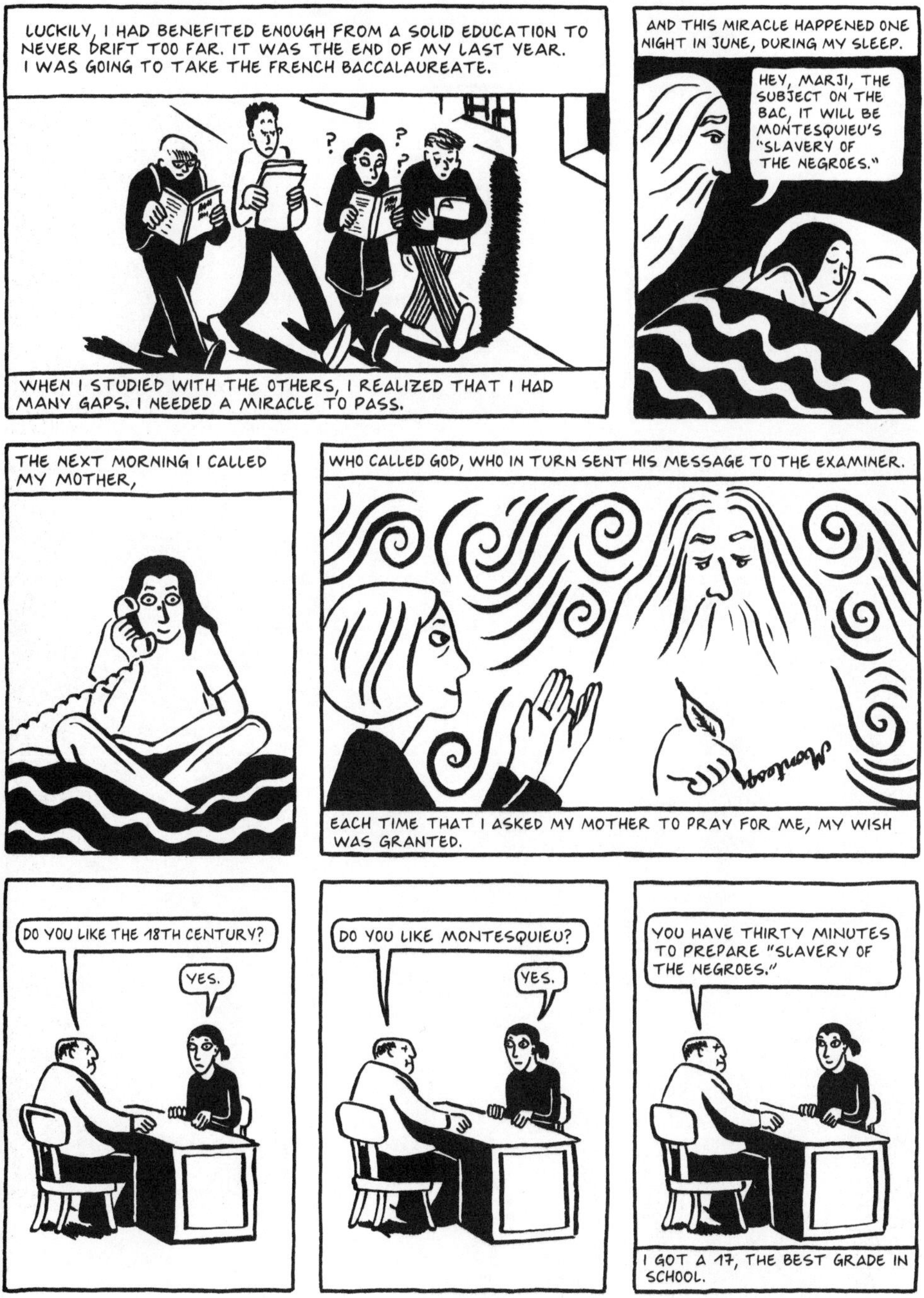

LUCKILY, I HAD BENEFITED ENOUGH FROM A SOLID EDUCATION TO NEVER DRIFT TOO FAR. IT WAS THE END OF MY LAST YEAR. I WAS GOING TO TAKE THE FRENCH BACCALAUREATE.
WHEN I STUDIED WITH THE OTHERS, I REALIZED THAT I HAD MANY GAPS. I NEEDED A MIRACLE TO PASS.
AND THIS MIRACLE HAPPENED ONE NIGHT IN JUNE, DURING MY SLEEP.
HEY, MARJI, THE SUBJECT ON THE BAC, IT WILL BE MONTESQUIEU'S "SLAVERY OF THE NEGROES."
THE NEXT MORNING I CALLED MY MOTHER,
WHO CALLED GOD, WHO IN TURN SENT HIS MESSAGE TO THE EXAMINER.
EACH TIME THAT I ASKED MY MOTHER TO PRAY FOR ME, MY WISH WAS GRANTED.
DO YOU LIKE THE 18TH CENTURY?
YES.
DO YOU LIKE MONTESQUIEU?
YES.
YOU HAVE THIRTY MINUTES TO PREPARE "SLAVERY OF THE NEGROES."
I GOT A 17, THE BEST GRADE IN SCHOOL.

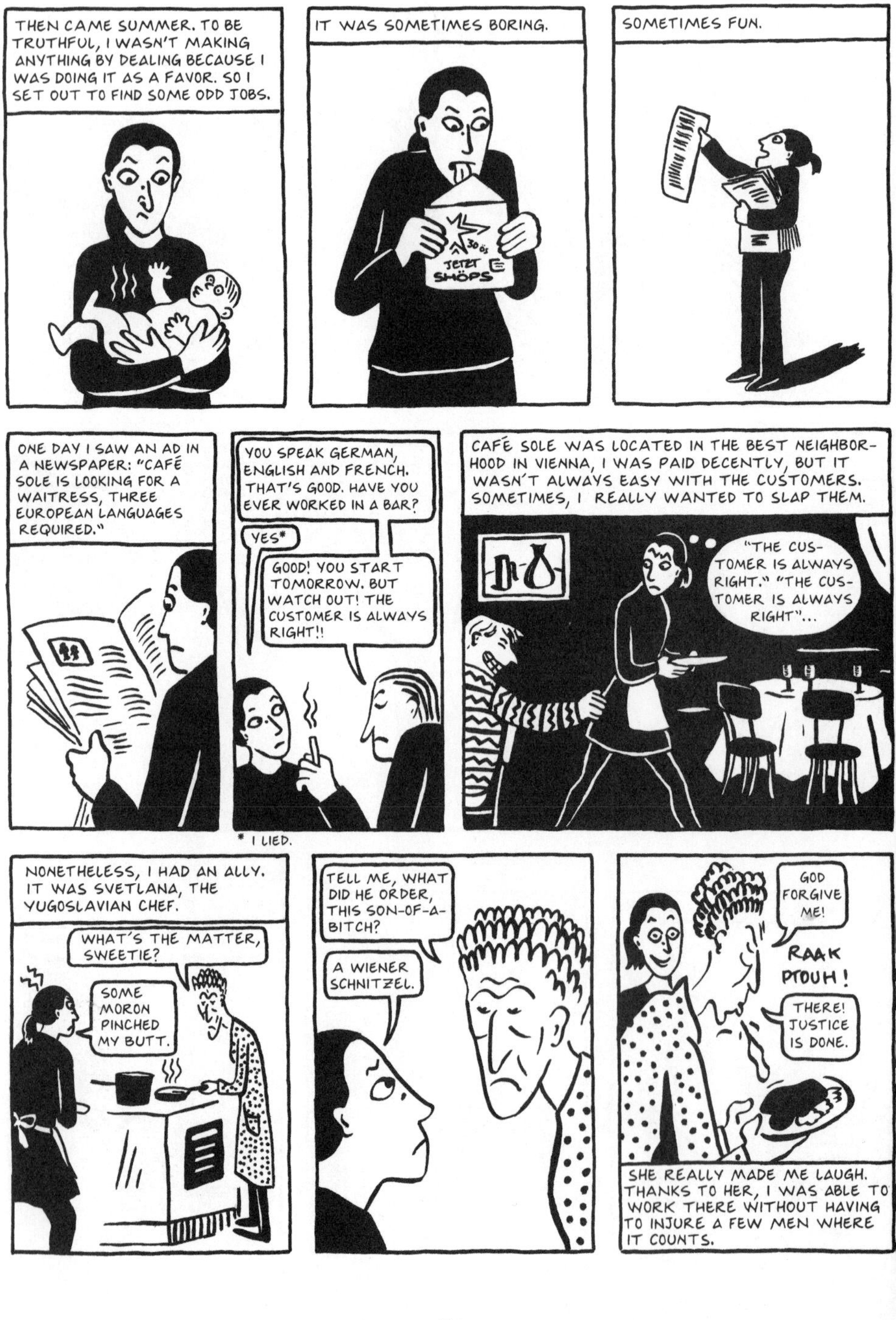
THEN CAME SUMMER. TO BE TRUTHFUL, I WASN'T MAKING ANYTHING BY DEALING BECAUSE I WAS DOING IT AS A FAVOR. SO I SET OUT TO FIND SOME ODD JOBS.
IT WAS SOMETIMES BORING.
30 ös
JETZT
SHÖPS
SOMETIMES FUN.
ONE DAY I SAW AN AD IN A NEWSPAPER: "CAFÉ SOLE IS LOOKING FOR A WAITRESS, THREE EUROPEAN LANGUAGES REQUIRED."
YOU SPEAK GERMAN, ENGLISH AND FRENCH. THAT'S GOOD. HAVE YOU EVER WORKED IN A BAR?
YES*
GOOD! YOU START TOMORROW. BUT WATCH OUT! THE CUSTOMER IS ALWAYS RIGHT!!
* I LIED.
CAFÉ SOLE WAS LOCATED IN THE BEST NEIGHBORHOOD IN VIENNA, I WAS PAID DECENTLY, BUT IT WASN'T ALWAYS EASY WITH THE CUSTOMERS. SOMETIMES, I REALLY WANTED TO SLAP THEM.
"THE CUSTOMER IS ALWAYS RIGHT." "THE CUSTOMER IS ALWAYS RIGHT"...
NONETHELESS, I HAD AN ALLY. IT WAS SVETLANA, THE YUGOSLAVIAN CHEF.
WHAT'S THE MATTER, SWEETIE?
SOME MORON PINCHED MY BUTT.
TELL ME, WHAT DID HE ORDER, THIS SON-OF-A-BITCH?
A WIENER SCHNITZEL.
GOD FORGIVE ME!
RAAK
PTOUH!
THERE! JUSTICE IS DONE.
SHE REALLY MADE ME LAUGH. THANKS TO HER, I WAS ABLE TO WORK THERE WITHOUT HAVING TO INJURE A FEW MEN WHERE IT COUNTS.

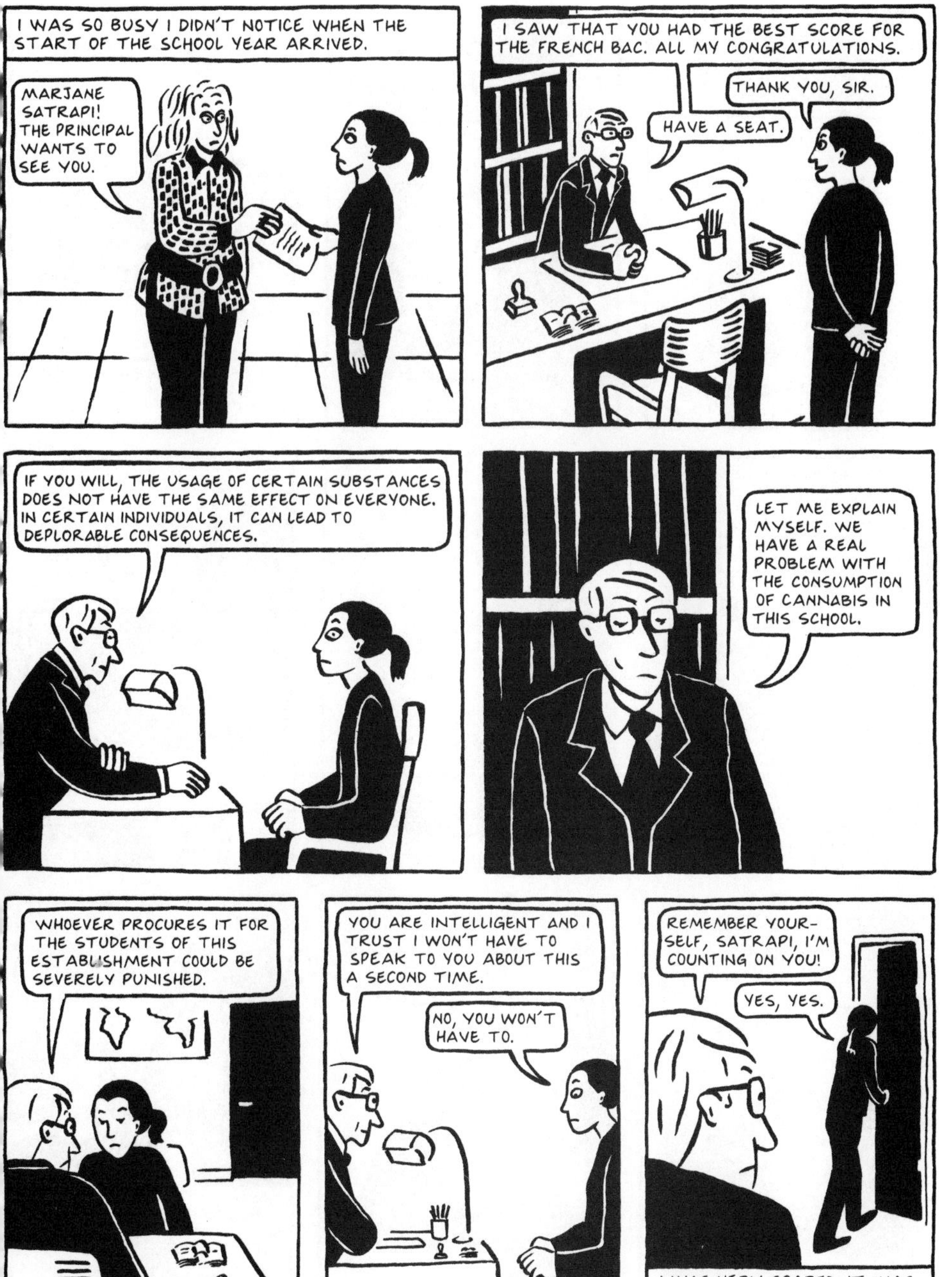
I WAS SO BUSY I DIDN'T NOTICE WHEN THE START OF THE SCHOOL YEAR ARRIVED.
MARJANE SATRAPI! THE PRINCIPAL WANTS TO SEE YOU.
I SAW THAT YOU HAD THE BEST SCORE FOR THE FRENCH BAC. ALL MY CONGRATULATIONS.
THANK YOU, SIR.
HAVE A SEAT.
IF YOU WILL, THE USAGE OF CERTAIN SUBSTANCES DOES NOT HAVE THE SAME EFFECT ON EVERYONE. IN CERTAIN INDIVIDUALS, IT CAN LEAD TO DEPLORABLE CONSEQUENCES.
LET ME EXPLAIN MYSELF. WE HAVE A REAL PROBLEM WITH THE CONSUMPTION OF CANNABIS IN THIS SCHOOL.
WHOEVER PROCURES IT FOR THE STUDENTS OF THIS ESTABLISHMENT COULD BE SEVERELY PUNISHED.
YOU ARE INTELLIGENT AND I TRUST I WON'T HAVE TO SPEAK TO YOU ABOUT THIS A SECOND TIME.
NO, YOU WON'T HAVE TO.
REMEMBER YOURSELF, SATRAPI, I'M COUNTING ON YOU!
YES, YES.
I WAS VERY SCARED. IT WAS THE END OF MY CAREER.

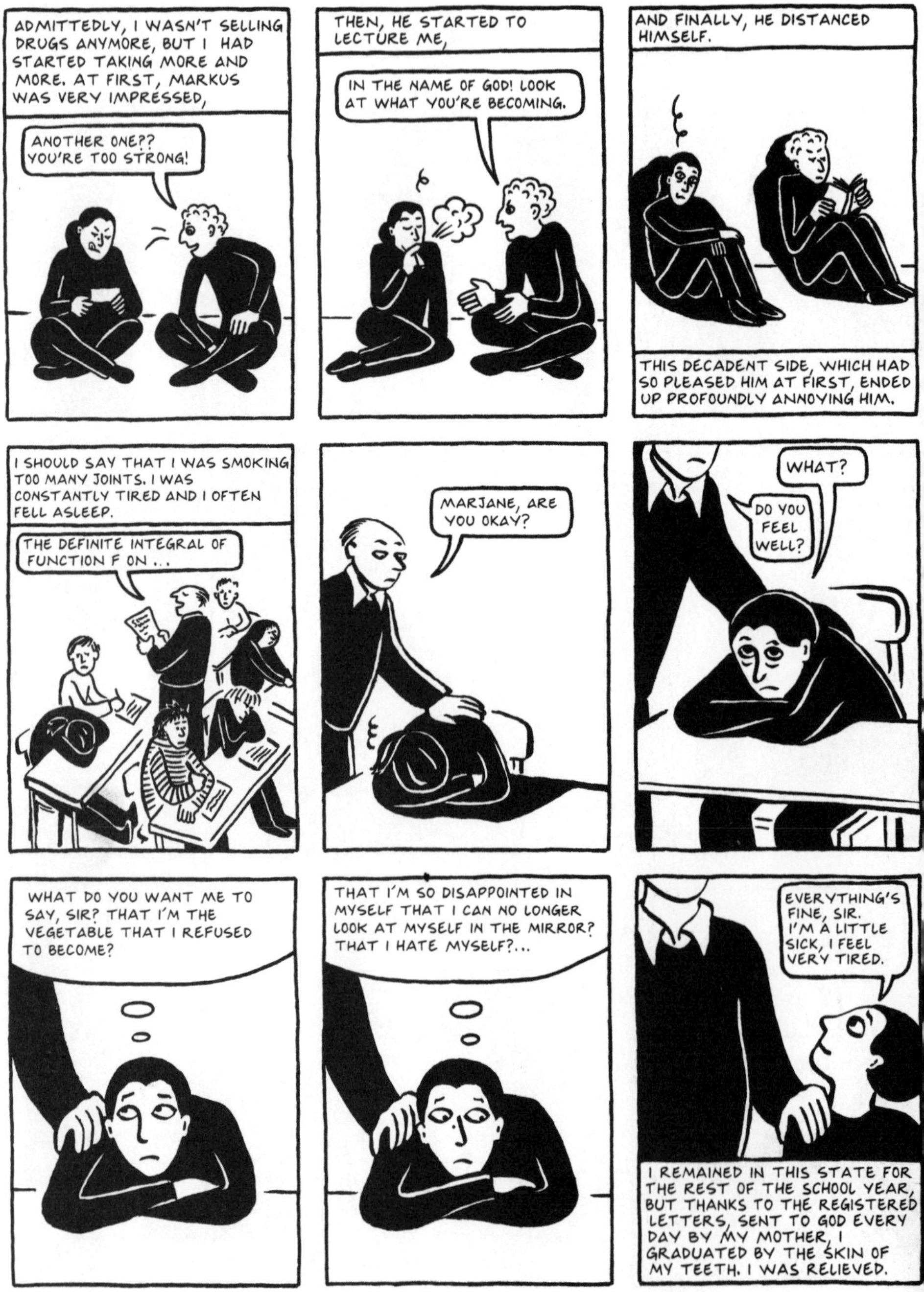
ADMITTEDLY, I WASN'T SELLING DRUGS ANYMORE, BUT I HAD STARTED TAKING MORE AND MORE. AT FIRST, MARKUS WAS VERY IMPRESSED,
ANOTHER ONE?? YOU'RE TOO STRONG!
THEN, HE STARTED TO LECTURE ME,
IN THE NAME OF GOD! LOOK AT WHAT YOU'RE BECOMING.
AND FINALLY, HE DISTANCED HIMSELF.
THIS DECADENT SIDE, WHICH HAD SO PLEASED HIM AT FIRST, ENDED UP PROFOUNDLY ANNOYING HIM.
I SHOULD SAY THAT I WAS SMOKING TOO MANY JOINTS. I WAS CONSTANTLY TIRED AND I OFTEN FELL ASLEEP.
THE DEFINITE INTEGRAL OF FUNCTION F ON . . .
MARJANE, ARE YOU OKAY?
DO YOU FEEL WELL?
WHAT?
WHAT DO YOU WANT ME TO SAY, SIR? THAT I'M THE VEGETABLE THAT I REFUSED TO BECOME?
THAT I'M SO DISAPPOINTED IN MYSELF THAT I CAN NO LONGER LOOK AT MYSELF IN THE MIRROR? THAT I HATE MYSELF?...
EVERYTHING'S FINE, SIR. I'M A LITTLE SICK, I FEEL VERY TIRED.
I REMAINED IN THIS STATE FOR THE REST OF THE SCHOOL YEAR, BUT THANKS TO THE REGISTERED LETTERS, SENT TO GOD EVERY DAY BY MY MOTHER, I GRADUATED BY THE SKIN OF MY TEETH. I WAS RELIEVED.

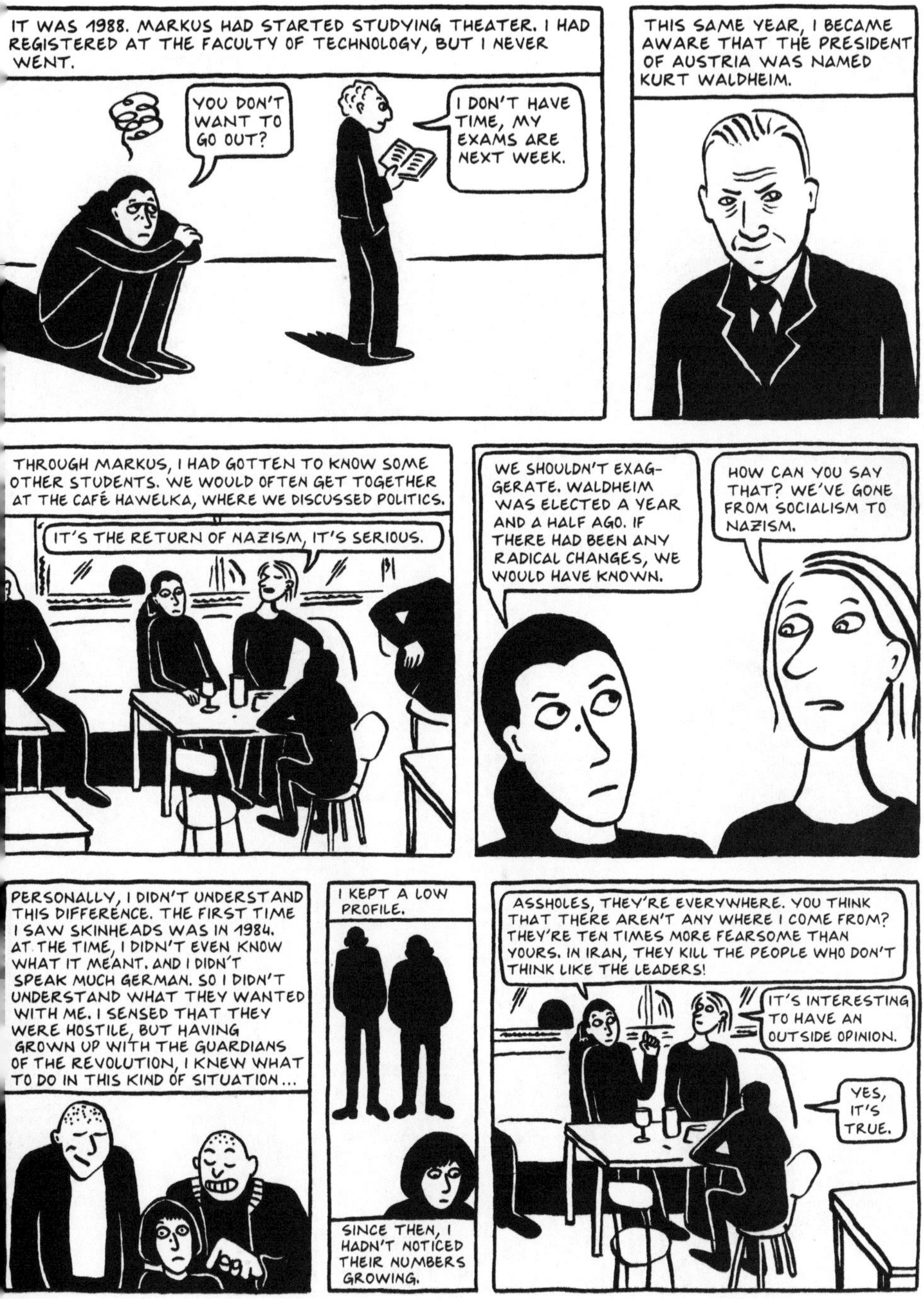
IT WAS 1988. MARKUS HAD STARTED STUDYING THEATER. I HAD REGISTERED AT THE FACULTY OF TECHNOLOGY, BUT I NEVER WENT.
YOU DON'T WANT TO GO OUT?
I DON'T HAVE TIME, MY EXAMS ARE NEXT WEEK.
THIS SAME YEAR, I BECAME AWARE THAT THE PRESIDENT OF AUSTRIA WAS NAMED KURT WALDHEIM.
THROUGH MARKUS, I HAD GOTTEN TO KNOW SOME OTHER STUDENTS. WE WOULD OFTEN GET TOGETHER AT THE CAFÉ HAWELKA, WHERE WE DISCUSSED POLITICS.
IT'S THE RETURN OF NAZISM, IT'S SERIOUS.
WE SHOULDN'T EXAGGERATE. WALDHEIM WAS ELECTED A YEAR AND A HALF AGO. IF THERE HAD BEEN ANY RADICAL CHANGES, WE WOULD HAVE KNOWN.
HOW CAN YOU SAY THAT? WE'VE GONE FROM SOCIALISM TO NAZISM.
PERSONALLY, I DIDN'T UNDERSTAND THIS DIFFERENCE. THE FIRST TIME I SAW SKINHEADS WAS IN 1984. AT THE TIME, I DIDN'T EVEN KNOW WHAT IT MEANT. AND I DIDN'T SPEAK MUCH GERMAN. SO I DIDN'T UNDERSTAND WHAT THEY WANTED WITH ME. I SENSED THAT THEY WERE HOSTILE, BUT HAVING GROWN UP WITH THE GUARDIANS OF THE REVOLUTION, I KNEW WHAT TO DO IN THIS KIND OF SITUATION...
I KEPT A LOW PROFILE.
SINCE THEN, I HADN'T NOTICED THEIR NUMBERS GROWING.
ASSHOLES, THEY'RE EVERYWHERE. YOU THINK THAT THERE AREN'T ANY WHERE I COME FROM? THEY'RE TEN TIMES MORE FEARSOME THAN YOURS. IN IRAN, THEY KILL THE PEOPLE WHO DON'T THINK LIKE THE LEADERS!
IT'S INTERESTING TO HAVE AN OUTSIDE OPINION.
YES, IT'S TRUE.

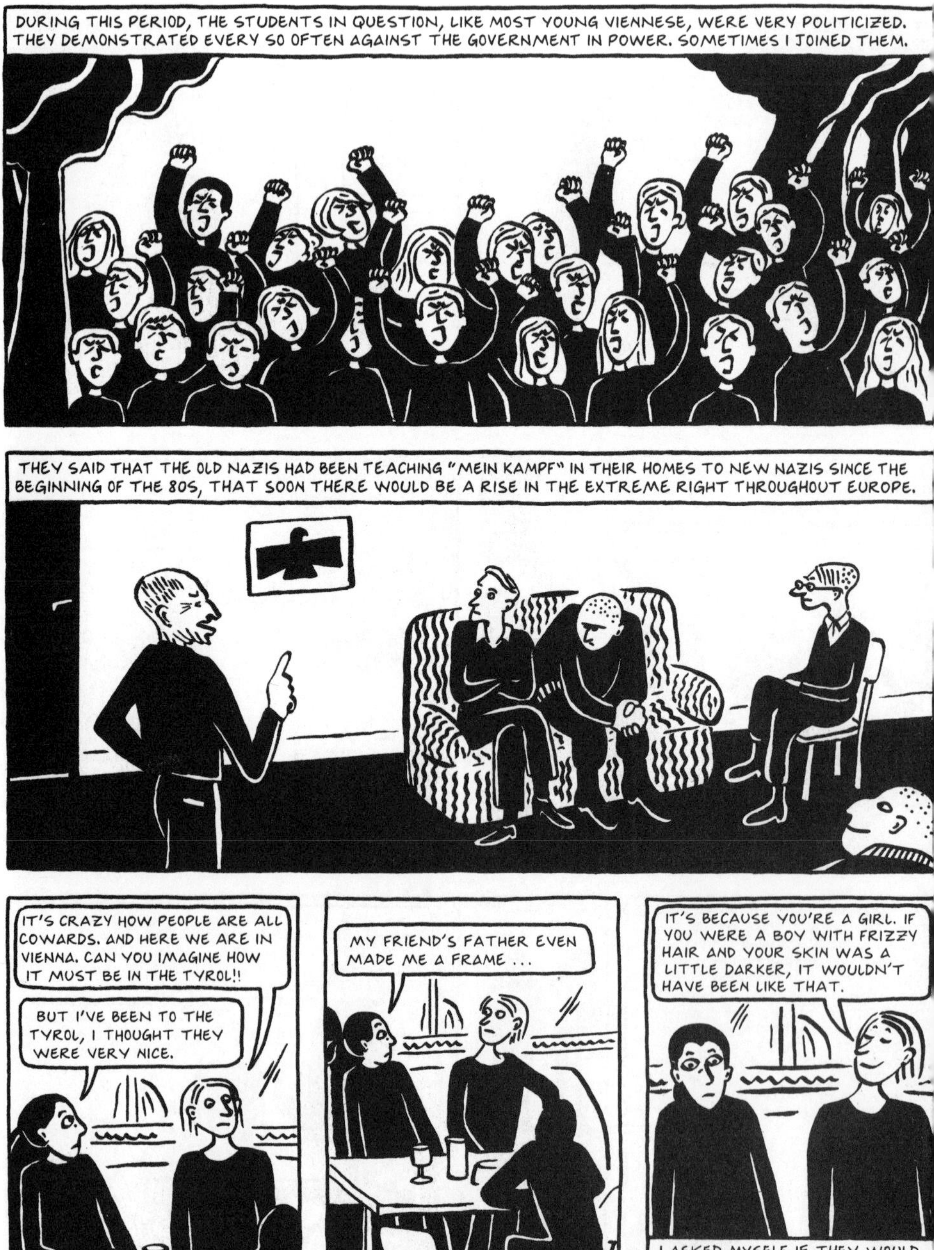
DURING THIS PERIOD, THE STUDENTS IN QUESTION, LIKE MOST YOUNG VIENNESE, WERE VERY POLITICIZED. THEY DEMONSTRATED EVERY SO OFTEN AGAINST THE GOVERNMENT IN POWER. SOMETIMES I JOINED THEM.
THEY SAID THAT THE OLD NAZIS HAD BEEN TEACHING "MEIN KAMPF" IN THEIR HOMES TO NEW NAZIS SINCE THE BEGINNING OF THE 80S, THAT SOON THERE WOULD BE A RISE IN THE EXTREME RIGHT THROUGHOUT EUROPE.
IT'S CRAZY HOW PEOPLE ARE ALL COWARDS. AND HERE WE ARE IN VIENNA. CAN YOU IMAGINE HOW IT MUST BE IN THE TYROL!!
BUT I'VE BEEN TO THE TYROL, I THOUGHT THEY WERE VERY NICE.
MY FRIEND'S FATHER EVEN MADE ME A FRAME ...
IT'S BECAUSE YOU'RE A GIRL. IF YOU WERE A BOY WITH FRIZZY HAIR AND YOUR SKIN WAS A LITTLE DARKER, IT WOULDN'T HAVE BEEN LIKE THAT.
I ASKED MYSELF IF THEY WOULD HAVE SAT BESIDE ME IF I HAD BEEN A FRIZZY-HAIRED AND DARK-SKINNED BOY?

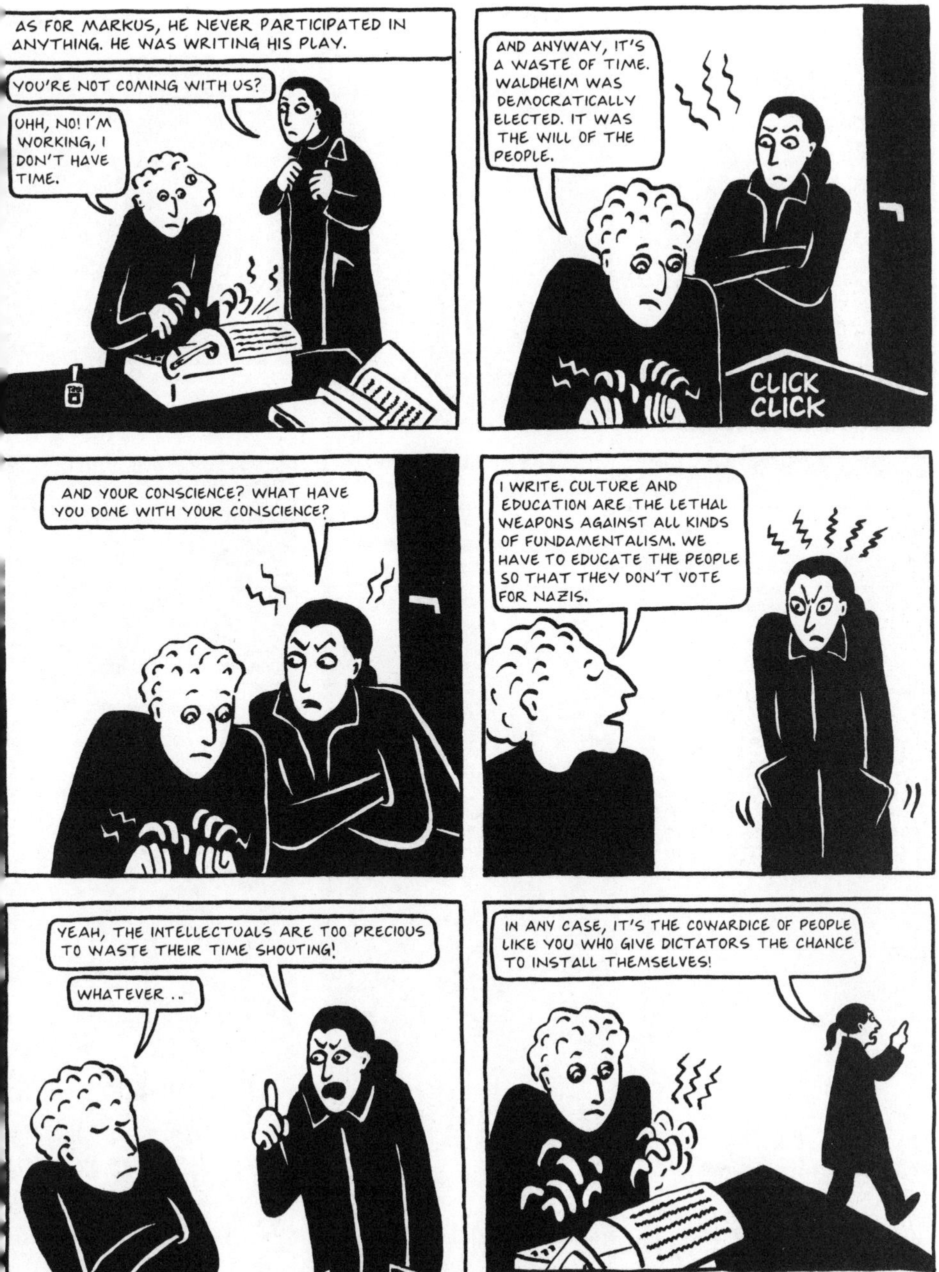
AS FOR MARKUS, HE NEVER PARTICIPATED IN ANYTHING. HE WAS WRITING HIS PLAY.
YOU'RE NOT COMING WITH US?
UHH, NO! I'M WORKING, I DON'T HAVE TIME.
AND ANYWAY, IT'S A WASTE OF TIME. WALDHEIM WAS DEMOCRATICALLY ELECTED. IT WAS THE WILL OF THE PEOPLE.
CLICK CLICK
AND YOUR CONSCIENCE? WHAT HAVE YOU DONE WITH YOUR CONSCIENCE?
I WRITE. CULTURE AND EDUCATION ARE THE LETHAL WEAPONS AGAINST ALL KINDS OF FUNDAMENTALISM. WE HAVE TO EDUCATE THE PEOPLE SO THAT THEY DON'T VOTE FOR NAZIS.
YEAH, THE INTELLECTUALS ARE TOO PRECIOUS TO WASTE THEIR TIME SHOUTING!
WHATEVER ..
IN ANY CASE, IT'S THE COWARDICE OF PEOPLE LIKE YOU WHO GIVE DICTATORS THE CHANCE TO INSTALL THEMSELVES!
THESE ARGUMENTS MARKED THE BEGINNING OF THE END OF OUR STORY.

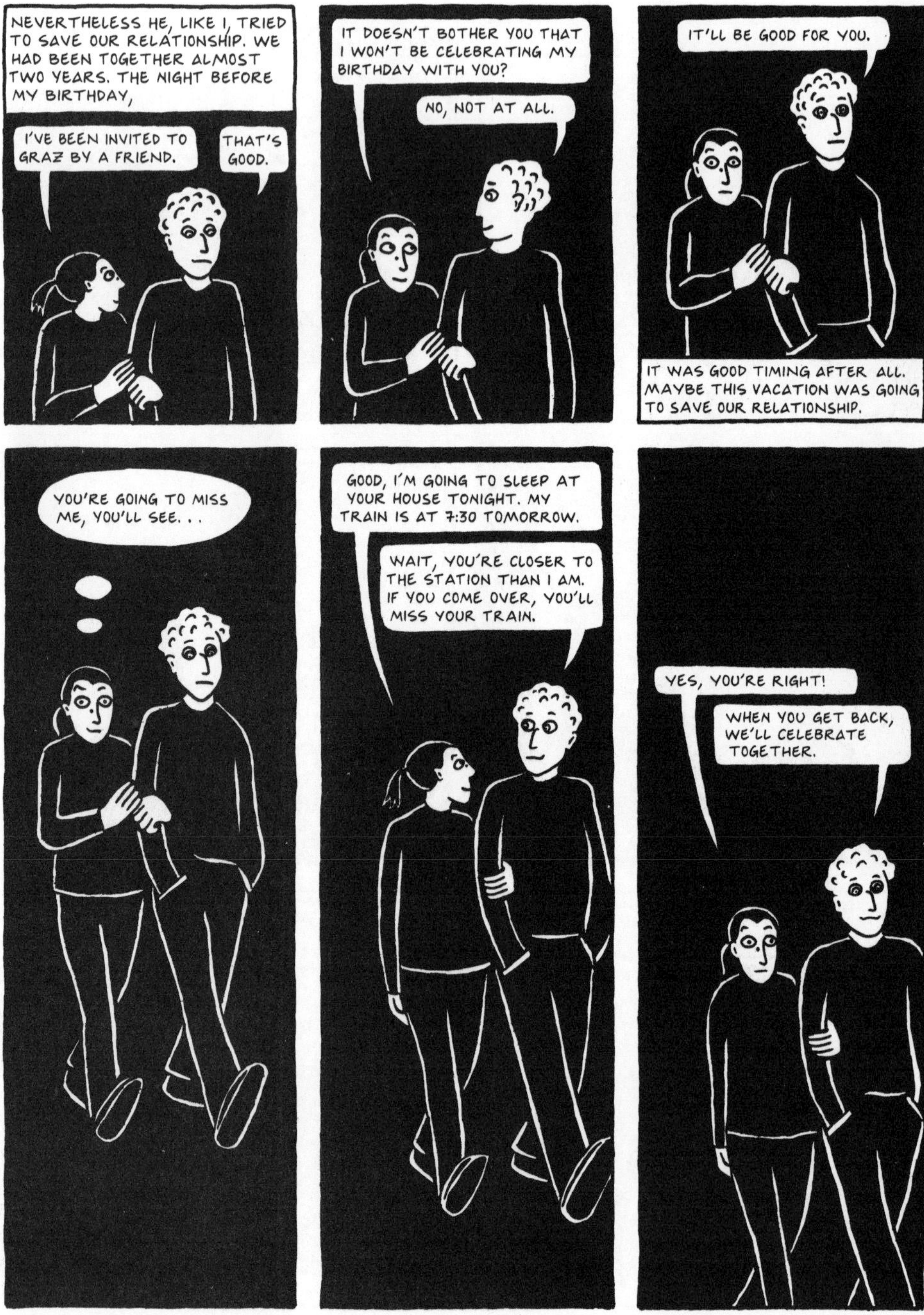
NEVERTHELESS HE, LIKE I, TRIED TO SAVE OUR RELATIONSHIP. WE HAD BEEN TOGETHER ALMOST TWO YEARS. THE NIGHT BEFORE MY BIRTHDAY,
I'VE BEEN INVITED TO GRAZ BY A FRIEND.
THAT'S GOOD.
IT DOESN'T BOTHER YOU THAT I WON'T BE CELEBRATING MY BIRTHDAY WITH YOU?
NO, NOT AT ALL.
IT'LL BE GOOD FOR YOU.
IT WAS GOOD TIMING AFTER ALL. MAYBE THIS VACATION WAS GOING TO SAVE OUR RELATIONSHIP.
YOU'RE GOING TO MISS ME, YOU'LL SEE. . .
GOOD, I'M GOING TO SLEEP AT YOUR HOUSE TONIGHT. MY TRAIN IS AT 7:30 TOMORROW.
WAIT, YOU'RE CLOSER TO THE STATION THAN I AM. IF YOU COME OVER, YOU'LL MISS YOUR TRAIN.
YES, YOU'RE RIGHT!
WHEN YOU GET BACK, WE'LL CELEBRATE TOGETHER.

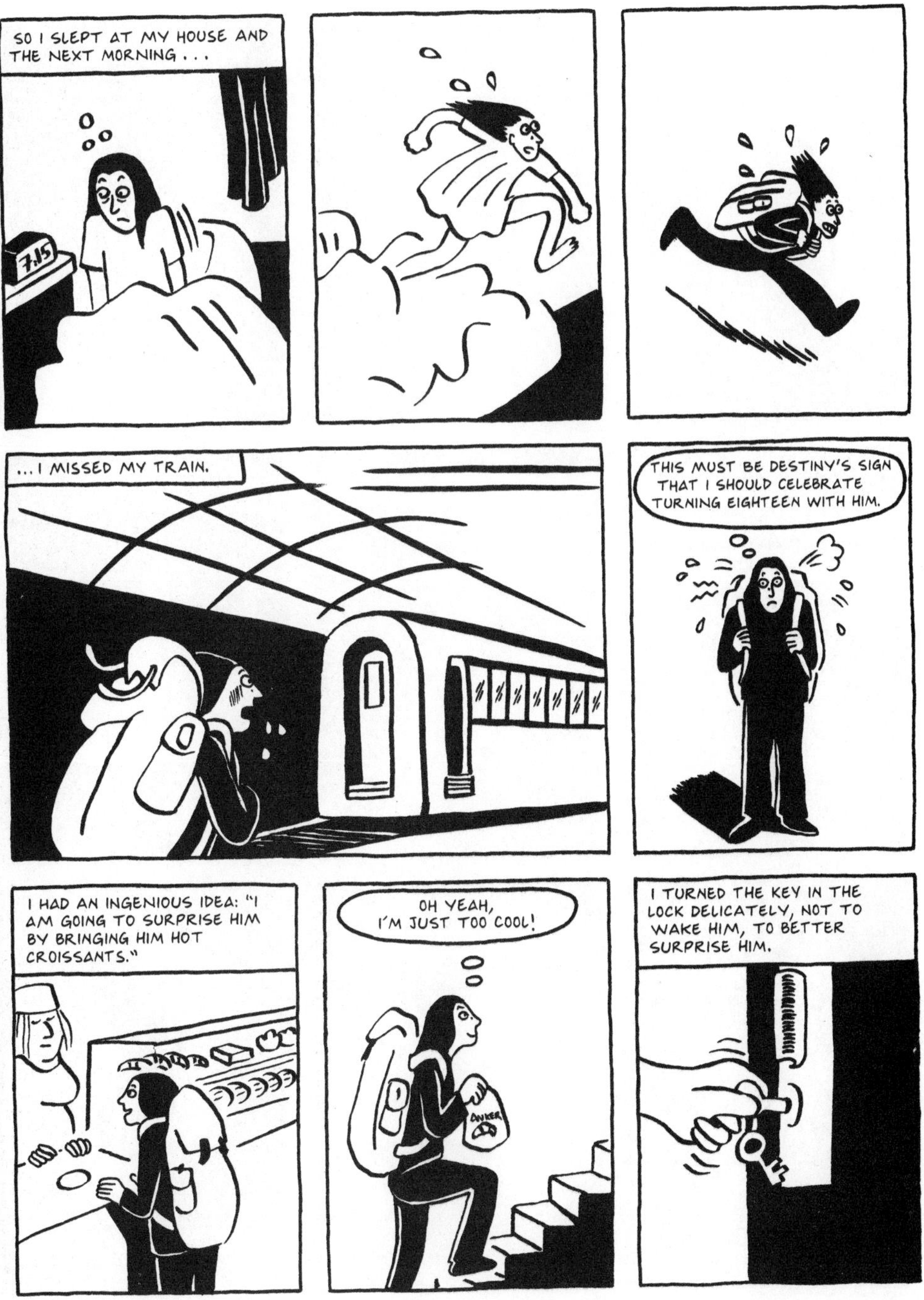
SO I SLEPT AT MY HOUSE AND THE NEXT MORNING . . .
7:15
. . . I MISSED MY TRAIN.
THIS MUST BE DESTINY'S SIGN THAT I SHOULD CELEBRATE TURNING EIGHTEEN WITH HIM.
I HAD AN INGENIOUS IDEA: "I AM GOING TO SURPRISE HIM BY BRINGING HIM HOT CROISSANTS."
OH YEAH, I'M JUST TOO COOL!
I TURNED THE KEY IN THE LOCK DELICATELY, NOT TO WAKE HIM, TO BETTER SURPRISE HIM.

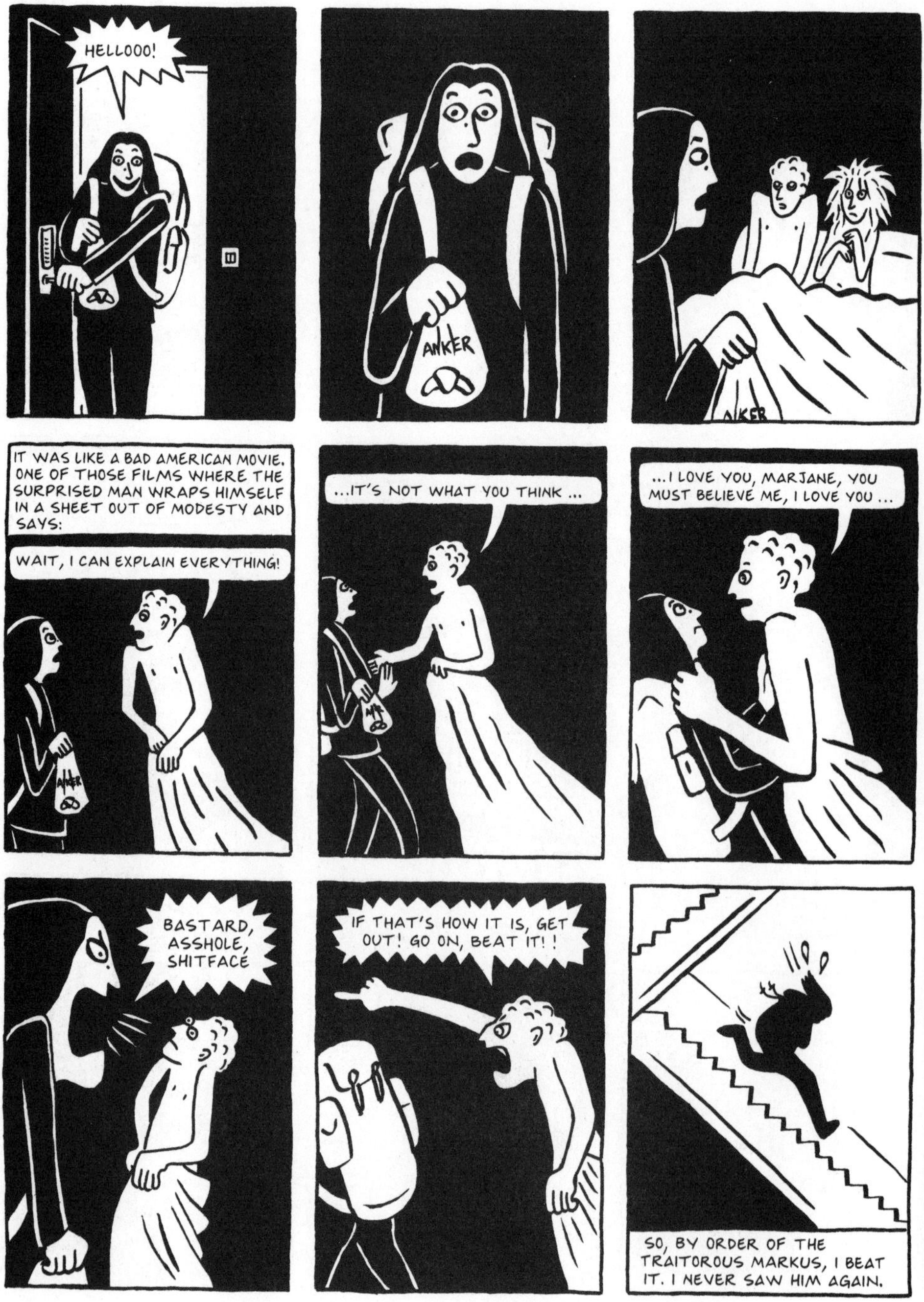
HELLOOO!
ANKER
IT WAS LIKE A BAD AMERICAN MOVIE. ONE OF THOSE FILMS WHERE THE SURPRISED MAN WRAPS HIMSELF IN A SHEET OUT OF MODESTY AND SAYS:
WAIT, I CAN EXPLAIN EVERYTHING!
...IT'S NOT WHAT YOU THINK ...
...I LOVE YOU, MARJANE, YOU MUST BELIEVE ME, I LOVE YOU ...
BASTARD, ASSHOLE, SHITFACE
IF THAT'S HOW IT IS, GET OUT! GO ON, BEAT IT!!
SO, BY ORDER OF THE TRAITOROUS MARKUS, I BEAT IT. I NEVER SAW HIM AGAIN.

THE VEIL

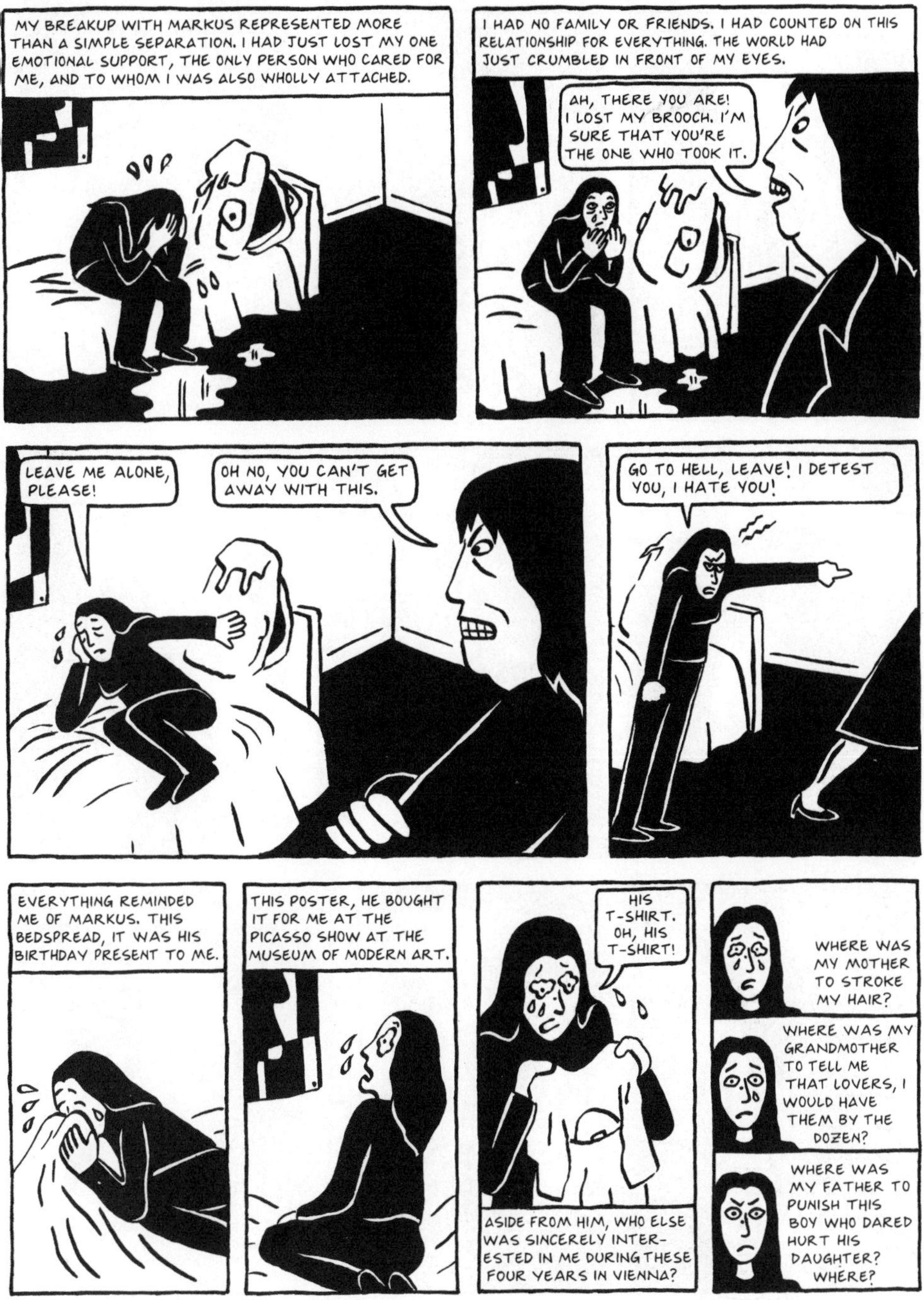

MY BREAKUP WITH MARKUS REPRESENTED MORE THAN A SIMPLE SEPARATION. I HAD JUST LOST MY ONE EMOTIONAL SUPPORT, THE ONLY PERSON WHO CARED FOR ME, AND TO WHOM I WAS ALSO WHOLLY ATTACHED.
I HAD NO FAMILY OR FRIENDS. I HAD COUNTED ON THIS RELATIONSHIP FOR EVERYTHING. THE WORLD HAD JUST CRUMBLED IN FRONT OF MY EYES.
AH, THERE YOU ARE! I LOST MY BROOCH. I'M SURE THAT YOU'RE THE ONE WHO TOOK IT.
LEAVE ME ALONE, PLEASE!
OH NO, YOU CAN'T GET AWAY WITH THIS.
GO TO HELL, LEAVE! I DETEST YOU, I HATE YOU!
EVERYTHING REMINDED ME OF MARKUS. THIS BEDSPREAD, IT WAS HIS BIRTHDAY PRESENT TO ME.
THIS POSTER, HE BOUGHT IT FOR ME AT THE PICASSO SHOW AT THE MUSEUM OF MODERN ART.
HIS T-SHIRT. OH, HIS T-SHIRT!
ASIDE FROM HIM, WHO ELSE WAS SINCERELY INTERESTED IN ME DURING THESE FOUR YEARS IN VIENNA?
WHERE WAS MY MOTHER TO STROKE MY HAIR?
WHERE WAS MY GRANDMOTHER TO TELL ME THAT LOVERS, I WOULD HAVE THEM BY THE DOZEN?
WHERE WAS MY FATHER TO PUNISH THIS BOY WHO DARED HURT HIS DAUGHTER? WHERE?

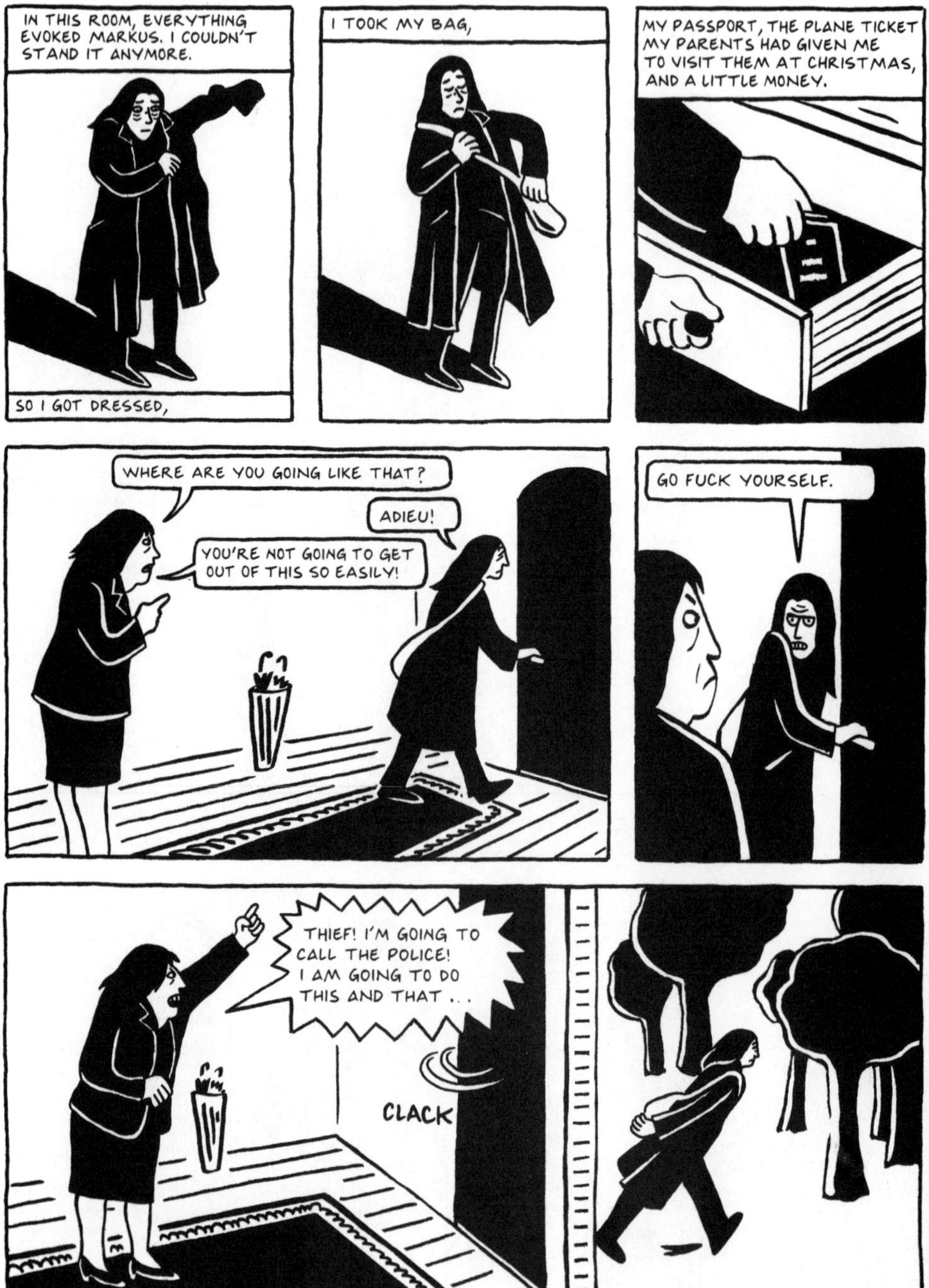
IN THIS ROOM, EVERYTHING EVOKED MARKUS. I COULDN'T STAND IT ANYMORE.
SO I GOT DRESSED,
I TOOK MY BAG,
MY PASSPORT, THE PLANE TICKET MY PARENTS HAD GIVEN ME TO VISIT THEM AT CHRISTMAS, AND A LITTLE MONEY.
WHERE ARE YOU GOING LIKE THAT?
ADIEU!
YOU'RE NOT GOING TO GET OUT OF THIS SO EASILY!
GO FUCK YOURSELF.
THIEF! I'M GOING TO CALL THE POLICE! I AM GOING TO DO THIS AND THAT . . .
CLACK

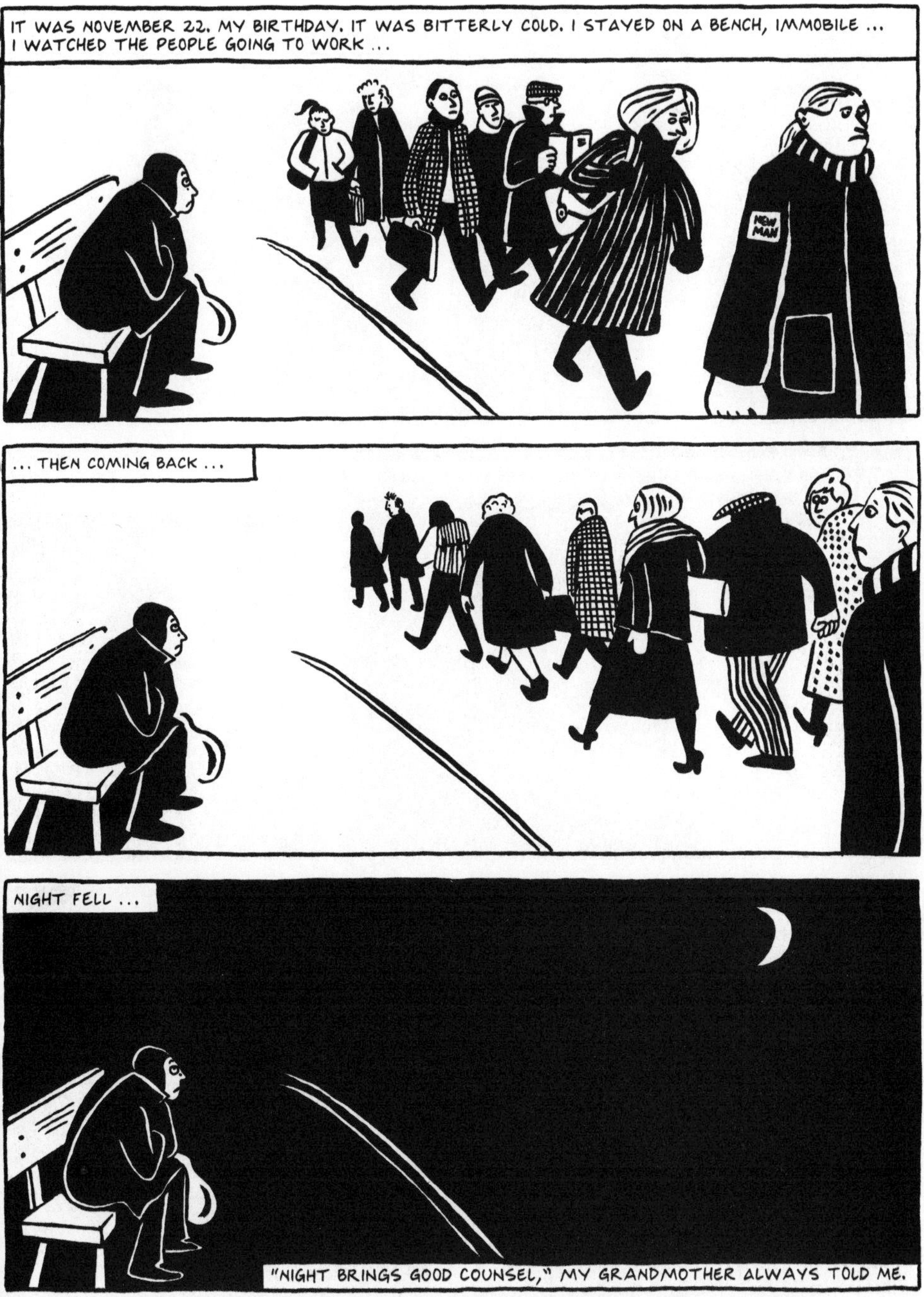
IT WAS NOVEMBER 22. MY BIRTHDAY. IT WAS BITTERLY COLD. I STAYED ON A BENCH, IMMOBILE ... I WATCHED THE PEOPLE GOING TO WORK ...
NEW MAN
... THEN COMING BACK ...
NIGHT FELL ...
"NIGHT BRINGS GOOD COUNSEL," MY GRANDMOTHER ALWAYS TOLD ME.

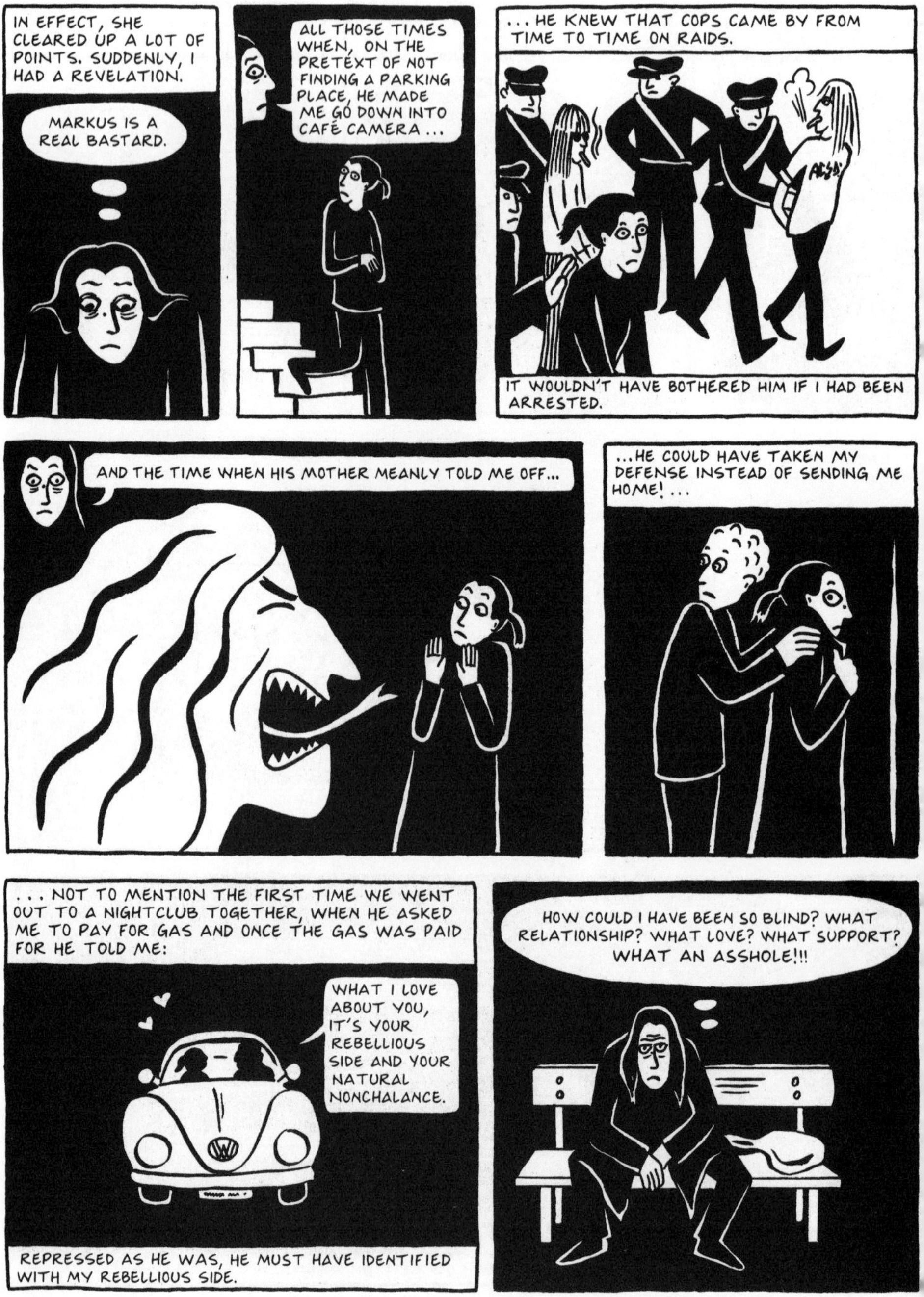
IN EFFECT, SHE CLEARED UP A LOT OF POINTS. SUDDENLY, I HAD A REVELATION.
MARKUS IS A REAL BASTARD.
ALL THOSE TIMES WHEN, ON THE PRETEXT OF NOT FINDING A PARKING PLACE, HE MADE ME GO DOWN INTO CAFÉ CAMERA . . .
. . . HE KNEW THAT COPS CAME BY FROM TIME TO TIME ON RAIDS.
IT WOULDN'T HAVE BOTHERED HIM IF I HAD BEEN ARRESTED.
AND THE TIME WHEN HIS MOTHER MEANLY TOLD ME OFF...
...HE COULD HAVE TAKEN MY DEFENSE INSTEAD OF SENDING ME HOME! . . .
. . . NOT TO MENTION THE FIRST TIME WE WENT OUT TO A NIGHTCLUB TOGETHER, WHEN HE ASKED ME TO PAY FOR GAS AND ONCE THE GAS WAS PAID FOR HE TOLD ME:
WHAT I LOVE ABOUT YOU, IT'S YOUR REBELLIOUS SIDE AND YOUR NATURAL NONCHALANCE.
REPRESSED AS HE WAS, HE MUST HAVE IDENTIFIED WITH MY REBELLIOUS SIDE.
HOW COULD I HAVE BEEN SO BLIND? WHAT RELATIONSHIP? WHAT LOVE? WHAT SUPPORT? WHAT AN ASSHOLE!!!

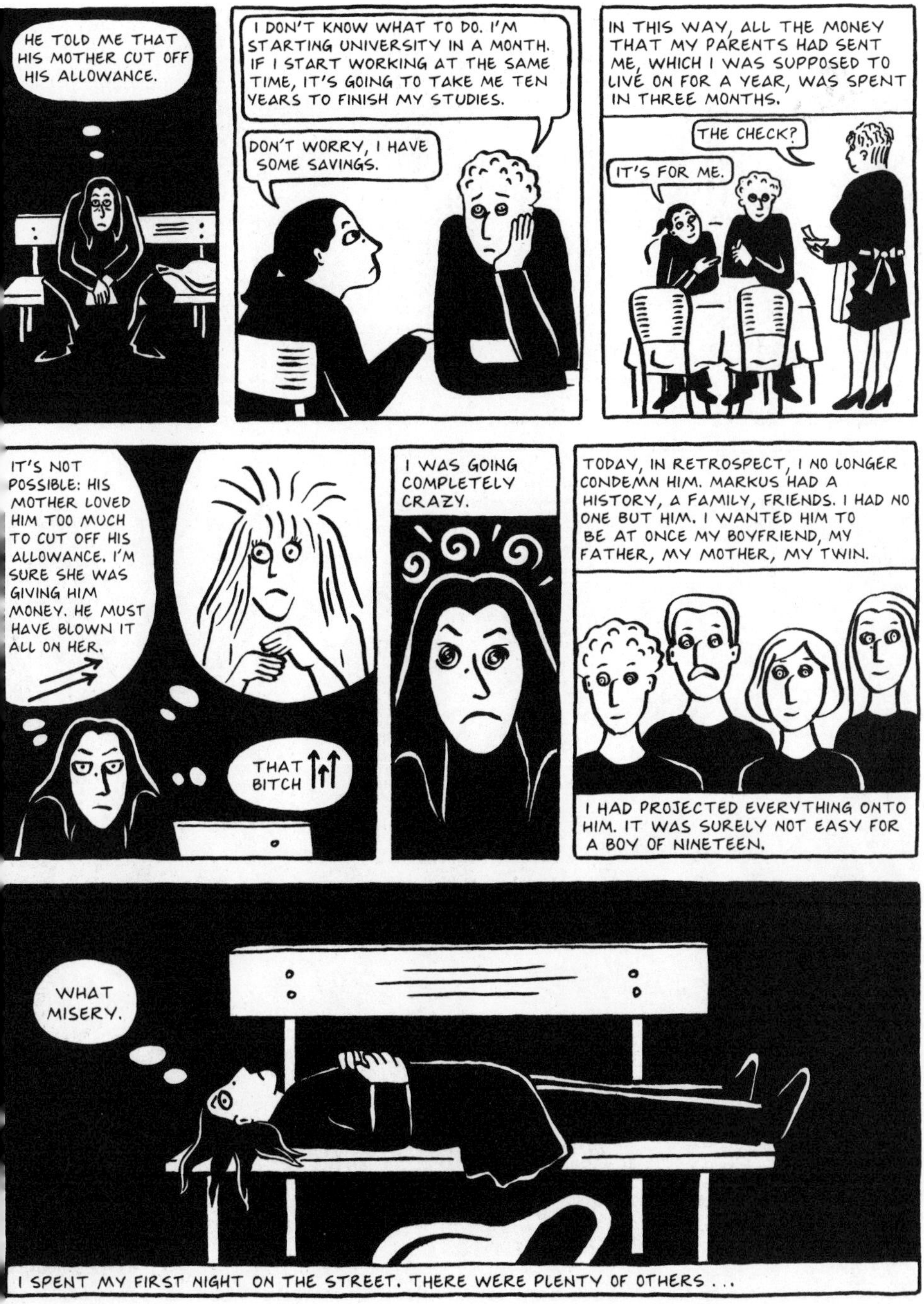
HE TOLD ME THAT HIS MOTHER CUT OFF HIS ALLOWANCE.
I DON'T KNOW WHAT TO DO. I'M STARTING UNIVERSITY IN A MONTH. IF I START WORKING AT THE SAME TIME, IT'S GOING TO TAKE ME TEN YEARS TO FINISH MY STUDIES.
DON'T WORRY, I HAVE SOME SAVINGS.
IN THIS WAY, ALL THE MONEY THAT MY PARENTS HAD SENT ME, WHICH I WAS SUPPOSED TO LIVE ON FOR A YEAR, WAS SPENT IN THREE MONTHS.
THE CHECK?
IT'S FOR ME.
IT'S NOT POSSIBLE: HIS MOTHER LOVED HIM TOO MUCH TO CUT OFF HIS ALLOWANCE. I'M SURE SHE WAS GIVING HIM MONEY. HE MUST HAVE BLOWN IT ALL ON HER.
THAT BITCH
I WAS GOING COMPLETELY CRAZY.
TODAY, IN RETROSPECT, I NO LONGER CONDEMN HIM. MARKUS HAD A HISTORY, A FAMILY, FRIENDS. I HAD NO ONE BUT HIM. I WANTED HIM TO BE AT ONCE MY BOYFRIEND, MY FATHER, MY MOTHER, MY TWIN.
I HAD PROJECTED EVERYTHING ONTO HIM. IT WAS SURELY NOT EASY FOR A BOY OF NINETEEN.
WHAT MISERY.
I SPENT MY FIRST NIGHT ON THE STREET. THERE WERE PLENTY OF OTHERS . . .

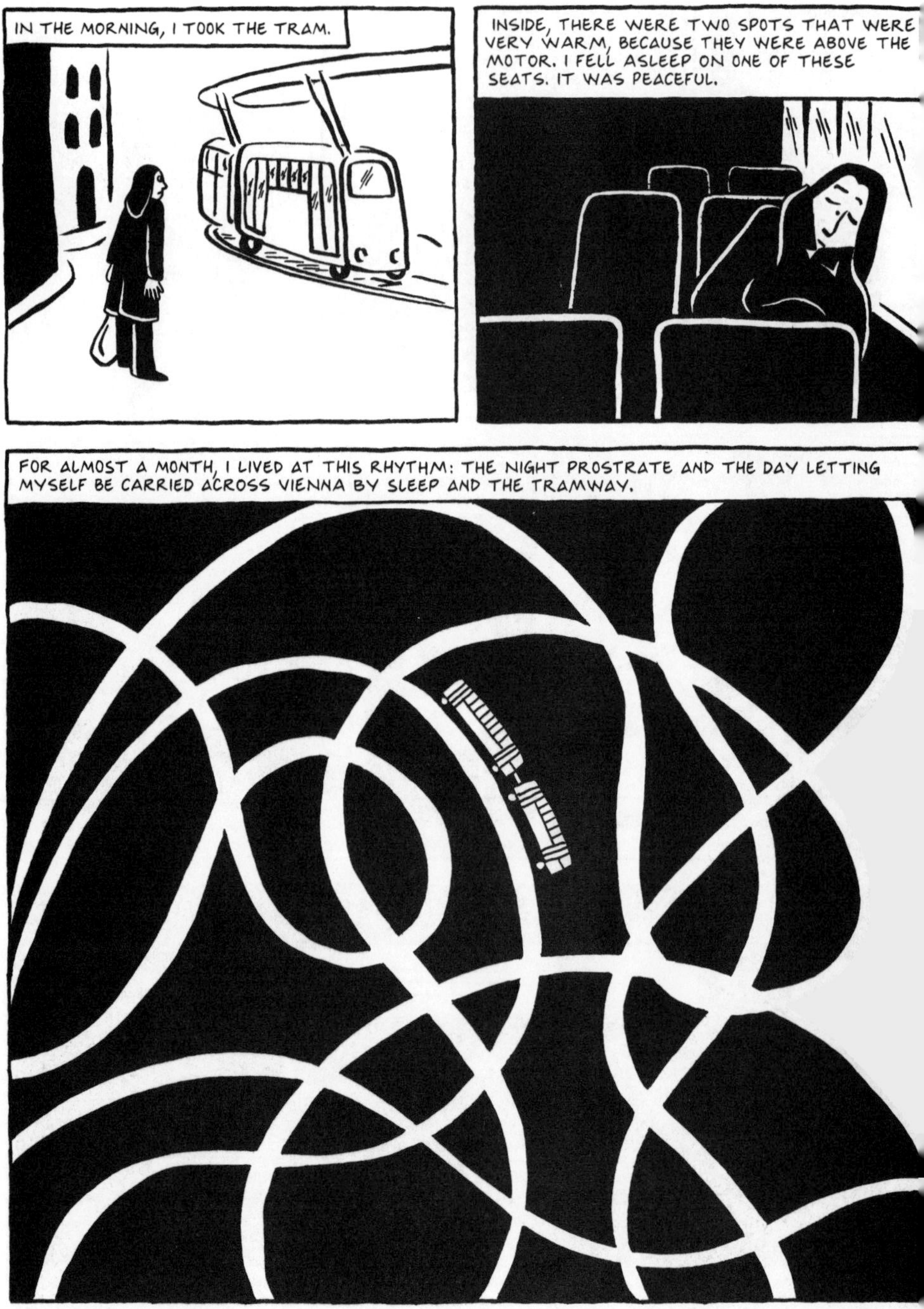
IN THE MORNING, I TOOK THE TRAM.
INSIDE, THERE WERE TWO SPOTS THAT WERE VERY WARM, BECAUSE THEY WERE ABOVE THE MOTOR. I FELL ASLEEP ON ONE OF THESE SEATS. IT WAS PEACEFUL.
FOR ALMOST A MONTH, I LIVED AT THIS RHYTHM: THE NIGHT PROSTRATE AND THE DAY LETTING MYSELF BE CARRIED ACROSS VIENNA BY SLEEP AND THE TRAMWAY.

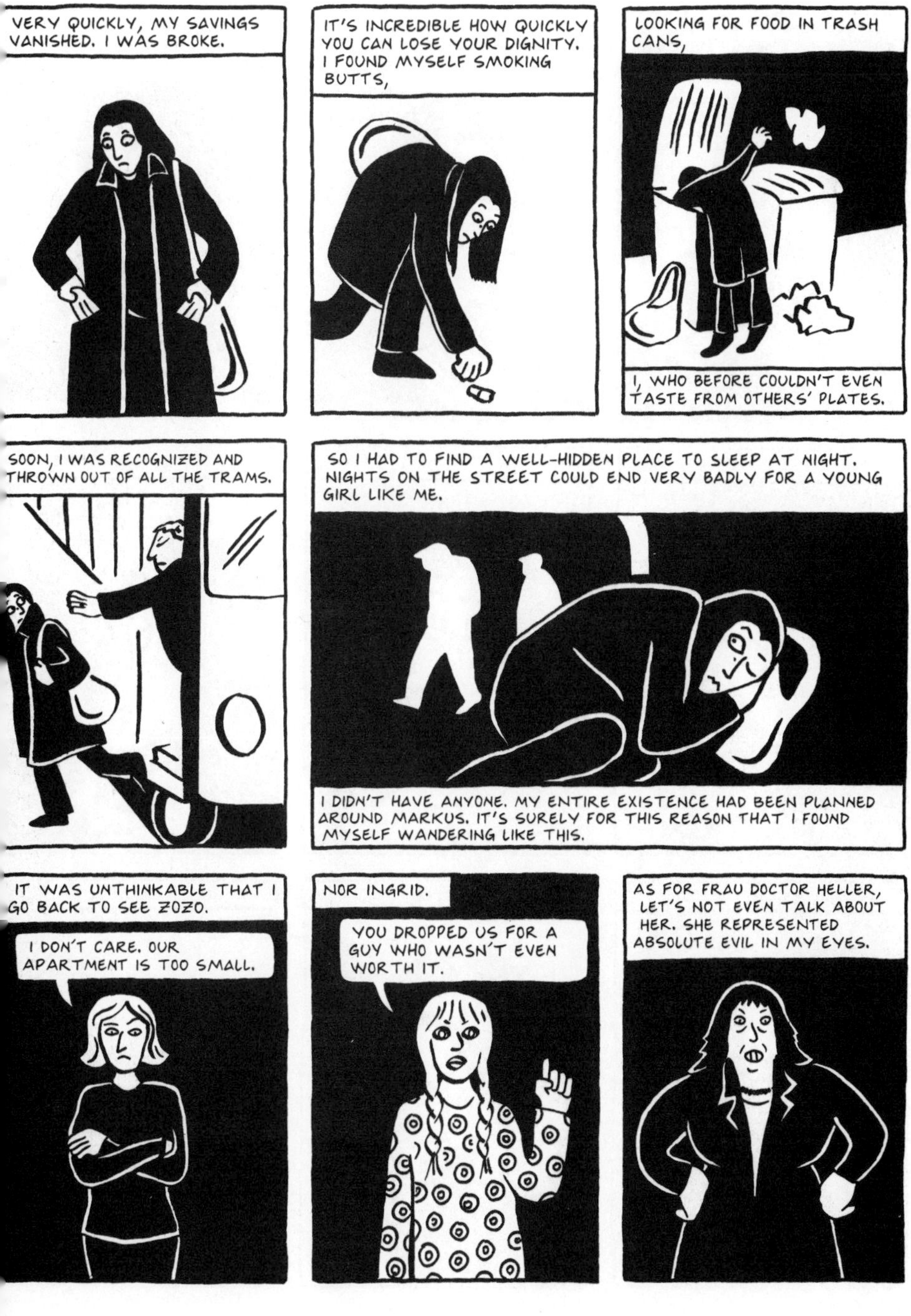
VERY QUICKLY, MY SAVINGS VANISHED. I WAS BROKE.
IT'S INCREDIBLE HOW QUICKLY YOU CAN LOSE YOUR DIGNITY. I FOUND MYSELF SMOKING BUTTS,
LOOKING FOR FOOD IN TRASH CANS,
I, WHO BEFORE COULDN'T EVEN TASTE FROM OTHERS' PLATES.
SOON, I WAS RECOGNIZED AND THROWN OUT OF ALL THE TRAMS.
SO I HAD TO FIND A WELL-HIDDEN PLACE TO SLEEP AT NIGHT. NIGHTS ON THE STREET COULD END VERY BADLY FOR A YOUNG GIRL LIKE ME.
I DIDN'T HAVE ANYONE. MY ENTIRE EXISTENCE HAD BEEN PLANNED AROUND MARKUS. IT'S SURELY FOR THIS REASON THAT I FOUND MYSELF WANDERING LIKE THIS.
IT WAS UNTHINKABLE THAT I GO BACK TO SEE ZOZO.
I DON'T CARE. OUR APARTMENT IS TOO SMALL.
NOR INGRID.
YOU DROPPED US FOR A GUY WHO WASN'T EVEN WORTH IT.
AS FOR FRAU DOCTOR HELLER, LET'S NOT EVEN TALK ABOUT HER. SHE REPRESENTED ABSOLUTE EVIL IN MY EYES.

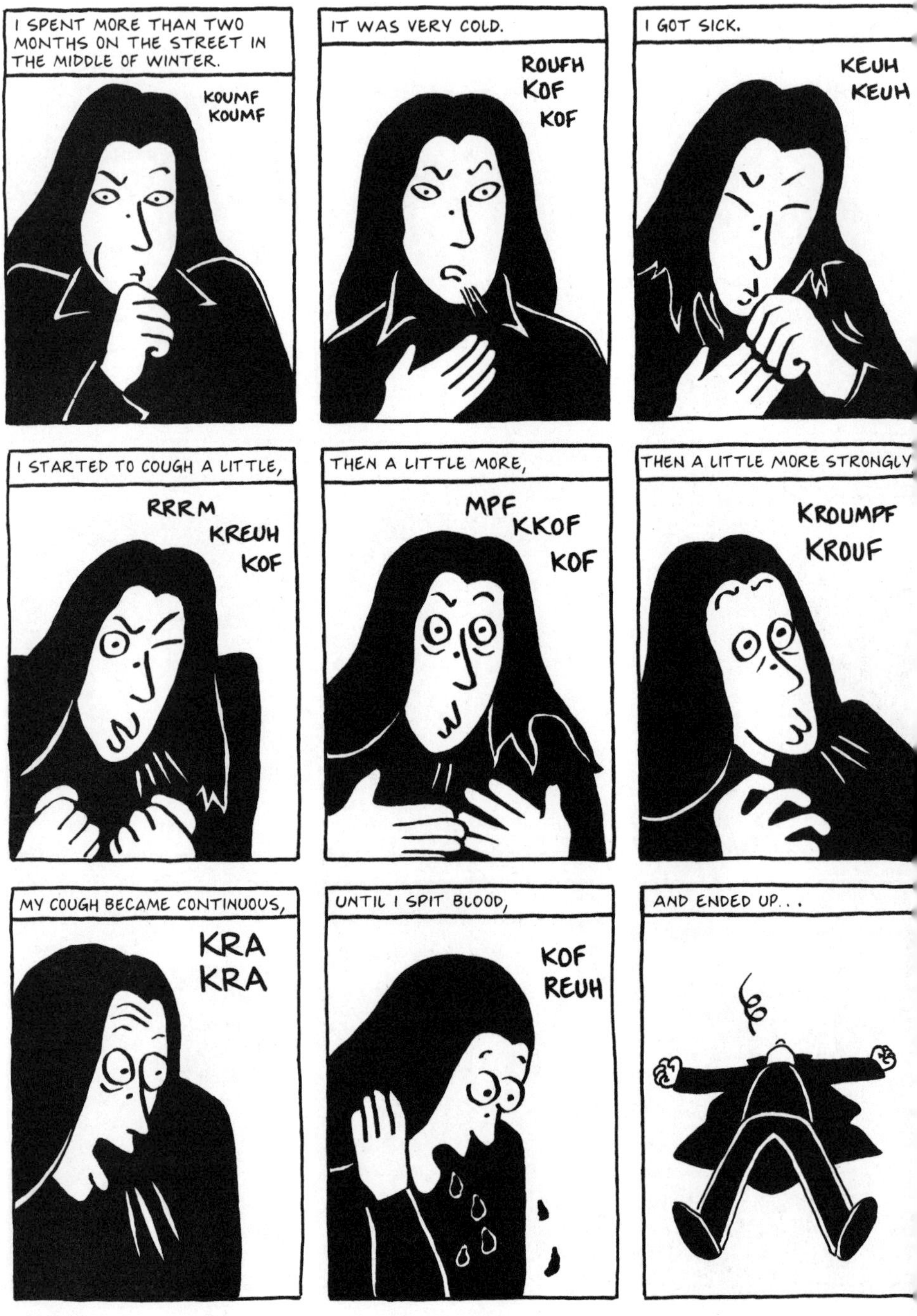
I SPENT MORE THAN TWO MONTHS ON THE STREET IN THE MIDDLE OF WINTER.
KOUMF KOUMF
IT WAS VERY COLD.
ROUFH KOF KOF
I GOT SICK.
KEUH KEUH
I STARTED TO COUGH A LITTLE,
RRRM KREUH KOF
THEN A LITTLE MORE,
MPF KKOF KOF
THEN A LITTLE MORE STRONGLY
KROUMPF KROUF
MY COUGH BECAME CONTINUOUS,
KRA KRA
UNTIL I SPIT BLOOD,
KOF REUH
AND ENDED UP. . .

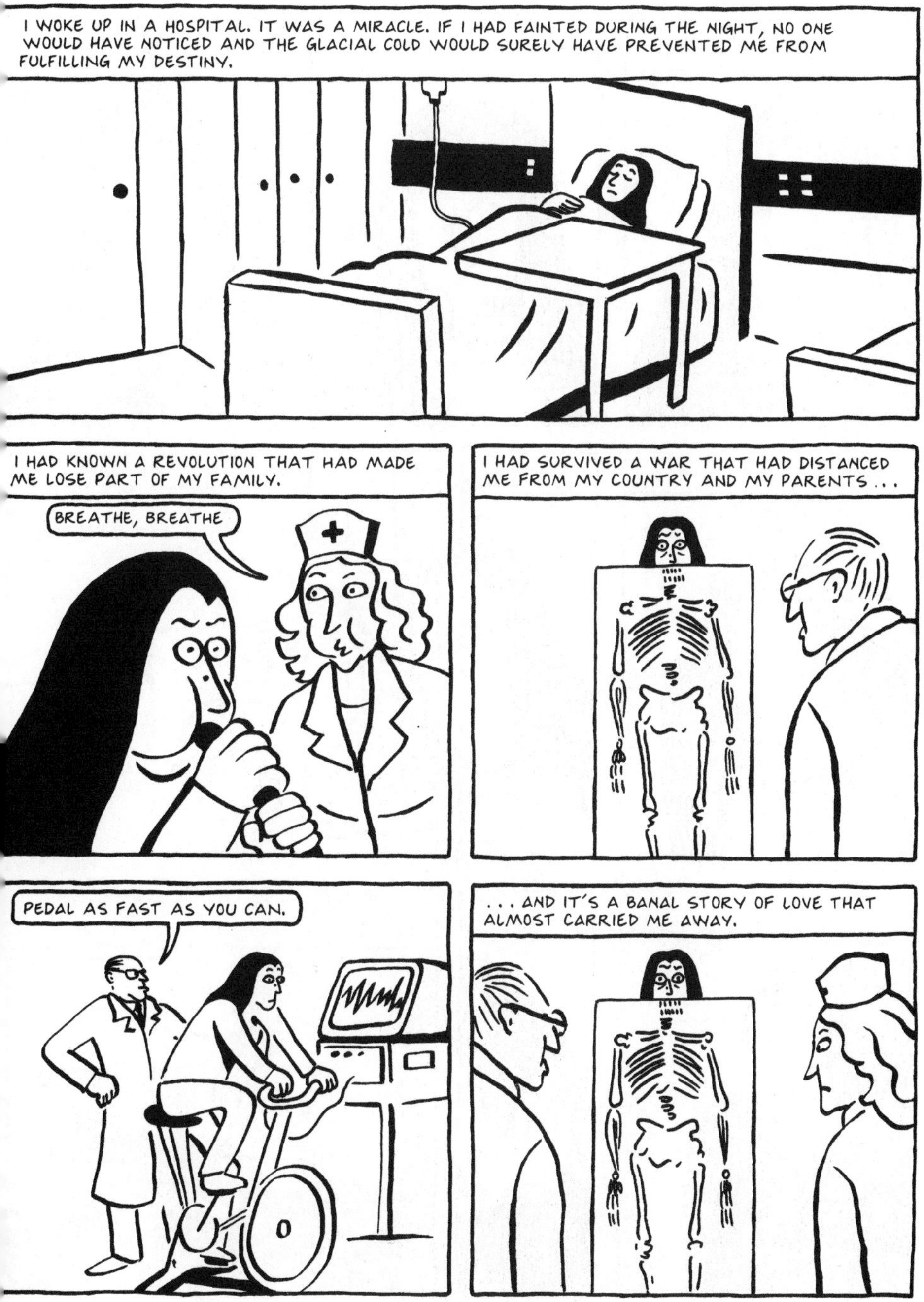
I WOKE UP IN A HOSPITAL. IT WAS A MIRACLE. IF I HAD FAINTED DURING THE NIGHT, NO ONE WOULD HAVE NOTICED AND THE GLACIAL COLD WOULD SURELY HAVE PREVENTED ME FROM FULFILLING MY DESTINY.
I HAD KNOWN A REVOLUTION THAT HAD MADE ME LOSE PART OF MY FAMILY.
BREATHE, BREATHE
I HAD SURVIVED A WAR THAT HAD DISTANCED ME FROM MY COUNTRY AND MY PARENTS . . .
PEDAL AS FAST AS YOU CAN.
. . . AND IT'S A BANAL STORY OF LOVE THAT ALMOST CARRIED ME AWAY.

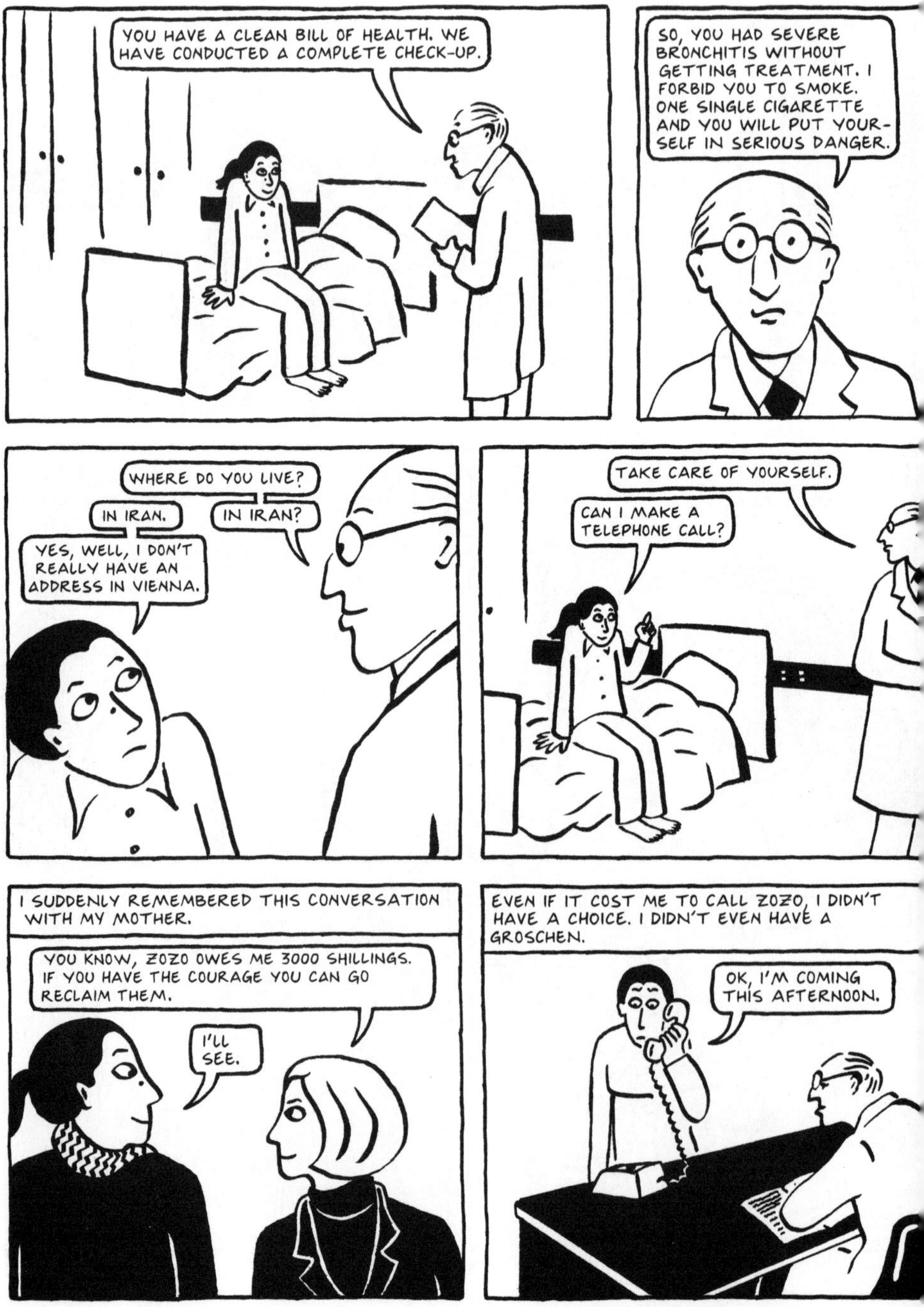
YOU HAVE A CLEAN BILL OF HEALTH. WE HAVE CONDUCTED A COMPLETE CHECK-UP.
SO, YOU HAD SEVERE BRONCHITIS WITHOUT GETTING TREATMENT. I FORBID YOU TO SMOKE. ONE SINGLE CIGARETTE AND YOU WILL PUT YOURSELF IN SERIOUS DANGER.
WHERE DO YOU LIVE?
IN IRAN.
IN IRAN?
YES, WELL, I DON'T REALLY HAVE AN ADDRESS IN VIENNA.
TAKE CARE OF YOURSELF.
CAN I MAKE A TELEPHONE CALL?
I SUDDENLY REMEMBERED THIS CONVERSATION WITH MY MOTHER.
YOU KNOW, ZOZO OWES ME 3000 SHILLINGS. IF YOU HAVE THE COURAGE YOU CAN GO RECLAIM THEM.
I'LL SEE.
EVEN IF IT COST ME TO CALL ZOZO, I DIDN'T HAVE A CHOICE. I DIDN'T EVEN HAVE A GROSCHEN.
OK, I'M COMING THIS AFTERNOON.

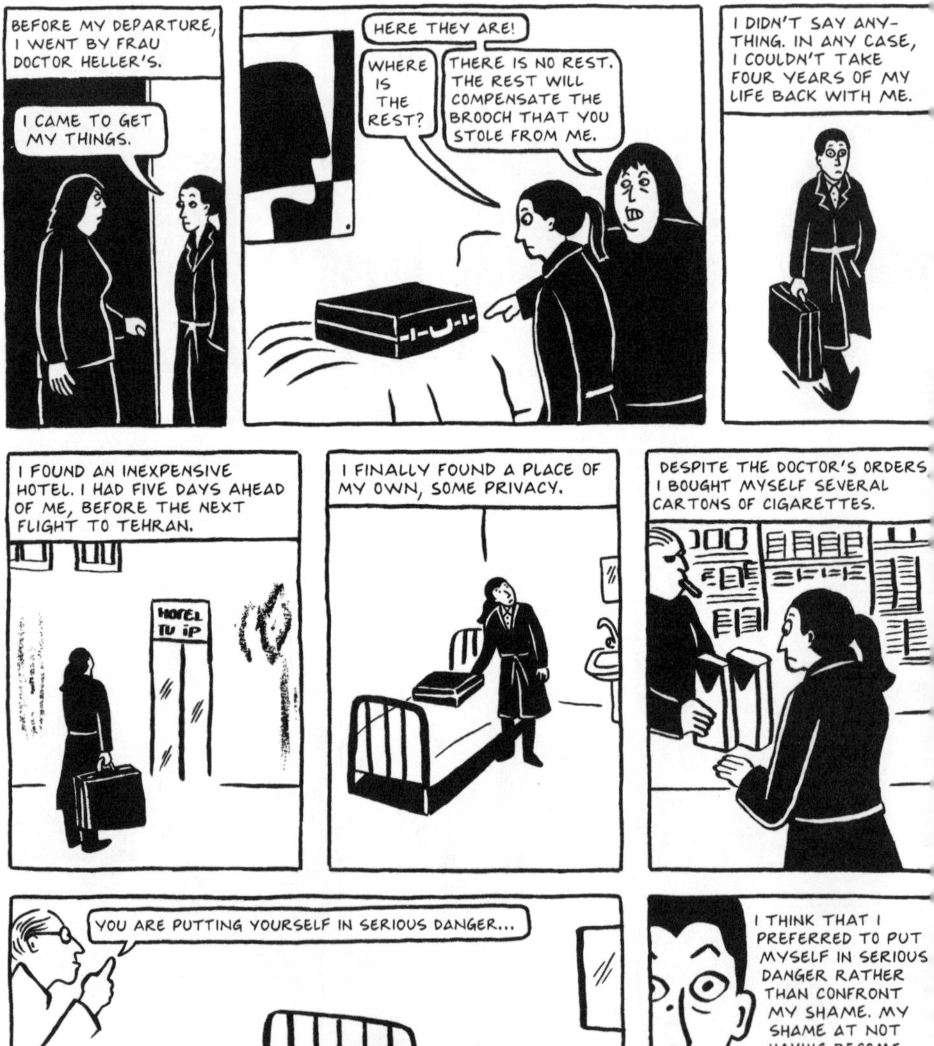
BEFORE MY DEPARTURE, I WENT BY FRAU DOCTOR HELLER'S.
I CAME TO GET MY THINGS.
HERE THEY ARE!
WHERE IS THE REST?
THERE IS NO REST. THE REST WILL COMPENSATE THE BROOCH THAT YOU STOLE FROM ME.
I DIDN'T SAY ANYTHING. IN ANY CASE, I COULDN'T TAKE FOUR YEARS OF MY LIFE BACK WITH ME.
I FOUND AN INEXPENSIVE HOTEL. I HAD FIVE DAYS AHEAD OF ME, BEFORE THE NEXT FLIGHT TO TEHRAN.
I FINALLY FOUND A PLACE OF MY OWN, SOME PRIVACY.
DESPITE THE DOCTOR'S ORDERS, I BOUGHT MYSELF SEVERAL CARTONS OF CIGARETTES.
YOU ARE PUTTING YOURSELF IN SERIOUS DANGER...
I THINK THAT I PREFERRED TO PUT MYSELF IN SERIOUS DANGER RATHER THAN CONFRONT MY SHAME. MY SHAME AT NOT HAVING BECOME SOMEONE, THE SHAME OF NOT HAVING MADE MY PARENTS PROUD AFTER ALL THE SACRIFICES THEY HAD MADE FOR ME. THE SHAME OF HAVING BECOME A MEDIOCRE NIHILIST.

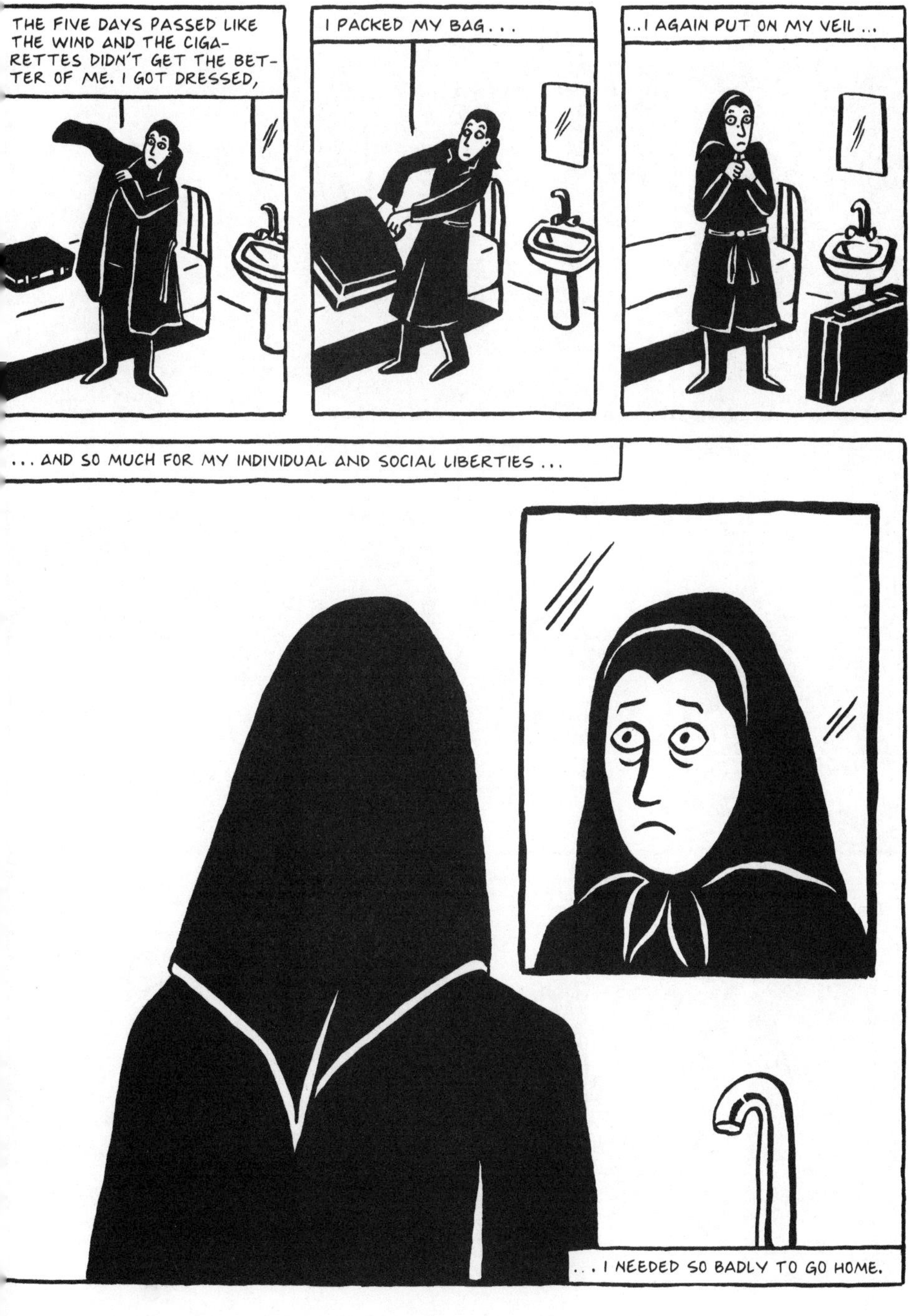
THE FIVE DAYS PASSED LIKE THE WIND AND THE CIGARETTES DIDN'T GET THE BETTER OF ME. I GOT DRESSED,
I PACKED MY BAG . . .
...I AGAIN PUT ON MY VEIL ...
. . . AND SO MUCH FOR MY INDIVIDUAL AND SOCIAL LIBERTIES . . .
. . . I NEEDED SO BADLY TO GO HOME.

THE RETURN

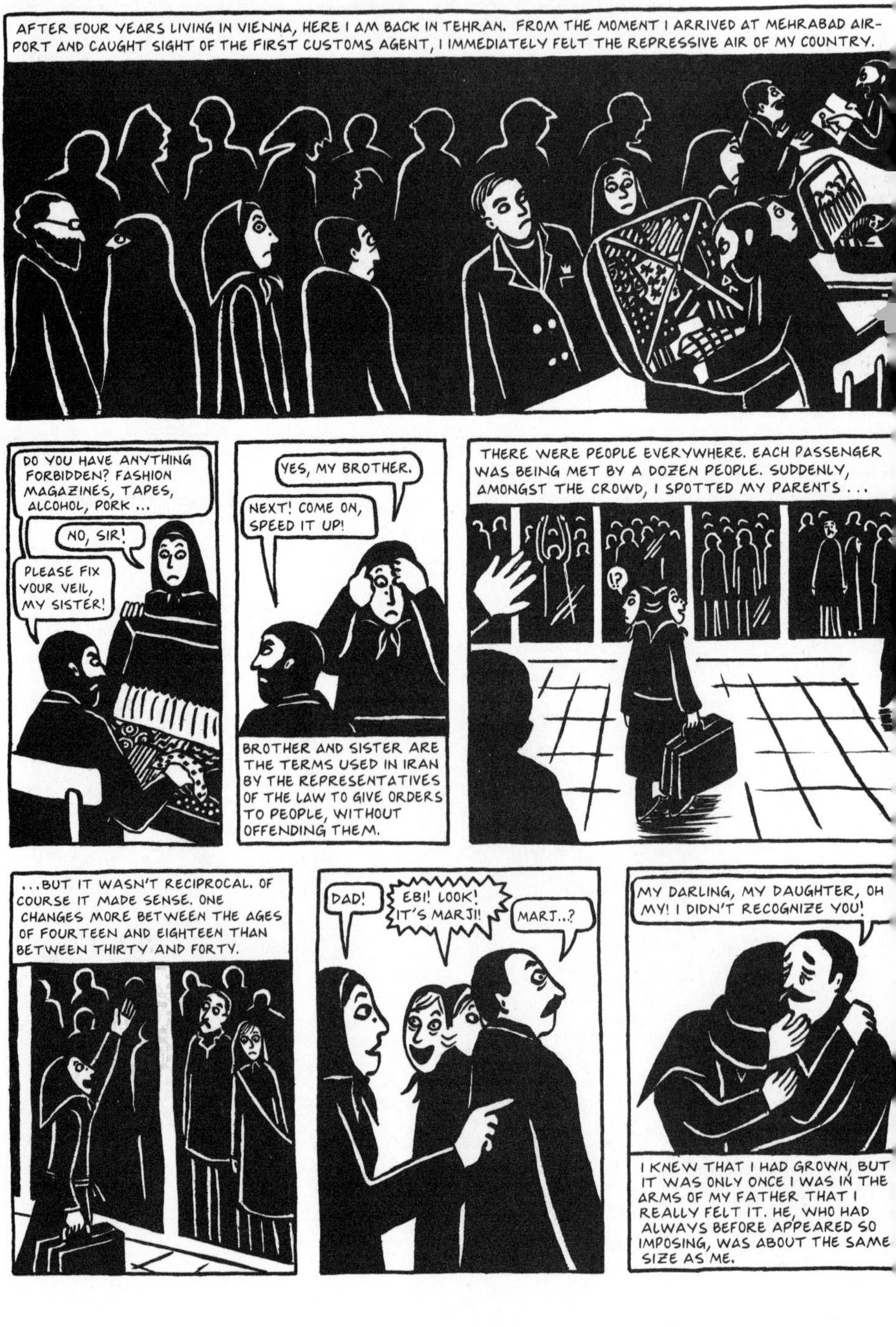

AFTER FOUR YEARS LIVING IN VIENNA, HERE I AM BACK IN TEHRAN. FROM THE MOMENT I ARRIVED AT MEHRABAD AIRPORT AND CAUGHT SIGHT OF THE FIRST CUSTOMS AGENT, I IMMEDIATELY FELT THE REPRESSIVE AIR OF MY COUNTRY.
DO YOU HAVE ANYTHING FORBIDDEN? FASHION MAGAZINES, TAPES, ALCOHOL, PORK ...
NO, SIR!
PLEASE FIX YOUR VEIL, MY SISTER!
YES, MY BROTHER.
NEXT! COME ON, SPEED IT UP!
BROTHER AND SISTER ARE THE TERMS USED IN IRAN BY THE REPRESENTATIVES OF THE LAW TO GIVE ORDERS TO PEOPLE, WITHOUT OFFENDING THEM.
THERE WERE PEOPLE EVERYWHERE. EACH PASSENGER WAS BEING MET BY A DOZEN PEOPLE. SUDDENLY, AMONGST THE CROWD, I SPOTTED MY PARENTS ...
!?
...BUT IT WASN'T RECIPROCAL. OF COURSE IT MADE SENSE. ONE CHANGES MORE BETWEEN THE AGES OF FOURTEEN AND EIGHTEEN THAN BETWEEN THIRTY AND FORTY.
DAD!
EBI! LOOK! IT'S MARJI!
MARJ...?
MY DARLING, MY DAUGHTER, OH MY! I DIDN'T RECOGNIZE YOU!
I KNEW THAT I HAD GROWN, BUT IT WAS ONLY ONCE I WAS IN THE ARMS OF MY FATHER THAT I REALLY FELT IT. HE, WHO HAD ALWAYS BEFORE APPEARED SO IMPOSING, WAS ABOUT THE SAME SIZE AS ME.

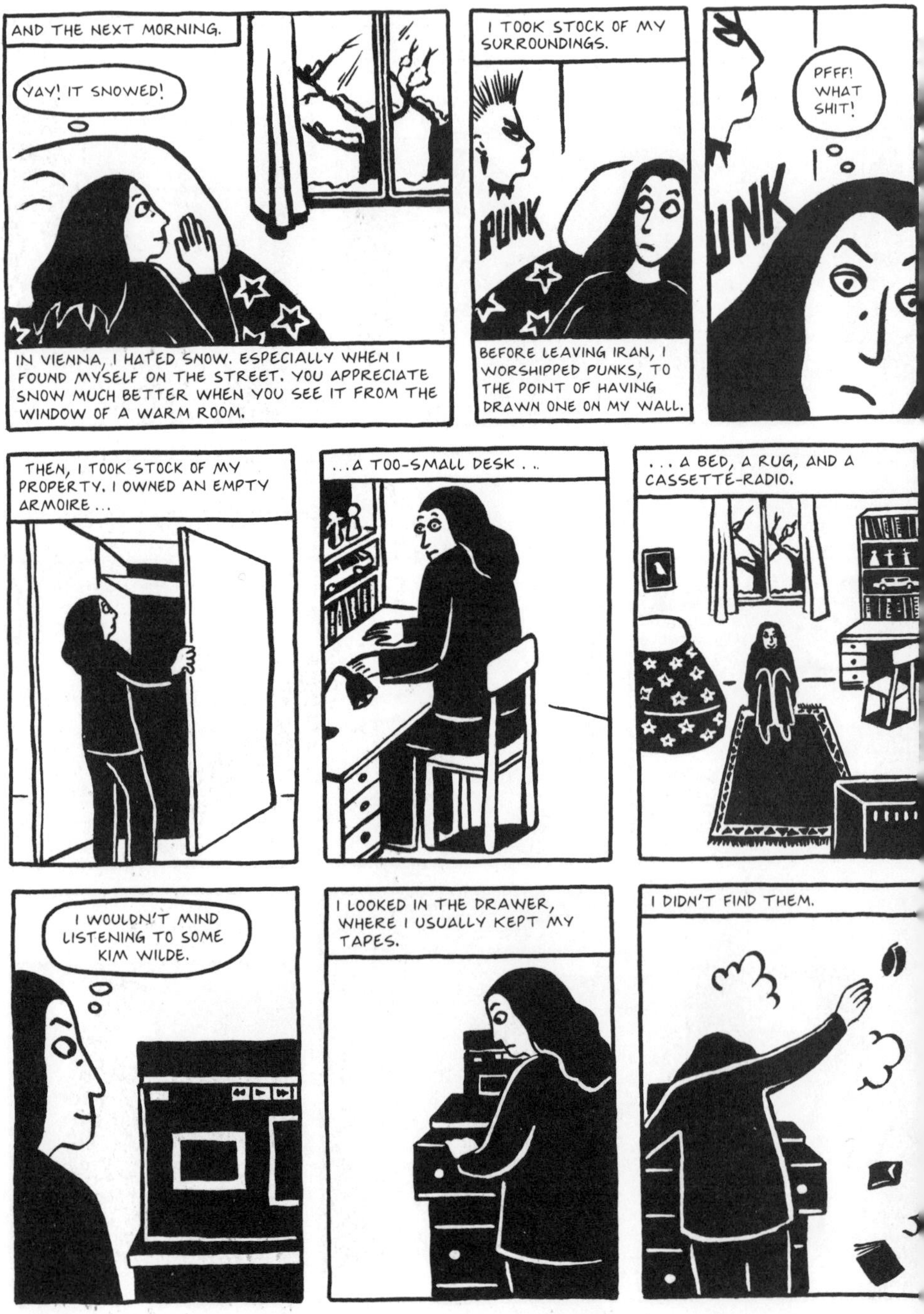
AND THE NEXT MORNING.
YAY! IT SNOWED!
IN VIENNA, I HATED SNOW. ESPECIALLY WHEN I FOUND MYSELF ON THE STREET. YOU APPRECIATE SNOW MUCH BETTER WHEN YOU SEE IT FROM THE WINDOW OF A WARM ROOM.
I TOOK STOCK OF MY SURROUNDINGS.
PUNK
BEFORE LEAVING IRAN, I WORSHIPPED PUNKS, TO THE POINT OF HAVING DRAWN ONE ON MY WALL.
UNK
PFFF! WHAT SHIT!
THEN, I TOOK STOCK OF MY PROPERTY. I OWNED AN EMPTY ARMOIRE ...
...A TOO-SMALL DESK . ..
. . . A BED, A RUG, AND A CASSETTE-RADIO.
I WOULDN'T MIND LISTENING TO SOME KIM WILDE.
I LOOKED IN THE DRAWER, WHERE I USUALLY KEPT MY TAPES.
I DIDN'T FIND THEM.

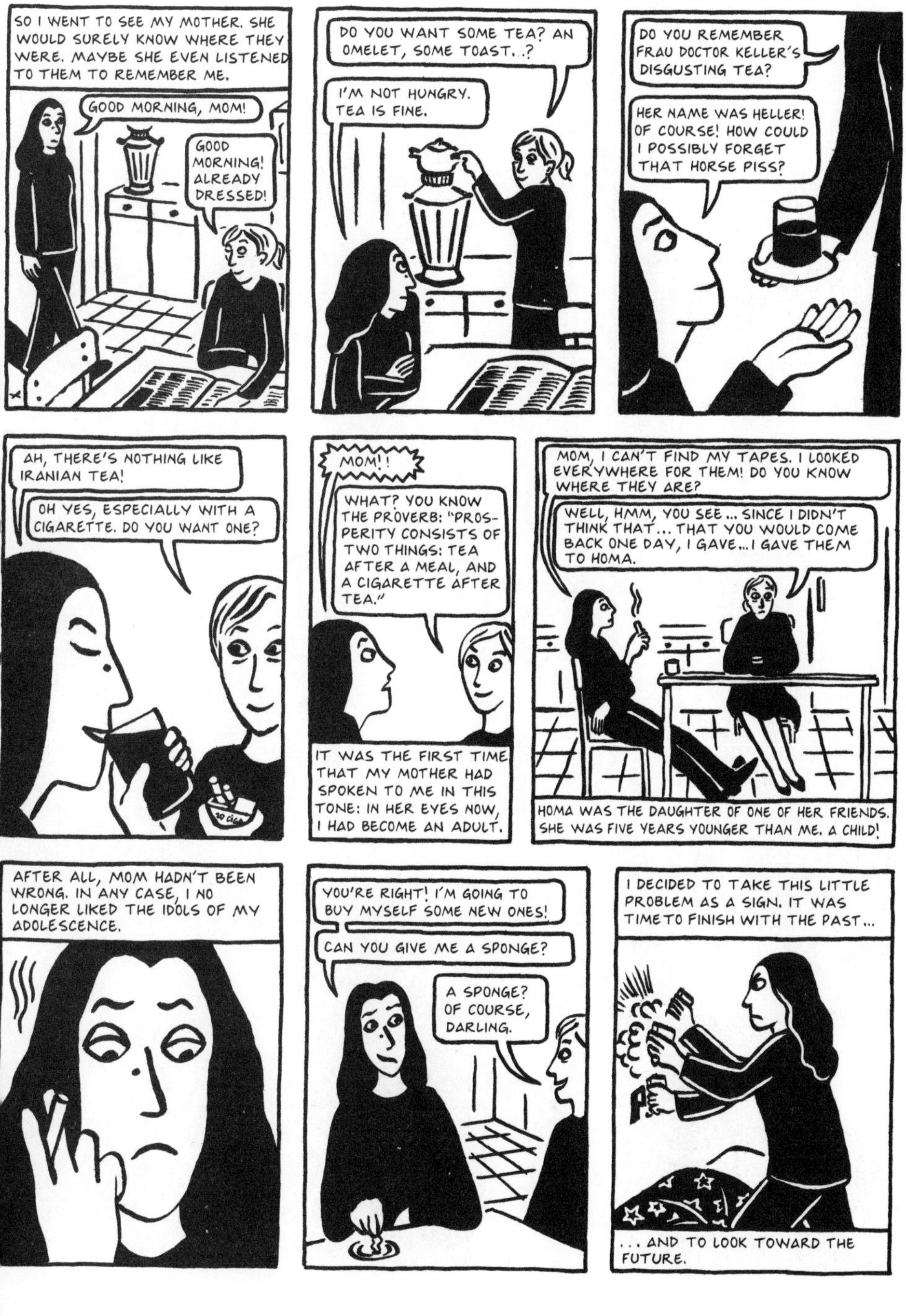
SO I WENT TO SEE MY MOTHER. SHE WOULD SURELY KNOW WHERE THEY WERE. MAYBE SHE EVEN LISTENED TO THEM TO REMEMBER ME.
GOOD MORNING, MOM!
GOOD MORNING! ALREADY DRESSED!
DO YOU WANT SOME TEA? AN OMELET, SOME TOAST...?
I'M NOT HUNGRY. TEA IS FINE.
DO YOU REMEMBER FRAU DOCTOR KELLER'S DISGUSTING TEA?
HER NAME WAS HELLER! OF COURSE! HOW COULD I POSSIBLY FORGET THAT HORSE PISS?
AH, THERE'S NOTHING LIKE IRANIAN TEA!
OH YES, ESPECIALLY WITH A CIGARETTE. DO YOU WANT ONE?
MOM!!
WHAT? YOU KNOW THE PROVERB: "PROSPERITY CONSISTS OF TWO THINGS: TEA AFTER A MEAL, AND A CIGARETTE AFTER TEA."
IT WAS THE FIRST TIME THAT MY MOTHER HAD SPOKEN TO ME IN THIS TONE: IN HER EYES NOW, I HAD BECOME AN ADULT.
MOM, I CAN'T FIND MY TAPES. I LOOKED EVERYWHERE FOR THEM! DO YOU KNOW WHERE THEY ARE?
WELL, HMM, YOU SEE... SINCE I DIDN'T THINK THAT... THAT YOU WOULD COME BACK ONE DAY, I GAVE... I GAVE THEM TO HOMA.
HOMA WAS THE DAUGHTER OF ONE OF HER FRIENDS. SHE WAS FIVE YEARS YOUNGER THAN ME. A CHILD!
AFTER ALL, MOM HADN'T BEEN WRONG. IN ANY CASE, I NO LONGER LIKED THE IDOLS OF MY ADOLESCENCE.
YOU'RE RIGHT! I'M GOING TO BUY MYSELF SOME NEW ONES!
CAN YOU GIVE ME A SPONGE?
A SPONGE? OF COURSE, DARLING.
I DECIDED TO TAKE THIS LITTLE PROBLEM AS A SIGN. IT WAS TIME TO FINISH WITH THE PAST...
... AND TO LOOK TOWARD THE FUTURE.

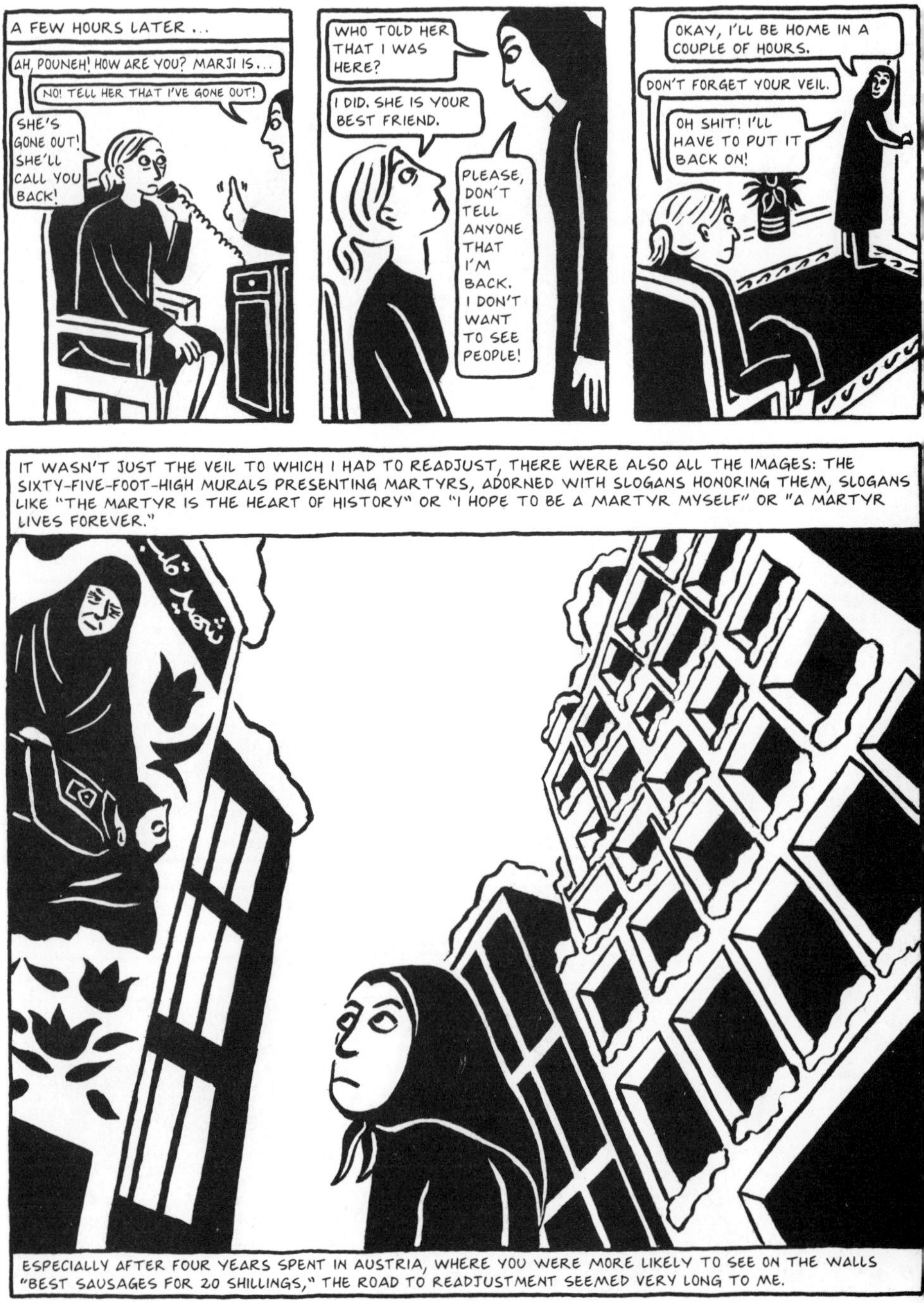
A FEW HOURS LATER...
AH, POUNEH! HOW ARE YOU? MARJI IS...
NO! TELL HER THAT I'VE GONE OUT!
SHE'S GONE OUT! SHE'LL CALL YOU BACK!
WHO TOLD HER THAT I WAS HERE?
I DID. SHE IS YOUR BEST FRIEND.
PLEASE, DON'T TELL ANYONE THAT I'M BACK. I DON'T WANT TO SEE PEOPLE!
OKAY, I'LL BE HOME IN A COUPLE OF HOURS.
DON'T FORGET YOUR VEIL.
OH SHIT! I'LL HAVE TO PUT IT BACK ON!
IT WASN'T JUST THE VEIL TO WHICH I HAD TO READJUST, THERE WERE ALSO ALL THE IMAGES: THE SIXTY-FIVE-FOOT-HIGH MURALS PRESENTING MARTYRS, ADORNED WITH SLOGANS HONORING THEM, SLOGANS LIKE "THE MARTYR IS THE HEART OF HISTORY" OR "I HOPE TO BE A MARTYR MYSELF" OR "A MARTYR LIVES FOREVER."
ESPECIALLY AFTER FOUR YEARS SPENT IN AUSTRIA, WHERE YOU WERE MORE LIKELY TO SEE ON THE WALLS "BEST SAUSAGES FOR 20 SHILLINGS," THE ROAD TO READJUSTMENT SEEMED VERY LONG TO ME.

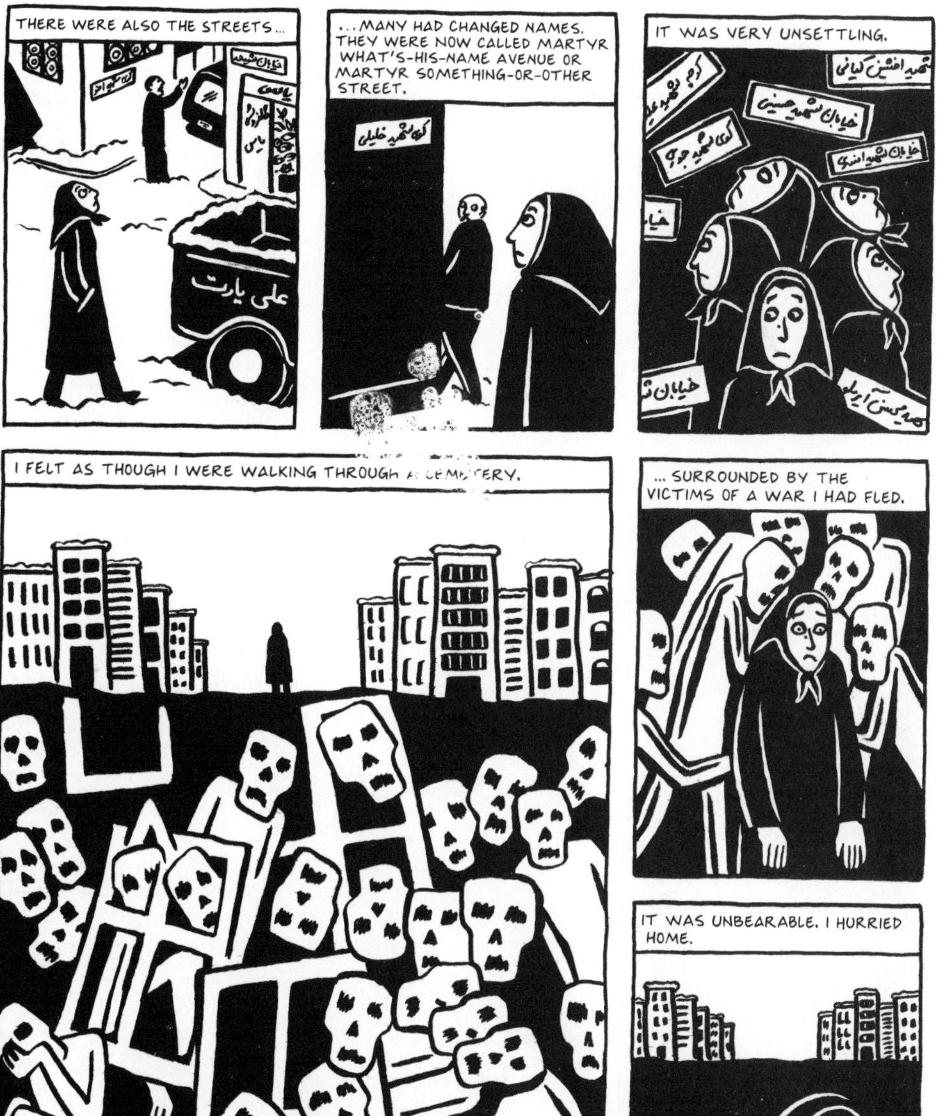
THERE WERE ALSO THE STREETS...
علی یارت
...MANY HAD CHANGED NAMES. THEY WERE NOW CALLED MARTYR WHAT'S-HIS-NAME AVENUE OR MARTYR SOMETHING-OR-OTHER STREET.
IT WAS VERY UNSETTLING.
I FELT AS THOUGH I WERE WALKING THROUGH A CEMETERY.
... SURROUNDED BY THE VICTIMS OF A WAR I HAD FLED.
IT WAS UNBEARABLE. I HURRIED HOME.

98

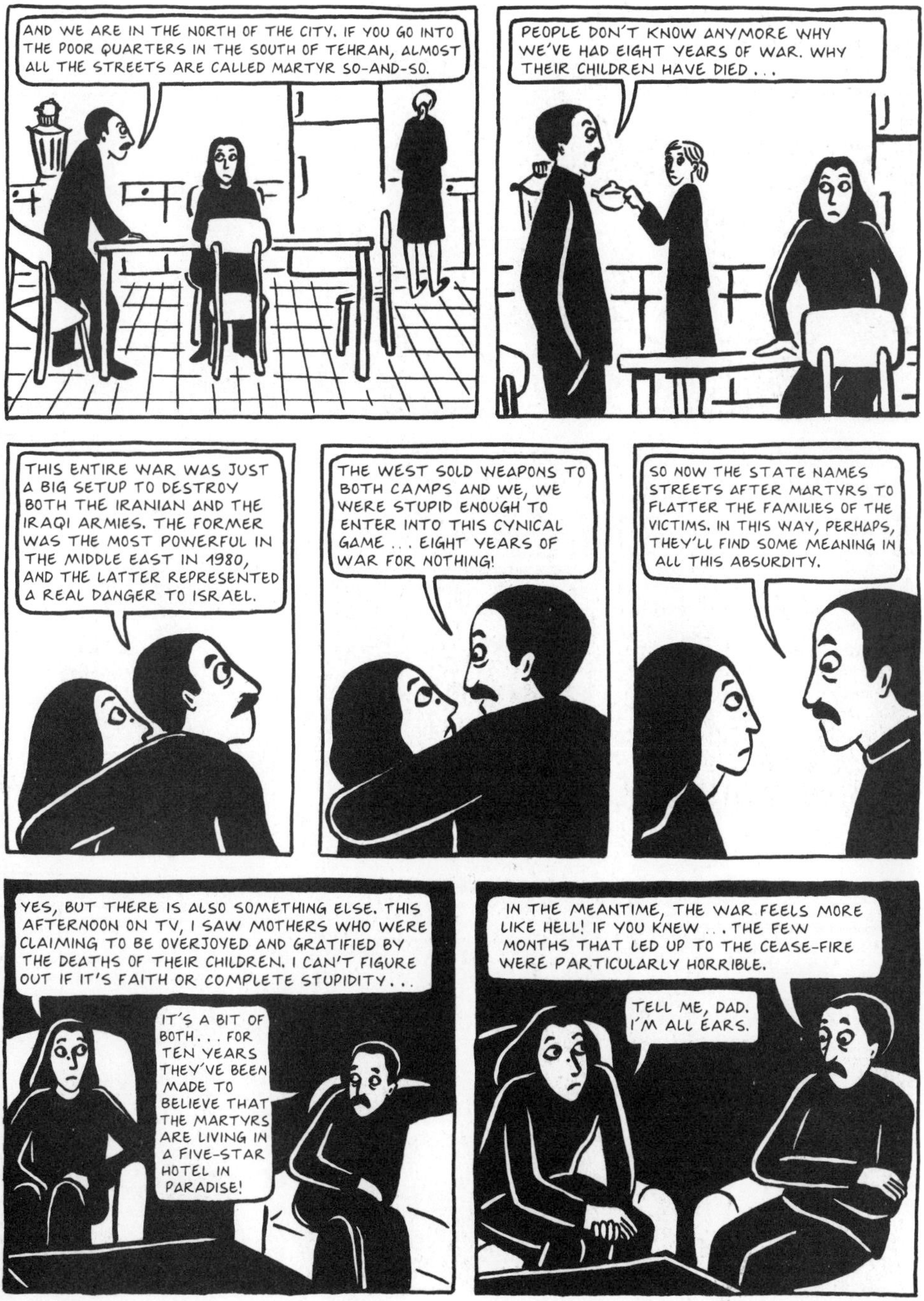
AND WE ARE IN THE NORTH OF THE CITY. IF YOU GO INTO THE POOR QUARTERS IN THE SOUTH OF TEHRAN, ALMOST ALL THE STREETS ARE CALLED MARTYR SO-AND-SO.
PEOPLE DON'T KNOW ANYMORE WHY WE'VE HAD EIGHT YEARS OF WAR. WHY THEIR CHILDREN HAVE DIED . . .
THIS ENTIRE WAR WAS JUST A BIG SETUP TO DESTROY BOTH THE IRANIAN AND THE IRAQI ARMIES. THE FORMER WAS THE MOST POWERFUL IN THE MIDDLE EAST IN 1980, AND THE LATTER REPRESENTED A REAL DANGER TO ISRAEL.
THE WEST SOLD WEAPONS TO BOTH CAMPS AND WE, WE WERE STUPID ENOUGH TO ENTER INTO THIS CYNICAL GAME . . . EIGHT YEARS OF WAR FOR NOTHING!
SO NOW THE STATE NAMES STREETS AFTER MARTYRS TO FLATTER THE FAMILIES OF THE VICTIMS. IN THIS WAY, PERHAPS, THEY'LL FIND SOME MEANING IN ALL THIS ABSURDITY.
YES, BUT THERE IS ALSO SOMETHING ELSE. THIS AFTERNOON ON TV, I SAW MOTHERS WHO WERE CLAIMING TO BE OVERJOYED AND GRATIFIED BY THE DEATHS OF THEIR CHILDREN. I CAN'T FIGURE OUT IF IT'S FAITH OR COMPLETE STUPIDITY . . .
IT'S A BIT OF BOTH . . . FOR TEN YEARS THEY'VE BEEN MADE TO BELIEVE THAT THE MARTYRS ARE LIVING IN A FIVE-STAR HOTEL IN PARADISE!
IN THE MEANTIME, THE WAR FEELS MORE LIKE HELL! IF YOU KNEW . . . THE FEW MONTHS THAT LED UP TO THE CEASE-FIRE WERE PARTICULARLY HORRIBLE.
TELL ME, DAD. I'M ALL EARS.

ONE MONTH BEFORE THE ARMISTICE, IRAQ BEGAN BOMBING TEHRAN EVERY DAY, AS IF IT WERE NECESSARY TO DESTROY AS MUCH AS POSSIBLE BEFORE IT WAS OVER...

...THE PEACE HADN'T YET BEEN ANNOUNCED WHEN THE ARMED GROUPS OPPOSED TO THE ISLAMIC REGIME, THE IRANIAN MUJAHIDEEN,* ENTERED THE COUNTRY FROM THE IRAQI BORDER WITH THE SUPPORT OF SADDAM HUSSEIN TO LIBERATE IRAN FROM THE HANDS OF ITS FUNDAMENTALIST LEADERS.

*THE TERM "MUJAHIDEEN" ISN'T SPECIFIC TO AFGHANISTAN. IT MEANS A COMBATANT.

YOU SURELY HEARD ABOUT IT.

NO, DAD, I DIDN'T KNOW.

WHAT DO YOU MEAN?

EBI!!! REALLY! SHE JUST SPENT FOUR YEARS IN EUROPE!

YES, OF COURSE.

WHAT WAS I SAYING?... RIGHT, THE MUJAHIDEEN THOUGHT THAT SINCE IT WAS THE END OF THE WAR, OUR ARMY WOULDN'T HAVE THE STRENGTH TO FIGHT ANYMORE.

100

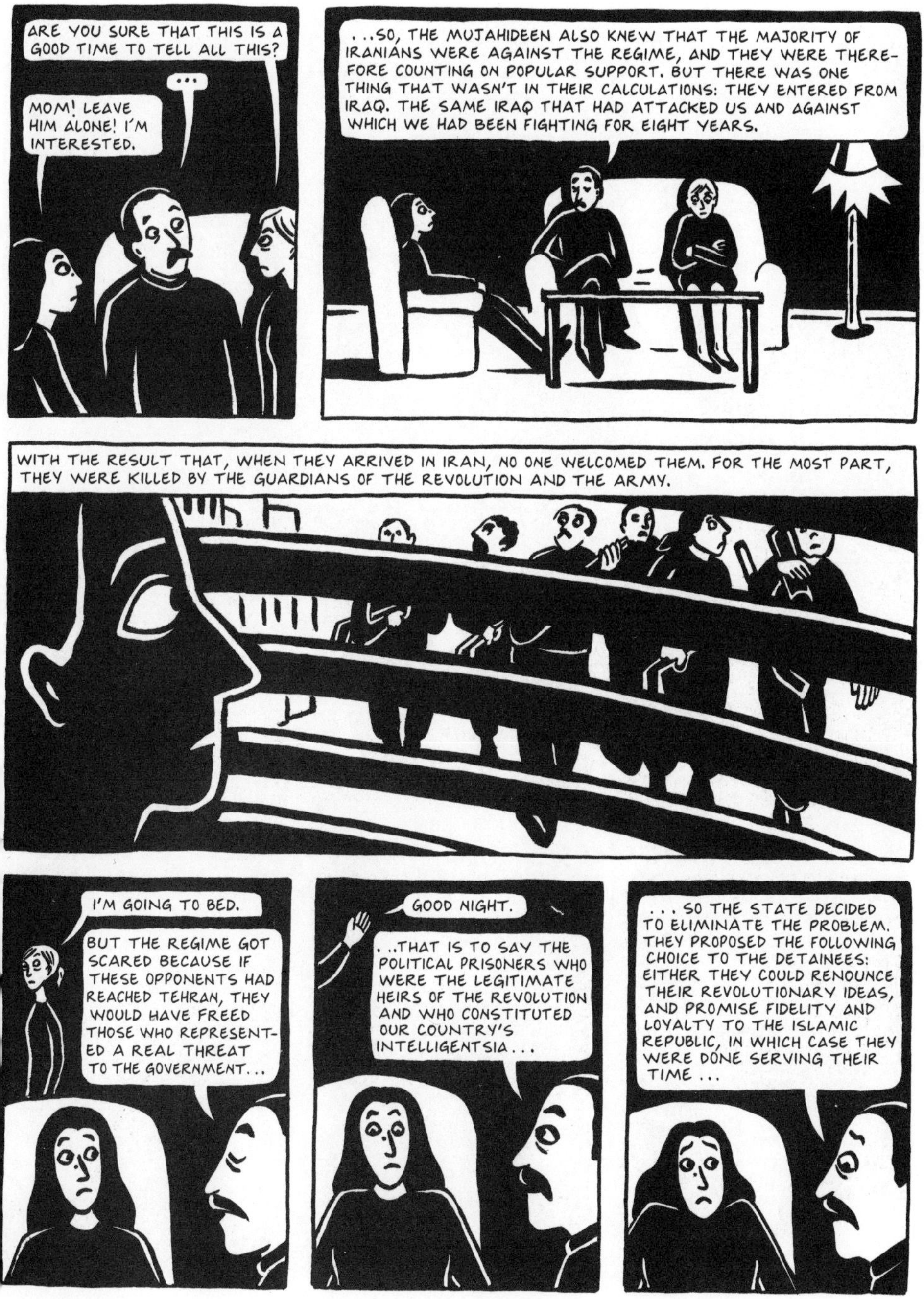
ARE YOU SURE THAT THIS IS A GOOD TIME TO TELL ALL THIS?
...
MOM! LEAVE HIM ALONE! I'M INTERESTED.
...SO, THE MUJAHIDEEN ALSO KNEW THAT THE MAJORITY OF IRANIANS WERE AGAINST THE REGIME, AND THEY WERE THEREFORE COUNTING ON POPULAR SUPPORT. BUT THERE WAS ONE THING THAT WASN'T IN THEIR CALCULATIONS: THEY ENTERED FROM IRAQ. THE SAME IRAQ THAT HAD ATTACKED US AND AGAINST WHICH WE HAD BEEN FIGHTING FOR EIGHT YEARS.
WITH THE RESULT THAT, WHEN THEY ARRIVED IN IRAN, NO ONE WELCOMED THEM. FOR THE MOST PART, THEY WERE KILLED BY THE GUARDIANS OF THE REVOLUTION AND THE ARMY.
I'M GOING TO BED.
BUT THE REGIME GOT SCARED BECAUSE IF THESE OPPONENTS HAD REACHED TEHRAN, THEY WOULD HAVE FREED THOSE WHO REPRESENTED A REAL THREAT TO THE GOVERNMENT...
GOOD NIGHT.
...THAT IS TO SAY THE POLITICAL PRISONERS WHO WERE THE LEGITIMATE HEIRS OF THE REVOLUTION AND WHO CONSTITUTED OUR COUNTRY'S INTELLIGENTSIA...
...SO THE STATE DECIDED TO ELIMINATE THE PROBLEM. THEY PROPOSED THE FOLLOWING CHOICE TO THE DETAINEES: EITHER THEY COULD RENOUNCE THEIR REVOLUTIONARY IDEAS, AND PROMISE FIDELITY AND LOYALTY TO THE ISLAMIC REPUBLIC, IN WHICH CASE THEY WERE DONE SERVING THEIR TIME...

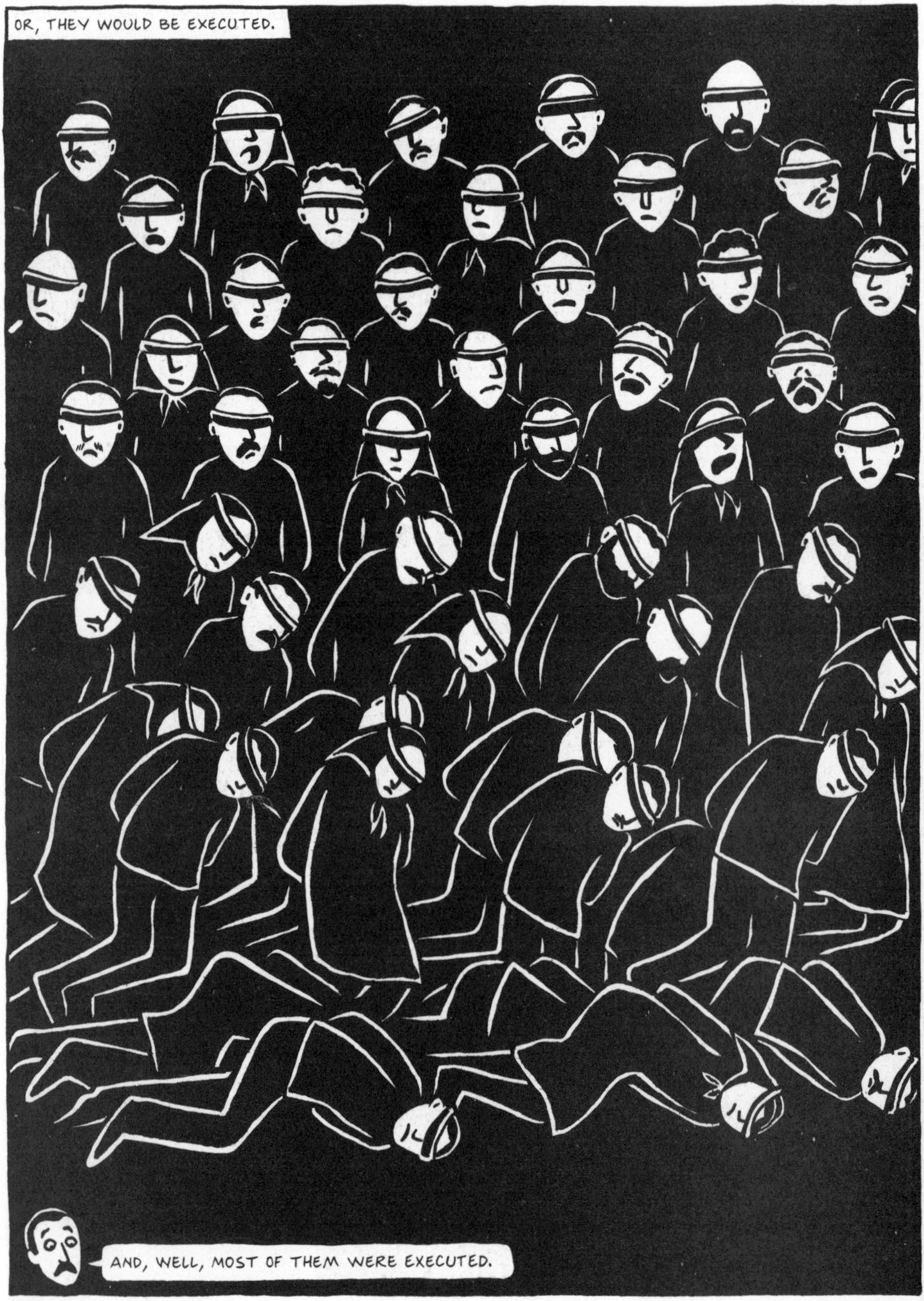
OR, THEY WOULD BE EXECUTED.
AND, WELL, MOST OF THEM WERE EXECUTED.

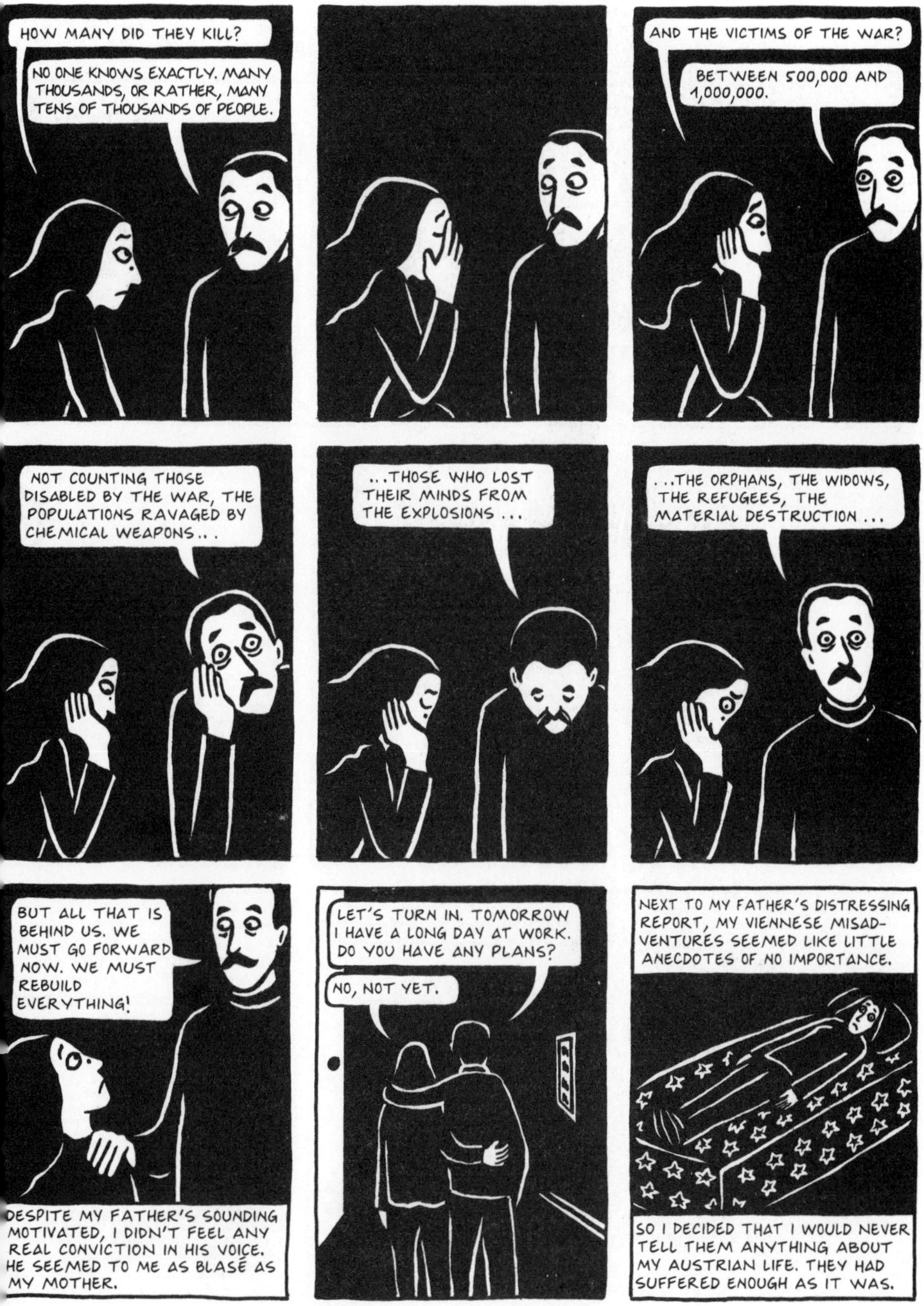
HOW MANY DID THEY KILL?
NO ONE KNOWS EXACTLY. MANY THOUSANDS, OR RATHER, MANY TENS OF THOUSANDS OF PEOPLE.
AND THE VICTIMS OF THE WAR?
BETWEEN 500,000 AND 1,000,000.
NOT COUNTING THOSE DISABLED BY THE WAR, THE POPULATIONS RAVAGED BY CHEMICAL WEAPONS...
...THOSE WHO LOST THEIR MINDS FROM THE EXPLOSIONS ...
...THE ORPHANS, THE WIDOWS, THE REFUGEES, THE MATERIAL DESTRUCTION ...
BUT ALL THAT IS BEHIND US. WE MUST GO FORWARD NOW. WE MUST REBUILD EVERYTHING!
DESPITE MY FATHER'S SOUNDING MOTIVATED, I DIDN'T FEEL ANY REAL CONVICTION IN HIS VOICE. HE SEEMED TO ME AS BLASÉ AS MY MOTHER.
LET'S TURN IN. TOMORROW I HAVE A LONG DAY AT WORK. DO YOU HAVE ANY PLANS?
NO, NOT YET.
NEXT TO MY FATHER'S DISTRESSING REPORT, MY VIENNESE MISAD-VENTURES SEEMED LIKE LITTLE ANECDOTES OF NO IMPORTANCE.
SO I DECIDED THAT I WOULD NEVER TELL THEM ANYTHING ABOUT MY AUSTRIAN LIFE. THEY HAD SUFFERED ENOUGH AS IT WAS.

THE JOKE

I HAD BEEN IN TEHRAN FOR TEN DAYS. DESPITE MY RELUCTANCE, IN THE END MY ENTIRE FAMILY CAME TO SEE ME. I DIDN'T KNOW WHETHER OR NOT THEY KNEW ABOUT MY EUROPEAN FAILURE. I WAS SCARED THAT THEY WOULD BE DISAPPOINTED.

YOU MUST SPEAK GOOD GERMAN NOW.

I KNOW HOW TO SAY "ICH LIEBE DICH" HEE HEE HEE!

YES, I SPEAK A LITTLE.

THANK YOU FOR THE FLOWERS.

THIS IS UNCLE ARDESHIR, MY MOTHER'S UNCLE. HE'S RETIRED FROM THE NATIONAL EDUCATION SYSTEM.

WHEN I THINK OF VIENNA, I IMMEDIATELY THINK OF SISSI. YOU MUST HAVE SEEN THE FILM STARRING ROMY!

YES.

THAT'S MINA, MY FIRST COUSIN. SHE'S AN IMBECILE. SHE TALKS ABOUT ROMY SCHNEIDER AS IF SHE WERE HER BEST FRIEND.

MARJANE, THE STARS SHINE IN THE SKY AND YOU IN MY HEART...

THESE ARE OUR NEIGHBORS. THEY'RE THE INCARNATION OF THE PERFECT FAMILY.

EVEN THOUGH I KNEW THAT THEY WERE COMING TO SEE ME OUT OF FRIEND-SHIP AND KINDNESS, I'D QUICKLY HAD ENOUGH OF RECEIVING THEM EVERY DAY.

BUT THERE WAS NOTHING TO BE DONE, THE VISITS CONTINUED ...

ASIDE FROM MY PARENTS, THE ONLY PERSON TO WHOM I REALLY WANTED TO TALK WAS MY GRANDMOTHER. BUT SHE CAME AFTER EVERYONE ELSE.

GRANDMA, WHERE WERE YOU?

I WAS WAITING FOR THE TRIBE TO GO FIRST! OH MY!! HOW YOU'VE GROWN. SOON YOU'LL BE CATCHING THE LORD'S BALLS.

SHE WAS STILL HER OLD SELF.

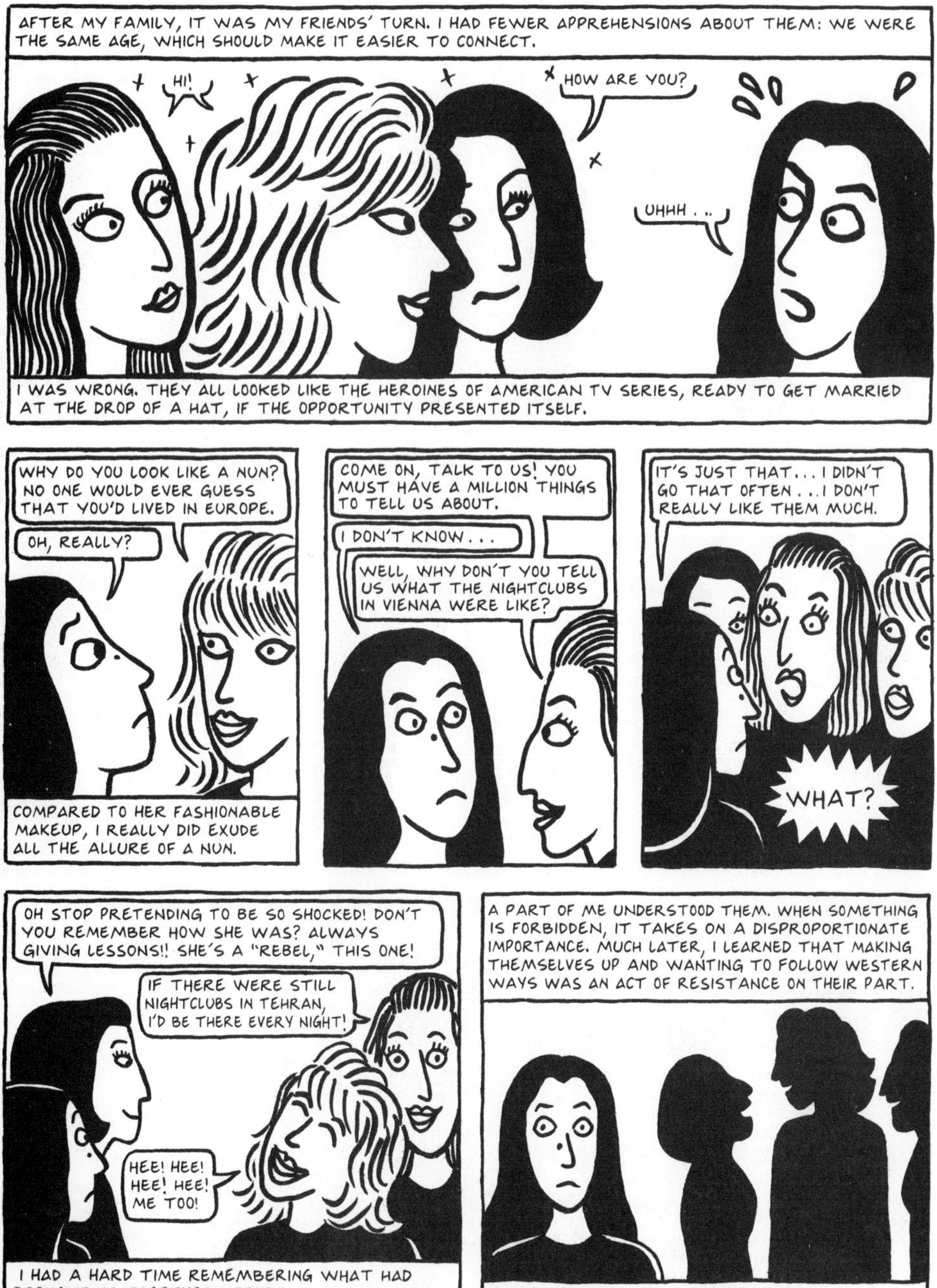
AFTER MY FAMILY, IT WAS MY FRIENDS' TURN. I HAD FEWER APPREHENSIONS ABOUT THEM: WE WERE THE SAME AGE, WHICH SHOULD MAKE IT EASIER TO CONNECT.
HI!
HOW ARE YOU?
UHHH . . .
I WAS WRONG. THEY ALL LOOKED LIKE THE HEROINES OF AMERICAN TV SERIES, READY TO GET MARRIED AT THE DROP OF A HAT, IF THE OPPORTUNITY PRESENTED ITSELF.
WHY DO YOU LOOK LIKE A NUN? NO ONE WOULD EVER GUESS THAT YOU'D LIVED IN EUROPE.
OH, REALLY?
COMPARED TO HER FASHIONABLE MAKEUP, I REALLY DID EXUDE ALL THE ALLURE OF A NUN.
COME ON, TALK TO US! YOU MUST HAVE A MILLION THINGS TO TELL US ABOUT.
I DON'T KNOW . . .
WELL, WHY DON'T YOU TELL US WHAT THE NIGHTCLUBS IN VIENNA WERE LIKE?
IT'S JUST THAT . . . I DIDN'T GO THAT OFTEN . . . I DON'T REALLY LIKE THEM MUCH.
WHAT?
OH STOP PRETENDING TO BE SO SHOCKED! DON'T YOU REMEMBER HOW SHE WAS? ALWAYS GIVING LESSONS!! SHE'S A "REBEL," THIS ONE!
IF THERE WERE STILL NIGHTCLUBS IN TEHRAN, I'D BE THERE EVERY NIGHT!
HEE! HEE! HEE! HEE! ME TOO!
I HAD A HARD TIME REMEMBERING WHAT HAD BROUGHT US TOGETHER BEFORE.
A PART OF ME UNDERSTOOD THEM. WHEN SOMETHING IS FORBIDDEN, IT TAKES ON A DISPROPORTIONATE IMPORTANCE. MUCH LATER, I LEARNED THAT MAKING THEMSELVES UP AND WANTING TO FOLLOW WESTERN WAYS WAS AN ACT OF RESISTANCE ON THEIR PART.
NEVERTHELESS, I FELT TERRIBLY ALONE.

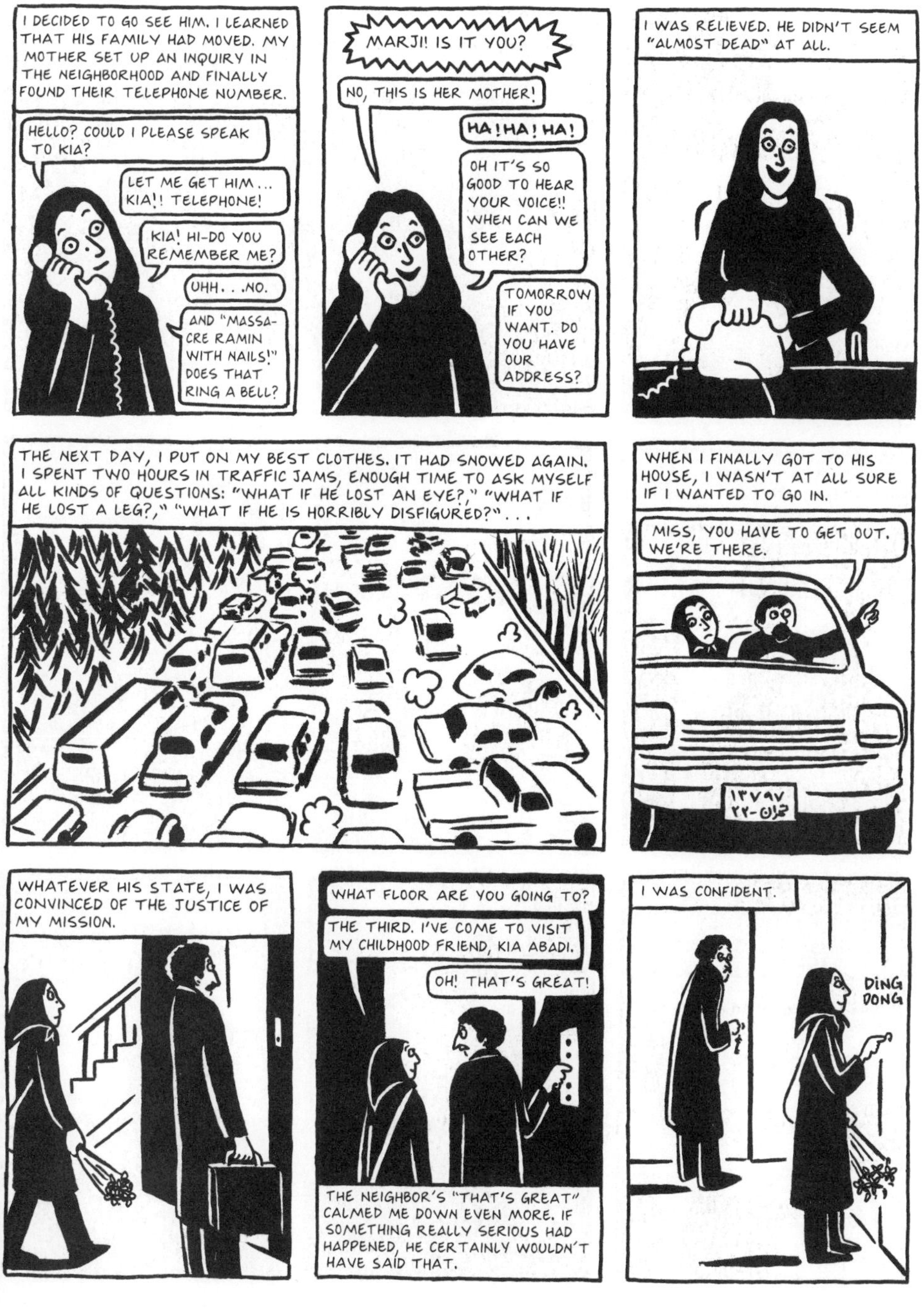
I DECIDED TO GO SEE HIM. I LEARNED THAT HIS FAMILY HAD MOVED. MY MOTHER SET UP AN INQUIRY IN THE NEIGHBORHOOD AND FINALLY FOUND THEIR TELEPHONE NUMBER.
HELLO? COULD I PLEASE SPEAK TO KIA?
LET ME GET HIM... KIA!! TELEPHONE!
KIA! HI-DO YOU REMEMBER ME?
UHH. . .NO.
AND "MASSA-CRE RAMIN WITH NAILS!" DOES THAT RING A BELL?
MARJI! IS IT YOU?
NO, THIS IS HER MOTHER!
HA! HA! HA!
OH IT'S SO GOOD TO HEAR YOUR VOICE!! WHEN CAN WE SEE EACH OTHER?
TOMORROW IF YOU WANT. DO YOU HAVE OUR ADDRESS?
I WAS RELIEVED. HE DIDN'T SEEM "ALMOST DEAD" AT ALL.
THE NEXT DAY, I PUT ON MY BEST CLOTHES. IT HAD SNOWED AGAIN. I SPENT TWO HOURS IN TRAFFIC JAMS, ENOUGH TIME TO ASK MYSELF ALL KINDS OF QUESTIONS: "WHAT IF HE LOST AN EYE?," "WHAT IF HE LOST A LEG?," "WHAT IF HE IS HORRIBLY DISFIGURED?" . . .
WHEN I FINALLY GOT TO HIS HOUSE, I WASN'T AT ALL SURE IF I WANTED TO GO IN.
MISS, YOU HAVE TO GET OUT. WE'RE THERE.
۱۳۷۹۷
تهران-۲۲
WHATEVER HIS STATE, I WAS CONVINCED OF THE JUSTICE OF MY MISSION.
WHAT FLOOR ARE YOU GOING TO?
THE THIRD. I'VE COME TO VISIT MY CHILDHOOD FRIEND, KIA ABADI.
OH! THAT'S GREAT!
THE NEIGHBOR'S "THAT'S GREAT" CALMED ME DOWN EVEN MORE. IF SOMETHING REALLY SERIOUS HAD HAPPENED, HE CERTAINLY WOULDN'T HAVE SAID THAT.
I WAS CONFIDENT.
DING DONG

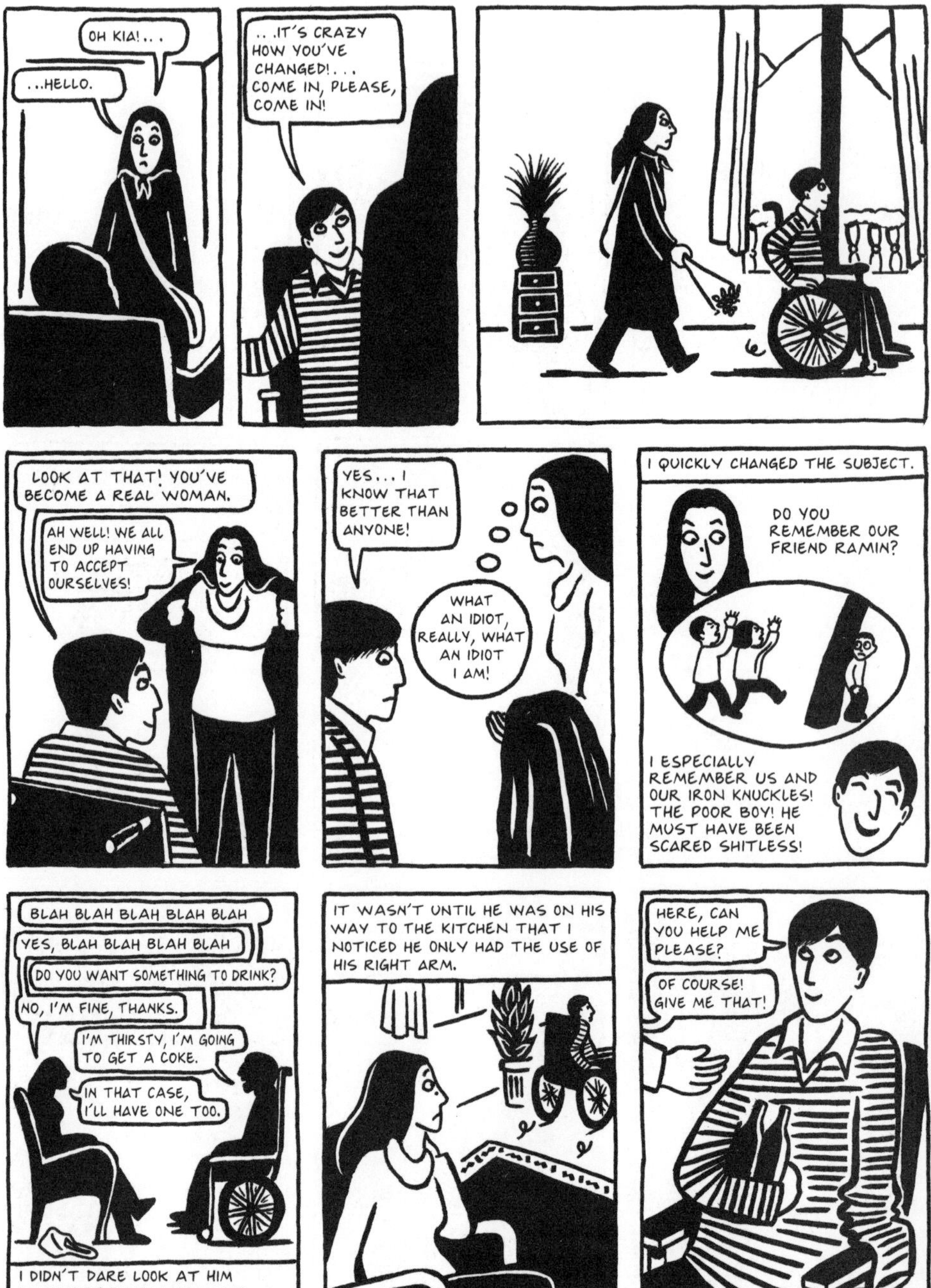

OH KIA!. . .
. . .HELLO.
. . .IT'S CRAZY HOW YOU'VE CHANGED!. . . COME IN, PLEASE, COME IN!
LOOK AT THAT! YOU'VE BECOME A REAL WOMAN.
AH WELL! WE ALL END UP HAVING TO ACCEPT OURSELVES!
YES. . . I KNOW THAT BETTER THAN ANYONE!
WHAT AN IDIOT, REALLY, WHAT AN IDIOT I AM!
I QUICKLY CHANGED THE SUBJECT.
DO YOU REMEMBER OUR FRIEND RAMIN?
I ESPECIALLY REMEMBER US AND OUR IRON KNUCKLES! THE POOR BOY! HE MUST HAVE BEEN SCARED SHITLESS!
BLAH BLAH BLAH BLAH BLAH
YES, BLAH BLAH BLAH BLAH
DO YOU WANT SOMETHING TO DRINK?
NO, I'M FINE, THANKS.
I'M THIRSTY, I'M GOING TO GET A COKE.
IN THAT CASE, I'LL HAVE ONE TOO.
I DIDN'T DARE LOOK AT HIM ANYWHERE BUT IN THE EYES.
IT WASN'T UNTIL HE WAS ON HIS WAY TO THE KITCHEN THAT I NOTICED HE ONLY HAD THE USE OF HIS RIGHT ARM.
HERE, CAN YOU HELP ME PLEASE?
OF COURSE! GIVE ME THAT!

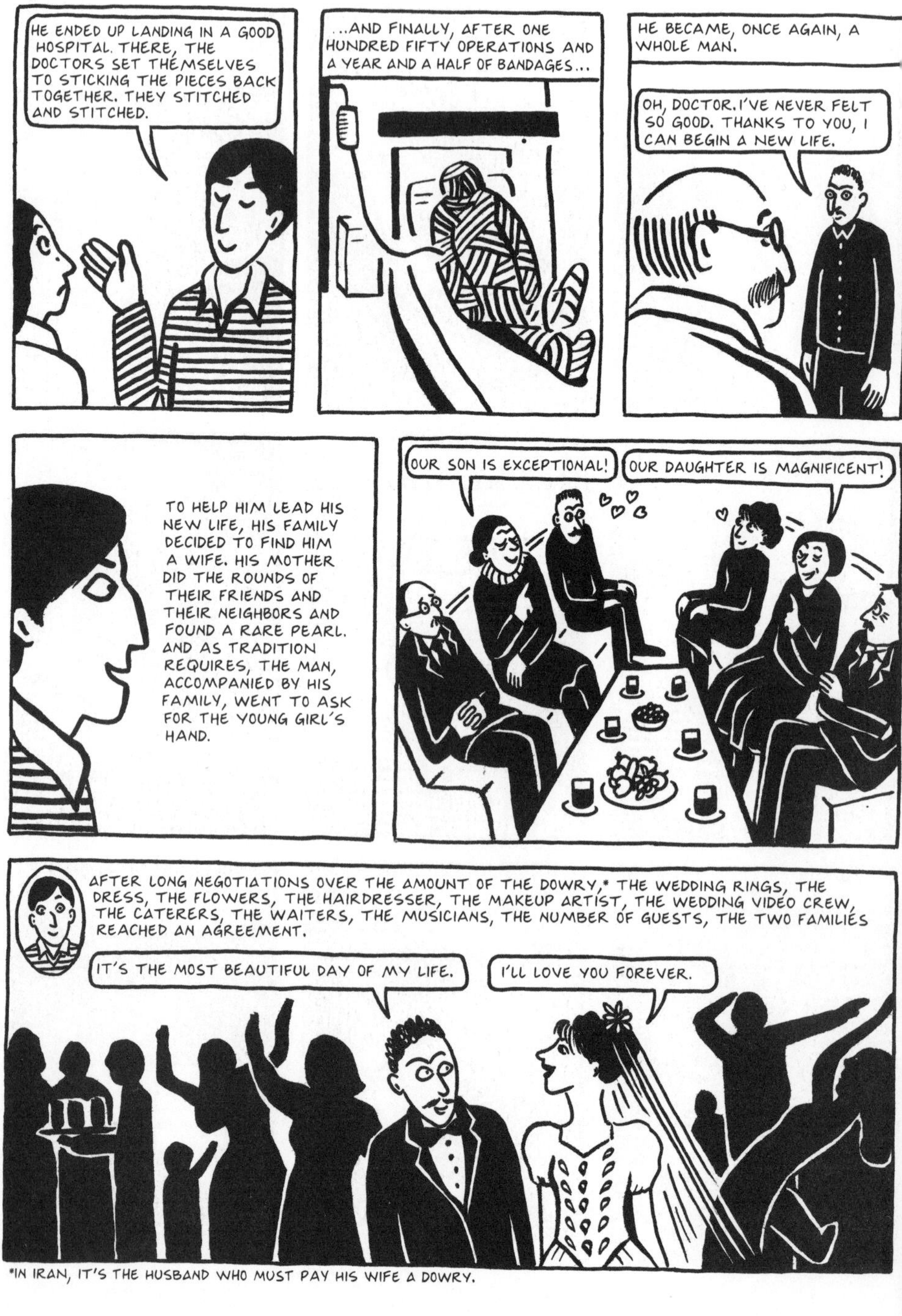
HE ENDED UP LANDING IN A GOOD HOSPITAL. THERE, THE DOCTORS SET THEMSELVES TO STICKING THE PIECES BACK TOGETHER. THEY STITCHED AND STITCHED.
...AND FINALLY, AFTER ONE HUNDRED FIFTY OPERATIONS AND A YEAR AND A HALF OF BANDAGES...
HE BECAME, ONCE AGAIN, A WHOLE MAN.
OH, DOCTOR. I'VE NEVER FELT SO GOOD. THANKS TO YOU, I CAN BEGIN A NEW LIFE.
TO HELP HIM LEAD HIS NEW LIFE, HIS FAMILY DECIDED TO FIND HIM A WIFE. HIS MOTHER DID THE ROUNDS OF THEIR FRIENDS AND THEIR NEIGHBORS AND FOUND A RARE PEARL. AND AS TRADITION REQUIRES, THE MAN, ACCOMPANIED BY HIS FAMILY, WENT TO ASK FOR THE YOUNG GIRL'S HAND.
OUR SON IS EXCEPTIONAL!
OUR DAUGHTER IS MAGNIFICENT!
AFTER LONG NEGOTIATIONS OVER THE AMOUNT OF THE DOWRY,* THE WEDDING RINGS, THE DRESS, THE FLOWERS, THE HAIRDRESSER, THE MAKEUP ARTIST, THE WEDDING VIDEO CREW, THE CATERERS, THE WAITERS, THE MUSICIANS, THE NUMBER OF GUESTS, THE TWO FAMILIES REACHED AN AGREEMENT.
IT'S THE MOST BEAUTIFUL DAY OF MY LIFE.
I'LL LOVE YOU FOREVER.

*IN IRAN, IT'S THE HUSBAND WHO MUST PAY HIS WIFE A DOWRY.

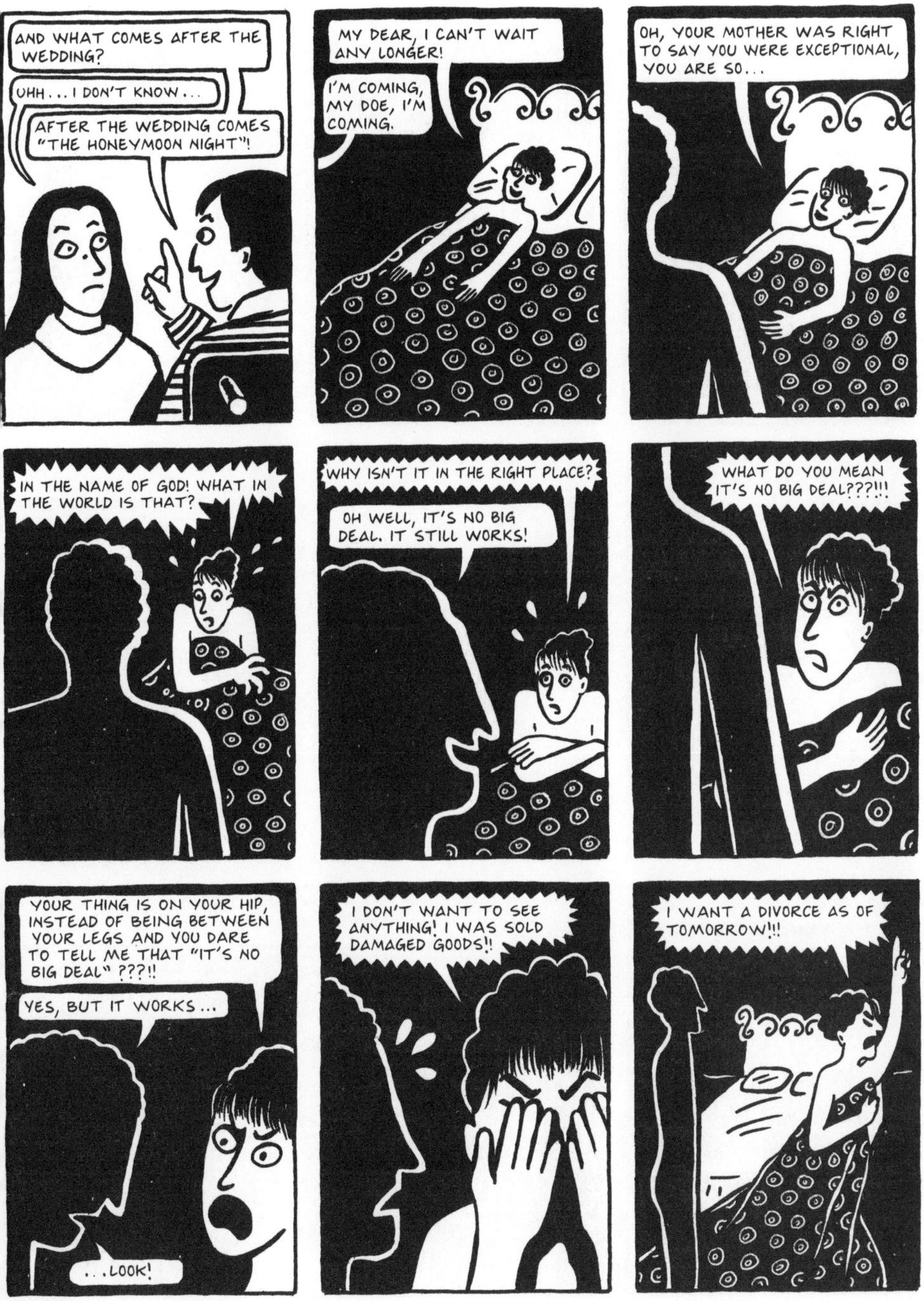
AND WHAT COMES AFTER THE WEDDING?
UHH... I DON'T KNOW...
AFTER THE WEDDING COMES "THE HONEYMOON NIGHT"!
MY DEAR, I CAN'T WAIT ANY LONGER!
I'M COMING, MY DOE, I'M COMING.
OH, YOUR MOTHER WAS RIGHT TO SAY YOU WERE EXCEPTIONAL, YOU ARE SO...
IN THE NAME OF GOD! WHAT IN THE WORLD IS THAT?
WHY ISN'T IT IN THE RIGHT PLACE?
OH WELL, IT'S NO BIG DEAL. IT STILL WORKS!
WHAT DO YOU MEAN IT'S NO BIG DEAL???!!!
YOUR THING IS ON YOUR HIP, INSTEAD OF BEING BETWEEN YOUR LEGS AND YOU DARE TO TELL ME THAT "IT'S NO BIG DEAL"???!!
YES, BUT IT WORKS...
...LOOK!
I DON'T WANT TO SEE ANYTHING! I WAS SOLD DAMAGED GOODS!!
I WANT A DIVORCE AS OF TOMORROW!!!

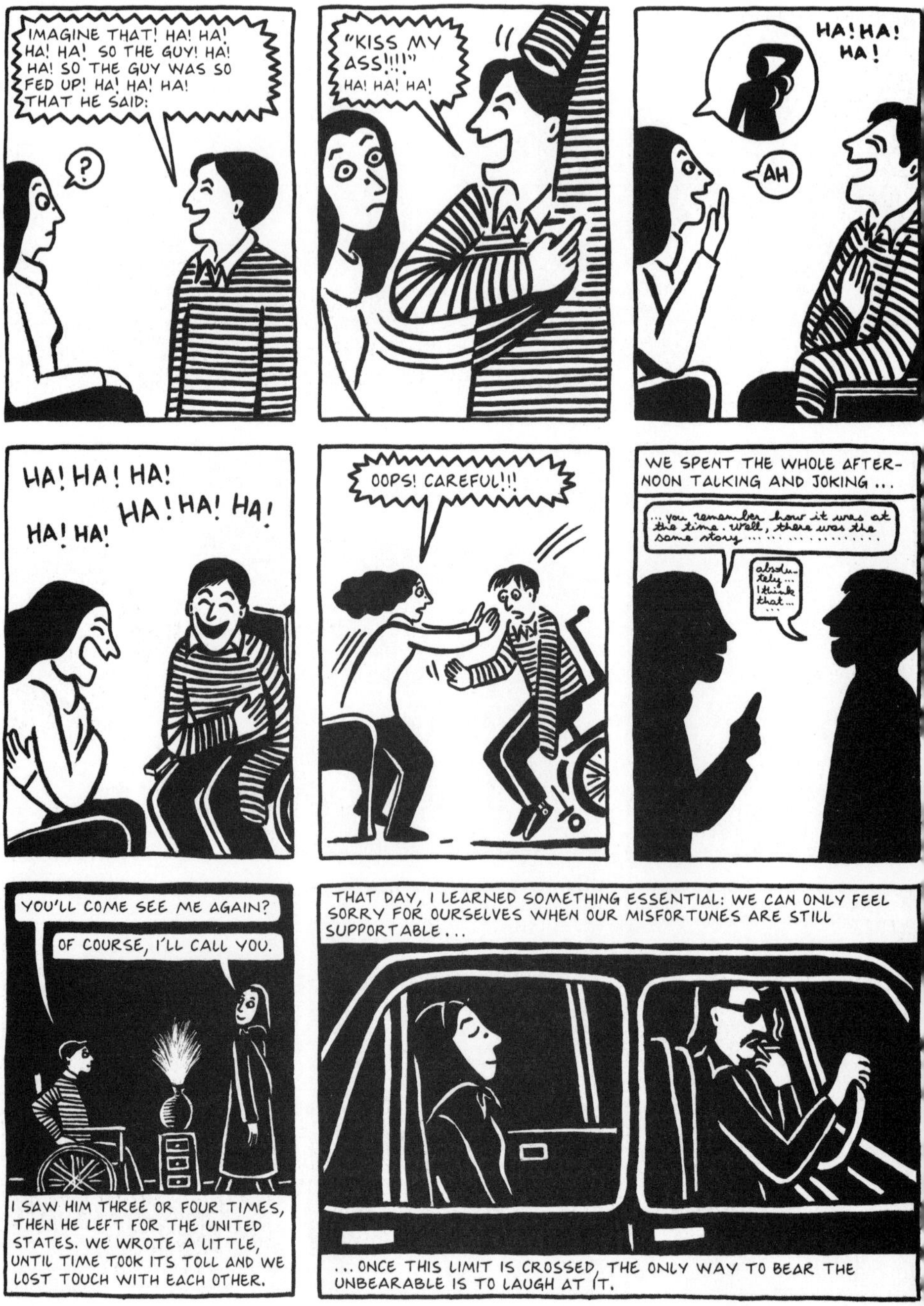
IMAGINE THAT! HA! HA! HA! HA! SO THE GUY! HA! HA! SO THE GUY WAS SO FED UP! HA! HA! HA! THAT HE SAID:
?
"KISS MY ASS!!!!" HA! HA! HA!
HA! HA! HA!
AH
HA! HA! HA! HA! HA! HA! HA! HA!
OOPS! CAREFUL!!!
WE SPENT THE WHOLE AFTERNOON TALKING AND JOKING ...
... you remember how it was at the time. Well, there was the same story ... ...
absolutely... I think that... ...
YOU'LL COME SEE ME AGAIN?
OF COURSE, I'LL CALL YOU.
I SAW HIM THREE OR FOUR TIMES, THEN HE LEFT FOR THE UNITED STATES. WE WROTE A LITTLE, UNTIL TIME TOOK ITS TOLL AND WE LOST TOUCH WITH EACH OTHER.
THAT DAY, I LEARNED SOMETHING ESSENTIAL: WE CAN ONLY FEEL SORRY FOR OURSELVES WHEN OUR MISFORTUNES ARE STILL SUPPORTABLE...
...ONCE THIS LIMIT IS CROSSED, THE ONLY WAY TO BEAR THE UNBEARABLE IS TO LAUGH AT IT.

SKIING

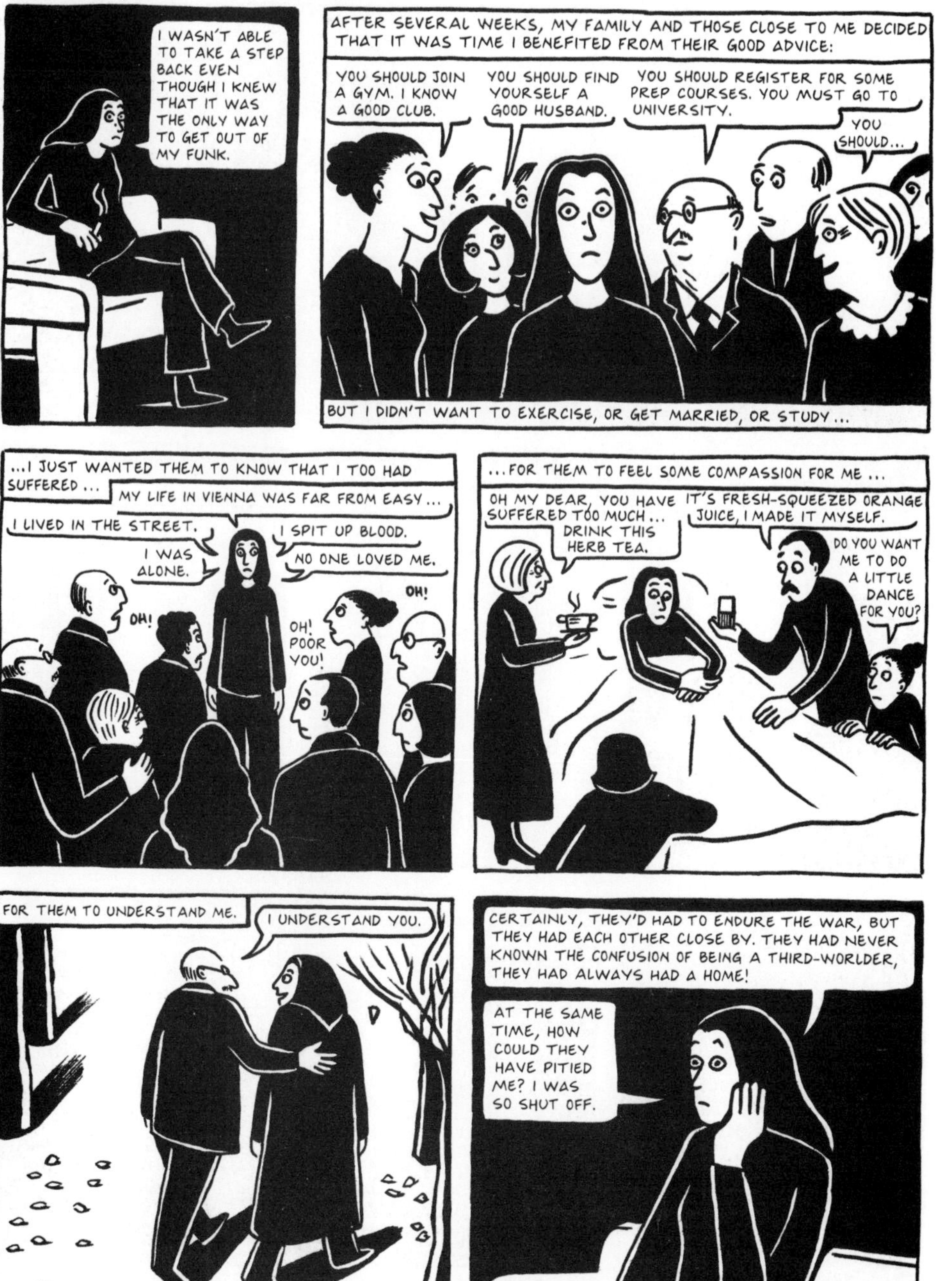

I WASN'T ABLE TO TAKE A STEP BACK EVEN THOUGH I KNEW THAT IT WAS THE ONLY WAY TO GET OUT OF MY FUNK.
AFTER SEVERAL WEEKS, MY FAMILY AND THOSE CLOSE TO ME DECIDED THAT IT WAS TIME I BENEFITED FROM THEIR GOOD ADVICE:
YOU SHOULD JOIN A GYM. I KNOW A GOOD CLUB.
YOU SHOULD FIND YOURSELF A GOOD HUSBAND.
YOU SHOULD REGISTER FOR SOME PREP COURSES. YOU MUST GO TO UNIVERSITY.
YOU SHOULD...
BUT I DIDN'T WANT TO EXERCISE, OR GET MARRIED, OR STUDY...
...I JUST WANTED THEM TO KNOW THAT I TOO HAD SUFFERED...
MY LIFE IN VIENNA WAS FAR FROM EASY...
I LIVED IN THE STREET.
I SPIT UP BLOOD.
I WAS ALONE.
NO ONE LOVED ME.
OH!
OH!
OH! POOR YOU!
...FOR THEM TO FEEL SOME COMPASSION FOR ME...
OH MY DEAR, YOU HAVE SUFFERED TOO MUCH... DRINK THIS HERB TEA.
IT'S FRESH-SQUEEZED ORANGE JUICE, I MADE IT MYSELF.
DO YOU WANT ME TO DO A LITTLE DANCE FOR YOU?
FOR THEM TO UNDERSTAND ME.
I UNDERSTAND YOU.
CERTAINLY, THEY'D HAD TO ENDURE THE WAR, BUT THEY HAD EACH OTHER CLOSE BY. THEY HAD NEVER KNOWN THE CONFUSION OF BEING A THIRD-WORLDER, THEY HAD ALWAYS HAD A HOME!
AT THE SAME TIME, HOW COULD THEY HAVE PITIED ME? I WAS SO SHUT OFF.
I KEPT REPEATING TO MYSELF THAT I MUSN'T CRACK UP.

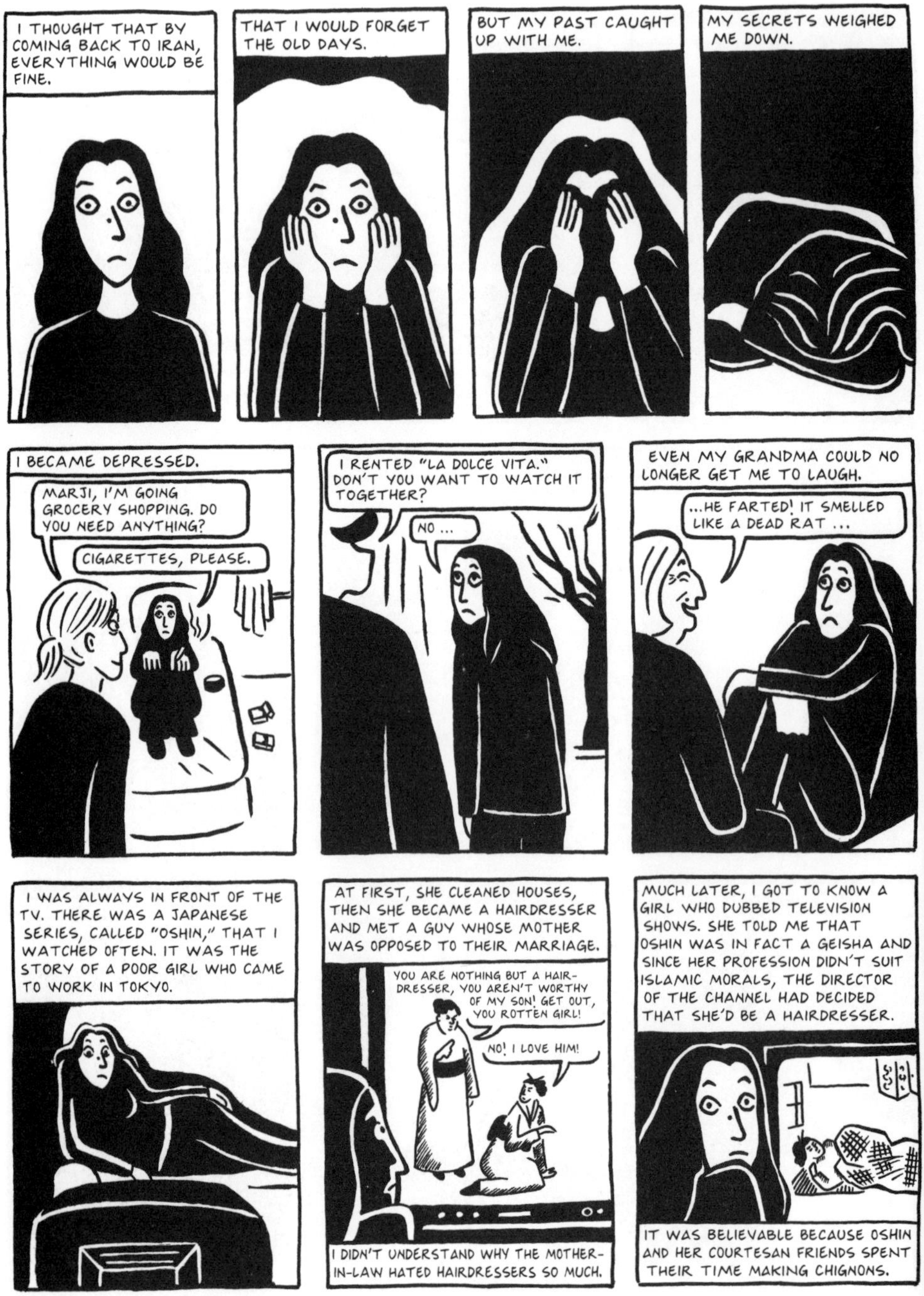
I THOUGHT THAT BY COMING BACK TO IRAN, EVERYTHING WOULD BE FINE.
THAT I WOULD FORGET THE OLD DAYS.
BUT MY PAST CAUGHT UP WITH ME.
MY SECRETS WEIGHED ME DOWN.
I BECAME DEPRESSED.
MARJI, I'M GOING GROCERY SHOPPING. DO YOU NEED ANYTHING?
CIGARETTES, PLEASE.
I RENTED "LA DOLCE VITA." DON'T YOU WANT TO WATCH IT TOGETHER?
NO ...
EVEN MY GRANDMA COULD NO LONGER GET ME TO LAUGH.
...HE FARTED! IT SMELLED LIKE A DEAD RAT ...
I WAS ALWAYS IN FRONT OF THE TV. THERE WAS A JAPANESE SERIES, CALLED "OSHIN," THAT I WATCHED OFTEN. IT WAS THE STORY OF A POOR GIRL WHO CAME TO WORK IN TOKYO.
AT FIRST, SHE CLEANED HOUSES, THEN SHE BECAME A HAIRDRESSER AND MET A GUY WHOSE MOTHER WAS OPPOSED TO THEIR MARRIAGE.
YOU ARE NOTHING BUT A HAIR-DRESSER, YOU AREN'T WORTHY OF MY SON! GET OUT, YOU ROTTEN GIRL!
NO! I LOVE HIM!
I DIDN'T UNDERSTAND WHY THE MOTHER-IN-LAW HATED HAIRDRESSERS SO MUCH.
MUCH LATER, I GOT TO KNOW A GIRL WHO DUBBED TELEVISION SHOWS. SHE TOLD ME THAT OSHIN WAS IN FACT A GEISHA AND SINCE HER PROFESSION DIDN'T SUIT ISLAMIC MORALS, THE DIRECTOR OF THE CHANNEL HAD DECIDED THAT SHE'D BE A HAIRDRESSER.
IT WAS BELIEVABLE BECAUSE OSHIN AND HER COURTESAN FRIENDS SPENT THEIR TIME MAKING CHIGNONS.

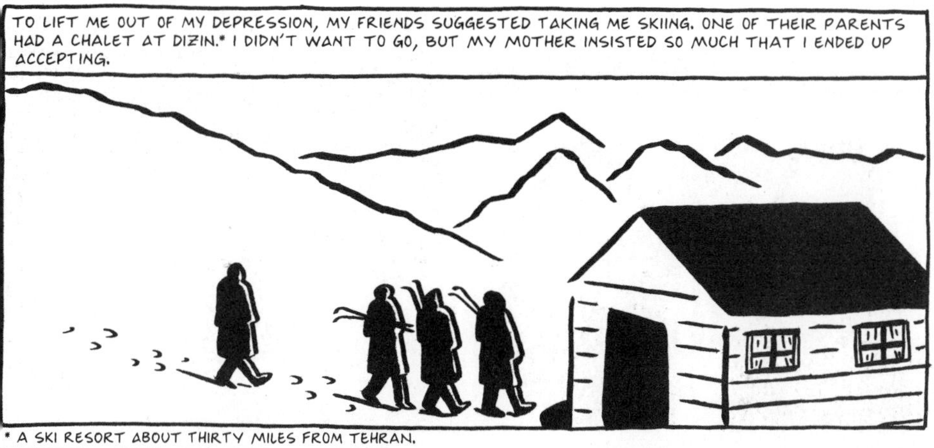
TO LIFT ME OUT OF MY DEPRESSION, MY FRIENDS SUGGESTED TAKING ME SKIING. ONE OF THEIR PARENTS HAD A CHALET AT DIZIN.* I DIDN'T WANT TO GO, BUT MY MOTHER INSISTED SO MUCH THAT I ENDED UP ACCEPTING.

* A SKI RESORT ABOUT THIRTY MILES FROM TEHRAN.

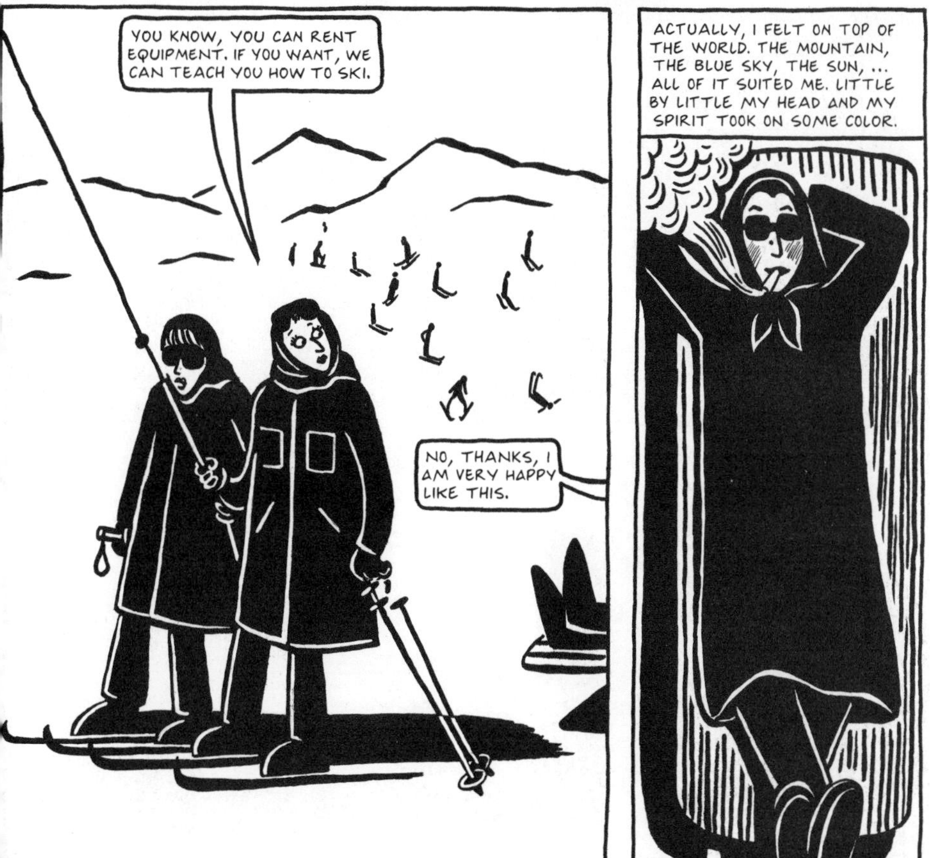
YOU KNOW, YOU CAN RENT EQUIPMENT. IF YOU WANT, WE CAN TEACH YOU HOW TO SKI.
NO, THANKS, I AM VERY HAPPY LIKE THIS.
ACTUALLY, I FELT ON TOP OF THE WORLD. THE MOUNTAIN, THE BLUE SKY, THE SUN, ... ALL OF IT SUITED ME. LITTLE BY LITTLE MY HEAD AND MY SPIRIT TOOK ON SOME COLOR.

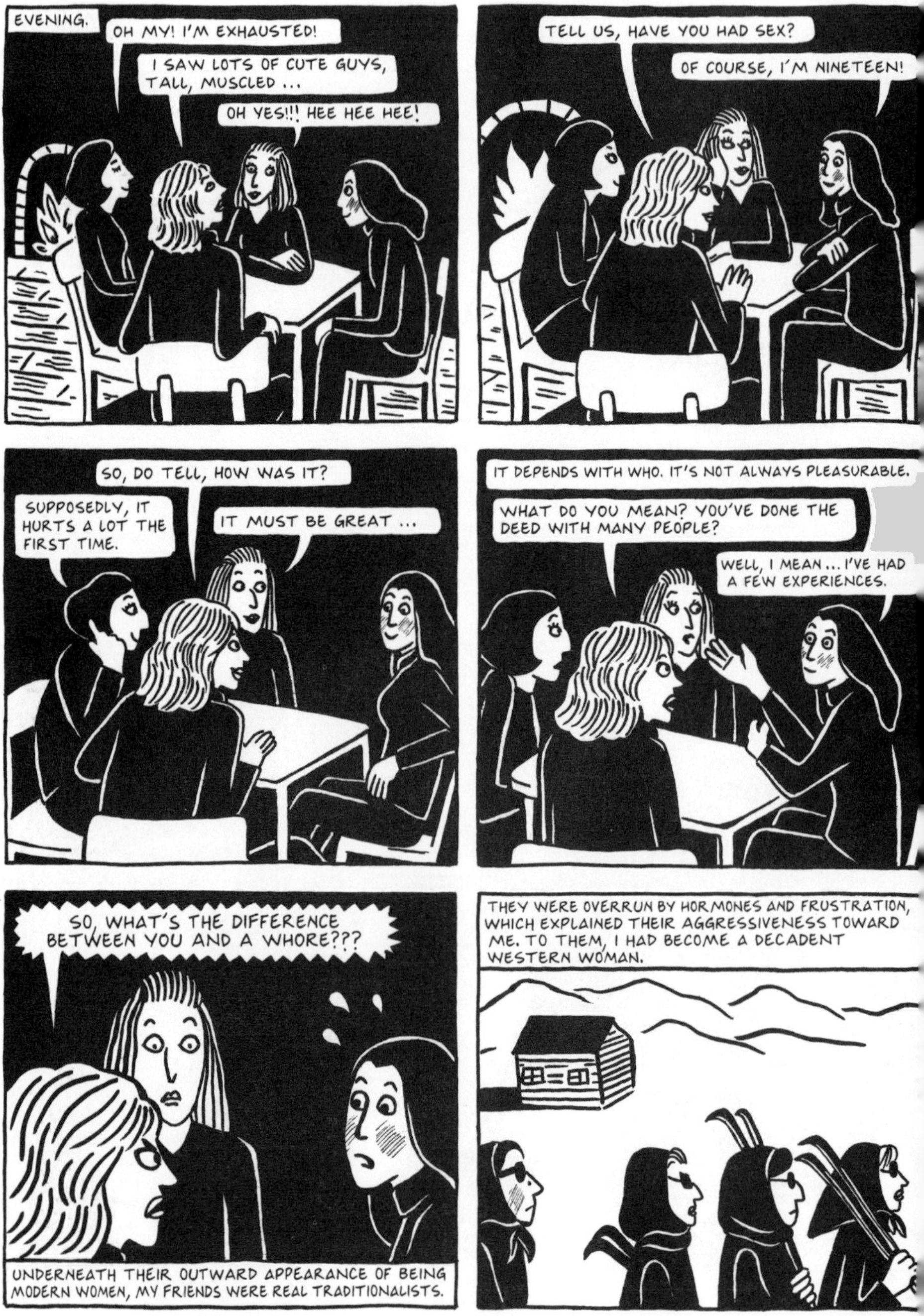
EVENING.
OH MY! I'M EXHAUSTED!
I SAW LOTS OF CUTE GUYS, TALL, MUSCLED ...
OH YES!!! HEE HEE HEE!
TELL US, HAVE YOU HAD SEX?
OF COURSE, I'M NINETEEN!
SO, DO TELL, HOW WAS IT?
SUPPOSEDLY, IT HURTS A LOT THE FIRST TIME.
IT MUST BE GREAT ...
IT DEPENDS WITH WHO. IT'S NOT ALWAYS PLEASURABLE.
WHAT DO YOU MEAN? YOU'VE DONE THE DEED WITH MANY PEOPLE?
WELL, I MEAN ... I'VE HAD A FEW EXPERIENCES.
SO, WHAT'S THE DIFFERENCE BETWEEN YOU AND A WHORE???
UNDERNEATH THEIR OUTWARD APPEARANCE OF BEING MODERN WOMEN, MY FRIENDS WERE REAL TRADITIONALISTS.
THEY WERE OVERRUN BY HORMONES AND FRUSTRATION, WHICH EXPLAINED THEIR AGGRESSIVENESS TOWARD ME. TO THEM, I HAD BECOME A DECADENT WESTERN WOMAN.

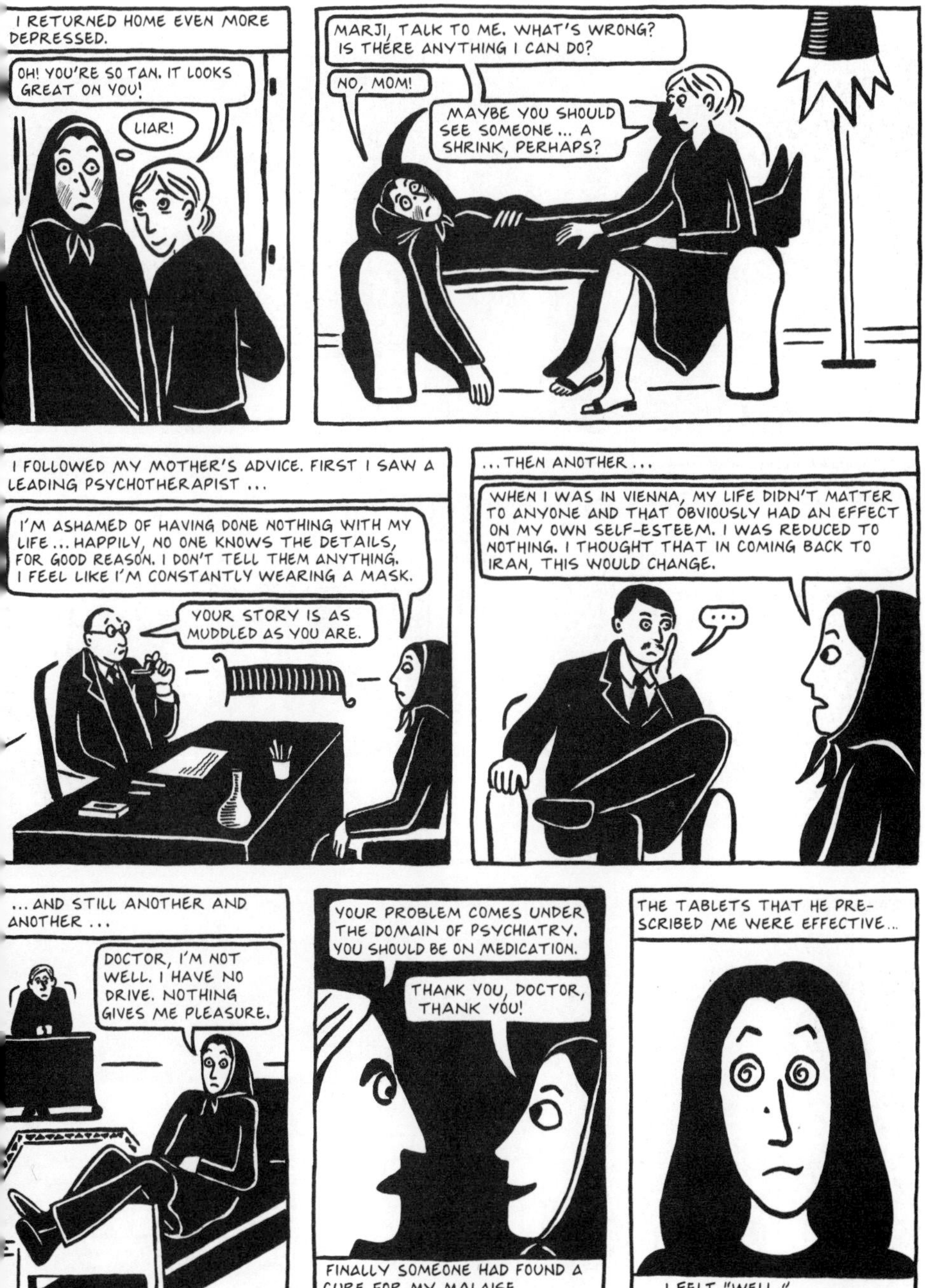
I RETURNED HOME EVEN MORE DEPRESSED.
OH! YOU'RE SO TAN. IT LOOKS GREAT ON YOU!
LIAR!
MARJI, TALK TO ME. WHAT'S WRONG? IS THERE ANYTHING I CAN DO?
NO, MOM!
MAYBE YOU SHOULD SEE SOMEONE... A SHRINK, PERHAPS?
I FOLLOWED MY MOTHER'S ADVICE. FIRST I SAW A LEADING PSYCHOTHERAPIST...
I'M ASHAMED OF HAVING DONE NOTHING WITH MY LIFE... HAPPILY, NO ONE KNOWS THE DETAILS, FOR GOOD REASON. I DON'T TELL THEM ANYTHING. I FEEL LIKE I'M CONSTANTLY WEARING A MASK.
YOUR STORY IS AS MUDDLED AS YOU ARE.
...THEN ANOTHER...
WHEN I WAS IN VIENNA, MY LIFE DIDN'T MATTER TO ANYONE AND THAT OBVIOUSLY HAD AN EFFECT ON MY OWN SELF-ESTEEM. I WAS REDUCED TO NOTHING. I THOUGHT THAT IN COMING BACK TO IRAN, THIS WOULD CHANGE.
...
...AND STILL ANOTHER AND ANOTHER...
DOCTOR, I'M NOT WELL. I HAVE NO DRIVE. NOTHING GIVES ME PLEASURE.
YOUR PROBLEM COMES UNDER THE DOMAIN OF PSYCHIATRY. YOU SHOULD BE ON MEDICATION.
THANK YOU, DOCTOR, THANK YOU!
FINALLY SOMEONE HAD FOUND A CURE FOR MY MALAISE.
THE TABLETS THAT HE PRESCRIBED ME WERE EFFECTIVE...
... I FELT "WELL."

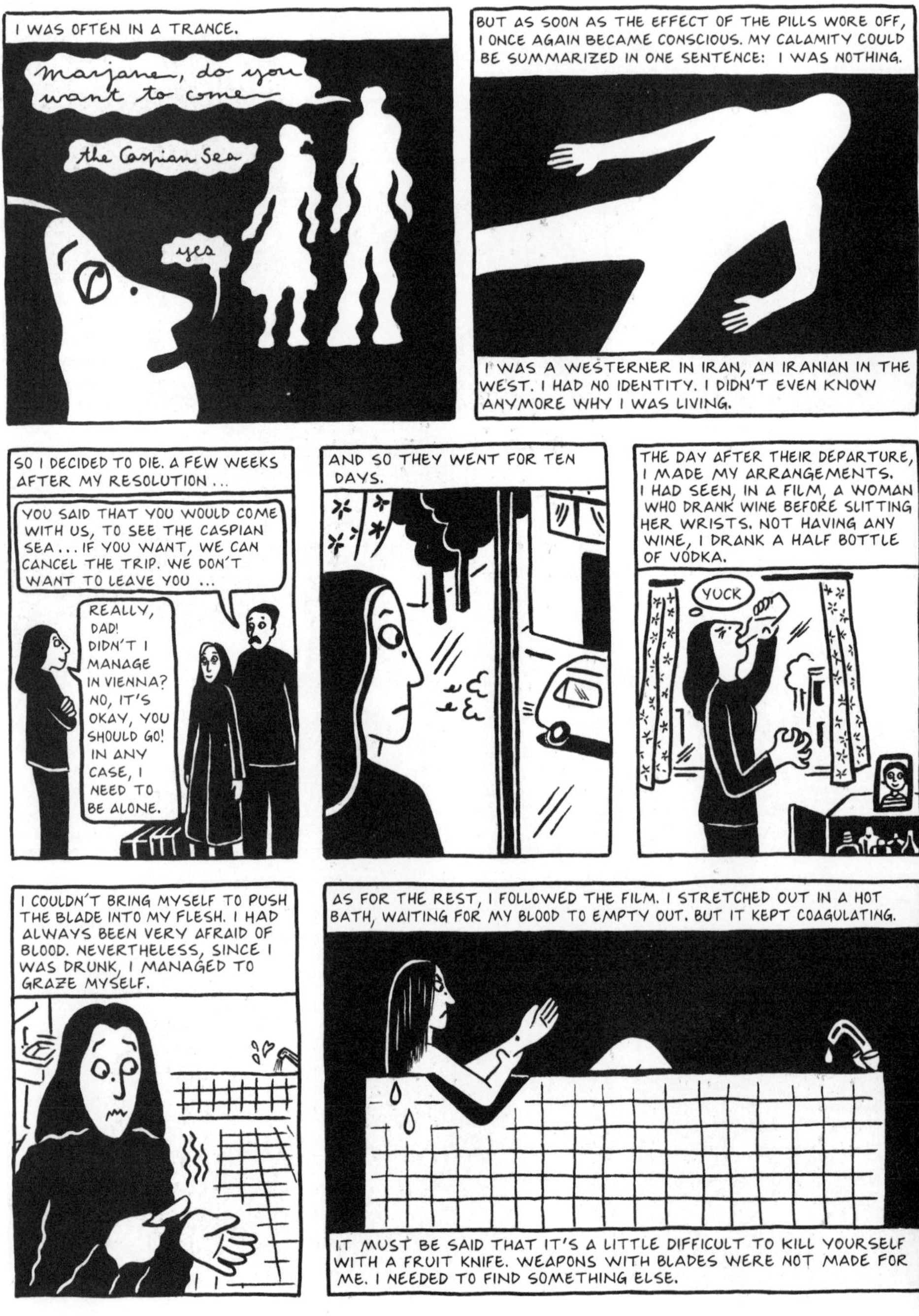
I WAS OFTEN IN A TRANCE.
marjane, do you want to come
the Caspian Sea
yes
BUT AS SOON AS THE EFFECT OF THE PILLS WORE OFF, I ONCE AGAIN BECAME CONSCIOUS. MY CALAMITY COULD BE SUMMARIZED IN ONE SENTENCE: I WAS NOTHING.
I WAS A WESTERNER IN IRAN, AN IRANIAN IN THE WEST. I HAD NO IDENTITY. I DIDN'T EVEN KNOW ANYMORE WHY I WAS LIVING.
SO I DECIDED TO DIE. A FEW WEEKS AFTER MY RESOLUTION ...
YOU SAID THAT YOU WOULD COME WITH US, TO SEE THE CASPIAN SEA... IF YOU WANT, WE CAN CANCEL THE TRIP. WE DON'T WANT TO LEAVE YOU ...
REALLY, DAD! DIDN'T I MANAGE IN VIENNA? NO, IT'S OKAY, YOU SHOULD GO! IN ANY CASE, I NEED TO BE ALONE.
AND SO THEY WENT FOR TEN DAYS.
THE DAY AFTER THEIR DEPARTURE, I MADE MY ARRANGEMENTS. I HAD SEEN, IN A FILM, A WOMAN WHO DRANK WINE BEFORE SLITTING HER WRISTS. NOT HAVING ANY WINE, I DRANK A HALF BOTTLE OF VODKA.
YUCK
I COULDN'T BRING MYSELF TO PUSH THE BLADE INTO MY FLESH. I HAD ALWAYS BEEN VERY AFRAID OF BLOOD. NEVERTHELESS, SINCE I WAS DRUNK, I MANAGED TO GRAZE MYSELF.
AS FOR THE REST, I FOLLOWED THE FILM. I STRETCHED OUT IN A HOT BATH, WAITING FOR MY BLOOD TO EMPTY OUT. BUT IT KEPT COAGULATING.
IT MUST BE SAID THAT IT'S A LITTLE DIFFICULT TO KILL YOURSELF WITH A FRUIT KNIFE. WEAPONS WITH BLADES WERE NOT MADE FOR ME. I NEEDED TO FIND SOMETHING ELSE.

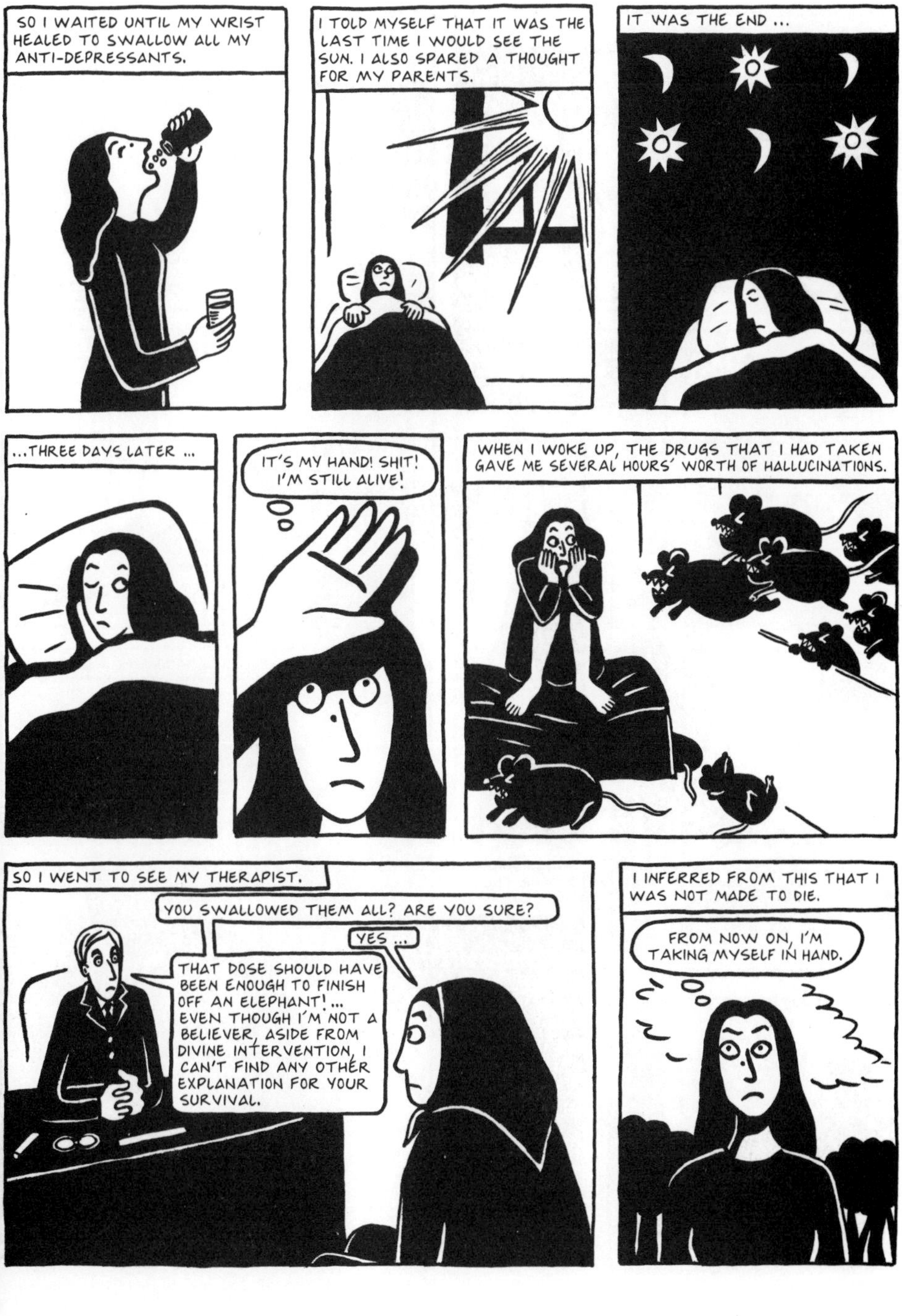
SO I WAITED UNTIL MY WRIST HEALED TO SWALLOW ALL MY ANTI-DEPRESSANTS.
I TOLD MYSELF THAT IT WAS THE LAST TIME I WOULD SEE THE SUN. I ALSO SPARED A THOUGHT FOR MY PARENTS.
IT WAS THE END...
...THREE DAYS LATER...
IT'S MY HAND! SHIT! I'M STILL ALIVE!
WHEN I WOKE UP, THE DRUGS THAT I HAD TAKEN GAVE ME SEVERAL HOURS' WORTH OF HALLUCINATIONS.
SO I WENT TO SEE MY THERAPIST.
YOU SWALLOWED THEM ALL? ARE YOU SURE?
YES...
THAT DOSE SHOULD HAVE BEEN ENOUGH TO FINISH OFF AN ELEPHANT!... EVEN THOUGH I'M NOT A BELIEVER, ASIDE FROM DIVINE INTERVENTION, I CAN'T FIND ANY OTHER EXPLANATION FOR YOUR SURVIVAL.
I INFERRED FROM THIS THAT I WAS NOT MADE TO DIE.
FROM NOW ON, I'M TAKING MYSELF IN HAND.

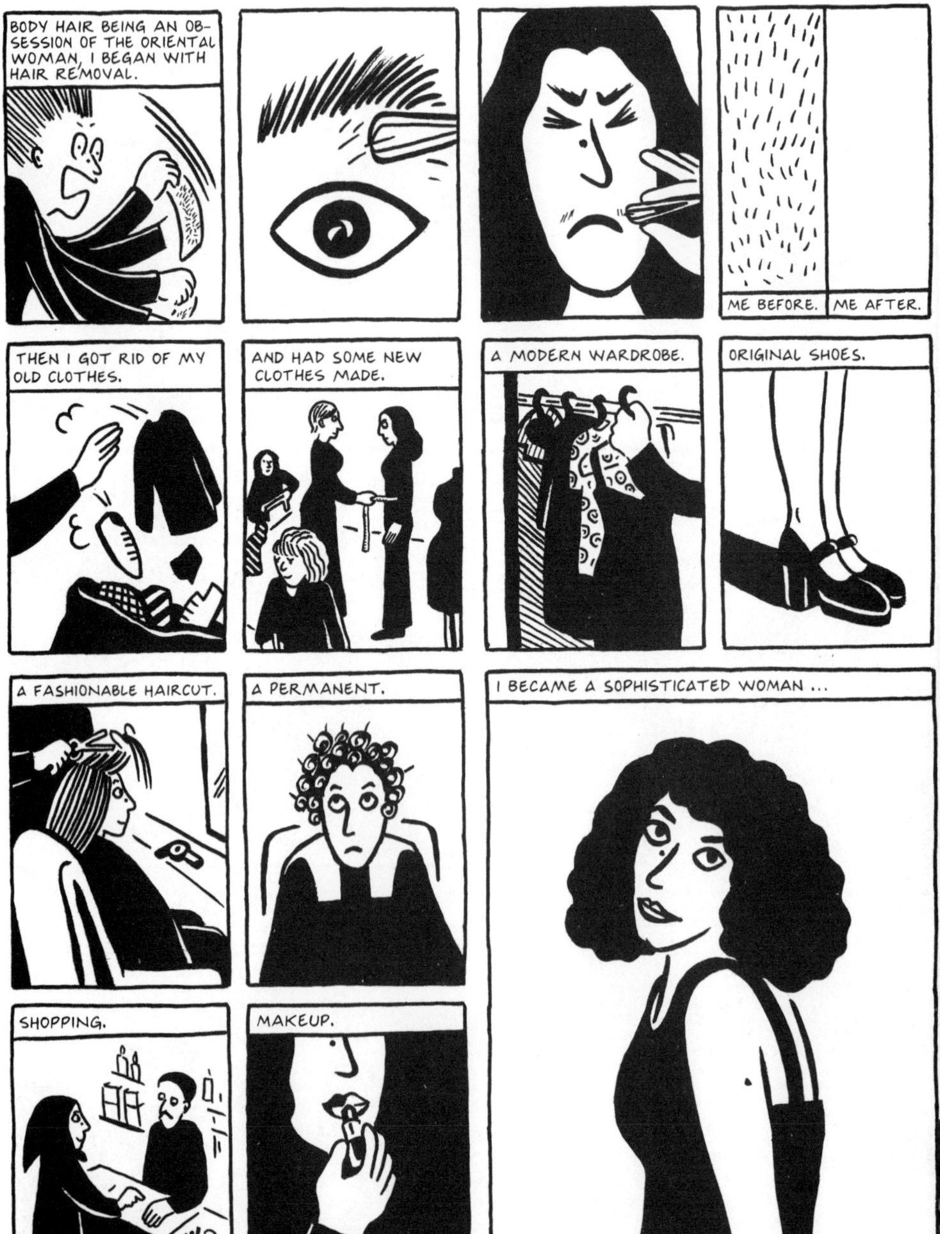
BODY HAIR BEING AN OBSESSION OF THE ORIENTAL WOMAN, I BEGAN WITH HAIR REMOVAL.
ME BEFORE.
ME AFTER.
THEN I GOT RID OF MY OLD CLOTHES.
AND HAD SOME NEW CLOTHES MADE.
A MODERN WARDROBE.
ORIGINAL SHOES.
A FASHIONABLE HAIRCUT.
A PERMANENT.
I BECAME A SOPHISTICATED WOMAN ...
SHOPPING.
MAKEUP.

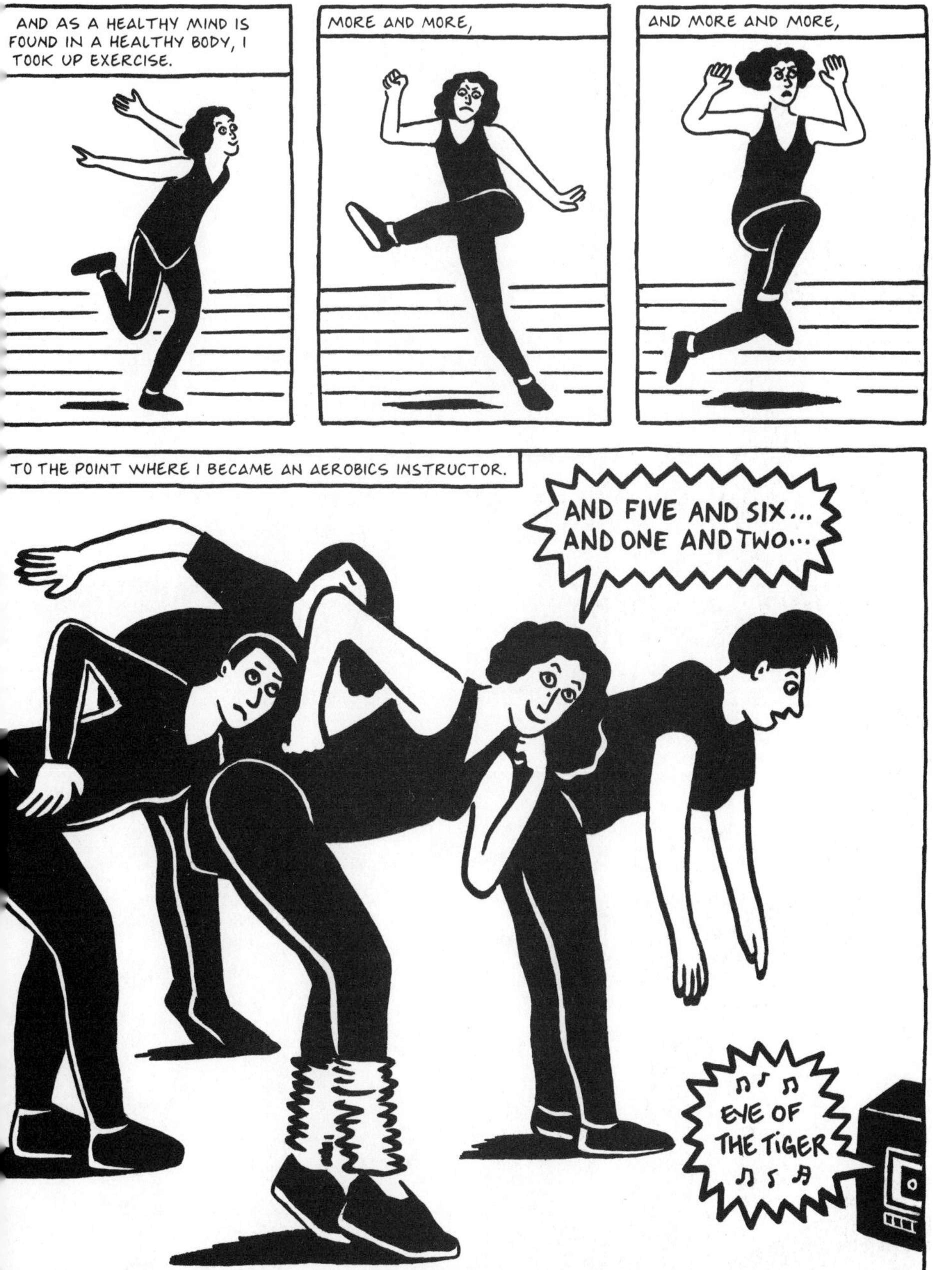
AND AS A HEALTHY MIND IS FOUND IN A HEALTHY BODY, I TOOK UP EXERCISE.
MORE AND MORE,
AND MORE AND MORE,
TO THE POINT WHERE I BECAME AN AEROBICS INSTRUCTOR.
AND FIVE AND SIX... AND ONE AND TWO...
EYE OF THE TIGER
STRONG AND INVINCIBLE LIKE THIS, I WAS GOING TO MEET MY NEW DESTINY.

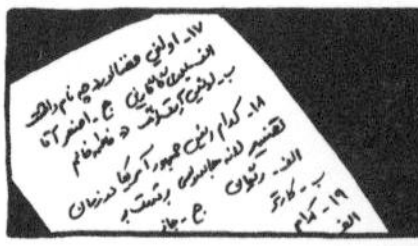

THE EXAM

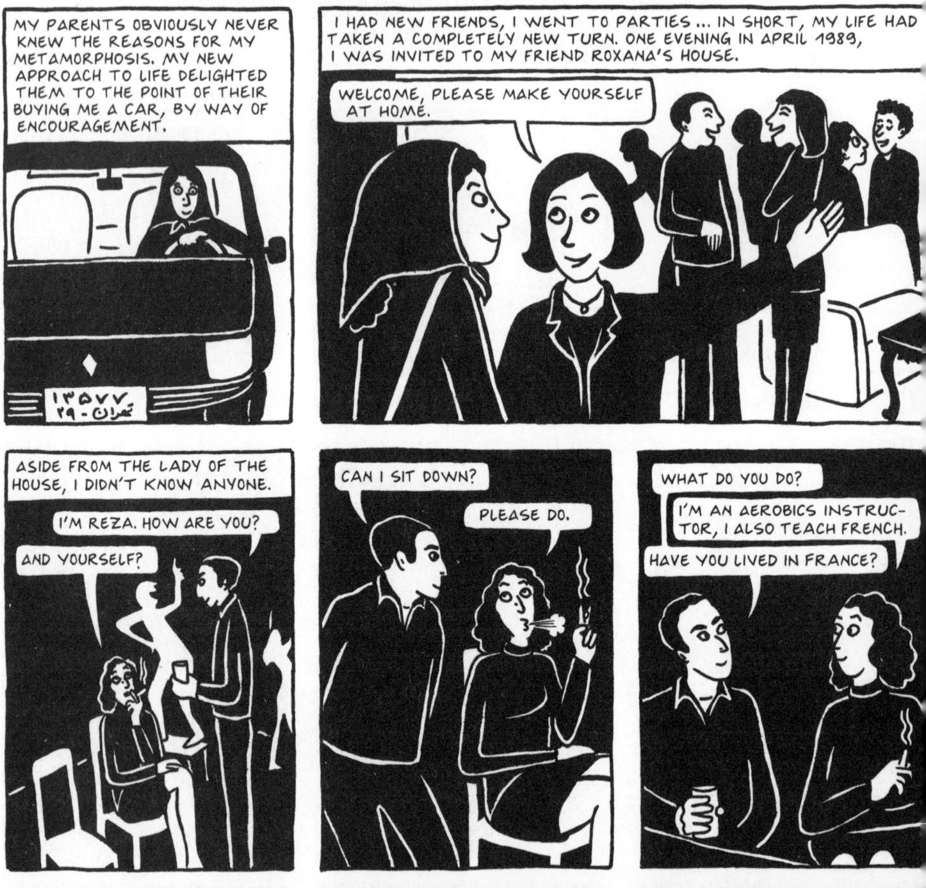
MY PARENTS OBVIOUSLY NEVER KNEW THE REASONS FOR MY METAMORPHOSIS. MY NEW APPROACH TO LIFE DELIGHTED THEM TO THE POINT OF THEIR BUYING ME A CAR, BY WAY OF ENCOURAGEMENT.
I HAD NEW FRIENDS, I WENT TO PARTIES... IN SHORT, MY LIFE HAD TAKEN A COMPLETELY NEW TURN. ONE EVENING IN APRIL 1989, I WAS INVITED TO MY FRIEND ROXANA'S HOUSE.
WELCOME, PLEASE MAKE YOURSELF AT HOME.
ASIDE FROM THE LADY OF THE HOUSE, I DIDN'T KNOW ANYONE.
I'M REZA. HOW ARE YOU?
AND YOURSELF?
CAN I SIT DOWN?
PLEASE DO.
WHAT DO YOU DO?
I'M AN AEROBICS INSTRUCTOR, I ALSO TEACH FRENCH.
HAVE YOU LIVED IN FRANCE?
NO, IN AUSTRIA, BUT I STUDIED AT THE LYCÉE FRANÇAIS IN TEHRAN AND IN VIENNA.
WERE YOU AT THE LYCÉE RAZI?*
YES, WERE YOU TOO?
NO, NOT ME, MY FRIENDS.
AND YOU? WHAT DO YOU DO?
PAINTING.
NO WAY! I PAINT TOO!!

*THE NAME OF THE LYCÉE FRANÇAIS IN TEHRAN.

OH YOU! EITHER YOU TALK OR YOU SMOKE! COME ON, COME DANCE A LITTLE!
WHO'S THAT GUY?
REZA? HE'S ONE OF OUR NEIGHBORS. BE CAREFUL! HE'S A LADIES' MAN . . .
. . . A MERCILESS SEDUCER!
OH REALLY? HE SEEMS VERY NICE.
OH YES, HE HIDES HIS GAME WELL!
OH, WHERE IS HE?
OUF!
ROXANA WAS WRONG.
HI AGAIN!
HI!
SORRY TO HAVE LEFT YOU BUT I HADN'T SEEN HAMID IN A WHILE.
WHO'S HAMID?
THAT GUY I WAS TALKING TO. WE WERE AT THE FRONT TOGETHER.
YOU WERE IN THE WAR?
YES, LIKE EVERYONE ELSE! BY THE WAY, HAVE YOU HEARD THE STORY OF THE SOLDIER WHO EXPLODED INTO A THOUSAND PIECES?
HE'S THE GUY WHO GETS MARRIED AND HAS HIS THING ON HIS HIP?
UHH . . . YEAH!
HEE, HEE, HEE ..HEE, HEE, HEE ...
IT'S TRUE THAT IT'S VERY FUNNY ...IT'S THE JOKE OF FORMER SOLDIERS.

*A MOUNTAIN CHAIN IN THE WEST OF IRAN

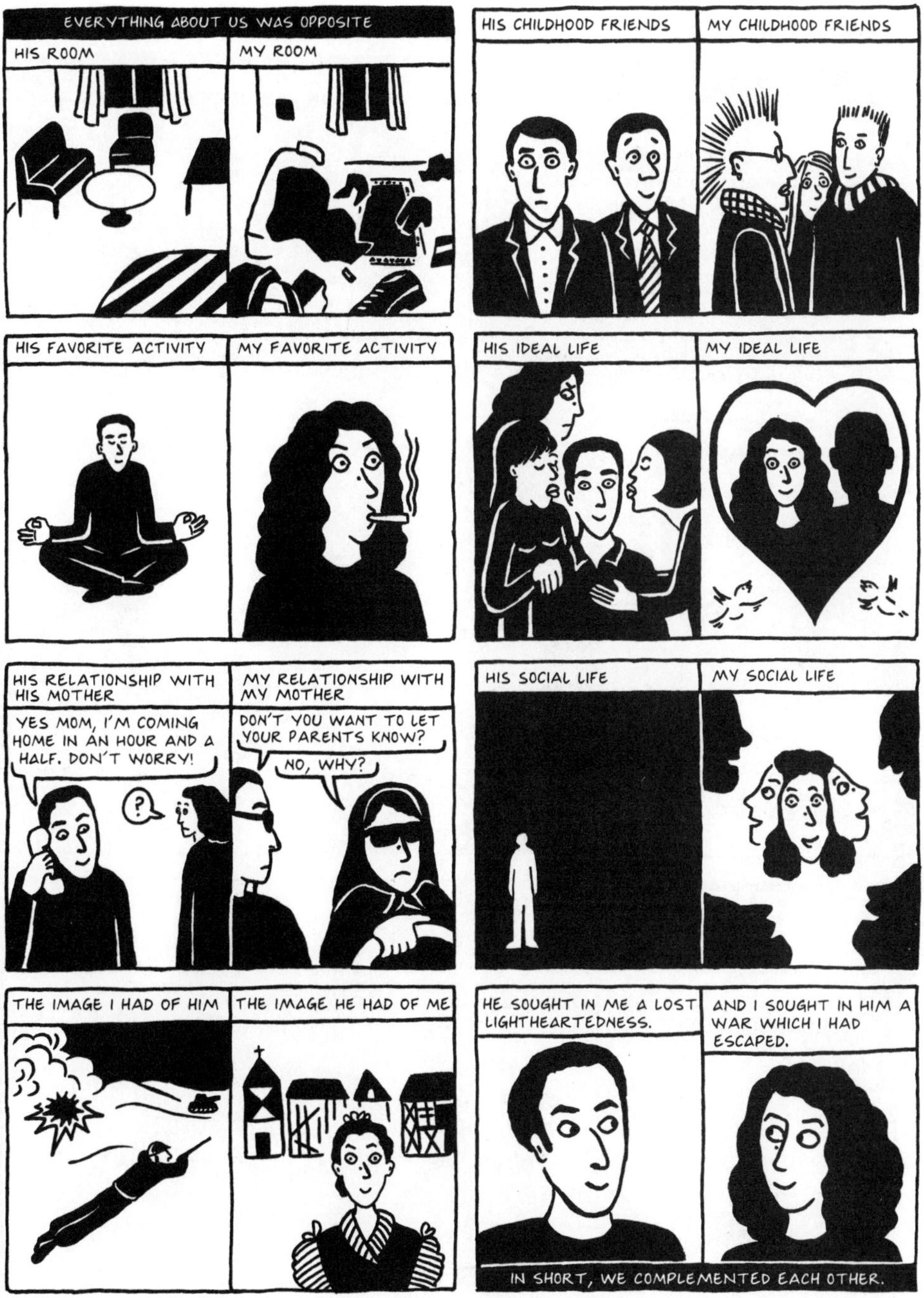
EVERYTHING ABOUT US WAS OPPOSITE
HIS ROOM
MY ROOM
HIS CHILDHOOD FRIENDS
MY CHILDHOOD FRIENDS
HIS FAVORITE ACTIVITY
MY FAVORITE ACTIVITY
HIS IDEAL LIFE
MY IDEAL LIFE
HIS RELATIONSHIP WITH HIS MOTHER
YES MOM, I'M COMING HOME IN AN HOUR AND A HALF. DON'T WORRY!
?
MY RELATIONSHIP WITH MY MOTHER
DON'T YOU WANT TO LET YOUR PARENTS KNOW?
NO, WHY?
HIS SOCIAL LIFE
MY SOCIAL LIFE
THE IMAGE I HAD OF HIM
THE IMAGE HE HAD OF ME
HE SOUGHT IN ME A LOST LIGHTHEARTEDNESS.
AND I SOUGHT IN HIM A WAR WHICH I HAD ESCAPED.
IN SHORT, WE COMPLEMENTED EACH OTHER.

WE NEEDED EACH OTHER SO MUCH THAT WE VERY QUICKLY STARTED TO TALK ABOUT OUR SHARED FUTURE.

WHAT DO YOU HAVE PLANNED FOR THE FUTURE?

I WANT TO LEAVE HERE. EITHER I'LL GO TO EUROPE, OR TO THE UNITED STATES, BUT I WON'T STAY HERE.

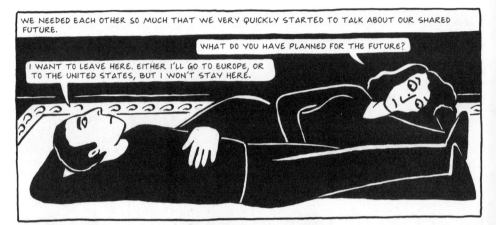

WHERE WILL YOU GO IN EUROPE?

ITALY, FRANCE, SWEDEN, SPAIN, ENGLAND... IT DOESN'T REALLY MATTER. I JUST DON'T WANT TO LIVE IN IRAN ANYMORE.

AND US?

YOU'LL COME WITH ME!

I DON'T WANT TO LEAVE THE COUNTRY RIGHT AWAY.

IT'S BECAUSE YOU ARE STILL NOSTALGIC. YOU'LL SEE, A YEAR FROM NOW PEOPLE WILL DISGUST YOU. ALWAYS INTERFERING IN THINGS THAT DON'T CONCERN THEM.

MAYBE SO, BUT IN THE WEST YOU CAN COLLAPSE IN THE STREET AND NO ONE WILL GIVE YOU A HAND.

DON'T WORRY! WE'LL FIND A SOLUTION!

HAPPILY, GETTING A VISA PROVED TO BE EXCEEDINGLY DIFFICULT. SO WE DECIDED TO STUDY FOR THE NATIONAL EXAM* SO AS NOT TO WASTE YEARS OF OUR LIVES DOING NOTHING. IT WAS VERY HARD! IT HAD BEEN SIX YEARS SINCE REZA HAD GRADUATED HIGH SCHOOL. HE WAS OUT OF PRACTICE FOR STUDYING. AS FOR ME, I HADN'T READ OR WRITTEN IN PERSIAN SINCE I WAS FOURTEEN.

* IN IRAN, YOU CAN'T ENTER UNIVERSITY WITHOUT HAVING PASSED THE NATIONAL EXAM.

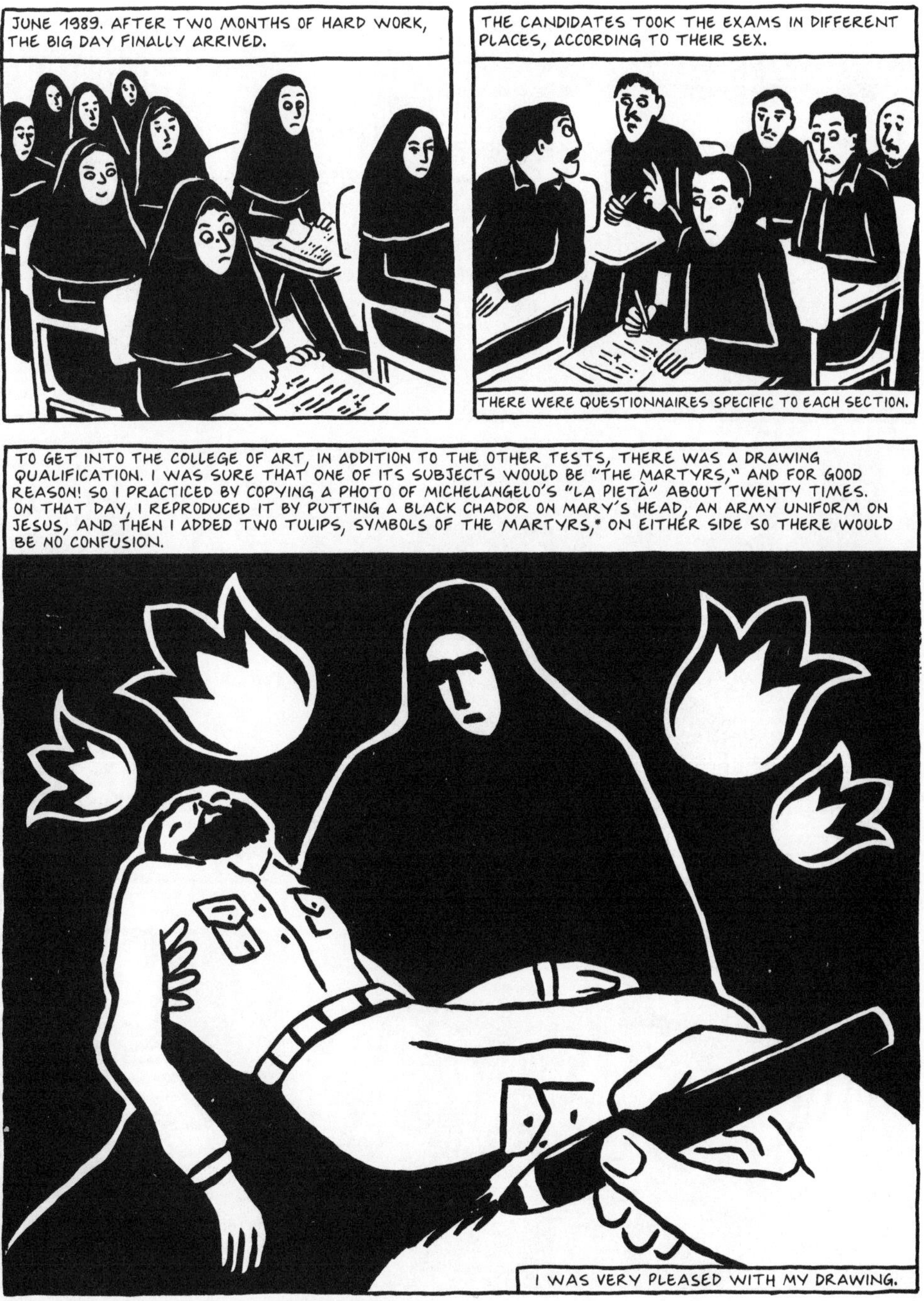
JUNE 1989. AFTER TWO MONTHS OF HARD WORK, THE BIG DAY FINALLY ARRIVED.
THE CANDIDATES TOOK THE EXAMS IN DIFFERENT PLACES, ACCORDING TO THEIR SEX.
THERE WERE QUESTIONNAIRES SPECIFIC TO EACH SECTION.
TO GET INTO THE COLLEGE OF ART, IN ADDITION TO THE OTHER TESTS, THERE WAS A DRAWING QUALIFICATION. I WAS SURE THAT ONE OF ITS SUBJECTS WOULD BE "THE MARTYRS," AND FOR GOOD REASON! SO I PRACTICED BY COPYING A PHOTO OF MICHELANGELO'S "LA PIETÀ" ABOUT TWENTY TIMES. ON THAT DAY, I REPRODUCED IT BY PUTTING A BLACK CHADOR ON MARY'S HEAD, AN ARMY UNIFORM ON JESUS, AND THEN I ADDED TWO TULIPS, SYMBOLS OF THE MARTYRS,* ON EITHER SIDE SO THERE WOULD BE NO CONFUSION.
I WAS VERY PLEASED WITH MY DRAWING.

*IT'S SAID THAT RED TULIPS GROW FROM THE BLOOD OF MARTYRS.

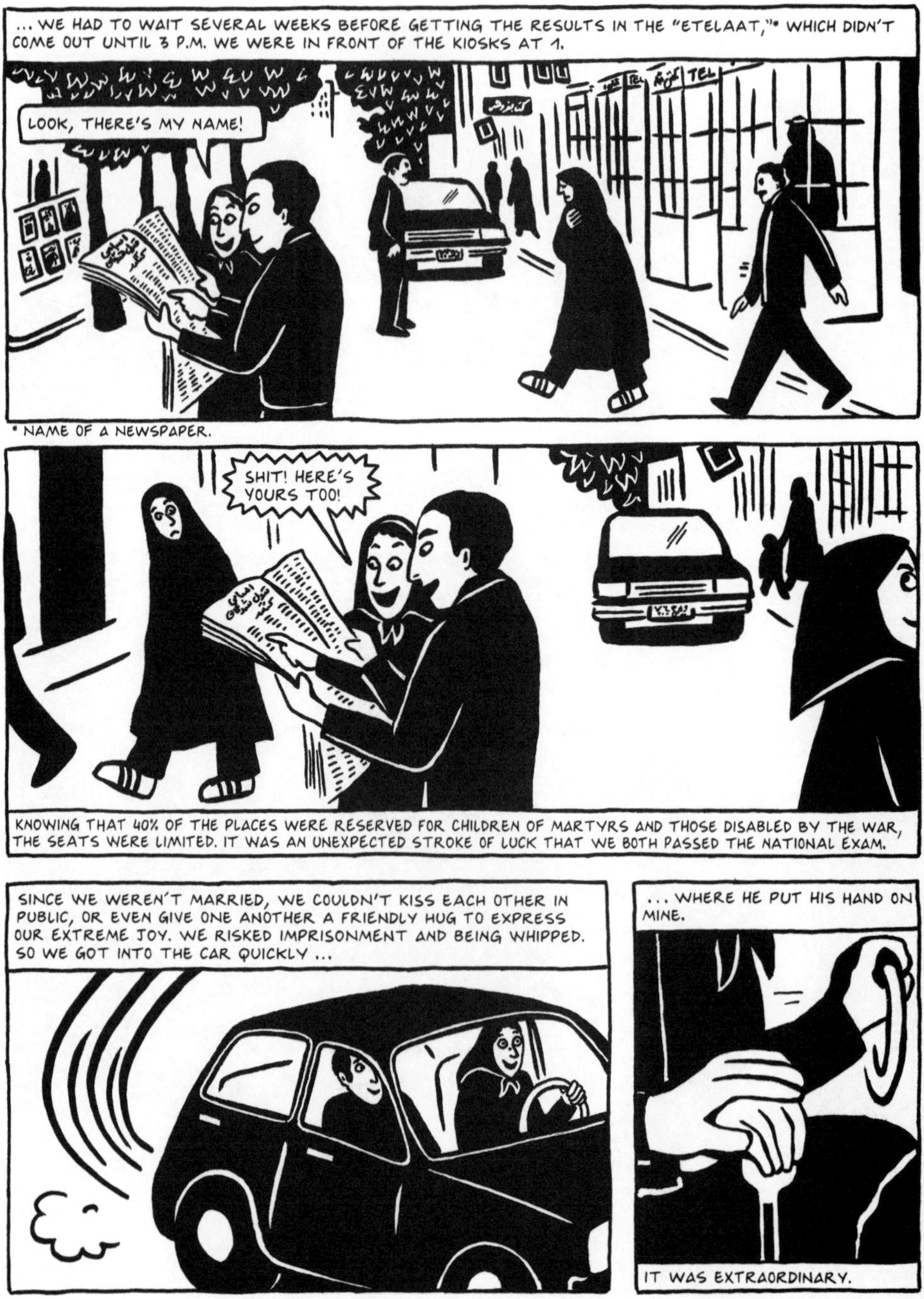
... WE HAD TO WAIT SEVERAL WEEKS BEFORE GETTING THE RESULTS IN THE "ETELAAT,"* WHICH DIDN'T COME OUT UNTIL 3 P.M. WE WERE IN FRONT OF THE KIOSKS AT 1.
TEL
LOOK, THERE'S MY NAME!
* NAME OF A NEWSPAPER.
SHIT! HERE'S YOURS TOO!
KNOWING THAT 40% OF THE PLACES WERE RESERVED FOR CHILDREN OF MARTYRS AND THOSE DISABLED BY THE WAR, THE SEATS WERE LIMITED. IT WAS AN UNEXPECTED STROKE OF LUCK THAT WE BOTH PASSED THE NATIONAL EXAM.
SINCE WE WEREN'T MARRIED, WE COULDN'T KISS EACH OTHER IN PUBLIC, OR EVEN GIVE ONE ANOTHER A FRIENDLY HUG TO EXPRESS OUR EXTREME JOY. WE RISKED IMPRISONMENT AND BEING WHIPPED. SO WE GOT INTO THE CAR QUICKLY ...
... WHERE HE PUT HIS HAND ON MINE.
IT WAS EXTRAORDINARY.

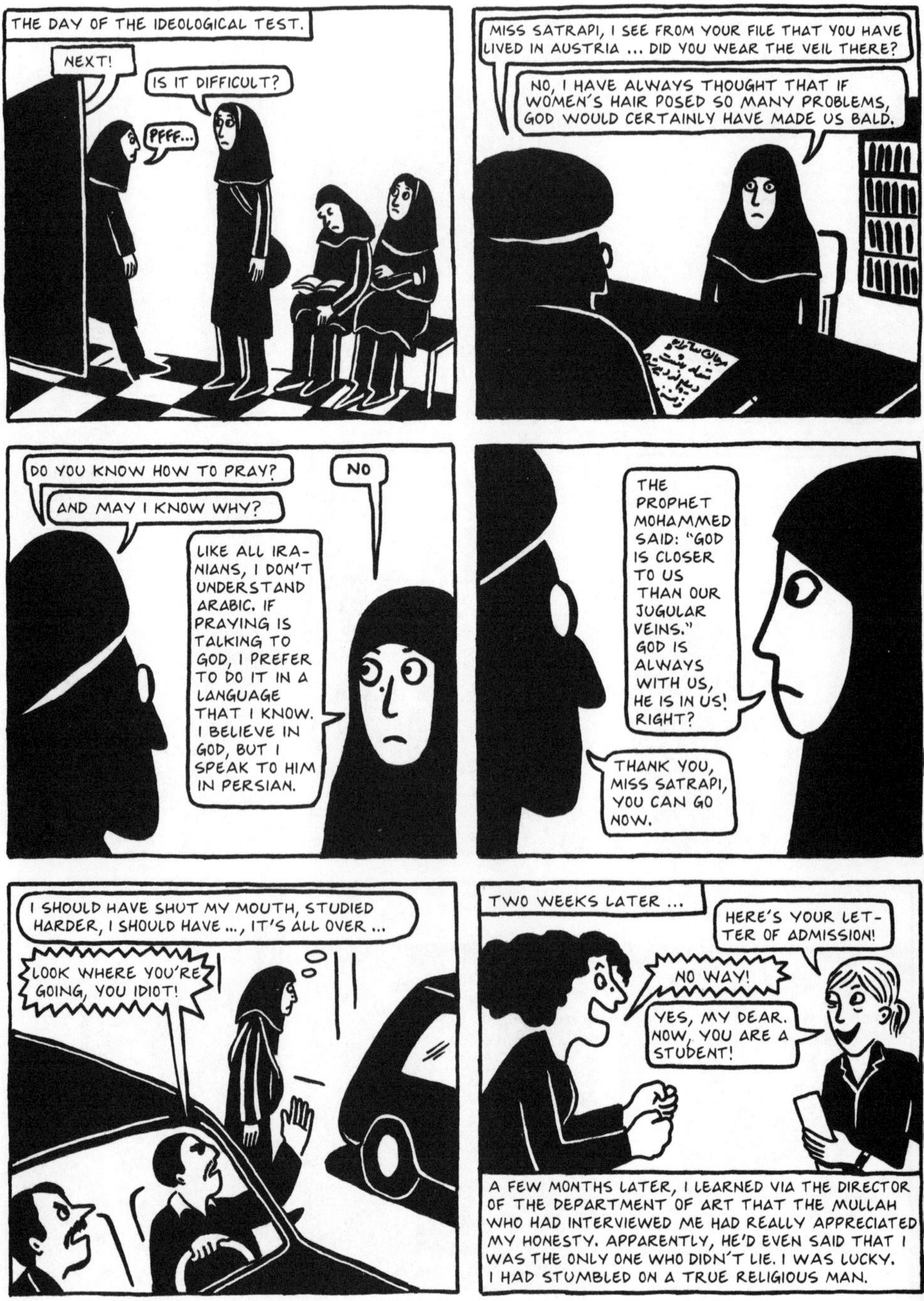
THE DAY OF THE IDEOLOGICAL TEST.
NEXT!
IS IT DIFFICULT?
PFFF...
MISS SATRAPI, I SEE FROM YOUR FILE THAT YOU HAVE LIVED IN AUSTRIA ... DID YOU WEAR THE VEIL THERE?
NO, I HAVE ALWAYS THOUGHT THAT IF WOMEN'S HAIR POSED SO MANY PROBLEMS, GOD WOULD CERTAINLY HAVE MADE US BALD.
DO YOU KNOW HOW TO PRAY?
NO
AND MAY I KNOW WHY?
LIKE ALL IRANIANS, I DON'T UNDERSTAND ARABIC. IF PRAYING IS TALKING TO GOD, I PREFER TO DO IT IN A LANGUAGE THAT I KNOW. I BELIEVE IN GOD, BUT I SPEAK TO HIM IN PERSIAN.
THE PROPHET MOHAMMED SAID: "GOD IS CLOSER TO US THAN OUR JUGULAR VEINS." GOD IS ALWAYS WITH US, HE IS IN US! RIGHT?
THANK YOU, MISS SATRAPI, YOU CAN GO NOW.
I SHOULD HAVE SHUT MY MOUTH, STUDIED HARDER, I SHOULD HAVE ..., IT'S ALL OVER ...
LOOK WHERE YOU'RE GOING, YOU IDIOT!
TWO WEEKS LATER ...
HERE'S YOUR LETTER OF ADMISSION!
NO WAY!
YES, MY DEAR. NOW, YOU ARE A STUDENT!
A FEW MONTHS LATER, I LEARNED VIA THE DIRECTOR OF THE DEPARTMENT OF ART THAT THE MULLAH WHO HAD INTERVIEWED ME HAD REALLY APPRECIATED MY HONESTY. APPARENTLY, HE'D EVEN SAID THAT I WAS THE ONLY ONE WHO DIDN'T LIE. I WAS LUCKY. I HAD STUMBLED ON A TRUE RELIGIOUS MAN.

THE MAKEUP

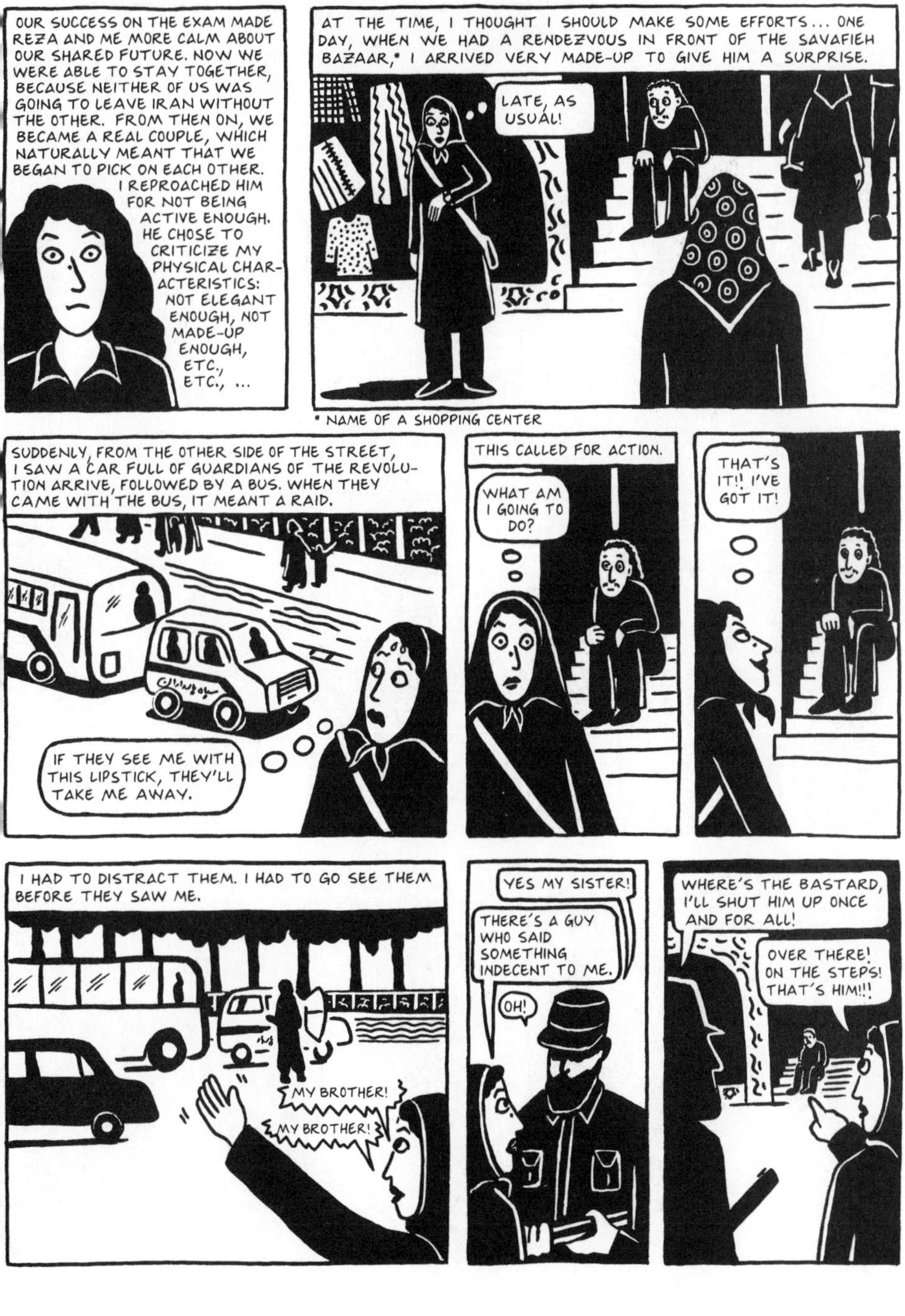
OUR SUCCESS ON THE EXAM MADE REZA AND ME MORE CALM ABOUT OUR SHARED FUTURE. NOW WE WERE ABLE TO STAY TOGETHER, BECAUSE NEITHER OF US WAS GOING TO LEAVE IRAN WITHOUT THE OTHER. FROM THEN ON, WE BECAME A REAL COUPLE, WHICH NATURALLY MEANT THAT WE BEGAN TO PICK ON EACH OTHER.
I REPROACHED HIM FOR NOT BEING ACTIVE ENOUGH. HE CHOSE TO CRITICIZE MY PHYSICAL CHARACTERISTICS: NOT ELEGANT ENOUGH, NOT MADE-UP ENOUGH, ETC., ETC., ...
AT THE TIME, I THOUGHT I SHOULD MAKE SOME EFFORTS... ONE DAY, WHEN WE HAD A RENDEZVOUS IN FRONT OF THE SAVAFIEH BAZAAR,* I ARRIVED VERY MADE-UP TO GIVE HIM A SURPRISE.
LATE, AS USUAL!
SUDDENLY, FROM THE OTHER SIDE OF THE STREET, I SAW A CAR FULL OF GUARDIANS OF THE REVOLUTION ARRIVE, FOLLOWED BY A BUS. WHEN THEY CAME WITH THE BUS, IT MEANT A RAID.
IF THEY SEE ME WITH THIS LIPSTICK, THEY'LL TAKE ME AWAY.
THIS CALLED FOR ACTION.
WHAT AM I GOING TO DO?
THAT'S IT!! I'VE GOT IT!
I HAD TO DISTRACT THEM. I HAD TO GO SEE THEM BEFORE THEY SAW ME.
MY BROTHER!
MY BROTHER!
YES MY SISTER!
THERE'S A GUY WHO SAID SOMETHING INDECENT TO ME.
OH!
WHERE'S THE BASTARD, I'LL SHUT HIM UP ONCE AND FOR ALL!
OVER THERE! ON THE STEPS! THAT'S HIM!!!

* NAME OF A SHOPPING CENTER

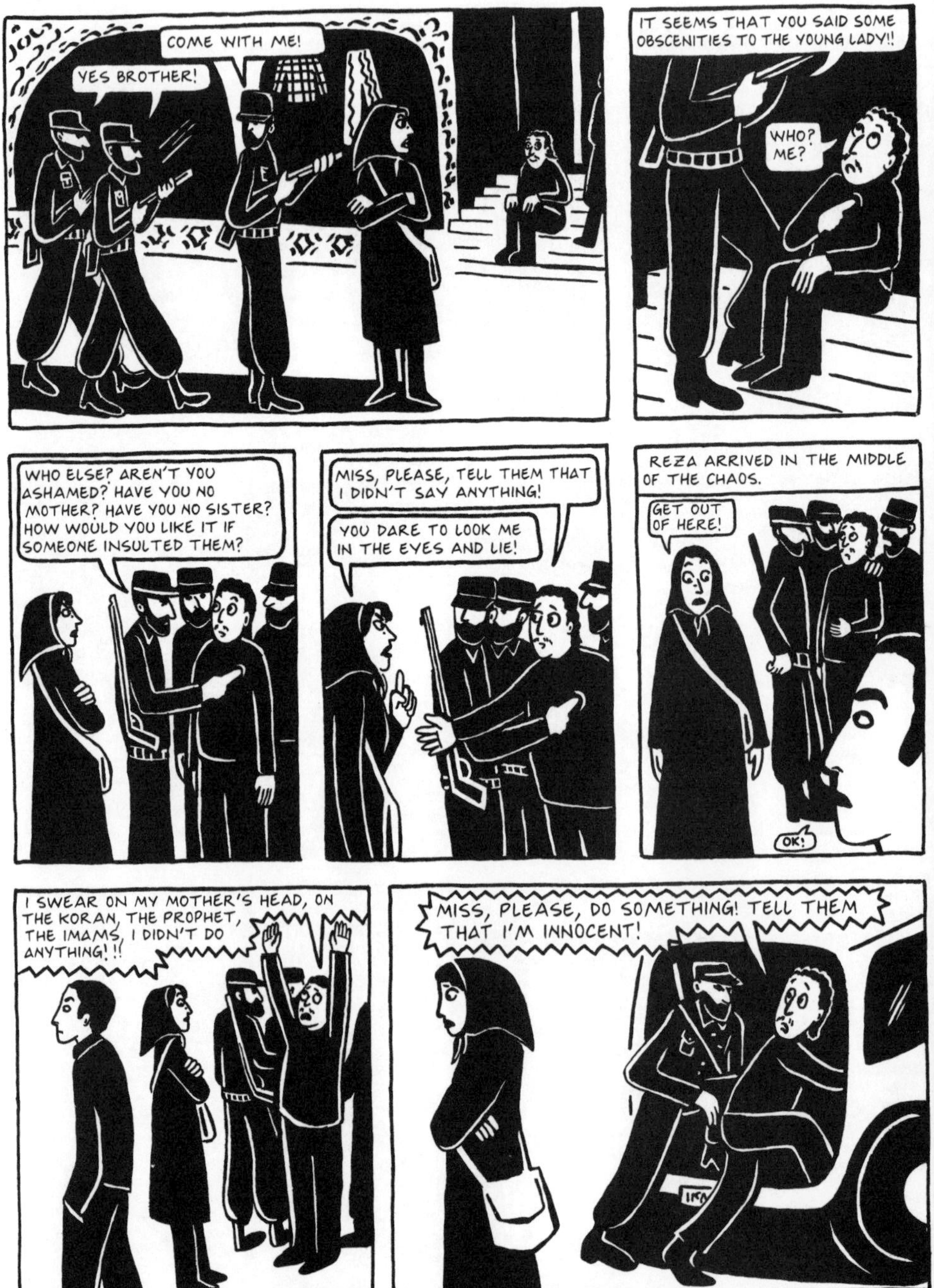
YES BROTHER!
COME WITH ME!
IT SEEMS THAT YOU SAID SOME OBSCENITIES TO THE YOUNG LADY!!
WHO? ME?
WHO ELSE? AREN'T YOU ASHAMED? HAVE YOU NO MOTHER? HAVE YOU NO SISTER? HOW WOULD YOU LIKE IT IF SOMEONE INSULTED THEM?
MISS, PLEASE, TELL THEM THAT I DIDN'T SAY ANYTHING!
YOU DARE TO LOOK ME IN THE EYES AND LIE!
REZA ARRIVED IN THE MIDDLE OF THE CHAOS.
GET OUT OF HERE!
OK!
I SWEAR ON MY MOTHER'S HEAD, ON THE KORAN, THE PROPHET, THE IMAMS, I DIDN'T DO ANYTHING!!!
MISS, PLEASE, DO SOMETHING! TELL THEM THAT I'M INNOCENT!

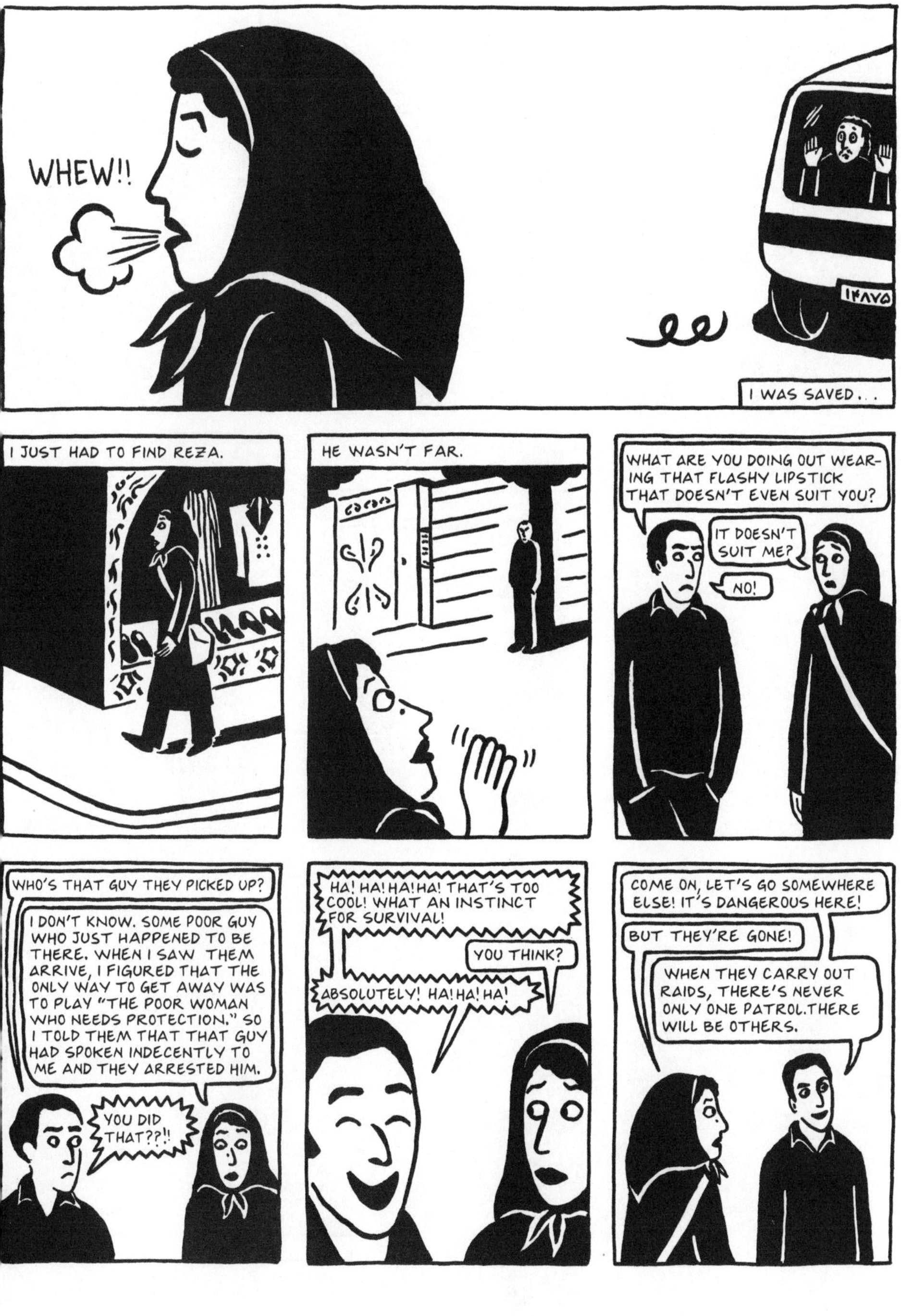
WHEW!!
I WAS SAVED...
I JUST HAD TO FIND REZA.
HE WASN'T FAR.
WHAT ARE YOU DOING OUT WEARING THAT FLASHY LIPSTICK THAT DOESN'T EVEN SUIT YOU?
IT DOESN'T SUIT ME?
NO!
WHO'S THAT GUY THEY PICKED UP?
I DON'T KNOW. SOME POOR GUY WHO JUST HAPPENED TO BE THERE. WHEN I SAW THEM ARRIVE, I FIGURED THAT THE ONLY WAY TO GET AWAY WAS TO PLAY "THE POOR WOMAN WHO NEEDS PROTECTION." SO I TOLD THEM THAT THAT GUY HAD SPOKEN INDECENTLY TO ME AND THEY ARRESTED HIM.
YOU DID THAT??!!
HA! HA! HA! HA! THAT'S TOO COOL! WHAT AN INSTINCT FOR SURVIVAL!
YOU THINK?
ABSOLUTELY! HA! HA! HA!
COME ON, LET'S GO SOMEWHERE ELSE! IT'S DANGEROUS HERE!
BUT THEY'RE GONE!
WHEN THEY CARRY OUT RAIDS, THERE'S NEVER ONLY ONE PATROL. THERE WILL BE OTHERS.

*THE COMMISSARIAT OF THE GUARDIANS OF THE REVOLUTION.
**AT THE TIME, THE MONTHLY SALARY OF A GOVERNMENT WORKER.

135

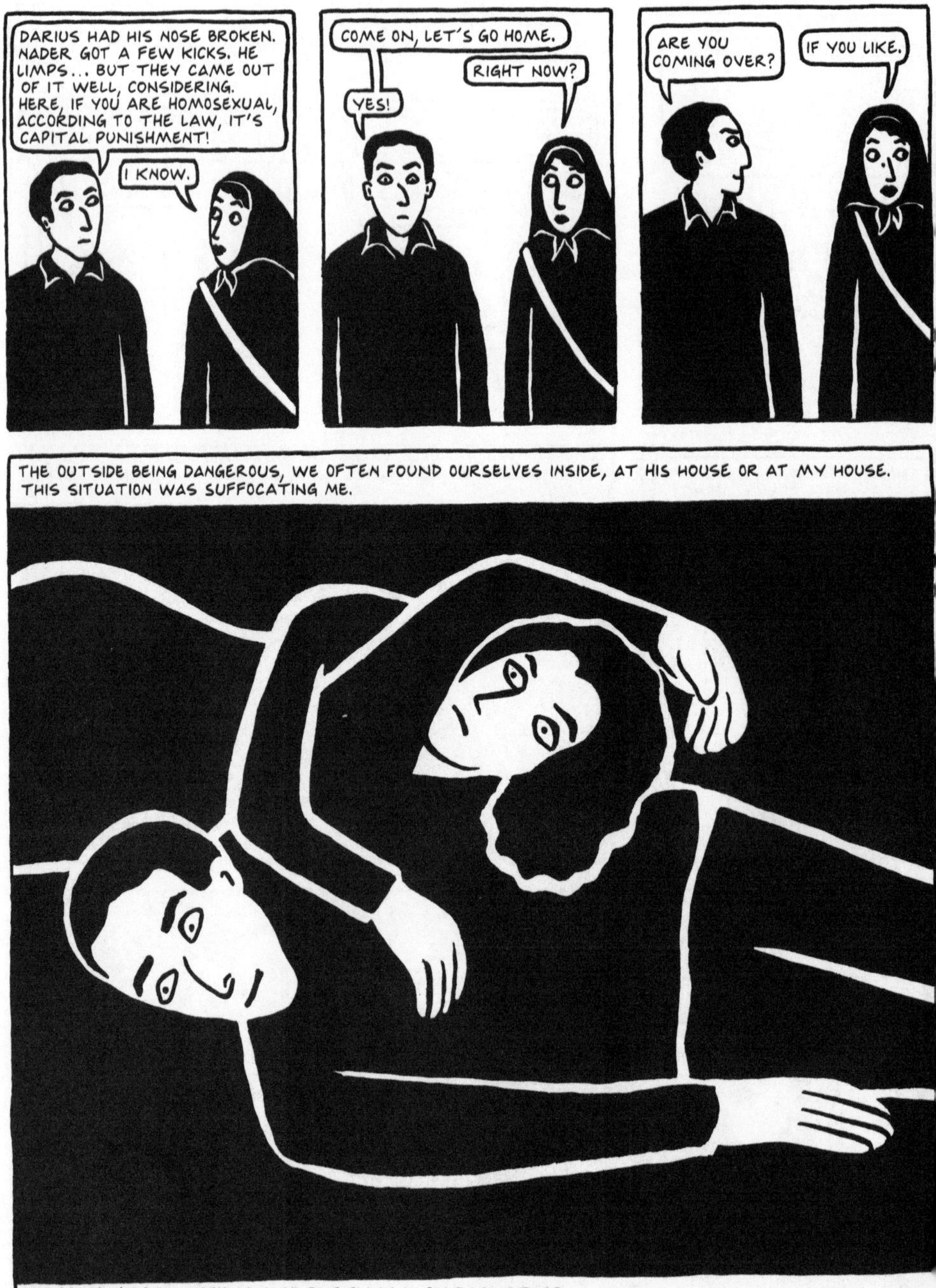
DARIUS HAD HIS NOSE BROKEN. NADER GOT A FEW KICKS. HE LIMPS... BUT THEY CAME OUT OF IT WELL, CONSIDERING. HERE, IF YOU ARE HOMOSEXUAL, ACCORDING TO THE LAW, IT'S CAPITAL PUNISHMENT!
I KNOW.
COME ON, LET'S GO HOME.
RIGHT NOW?
YES!
ARE YOU COMING OVER?
IF YOU LIKE.
THE OUTSIDE BEING DANGEROUS, WE OFTEN FOUND OURSELVES INSIDE, AT HIS HOUSE OR AT MY HOUSE. THIS SITUATION WAS SUFFOCATING ME.
WE COULDN'T DO ANYTHING ELSE BUT CLOSE IN ON EACH OTHER.

THE CONVOCATION

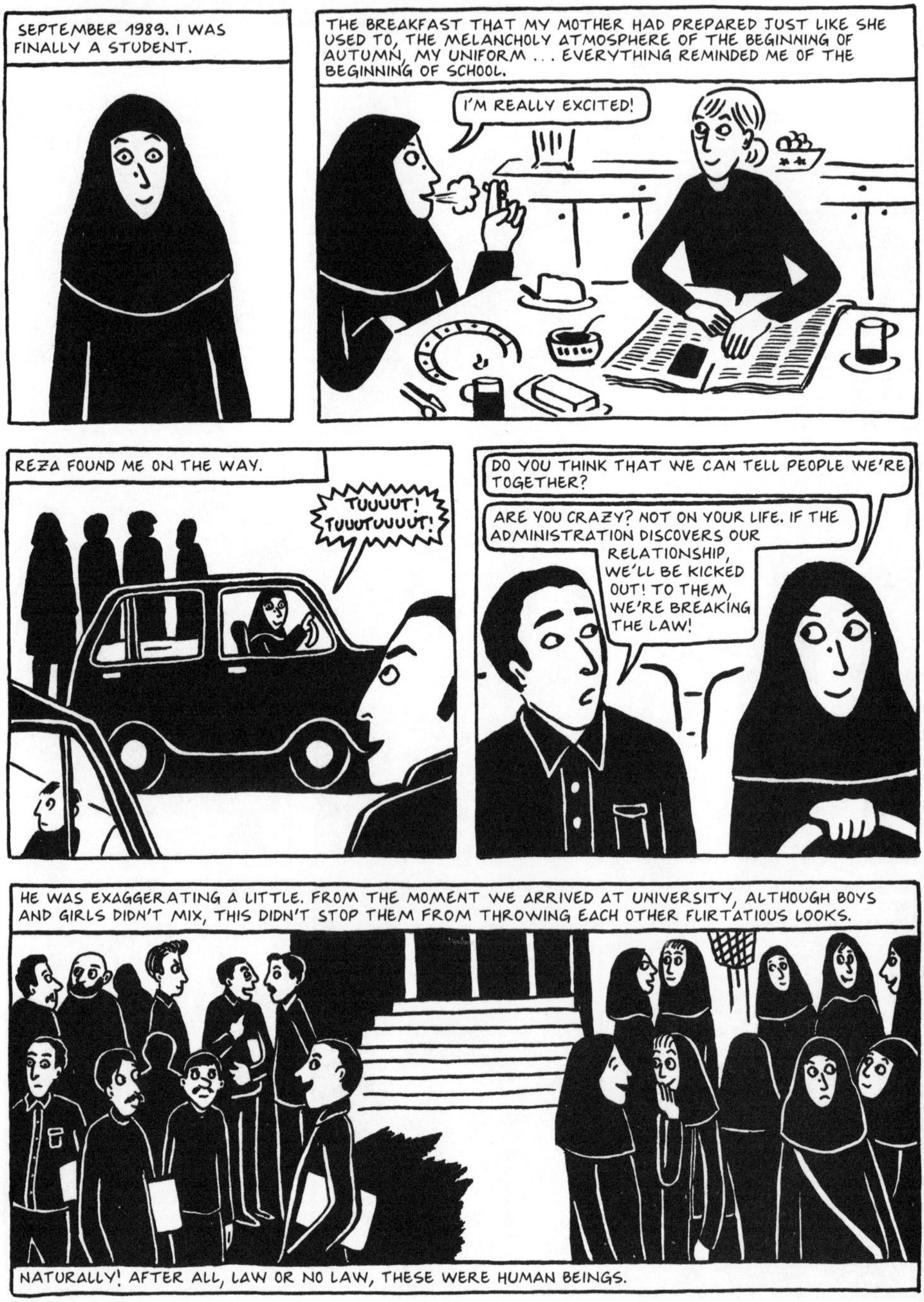
SEPTEMBER 1989. I WAS FINALLY A STUDENT.
THE BREAKFAST THAT MY MOTHER HAD PREPARED JUST LIKE SHE USED TO, THE MELANCHOLY ATMOSPHERE OF THE BEGINNING OF AUTUMN, MY UNIFORM . . . EVERYTHING REMINDED ME OF THE BEGINNING OF SCHOOL.
I'M REALLY EXCITED!
REZA FOUND ME ON THE WAY.
TUUUUT! TUUUTUUUUT!
DO YOU THINK THAT WE CAN TELL PEOPLE WE'RE TOGETHER?
ARE YOU CRAZY? NOT ON YOUR LIFE. IF THE ADMINISTRATION DISCOVERS OUR RELATIONSHIP, WE'LL BE KICKED OUT! TO THEM, WE'RE BREAKING THE LAW!
HE WAS EXAGGERATING A LITTLE. FROM THE MOMENT WE ARRIVED AT UNIVERSITY, ALTHOUGH BOYS AND GIRLS DIDN'T MIX, THIS DIDN'T STOP THEM FROM THROWING EACH OTHER FLIRTATIOUS LOOKS.
NATURALLY! AFTER ALL, LAW OR NO LAW, THESE WERE HUMAN BEINGS.

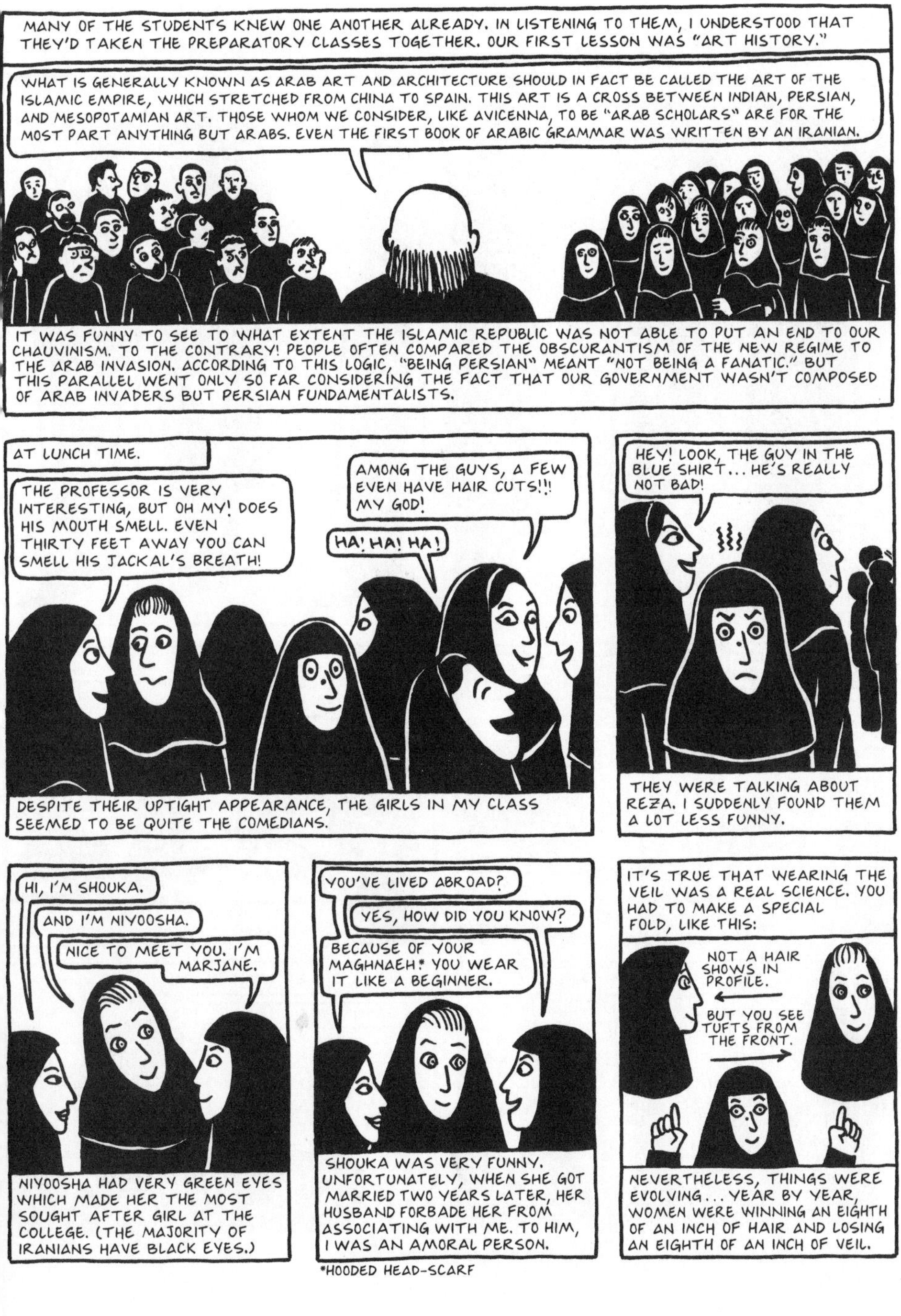
MANY OF THE STUDENTS KNEW ONE ANOTHER ALREADY. IN LISTENING TO THEM, I UNDERSTOOD THAT THEY'D TAKEN THE PREPARATORY CLASSES TOGETHER. OUR FIRST LESSON WAS "ART HISTORY."
WHAT IS GENERALLY KNOWN AS ARAB ART AND ARCHITECTURE SHOULD IN FACT BE CALLED THE ART OF THE ISLAMIC EMPIRE, WHICH STRETCHED FROM CHINA TO SPAIN. THIS ART IS A CROSS BETWEEN INDIAN, PERSIAN, AND MESOPOTAMIAN ART. THOSE WHOM WE CONSIDER, LIKE AVICENNA, TO BE "ARAB SCHOLARS" ARE FOR THE MOST PART ANYTHING BUT ARABS. EVEN THE FIRST BOOK OF ARABIC GRAMMAR WAS WRITTEN BY AN IRANIAN.
IT WAS FUNNY TO SEE TO WHAT EXTENT THE ISLAMIC REPUBLIC WAS NOT ABLE TO PUT AN END TO OUR CHAUVINISM. TO THE CONTRARY! PEOPLE OFTEN COMPARED THE OBSCURANTISM OF THE NEW REGIME TO THE ARAB INVASION. ACCORDING TO THIS LOGIC, "BEING PERSIAN" MEANT "NOT BEING A FANATIC." BUT THIS PARALLEL WENT ONLY SO FAR CONSIDERING THE FACT THAT OUR GOVERNMENT WASN'T COMPOSED OF ARAB INVADERS BUT PERSIAN FUNDAMENTALISTS.
AT LUNCH TIME.
THE PROFESSOR IS VERY INTERESTING, BUT OH MY! DOES HIS MOUTH SMELL. EVEN THIRTY FEET AWAY YOU CAN SMELL HIS JACKAL'S BREATH!
AMONG THE GUYS, A FEW EVEN HAVE HAIR CUTS!!! MY GOD!
HA! HA! HA!
DESPITE THEIR UPTIGHT APPEARANCE, THE GIRLS IN MY CLASS SEEMED TO BE QUITE THE COMEDIANS.
HEY! LOOK, THE GUY IN THE BLUE SHIRT... HE'S REALLY NOT BAD!
THEY WERE TALKING ABOUT REZA. I SUDDENLY FOUND THEM A LOT LESS FUNNY.
HI, I'M SHOUKA.
AND I'M NIYOOSHA.
NICE TO MEET YOU. I'M MARJANE.
NIYOOSHA HAD VERY GREEN EYES WHICH MADE HER THE MOST SOUGHT AFTER GIRL AT THE COLLEGE. (THE MAJORITY OF IRANIANS HAVE BLACK EYES.)
YOU'VE LIVED ABROAD?
YES, HOW DID YOU KNOW?
BECAUSE OF YOUR MAGHNAEH* YOU WEAR IT LIKE A BEGINNER.
SHOUKA WAS VERY FUNNY. UNFORTUNATELY, WHEN SHE GOT MARRIED TWO YEARS LATER, HER HUSBAND FORBADE HER FROM ASSOCIATING WITH ME. TO HIM, I WAS AN AMORAL PERSON.
IT'S TRUE THAT WEARING THE VEIL WAS A REAL SCIENCE. YOU HAD TO MAKE A SPECIAL FOLD, LIKE THIS:
NOT A HAIR SHOWS IN PROFILE.
BUT YOU SEE TUFTS FROM THE FRONT.
NEVERTHELESS, THINGS WERE EVOLVING... YEAR BY YEAR, WOMEN WERE WINNING AN EIGHTH OF AN INCH OF HAIR AND LOSING AN EIGHTH OF AN INCH OF VEIL.

*HOODED HEAD-SCARF

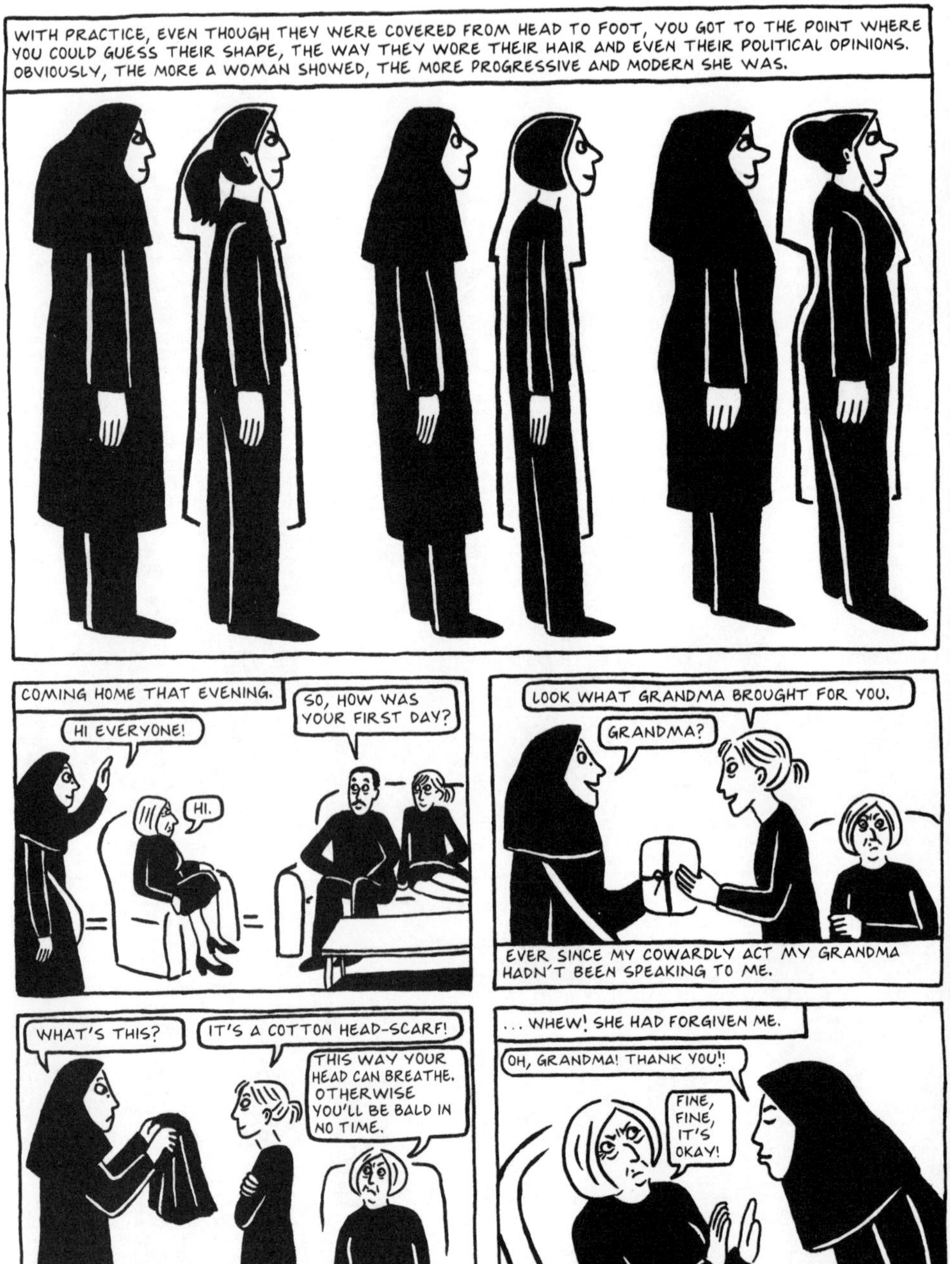
WITH PRACTICE, EVEN THOUGH THEY WERE COVERED FROM HEAD TO FOOT, YOU GOT TO THE POINT WHERE YOU COULD GUESS THEIR SHAPE, THE WAY THEY WORE THEIR HAIR AND EVEN THEIR POLITICAL OPINIONS. OBVIOUSLY, THE MORE A WOMAN SHOWED, THE MORE PROGRESSIVE AND MODERN SHE WAS.
COMING HOME THAT EVENING.
HI EVERYONE!
SO, HOW WAS YOUR FIRST DAY?
HI.
LOOK WHAT GRANDMA BROUGHT FOR YOU.
GRANDMA?
EVER SINCE MY COWARDLY ACT MY GRANDMA HADN'T BEEN SPEAKING TO ME.
WHAT'S THIS?
IT'S A COTTON HEAD-SCARF!
THIS WAY YOUR HEAD CAN BREATHE. OTHERWISE YOU'LL BE BALD IN NO TIME.
SHE HAD GIVEN ME A GIFT, SHE HAD THOUGHT OF MY HAIR, SHE WAS TALKING TO ME ...
... WHEW! SHE HAD FORGIVEN ME.
OH, GRANDMA! THANK YOU!!
FINE, FINE, IT'S OKAY!
I HAD FORGOTTEN HER EXTREME INTRANSIGENCE.

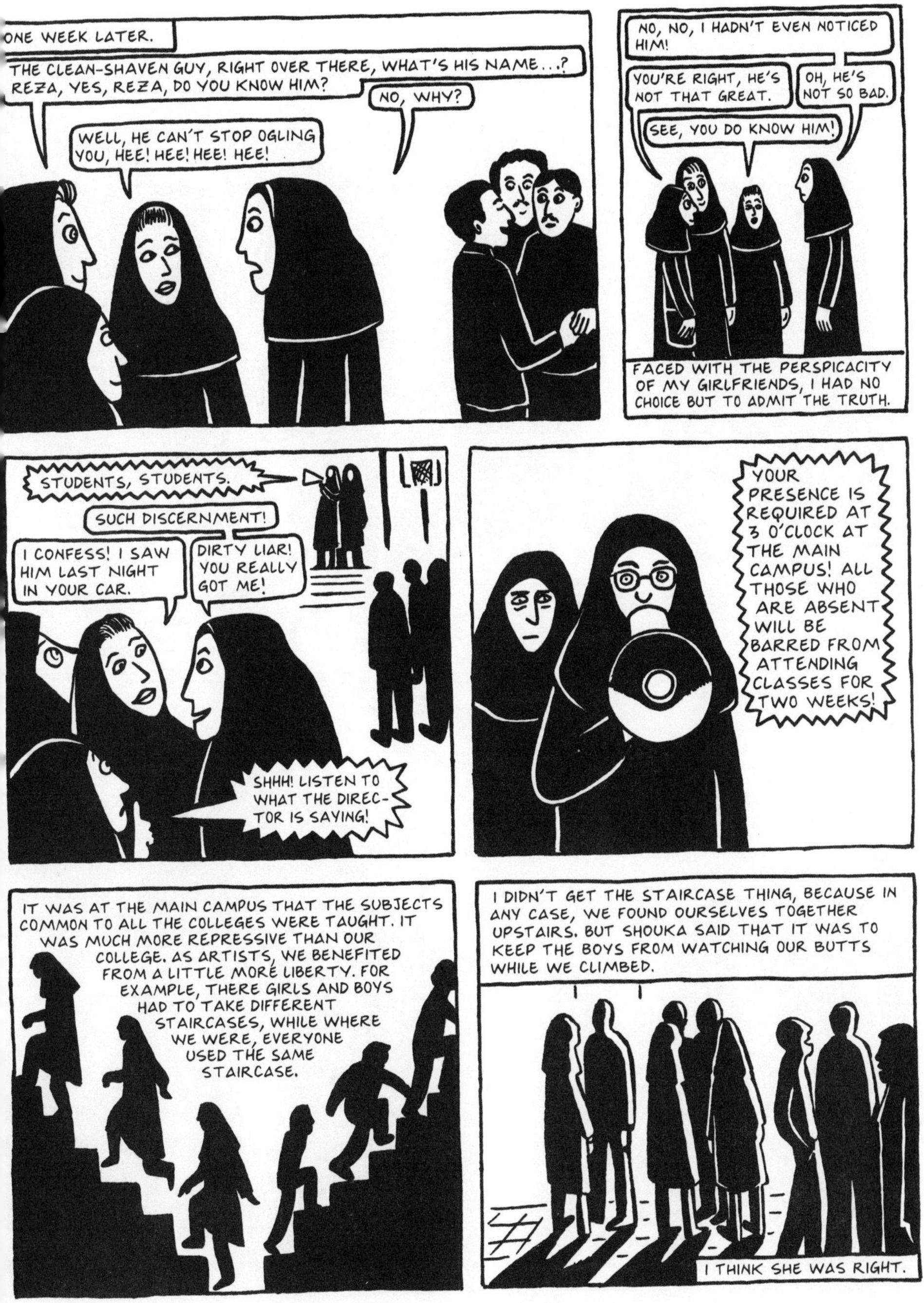
ONE WEEK LATER.
THE CLEAN-SHAVEN GUY, RIGHT OVER THERE, WHAT'S HIS NAME...? REZA, YES, REZA, DO YOU KNOW HIM?
NO, WHY?
WELL, HE CAN'T STOP OGLING YOU, HEE! HEE! HEE! HEE!
NO, NO, I HADN'T EVEN NOTICED HIM!
YOU'RE RIGHT, HE'S NOT THAT GREAT.
OH, HE'S NOT SO BAD.
SEE, YOU DO KNOW HIM!
FACED WITH THE PERSPICACITY OF MY GIRLFRIENDS, I HAD NO CHOICE BUT TO ADMIT THE TRUTH.
STUDENTS, STUDENTS.
SUCH DISCERNMENT!
I CONFESS! I SAW HIM LAST NIGHT IN YOUR CAR.
DIRTY LIAR! YOU REALLY GOT ME!
SHHH! LISTEN TO WHAT THE DIRECTOR IS SAYING!
YOUR PRESENCE IS REQUIRED AT 3 O'CLOCK AT THE MAIN CAMPUS! ALL THOSE WHO ARE ABSENT WILL BE BARRED FROM ATTENDING CLASSES FOR TWO WEEKS!
IT WAS AT THE MAIN CAMPUS THAT THE SUBJECTS COMMON TO ALL THE COLLEGES WERE TAUGHT. IT WAS MUCH MORE REPRESSIVE THAN OUR COLLEGE. AS ARTISTS, WE BENEFITED FROM A LITTLE MORE LIBERTY. FOR EXAMPLE, THERE GIRLS AND BOYS HAD TO TAKE DIFFERENT STAIRCASES, WHILE WHERE WE WERE, EVERYONE USED THE SAME STAIRCASE.
I DIDN'T GET THE STAIRCASE THING, BECAUSE IN ANY CASE, WE FOUND OURSELVES TOGETHER UPSTAIRS. BUT SHOUKA SAID THAT IT WAS TO KEEP THE BOYS FROM WATCHING OUR BUTTS WHILE WE CLIMBED.
I THINK SHE WAS RIGHT.

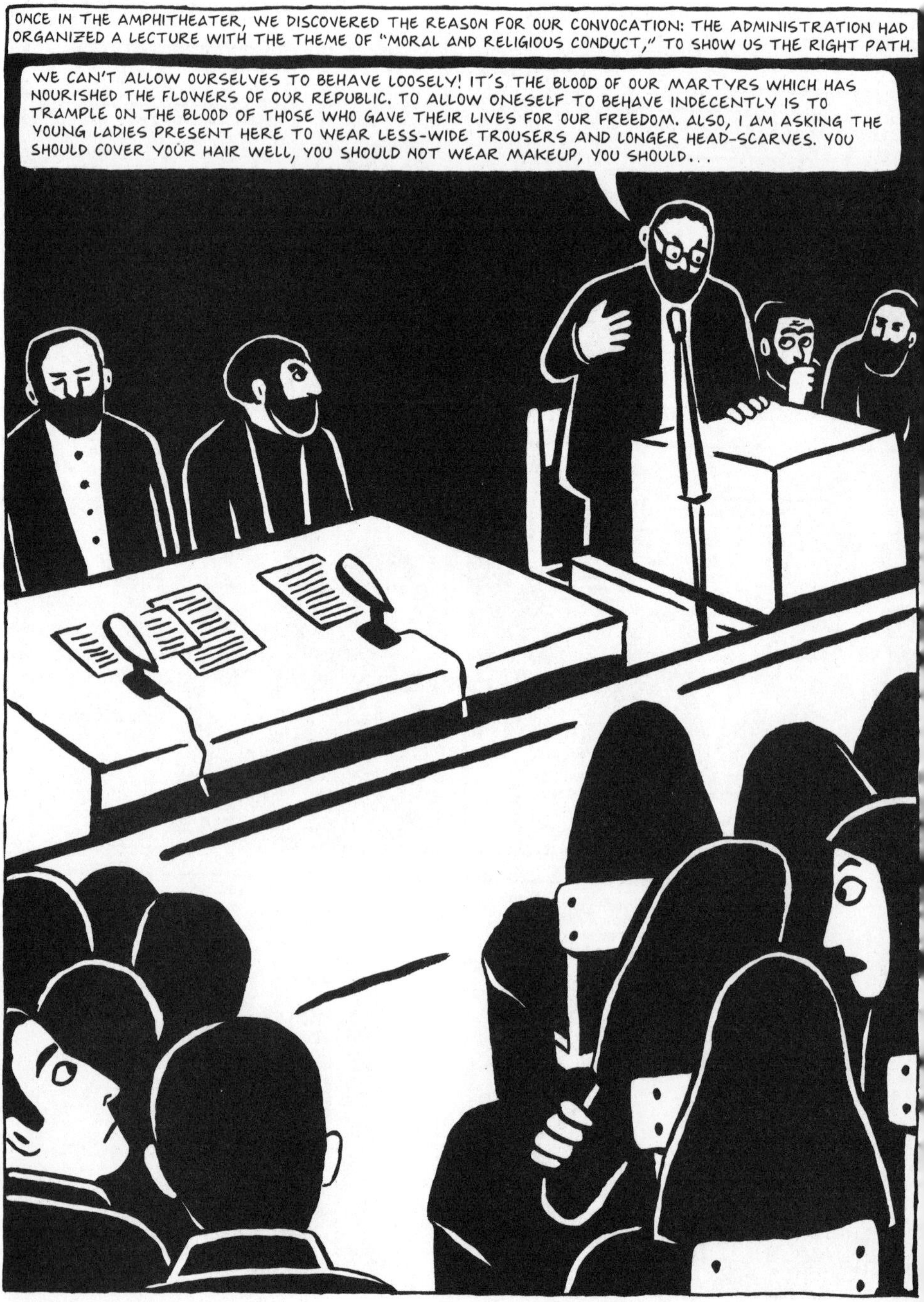
ONCE IN THE AMPHITHEATER, WE DISCOVERED THE REASON FOR OUR CONVOCATION: THE ADMINISTRATION HAD ORGANIZED A LECTURE WITH THE THEME OF "MORAL AND RELIGIOUS CONDUCT," TO SHOW US THE RIGHT PATH.
WE CAN'T ALLOW OURSELVES TO BEHAVE LOOSELY! IT'S THE BLOOD OF OUR MARTYRS WHICH HAS NOURISHED THE FLOWERS OF OUR REPUBLIC. TO ALLOW ONESELF TO BEHAVE INDECENTLY IS TO TRAMPLE ON THE BLOOD OF THOSE WHO GAVE THEIR LIVES FOR OUR FREEDOM. ALSO, I AM ASKING THE YOUNG LADIES PRESENT HERE TO WEAR LESS-WIDE TROUSERS AND LONGER HEAD-SCARVES. YOU SHOULD COVER YOUR HAIR WELL, YOU SHOULD NOT WEAR MAKEUP, YOU SHOULD...

THE SOCKS

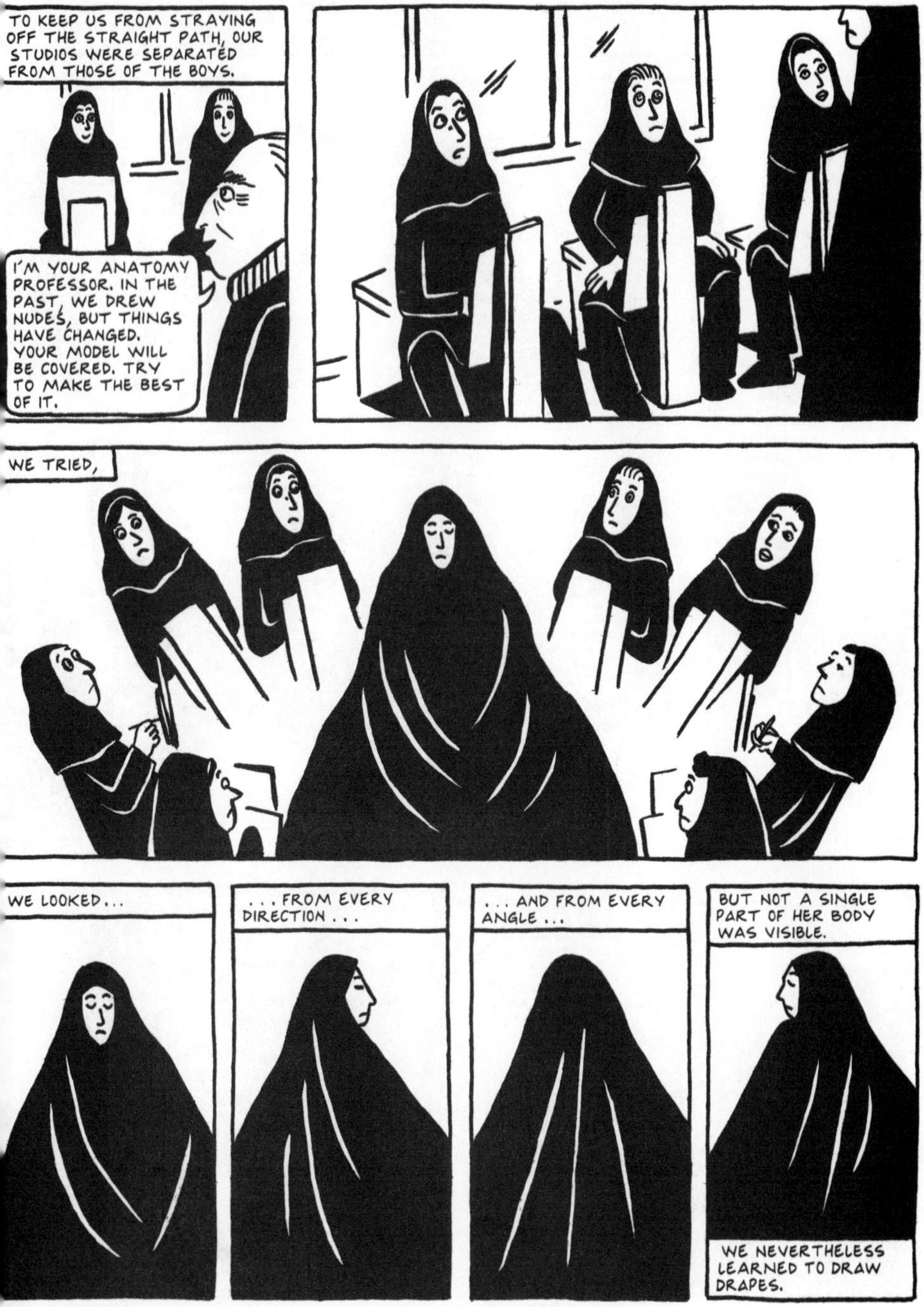
TO KEEP US FROM STRAYING OFF THE STRAIGHT PATH, OUR STUDIOS WERE SEPARATED FROM THOSE OF THE BOYS.
I'M YOUR ANATOMY PROFESSOR. IN THE PAST, WE DREW NUDES, BUT THINGS HAVE CHANGED. YOUR MODEL WILL BE COVERED. TRY TO MAKE THE BEST OF IT.
WE TRIED,
WE LOOKED...
...FROM EVERY DIRECTION...
...AND FROM EVERY ANGLE...
BUT NOT A SINGLE PART OF HER BODY WAS VISIBLE.
WE NEVERTHELESS LEARNED TO DRAW DRAPES.

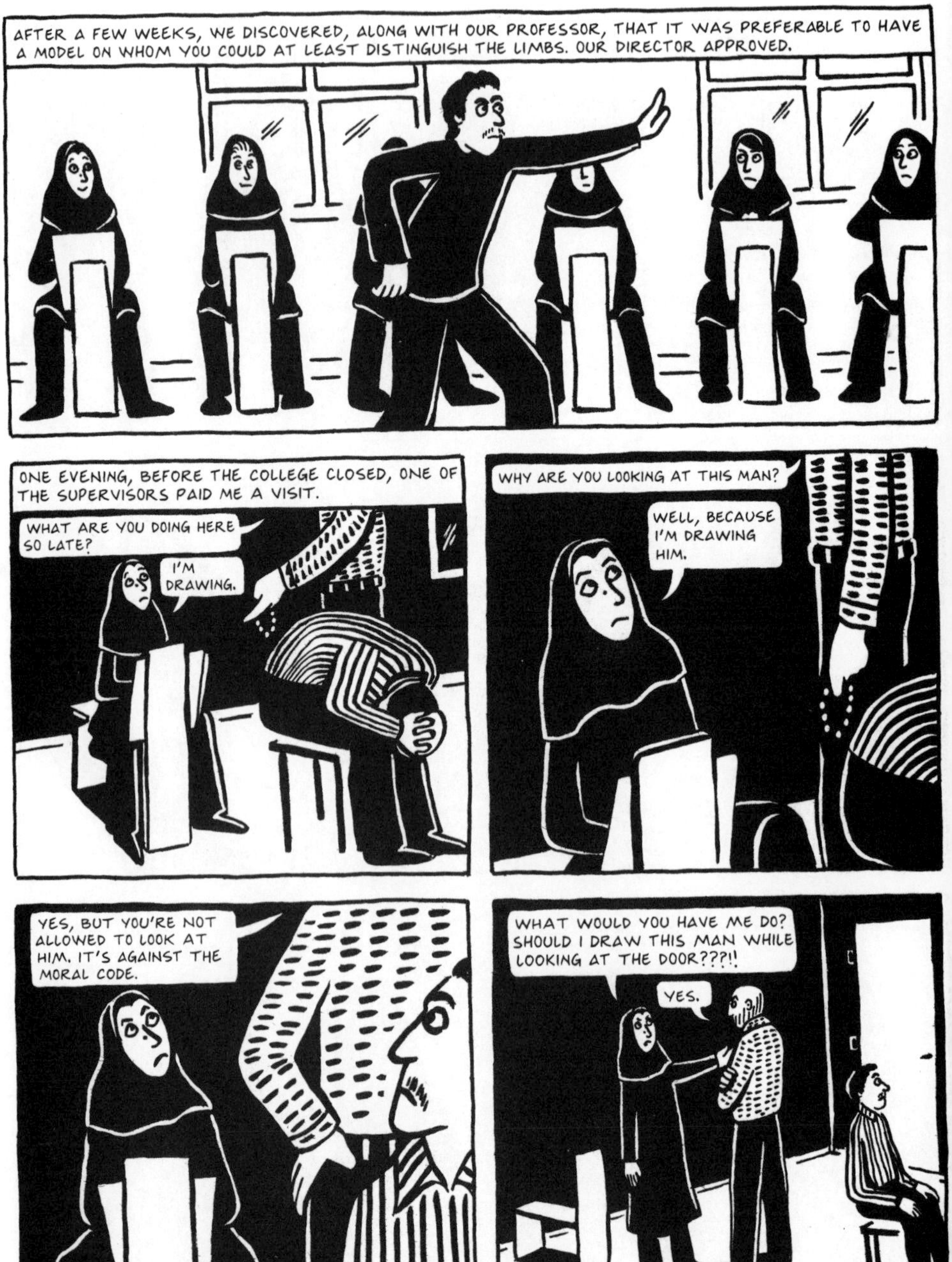
AFTER A FEW WEEKS, WE DISCOVERED, ALONG WITH OUR PROFESSOR, THAT IT WAS PREFERABLE TO HAVE A MODEL ON WHOM YOU COULD AT LEAST DISTINGUISH THE LIMBS. OUR DIRECTOR APPROVED.
ONE EVENING, BEFORE THE COLLEGE CLOSED, ONE OF THE SUPERVISORS PAID ME A VISIT.
WHAT ARE YOU DOING HERE SO LATE?
I'M DRAWING.
WHY ARE YOU LOOKING AT THIS MAN?
WELL, BECAUSE I'M DRAWING HIM.
YES, BUT YOU'RE NOT ALLOWED TO LOOK AT HIM. IT'S AGAINST THE MORAL CODE.
WHAT WOULD YOU HAVE ME DO? SHOULD I DRAW THIS MAN WHILE LOOKING AT THE DOOR???!!
YES.

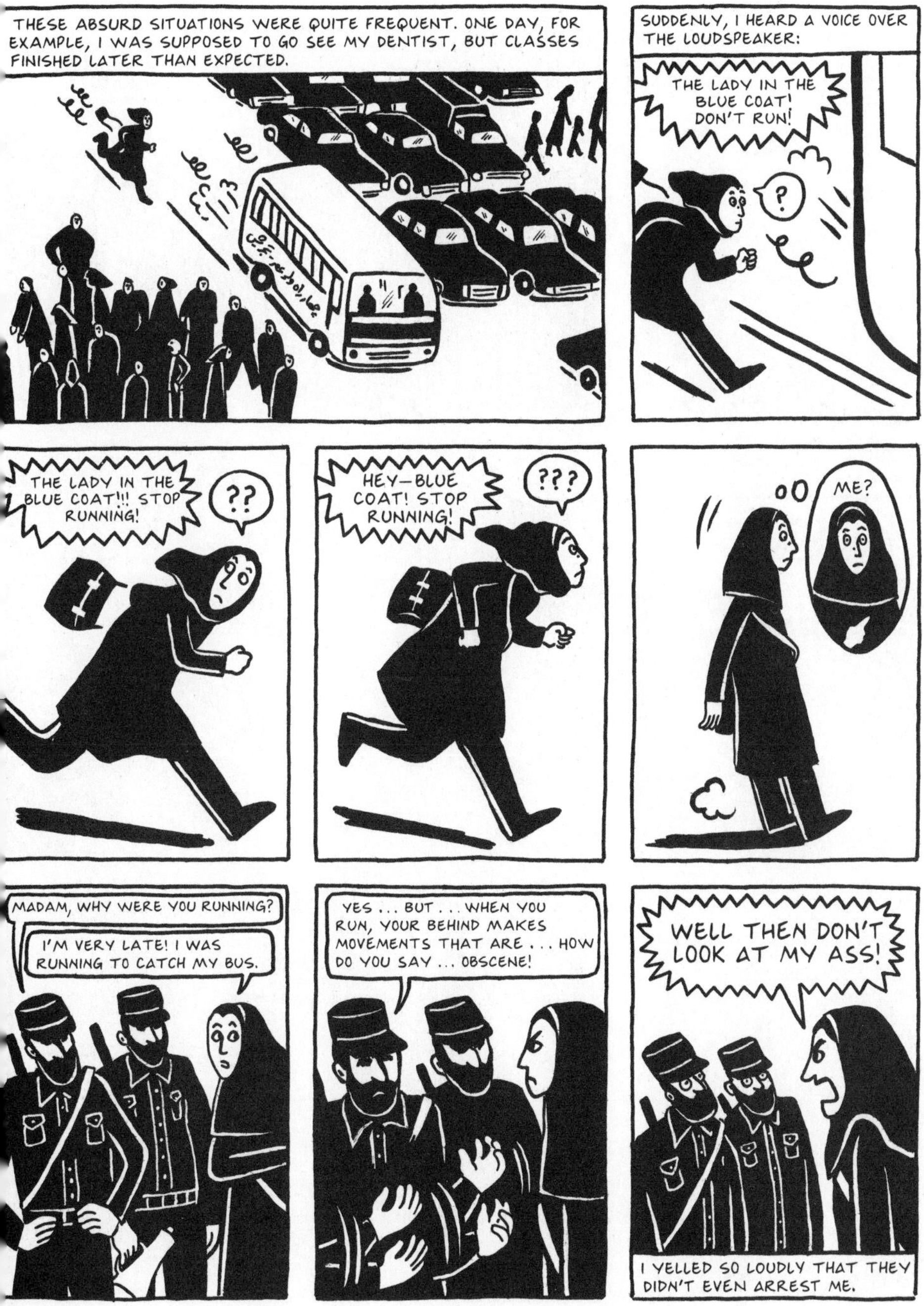
THESE ABSURD SITUATIONS WERE QUITE FREQUENT. ONE DAY, FOR EXAMPLE, I WAS SUPPOSED TO GO SEE MY DENTIST, BUT CLASSES FINISHED LATER THAN EXPECTED.
SUDDENLY, I HEARD A VOICE OVER THE LOUDSPEAKER:
THE LADY IN THE BLUE COAT! DON'T RUN!
?
THE LADY IN THE BLUE COAT!!! STOP RUNNING!
??
HEY—BLUE COAT! STOP RUNNING!
???
ME?
MADAM, WHY WERE YOU RUNNING?
I'M VERY LATE! I WAS RUNNING TO CATCH MY BUS.
YES . . . BUT . . . WHEN YOU RUN, YOUR BEHIND MAKES MOVEMENTS THAT ARE . . . HOW DO YOU SAY . . . OBSCENE!
WELL THEN DON'T LOOK AT MY ASS!
I YELLED SO LOUDLY THAT THEY DIDN'T EVEN ARREST ME.

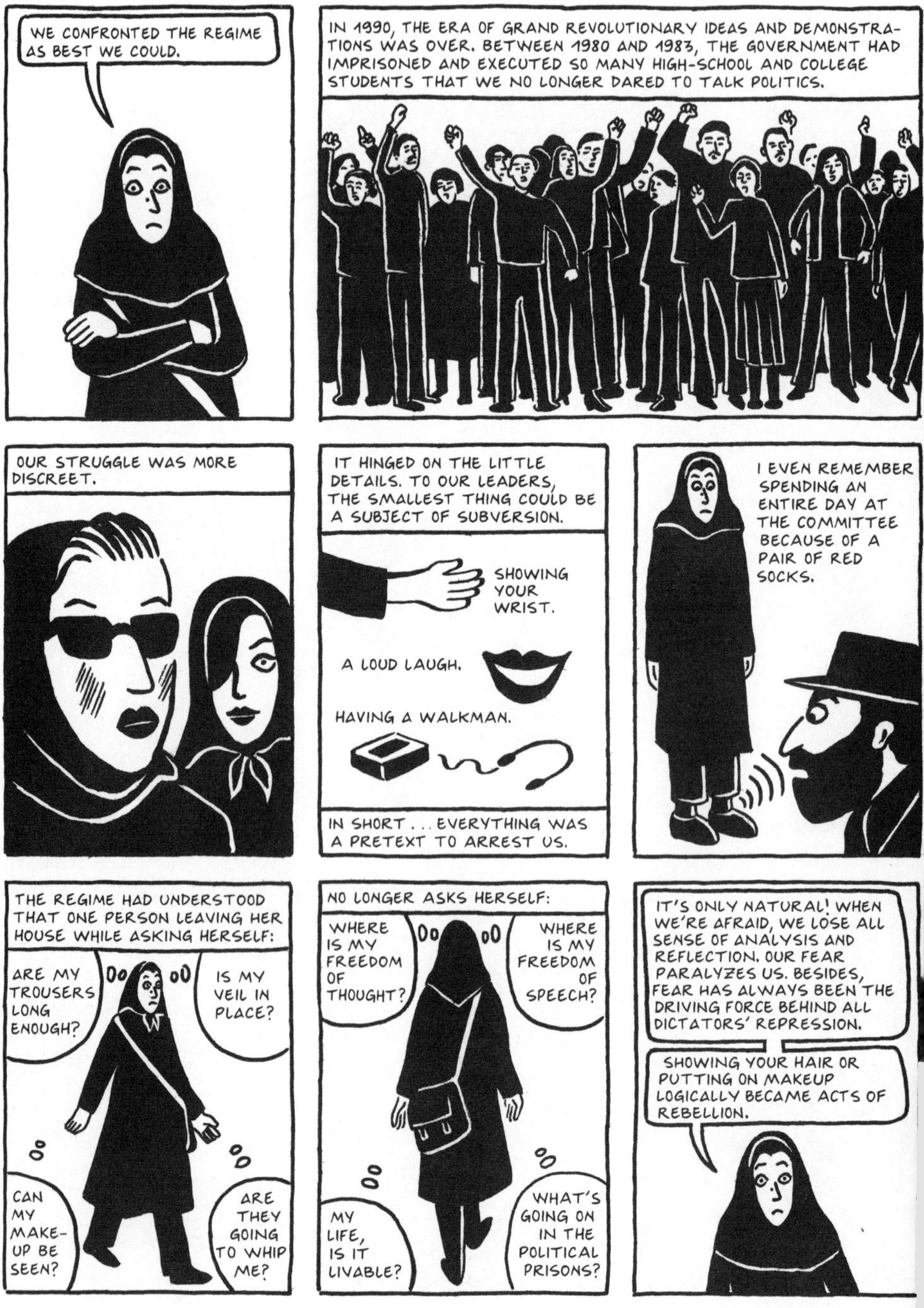
WE CONFRONTED THE REGIME AS BEST WE COULD.
IN 1990, THE ERA OF GRAND REVOLUTIONARY IDEAS AND DEMONSTRATIONS WAS OVER. BETWEEN 1980 AND 1983, THE GOVERNMENT HAD IMPRISONED AND EXECUTED SO MANY HIGH-SCHOOL AND COLLEGE STUDENTS THAT WE NO LONGER DARED TO TALK POLITICS.
OUR STRUGGLE WAS MORE DISCREET.
IT HINGED ON THE LITTLE DETAILS. TO OUR LEADERS, THE SMALLEST THING COULD BE A SUBJECT OF SUBVERSION.
SHOWING YOUR WRIST.
A LOUD LAUGH.
HAVING A WALKMAN.
IN SHORT . . . EVERYTHING WAS A PRETEXT TO ARREST US.
I EVEN REMEMBER SPENDING AN ENTIRE DAY AT THE COMMITTEE BECAUSE OF A PAIR OF RED SOCKS.
THE REGIME HAD UNDERSTOOD THAT ONE PERSON LEAVING HER HOUSE WHILE ASKING HERSELF:
ARE MY TROUSERS LONG ENOUGH?
IS MY VEIL IN PLACE?
CAN MY MAKE-UP BE SEEN?
ARE THEY GOING TO WHIP ME?
NO LONGER ASKS HERSELF:
WHERE IS MY FREEDOM OF THOUGHT?
WHERE IS MY FREEDOM OF SPEECH?
MY LIFE, IS IT LIVABLE?
WHAT'S GOING ON IN THE POLITICAL PRISONS?
IT'S ONLY NATURAL! WHEN WE'RE AFRAID, WE LOSE ALL SENSE OF ANALYSIS AND REFLECTION. OUR FEAR PARALYZES US. BESIDES, FEAR HAS ALWAYS BEEN THE DRIVING FORCE BEHIND ALL DICTATORS' REPRESSION.
SHOWING YOUR HAIR OR PUTTING ON MAKEUP LOGICALLY BECAME ACTS OF REBELLION.

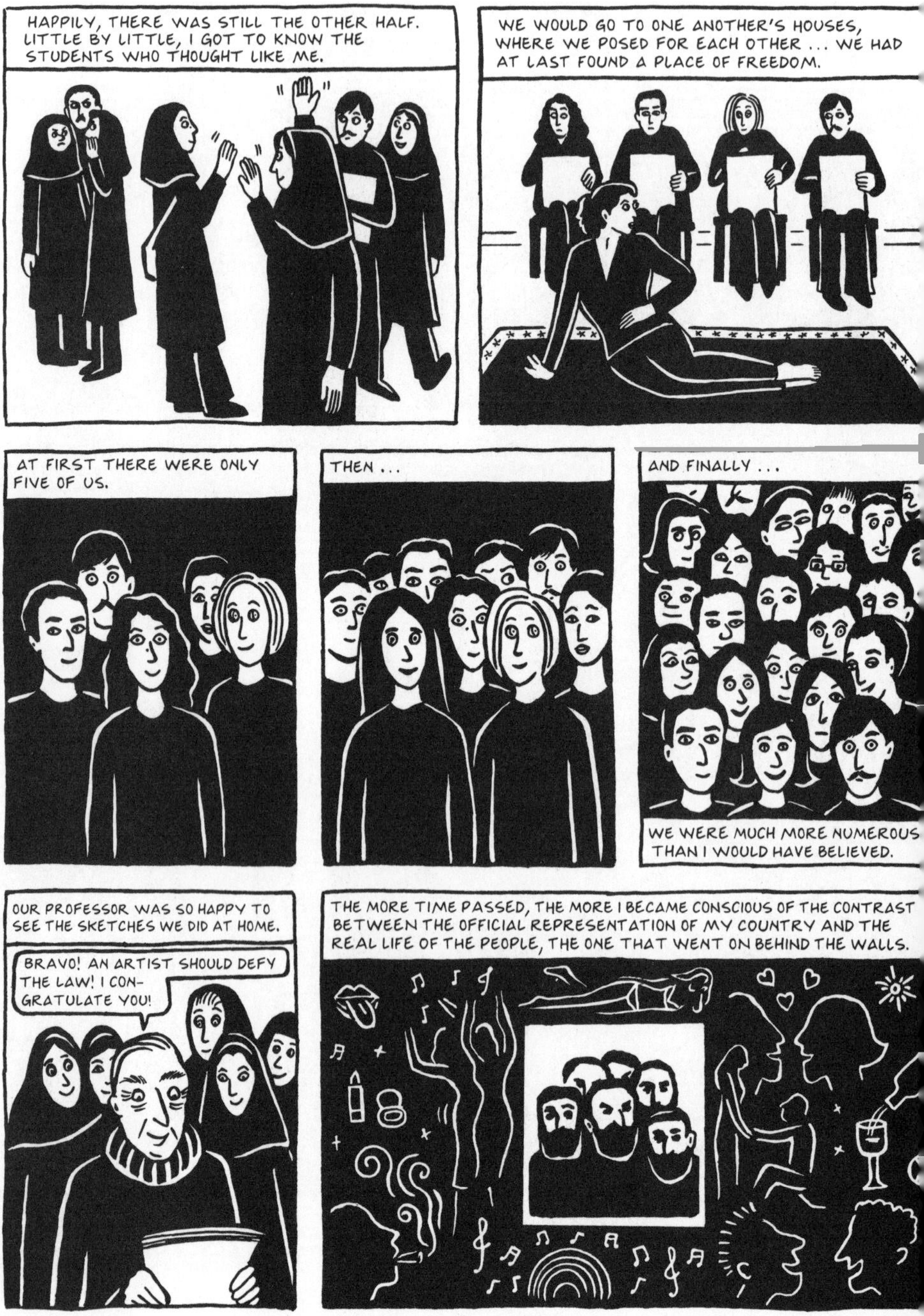

HAPPILY, THERE WAS STILL THE OTHER HALF. LITTLE BY LITTLE, I GOT TO KNOW THE STUDENTS WHO THOUGHT LIKE ME.
WE WOULD GO TO ONE ANOTHER'S HOUSES, WHERE WE POSED FOR EACH OTHER ... WE HAD AT LAST FOUND A PLACE OF FREEDOM.
AT FIRST THERE WERE ONLY FIVE OF US.
THEN ...
AND FINALLY ...
WE WERE MUCH MORE NUMEROUS THAN I WOULD HAVE BELIEVED.
OUR PROFESSOR WAS SO HAPPY TO SEE THE SKETCHES WE DID AT HOME.
BRAVO! AN ARTIST SHOULD DEFY THE LAW! I CONGRATULATE YOU!
THE MORE TIME PASSED, THE MORE I BECAME CONSCIOUS OF THE CONTRAST BETWEEN THE OFFICIAL REPRESENTATION OF MY COUNTRY AND THE REAL LIFE OF THE PEOPLE, THE ONE THAT WENT ON BEHIND THE WALLS.

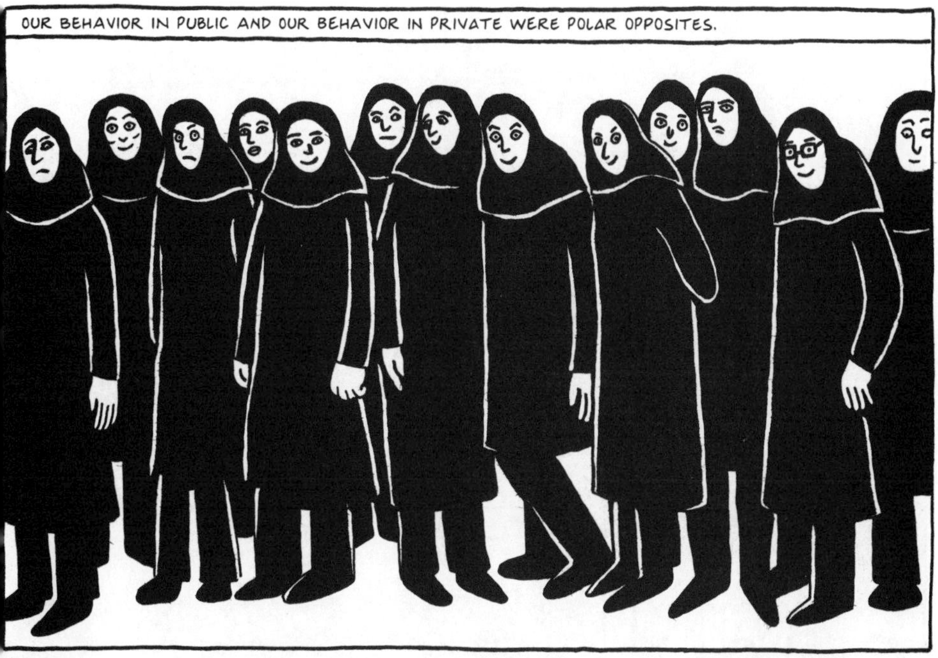
OUR BEHAVIOR IN PUBLIC AND OUR BEHAVIOR IN PRIVATE WERE POLAR OPPOSITES.

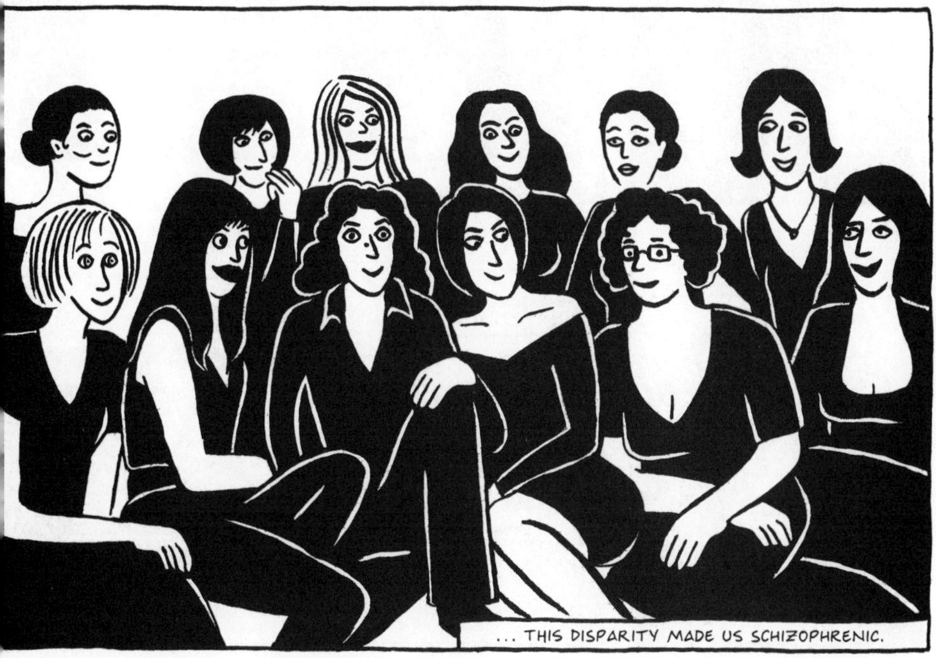
... THIS DISPARITY MADE US SCHIZOPHRENIC.

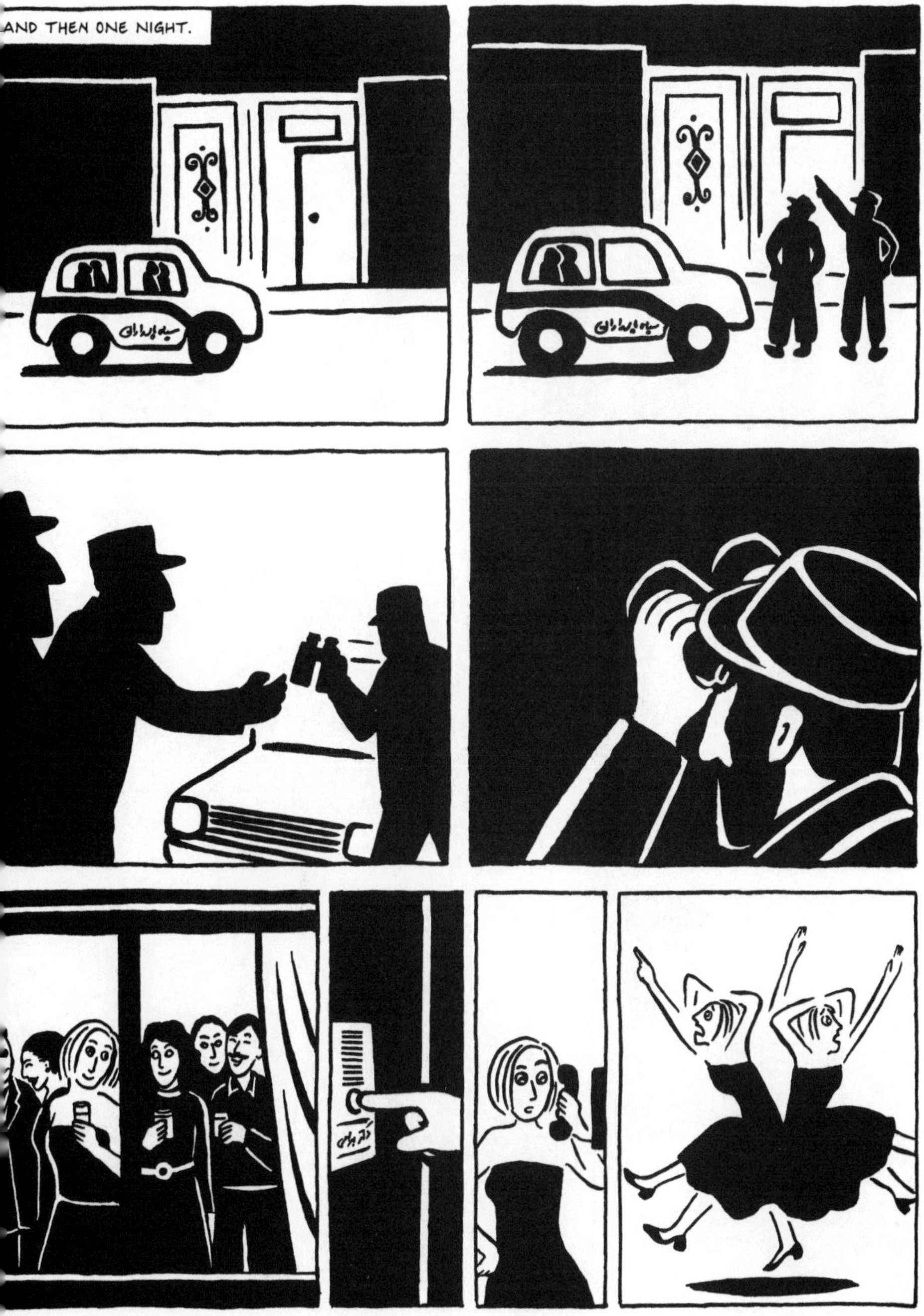
AND THEN ONE NIGHT.

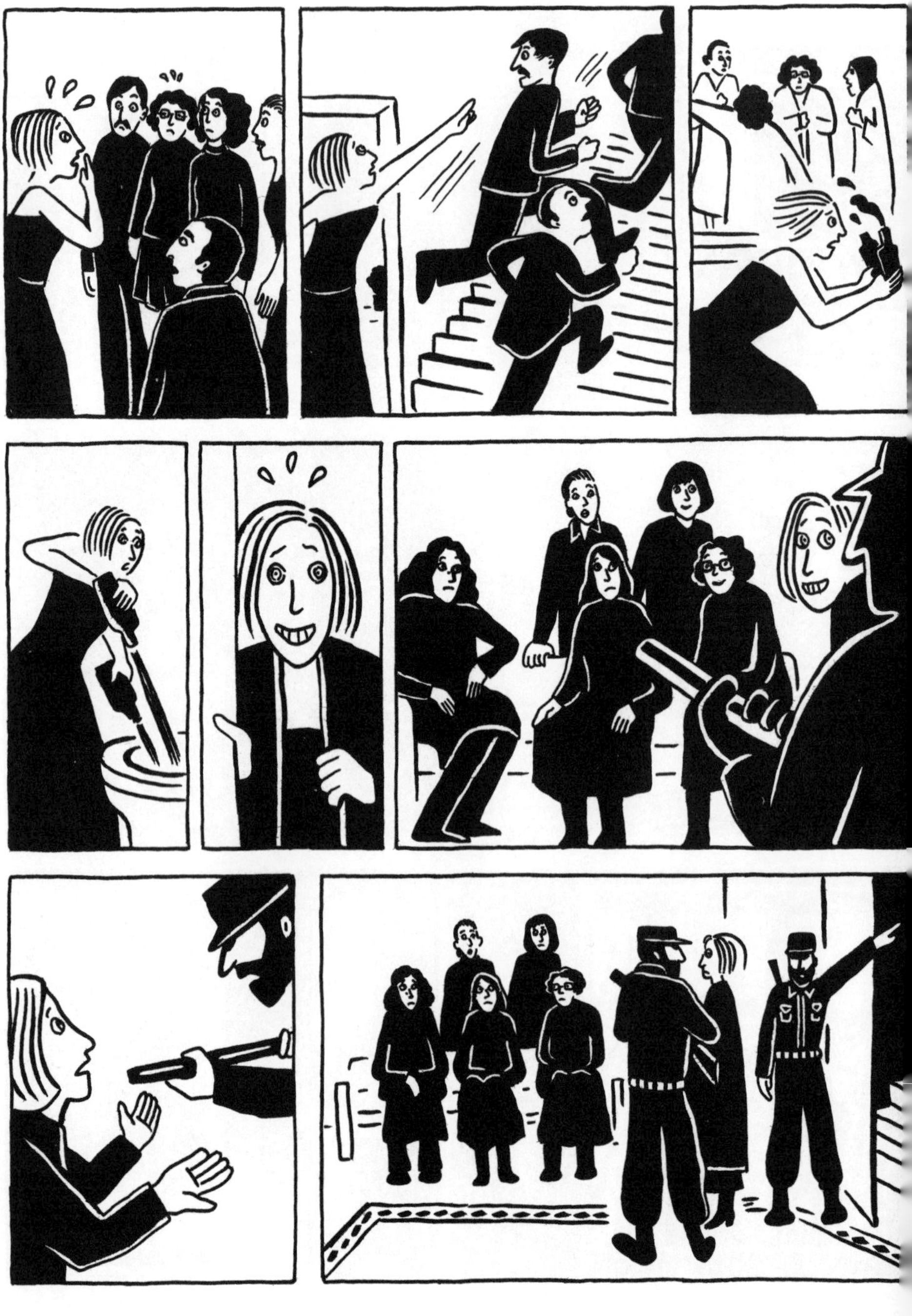

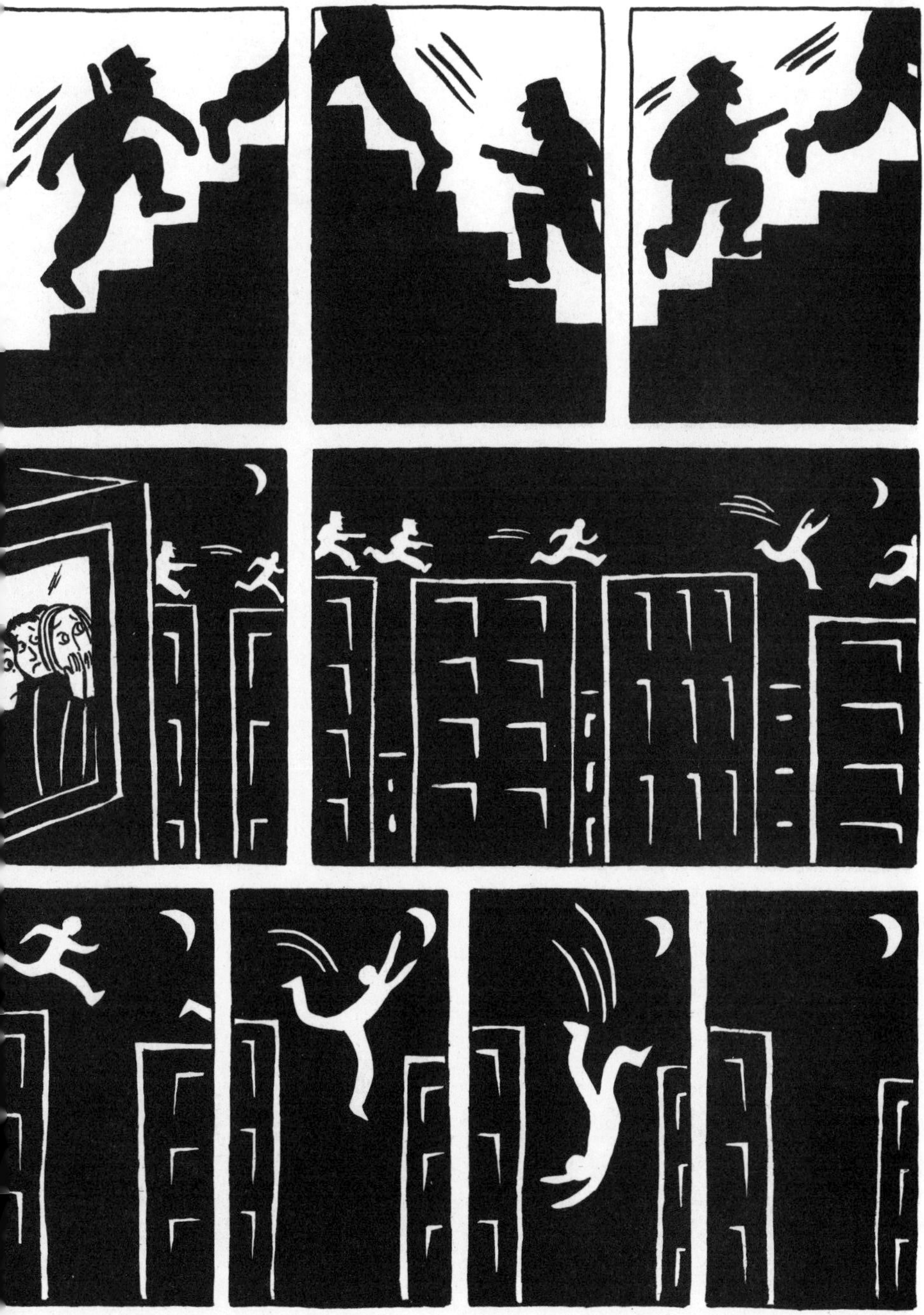

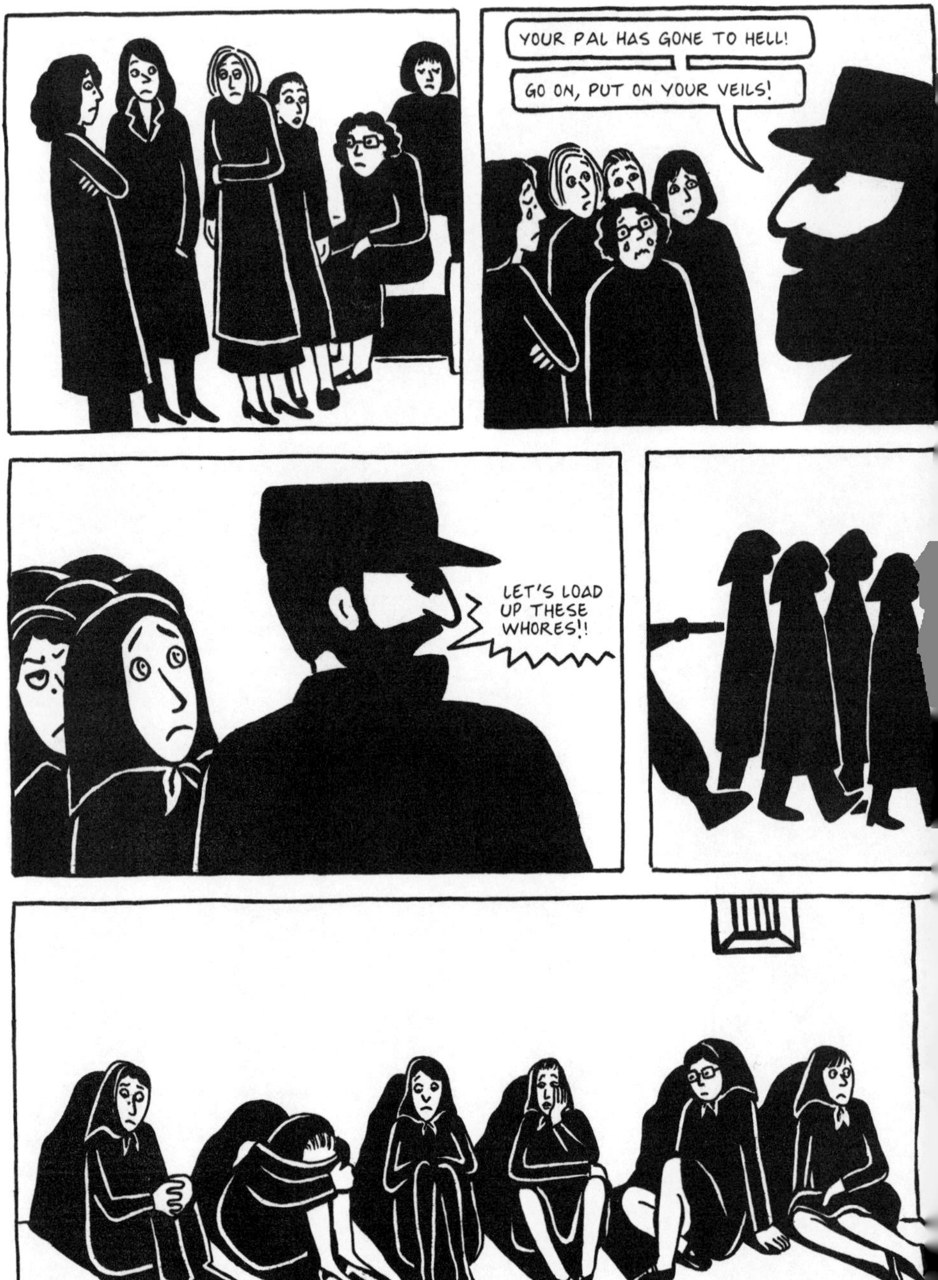
YOUR PAL HAS GONE TO HELL!
GO ON, PUT ON YOUR VEILS!
LET'S LOAD UP THESE WHORES!!

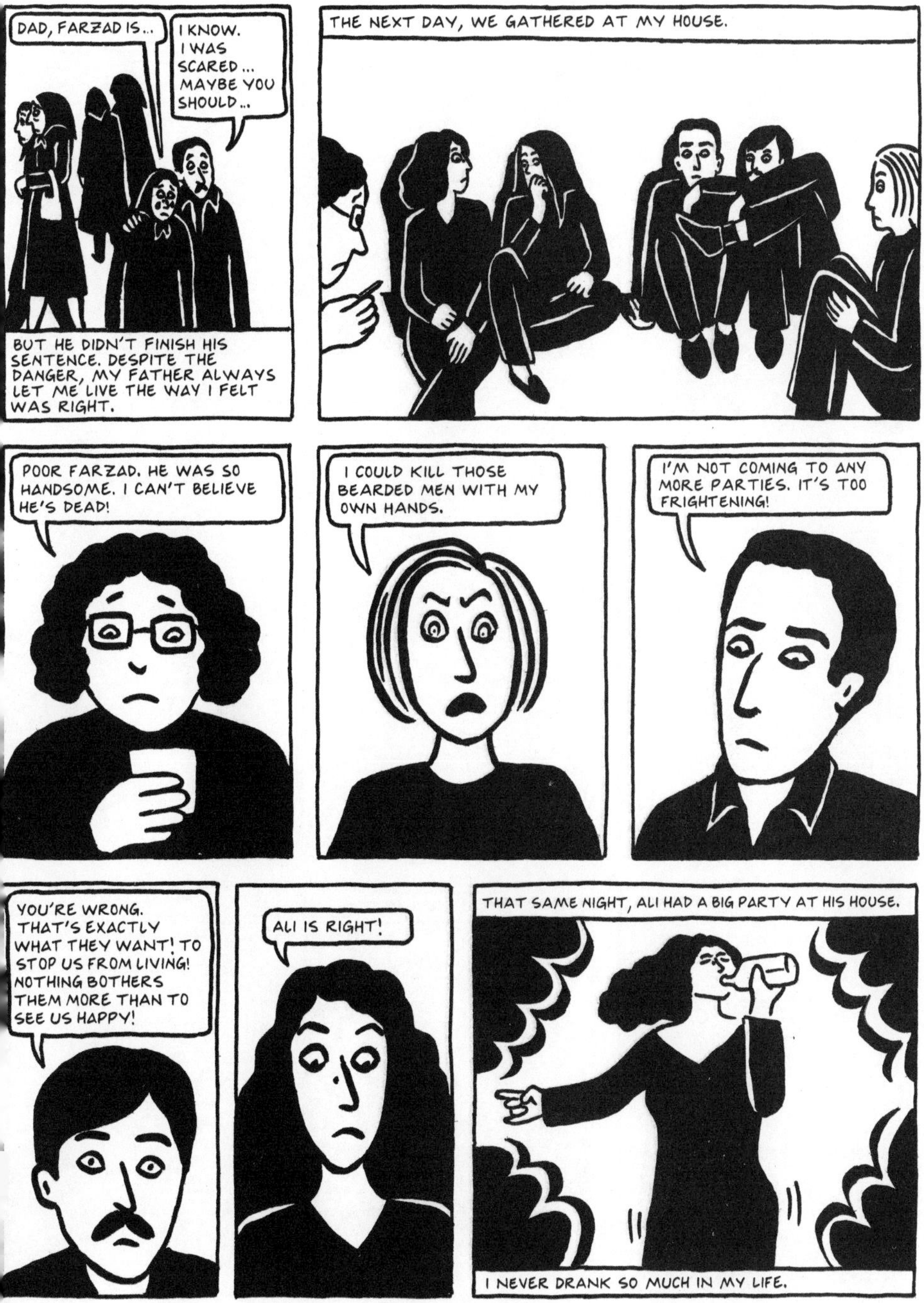
DAD, FARZAD IS...
I KNOW. I WAS SCARED... MAYBE YOU SHOULD...
BUT HE DIDN'T FINISH HIS SENTENCE. DESPITE THE DANGER, MY FATHER ALWAYS LET ME LIVE THE WAY I FELT WAS RIGHT.
THE NEXT DAY, WE GATHERED AT MY HOUSE.
POOR FARZAD. HE WAS SO HANDSOME. I CAN'T BELIEVE HE'S DEAD!
I COULD KILL THOSE BEARDED MEN WITH MY OWN HANDS.
I'M NOT COMING TO ANY MORE PARTIES. IT'S TOO FRIGHTENING!
YOU'RE WRONG. THAT'S EXACTLY WHAT THEY WANT! TO STOP US FROM LIVING! NOTHING BOTHERS THEM MORE THAN TO SEE US HAPPY!
ALI IS RIGHT!
THAT SAME NIGHT, ALI HAD A BIG PARTY AT HIS HOUSE.
I NEVER DRANK SO MUCH IN MY LIFE.

THE WEDDING

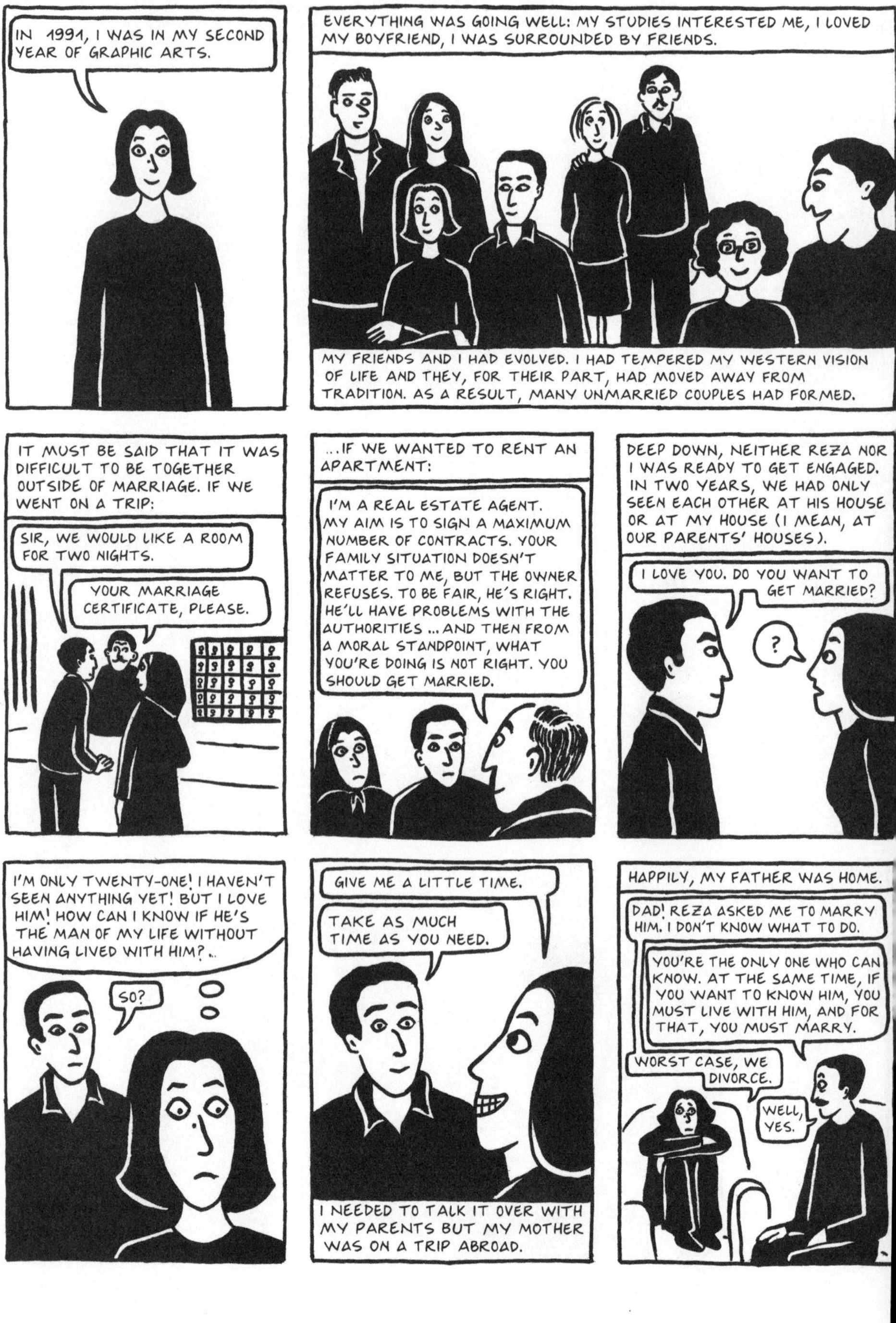
IN 1991, I WAS IN MY SECOND YEAR OF GRAPHIC ARTS.
EVERYTHING WAS GOING WELL: MY STUDIES INTERESTED ME, I LOVED MY BOYFRIEND, I WAS SURROUNDED BY FRIENDS.
MY FRIENDS AND I HAD EVOLVED. I HAD TEMPERED MY WESTERN VISION OF LIFE AND THEY, FOR THEIR PART, HAD MOVED AWAY FROM TRADITION. AS A RESULT, MANY UNMARRIED COUPLES HAD FORMED.
IT MUST BE SAID THAT IT WAS DIFFICULT TO BE TOGETHER OUTSIDE OF MARRIAGE. IF WE WENT ON A TRIP:
SIR, WE WOULD LIKE A ROOM FOR TWO NIGHTS.
YOUR MARRIAGE CERTIFICATE, PLEASE.
...IF WE WANTED TO RENT AN APARTMENT:
I'M A REAL ESTATE AGENT. MY AIM IS TO SIGN A MAXIMUM NUMBER OF CONTRACTS. YOUR FAMILY SITUATION DOESN'T MATTER TO ME, BUT THE OWNER REFUSES. TO BE FAIR, HE'S RIGHT. HE'LL HAVE PROBLEMS WITH THE AUTHORITIES ... AND THEN FROM A MORAL STANDPOINT, WHAT YOU'RE DOING IS NOT RIGHT. YOU SHOULD GET MARRIED.
DEEP DOWN, NEITHER REZA NOR I WAS READY TO GET ENGAGED. IN TWO YEARS, WE HAD ONLY SEEN EACH OTHER AT HIS HOUSE OR AT MY HOUSE (I MEAN, AT OUR PARENTS' HOUSES).
I LOVE YOU. DO YOU WANT TO GET MARRIED?
?
I'M ONLY TWENTY-ONE! I HAVEN'T SEEN ANYTHING YET! BUT I LOVE HIM! HOW CAN I KNOW IF HE'S THE MAN OF MY LIFE WITHOUT HAVING LIVED WITH HIM?..
SO?
GIVE ME A LITTLE TIME.
TAKE AS MUCH TIME AS YOU NEED.
I NEEDED TO TALK IT OVER WITH MY PARENTS BUT MY MOTHER WAS ON A TRIP ABROAD.
HAPPILY, MY FATHER WAS HOME.
DAD! REZA ASKED ME TO MARRY HIM. I DON'T KNOW WHAT TO DO.
YOU'RE THE ONLY ONE WHO CAN KNOW. AT THE SAME TIME, IF YOU WANT TO KNOW HIM, YOU MUST LIVE WITH HIM, AND FOR THAT, YOU MUST MARRY.
WORST CASE, WE DIVORCE.
WELL, YES.

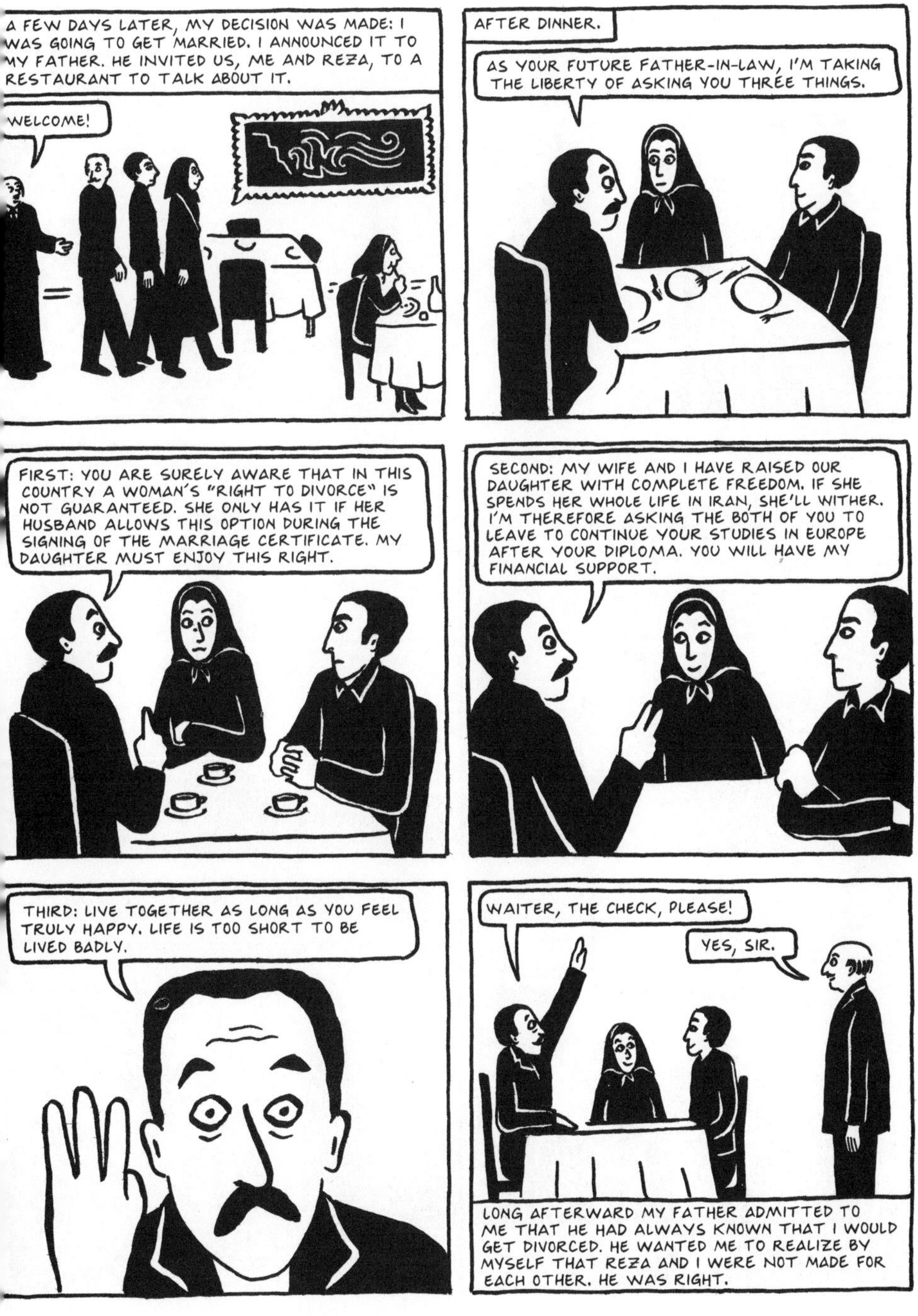
A FEW DAYS LATER, MY DECISION WAS MADE: I WAS GOING TO GET MARRIED. I ANNOUNCED IT TO MY FATHER. HE INVITED US, ME AND REZA, TO A RESTAURANT TO TALK ABOUT IT.
WELCOME!
AFTER DINNER.
AS YOUR FUTURE FATHER-IN-LAW, I'M TAKING THE LIBERTY OF ASKING YOU THREE THINGS.
FIRST: YOU ARE SURELY AWARE THAT IN THIS COUNTRY A WOMAN'S "RIGHT TO DIVORCE" IS NOT GUARANTEED. SHE ONLY HAS IT IF HER HUSBAND ALLOWS THIS OPTION DURING THE SIGNING OF THE MARRIAGE CERTIFICATE. MY DAUGHTER MUST ENJOY THIS RIGHT.
SECOND: MY WIFE AND I HAVE RAISED OUR DAUGHTER WITH COMPLETE FREEDOM. IF SHE SPENDS HER WHOLE LIFE IN IRAN, SHE'LL WITHER. I'M THEREFORE ASKING THE BOTH OF YOU TO LEAVE TO CONTINUE YOUR STUDIES IN EUROPE AFTER YOUR DIPLOMA. YOU WILL HAVE MY FINANCIAL SUPPORT.
THIRD: LIVE TOGETHER AS LONG AS YOU FEEL TRULY HAPPY. LIFE IS TOO SHORT TO BE LIVED BADLY.
WAITER, THE CHECK, PLEASE!
YES, SIR.
LONG AFTERWARD MY FATHER ADMITTED TO ME THAT HE HAD ALWAYS KNOWN THAT I WOULD GET DIVORCED. HE WANTED ME TO REALIZE BY MYSELF THAT REZA AND I WERE NOT MADE FOR EACH OTHER. HE WAS RIGHT.

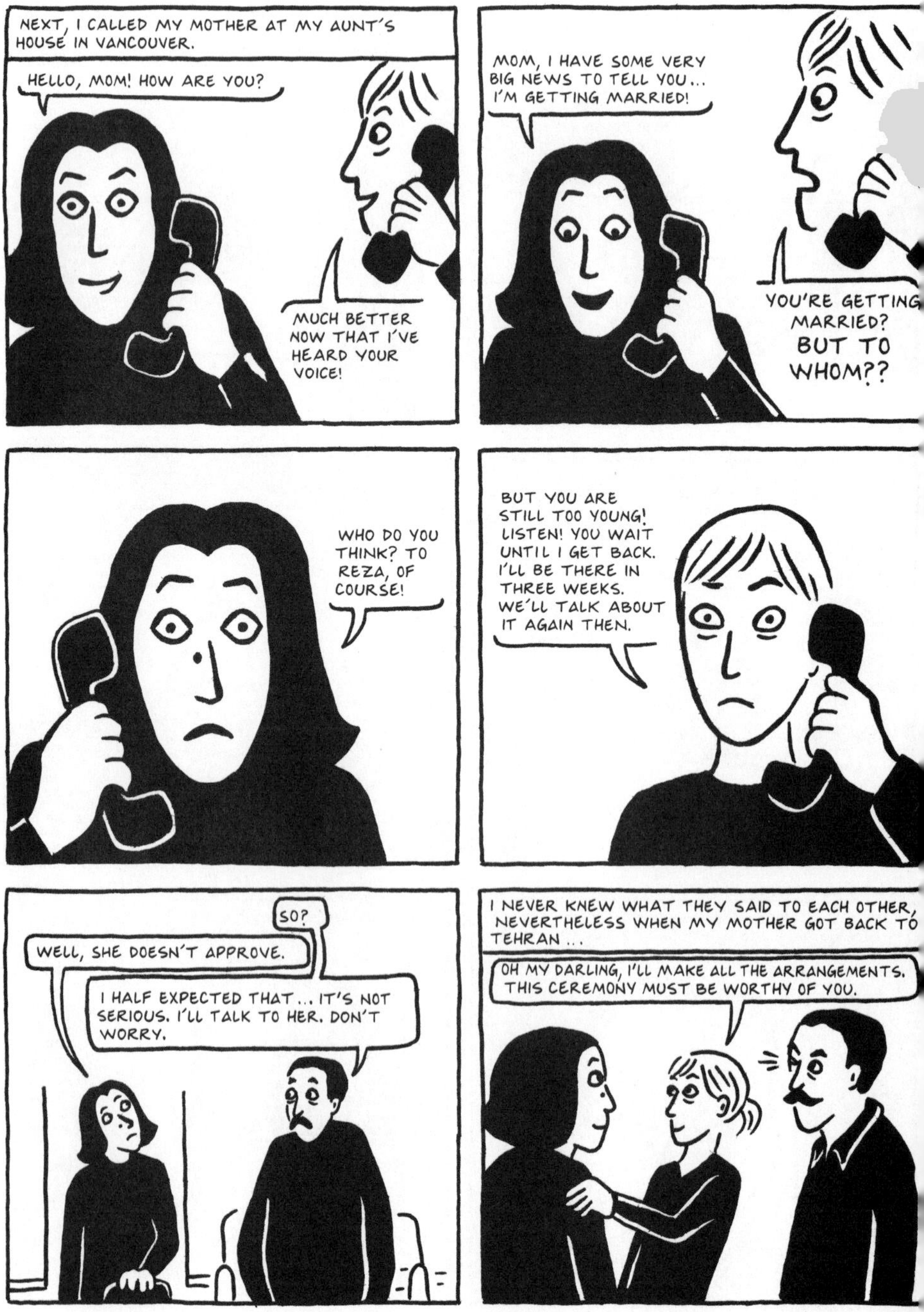
NEXT, I CALLED MY MOTHER AT MY AUNT'S HOUSE IN VANCOUVER.
HELLO, MOM! HOW ARE YOU?
MUCH BETTER NOW THAT I'VE HEARD YOUR VOICE!
MOM, I HAVE SOME VERY BIG NEWS TO TELL YOU... I'M GETTING MARRIED!
YOU'RE GETTING MARRIED? BUT TO WHOM??
WHO DO YOU THINK? TO REZA, OF COURSE!
BUT YOU ARE STILL TOO YOUNG! LISTEN! YOU WAIT UNTIL I GET BACK. I'LL BE THERE IN THREE WEEKS. WE'LL TALK ABOUT IT AGAIN THEN.
SO?
WELL, SHE DOESN'T APPROVE.
I HALF EXPECTED THAT... IT'S NOT SERIOUS. I'LL TALK TO HER. DON'T WORRY.
I NEVER KNEW WHAT THEY SAID TO EACH OTHER, NEVERTHELESS WHEN MY MOTHER GOT BACK TO TEHRAN...
OH MY DARLING, I'LL MAKE ALL THE ARRANGEMENTS. THIS CEREMONY MUST BE WORTHY OF YOU.

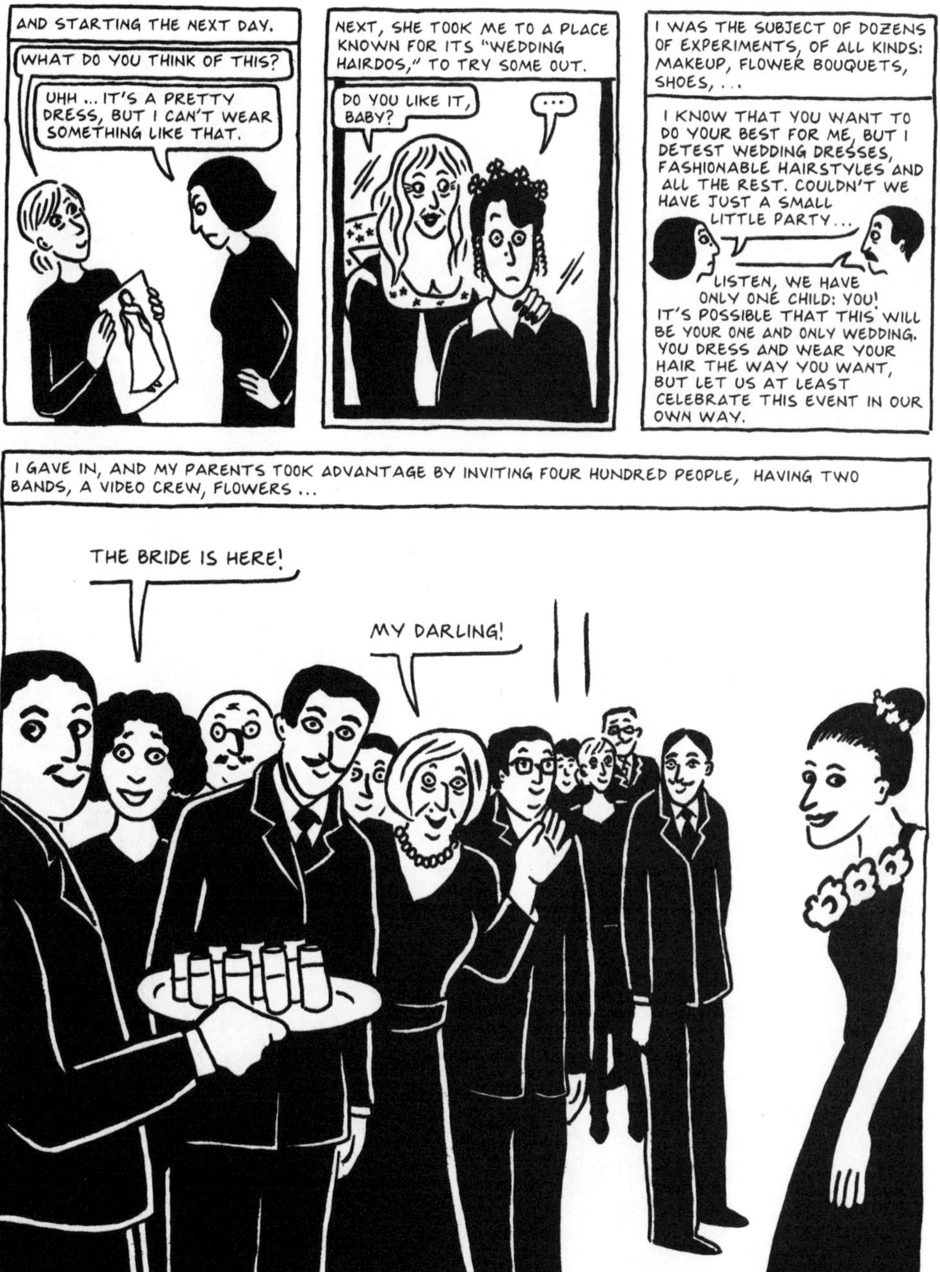
AND STARTING THE NEXT DAY.
WHAT DO YOU THINK OF THIS?
UHH ... IT'S A PRETTY DRESS, BUT I CAN'T WEAR SOMETHING LIKE THAT.
NEXT, SHE TOOK ME TO A PLACE KNOWN FOR ITS "WEDDING HAIRDOS," TO TRY SOME OUT.
DO YOU LIKE IT, BABY?
...
I WAS THE SUBJECT OF DOZENS OF EXPERIMENTS, OF ALL KINDS: MAKEUP, FLOWER BOUQUETS, SHOES, . . .
I KNOW THAT YOU WANT TO DO YOUR BEST FOR ME, BUT I DETEST WEDDING DRESSES, FASHIONABLE HAIRSTYLES AND ALL THE REST. COULDN'T WE HAVE JUST A SMALL LITTLE PARTY...
LISTEN, WE HAVE ONLY ONE CHILD: YOU! IT'S POSSIBLE THAT THIS WILL BE YOUR ONE AND ONLY WEDDING. YOU DRESS AND WEAR YOUR HAIR THE WAY YOU WANT, BUT LET US AT LEAST CELEBRATE THIS EVENT IN OUR OWN WAY.
I GAVE IN, AND MY PARENTS TOOK ADVANTAGE BY INVITING FOUR HUNDRED PEOPLE, HAVING TWO BANDS, A VIDEO CREW, FLOWERS ...
THE BRIDE IS HERE!
MY DARLING!

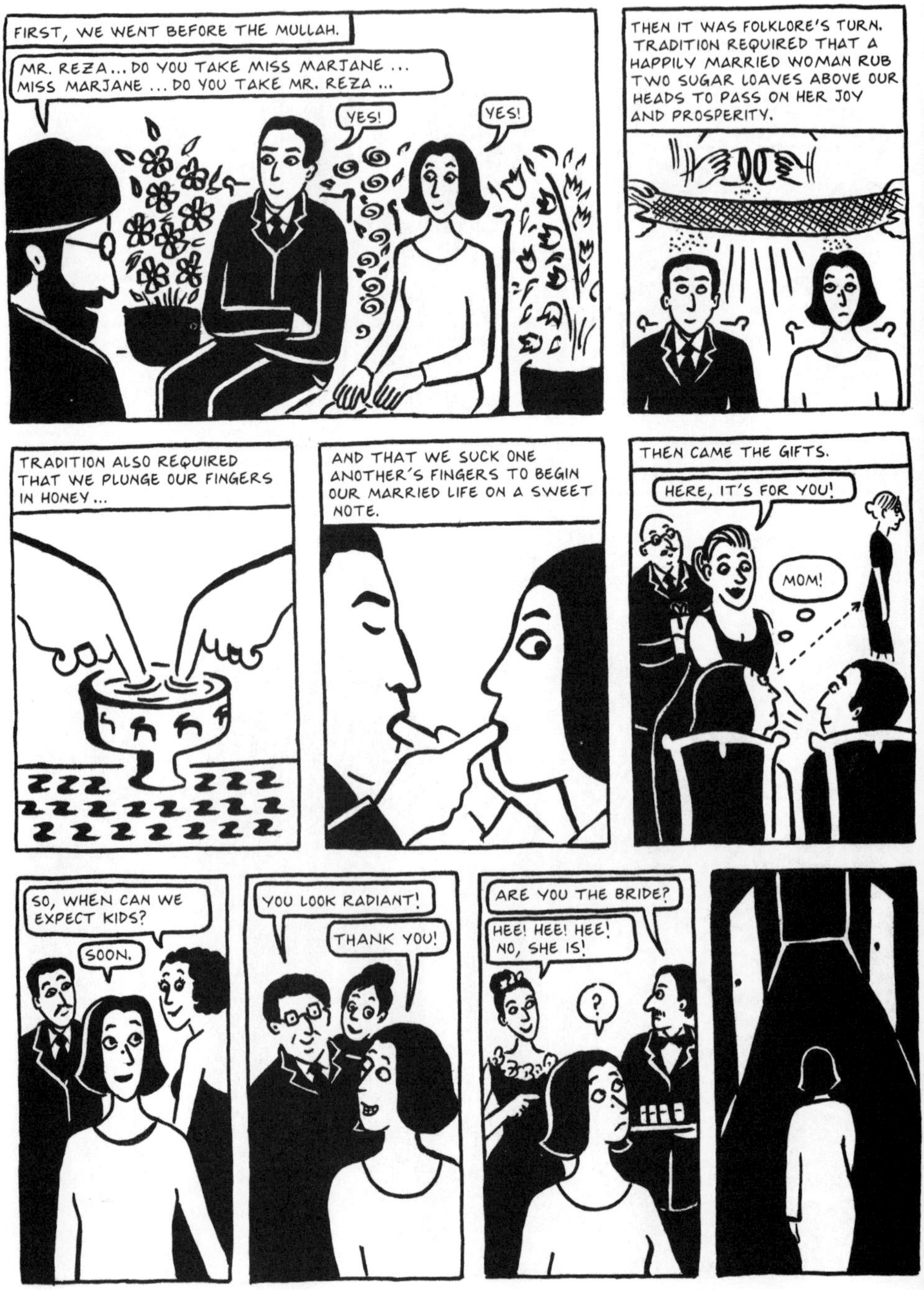
FIRST, WE WENT BEFORE THE MULLAH.
MR. REZA... DO YOU TAKE MISS MARJANE ... MISS MARJANE ... DO YOU TAKE MR. REZA ...
YES!
YES!
THEN IT WAS FOLKLORE'S TURN. TRADITION REQUIRED THAT A HAPPILY MARRIED WOMAN RUB TWO SUGAR LOAVES ABOVE OUR HEADS TO PASS ON HER JOY AND PROSPERITY.
TRADITION ALSO REQUIRED THAT WE PLUNGE OUR FINGERS IN HONEY ...
AND THAT WE SUCK ONE ANOTHER'S FINGERS TO BEGIN OUR MARRIED LIFE ON A SWEET NOTE.
THEN CAME THE GIFTS.
HERE, IT'S FOR YOU!
MOM!
SO, WHEN CAN WE EXPECT KIDS?
SOON.
YOU LOOK RADIANT!
THANK YOU!
ARE YOU THE BRIDE?
HEE! HEE! HEE! NO, SHE IS!
?

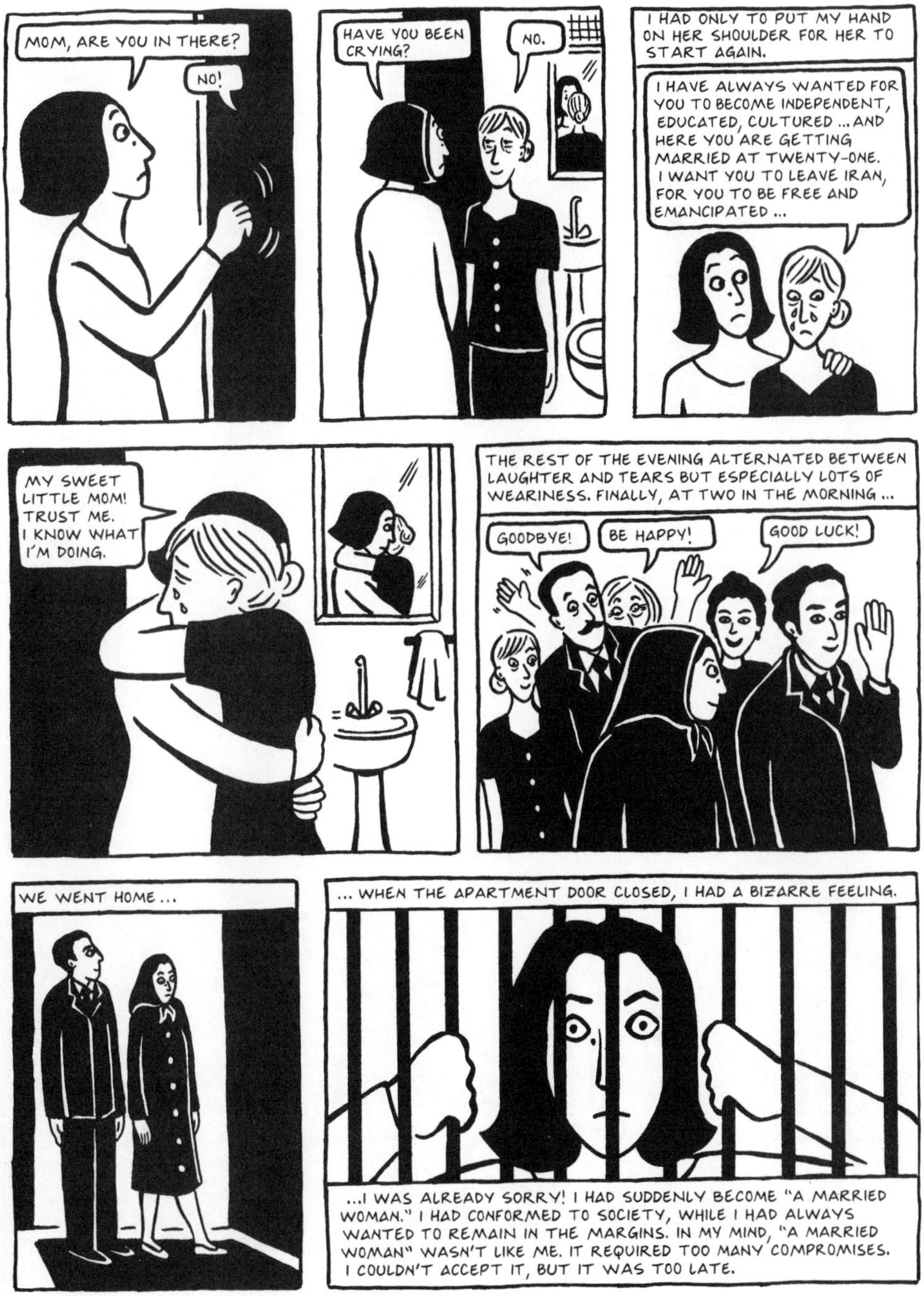
MOM, ARE YOU IN THERE?
NO!
HAVE YOU BEEN CRYING?
NO.
I HAD ONLY TO PUT MY HAND ON HER SHOULDER FOR HER TO START AGAIN.
I HAVE ALWAYS WANTED FOR YOU TO BECOME INDEPENDENT, EDUCATED, CULTURED ... AND HERE YOU ARE GETTING MARRIED AT TWENTY-ONE. I WANT YOU TO LEAVE IRAN, FOR YOU TO BE FREE AND EMANCIPATED ...
MY SWEET LITTLE MOM! TRUST ME. I KNOW WHAT I'M DOING.
THE REST OF THE EVENING ALTERNATED BETWEEN LAUGHTER AND TEARS BUT ESPECIALLY LOTS OF WEARINESS. FINALLY, AT TWO IN THE MORNING ...
GOODBYE!
BE HAPPY!
GOOD LUCK!
WE WENT HOME ...
... WHEN THE APARTMENT DOOR CLOSED, I HAD A BIZARRE FEELING.
...I WAS ALREADY SORRY! I HAD SUDDENLY BECOME "A MARRIED WOMAN." I HAD CONFORMED TO SOCIETY, WHILE I HAD ALWAYS WANTED TO REMAIN IN THE MARGINS. IN MY MIND, "A MARRIED WOMAN" WASN'T LIKE ME. IT REQUIRED TOO MANY COMPROMISES. I COULDN'T ACCEPT IT, BUT IT WAS TOO LATE.

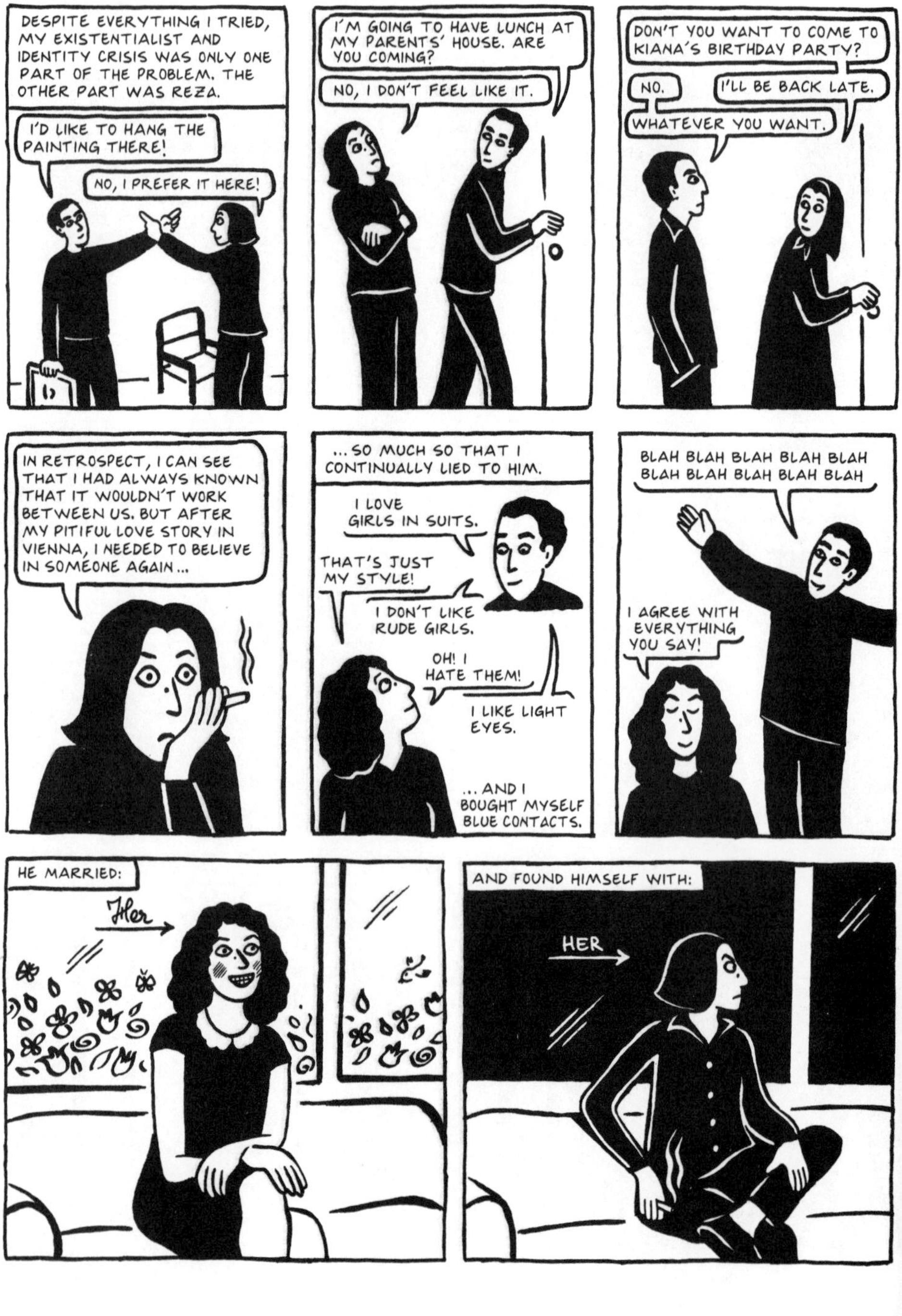
DESPITE EVERYTHING I TRIED, MY EXISTENTIALIST AND IDENTITY CRISIS WAS ONLY ONE PART OF THE PROBLEM. THE OTHER PART WAS REZA.
I'D LIKE TO HANG THE PAINTING THERE!
NO, I PREFER IT HERE!
I'M GOING TO HAVE LUNCH AT MY PARENTS' HOUSE. ARE YOU COMING?
NO, I DON'T FEEL LIKE IT.
DON'T YOU WANT TO COME TO KIANA'S BIRTHDAY PARTY?
NO.
I'LL BE BACK LATE.
WHATEVER YOU WANT.
IN RETROSPECT, I CAN SEE THAT I HAD ALWAYS KNOWN THAT IT WOULDN'T WORK BETWEEN US. BUT AFTER MY PITIFUL LOVE STORY IN VIENNA, I NEEDED TO BELIEVE IN SOMEONE AGAIN...
...SO MUCH SO THAT I CONTINUALLY LIED TO HIM.
I LOVE GIRLS IN SUITS.
THAT'S JUST MY STYLE!
I DON'T LIKE RUDE GIRLS.
OH! I HATE THEM!
I LIKE LIGHT EYES.
...AND I BOUGHT MYSELF BLUE CONTACTS.
BLAH BLAH BLAH BLAH BLAH BLAH BLAH BLAH BLAH BLAH
I AGREE WITH EVERYTHING YOU SAY!
HE MARRIED:
Her
AND FOUND HIMSELF WITH:
HER

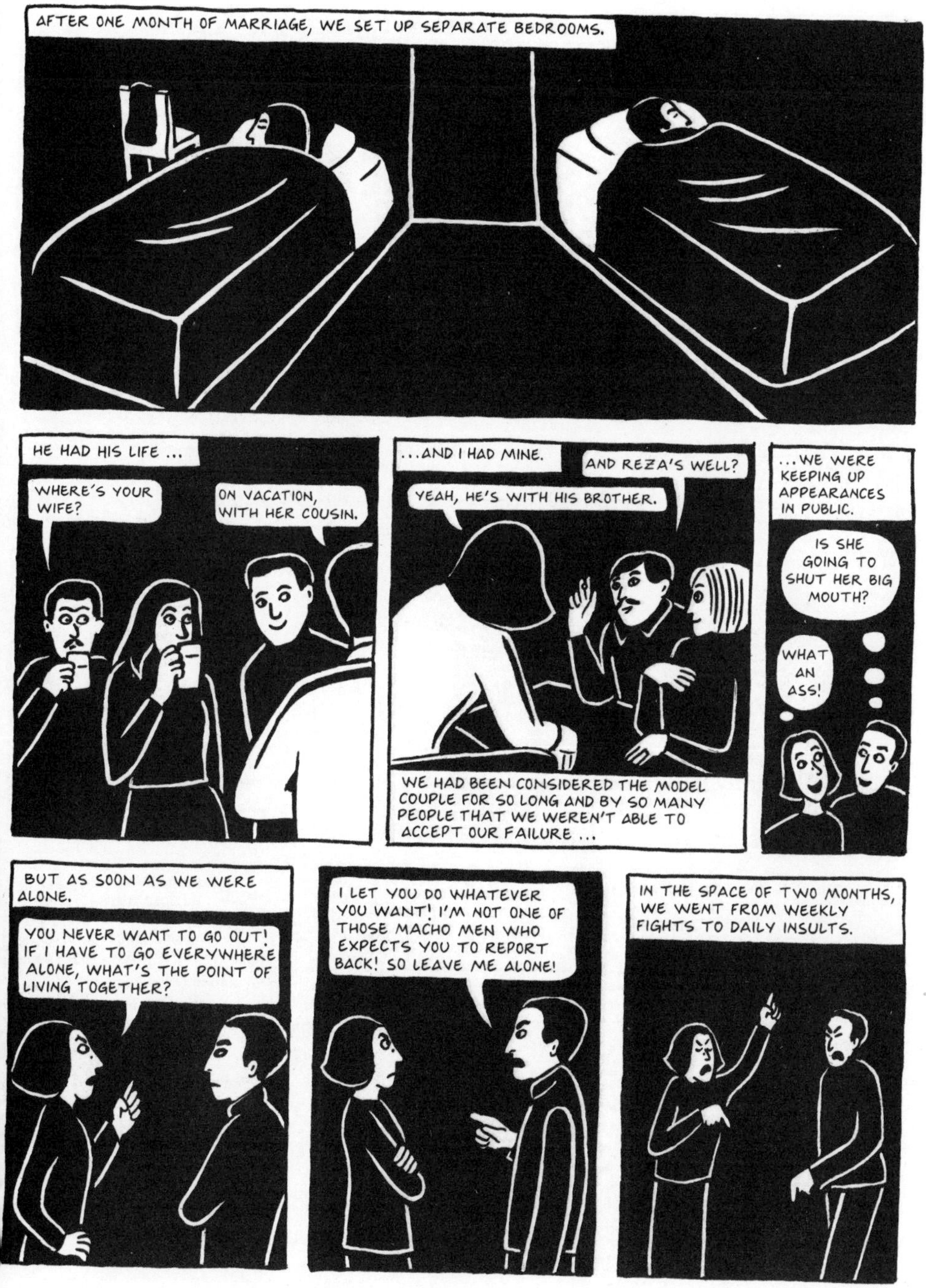

AFTER ONE MONTH OF MARRIAGE, WE SET UP SEPARATE BEDROOMS.
HE HAD HIS LIFE ...
WHERE'S YOUR WIFE?
ON VACATION, WITH HER COUSIN.
...AND I HAD MINE.
AND REZA'S WELL?
YEAH, HE'S WITH HIS BROTHER.
WE HAD BEEN CONSIDERED THE MODEL COUPLE FOR SO LONG AND BY SO MANY PEOPLE THAT WE WEREN'T ABLE TO ACCEPT OUR FAILURE ...
...WE WERE KEEPING UP APPEARANCES IN PUBLIC.
IS SHE GOING TO SHUT HER BIG MOUTH?
WHAT AN ASS!
BUT AS SOON AS WE WERE ALONE.
YOU NEVER WANT TO GO OUT! IF I HAVE TO GO EVERYWHERE ALONE, WHAT'S THE POINT OF LIVING TOGETHER?
I LET YOU DO WHATEVER YOU WANT! I'M NOT ONE OF THOSE MACHO MEN WHO EXPECTS YOU TO REPORT BACK! SO LEAVE ME ALONE!
IN THE SPACE OF TWO MONTHS, WE WENT FROM WEEKLY FIGHTS TO DAILY INSULTS.

THE SATELLITE

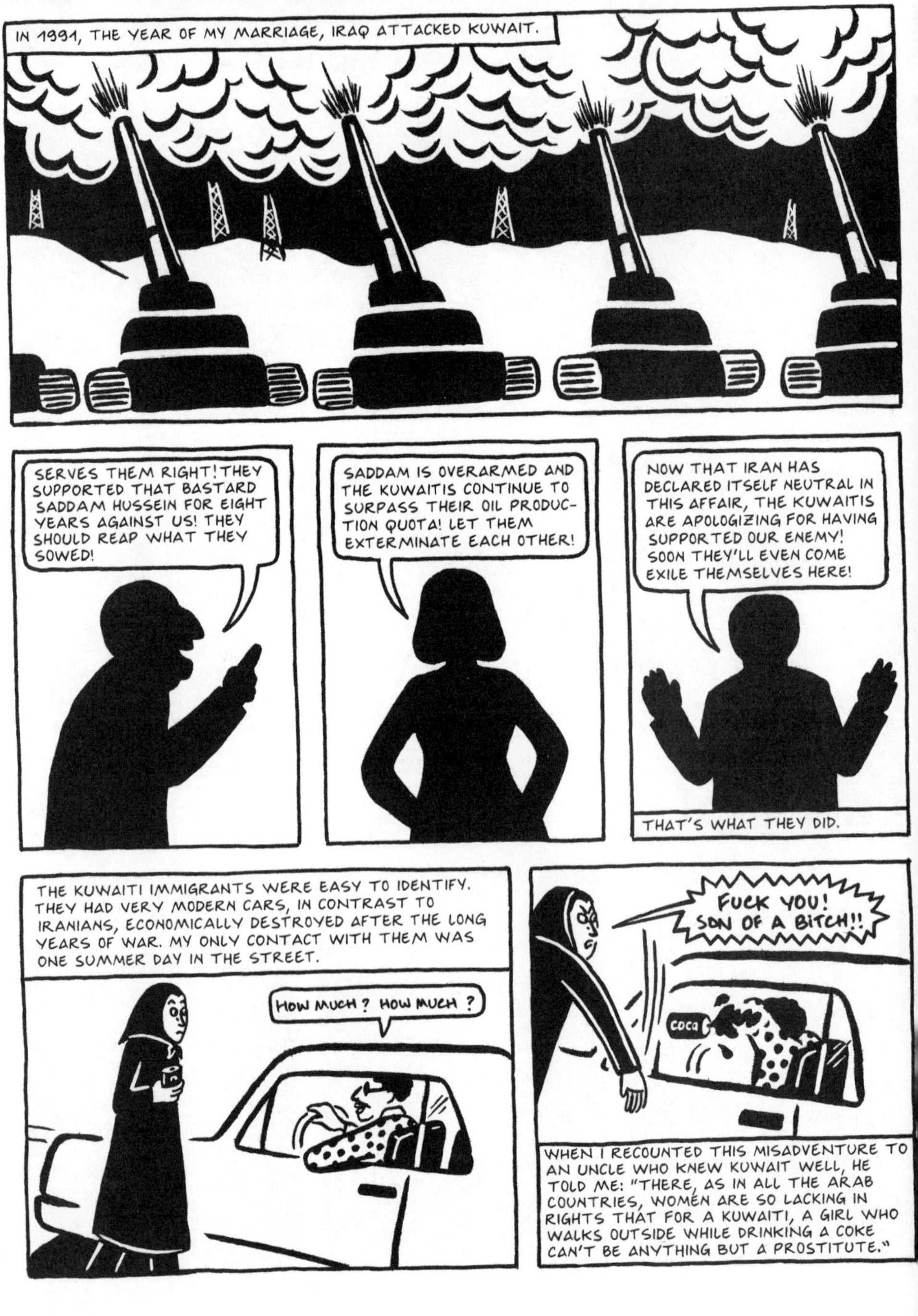
IN 1991, THE YEAR OF MY MARRIAGE, IRAQ ATTACKED KUWAIT.
SERVES THEM RIGHT! THEY SUPPORTED THAT BASTARD SADDAM HUSSEIN FOR EIGHT YEARS AGAINST US! THEY SHOULD REAP WHAT THEY SOWED!
SADDAM IS OVERARMED AND THE KUWAITIS CONTINUE TO SURPASS THEIR OIL PRODUCTION QUOTA! LET THEM EXTERMINATE EACH OTHER!
NOW THAT IRAN HAS DECLARED ITSELF NEUTRAL IN THIS AFFAIR, THE KUWAITIS ARE APOLOGIZING FOR HAVING SUPPORTED OUR ENEMY! SOON THEY'LL EVEN COME EXILE THEMSELVES HERE!
THAT'S WHAT THEY DID.
THE KUWAITI IMMIGRANTS WERE EASY TO IDENTIFY. THEY HAD VERY MODERN CARS, IN CONTRAST TO IRANIANS, ECONOMICALLY DESTROYED AFTER THE LONG YEARS OF WAR. MY ONLY CONTACT WITH THEM WAS ONE SUMMER DAY IN THE STREET.
HOW MUCH? HOW MUCH?
FUCK YOU! SON OF A BITCH!!
COCA
WHEN I RECOUNTED THIS MISADVENTURE TO AN UNCLE WHO KNEW KUWAIT WELL, HE TOLD ME: "THERE, AS IN ALL THE ARAB COUNTRIES, WOMEN ARE SO LACKING IN RIGHTS THAT FOR A KUWAITI, A GIRL WHO WALKS OUTSIDE WHILE DRINKING A COKE CAN'T BE ANYTHING BUT A PROSTITUTE."

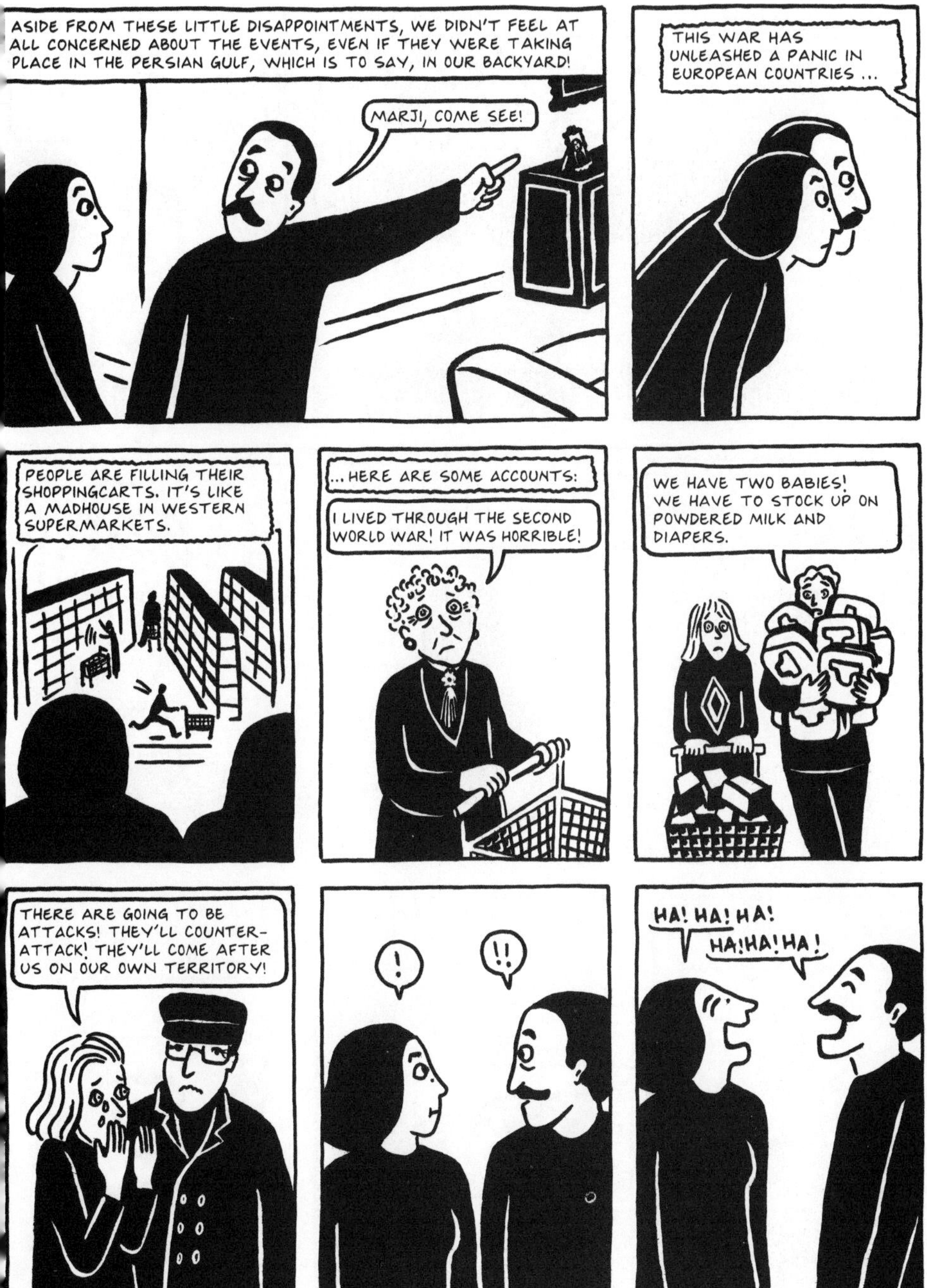

ASIDE FROM THESE LITTLE DISAPPOINTMENTS, WE DIDN'T FEEL AT ALL CONCERNED ABOUT THE EVENTS, EVEN IF THEY WERE TAKING PLACE IN THE PERSIAN GULF, WHICH IS TO SAY, IN OUR BACKYARD!
MARJI, COME SEE!
THIS WAR HAS UNLEASHED A PANIC IN EUROPEAN COUNTRIES ...
PEOPLE ARE FILLING THEIR SHOPPINGCARTS. IT'S LIKE A MADHOUSE IN WESTERN SUPERMARKETS.
... HERE ARE SOME ACCOUNTS:
I LIVED THROUGH THE SECOND WORLD WAR! IT WAS HORRIBLE!
WE HAVE TWO BABIES! WE HAVE TO STOCK UP ON POWDERED MILK AND DIAPERS.
THERE ARE GOING TO BE ATTACKS! THEY'LL COUNTER-ATTACK! THEY'LL COME AFTER US ON OUR OWN TERRITORY!
!
!!
HA! HA! HA!
HA! HA! HA!

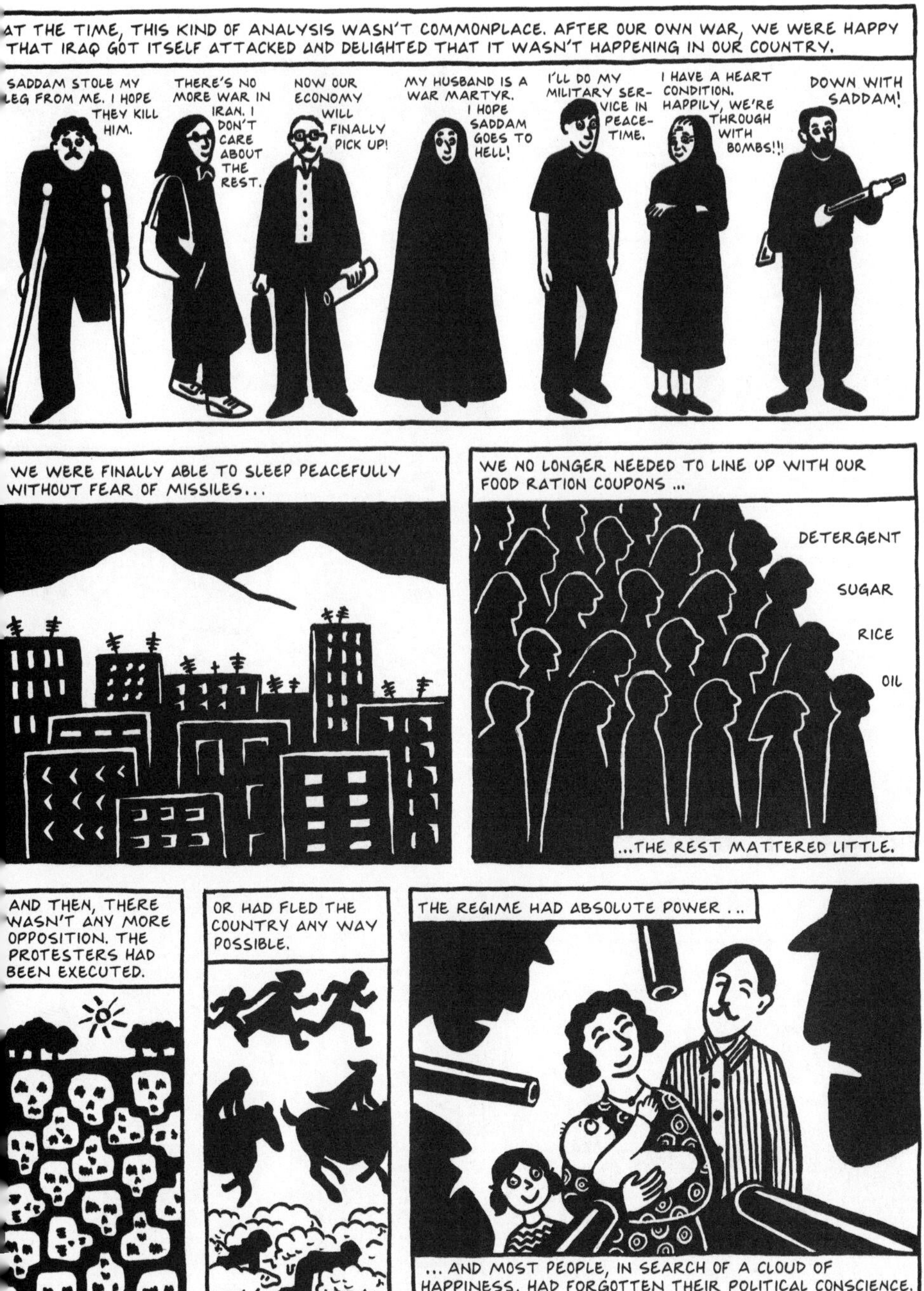
AT THE TIME, THIS KIND OF ANALYSIS WASN'T COMMONPLACE. AFTER OUR OWN WAR, WE WERE HAPPY THAT IRAQ GOT ITSELF ATTACKED AND DELIGHTED THAT IT WASN'T HAPPENING IN OUR COUNTRY.
SADDAM STOLE MY LEG FROM ME. I HOPE THEY KILL HIM.
THERE'S NO MORE WAR IN IRAN. I DON'T CARE ABOUT THE REST.
NOW OUR ECONOMY WILL FINALLY PICK UP!
MY HUSBAND IS A WAR MARTYR. I HOPE SADDAM GOES TO HELL!
I'LL DO MY MILITARY SERVICE IN PEACE-TIME.
I HAVE A HEART CONDITION. HAPPILY, WE'RE THROUGH WITH BOMBS!!!
DOWN WITH SADDAM!
WE WERE FINALLY ABLE TO SLEEP PEACEFULLY WITHOUT FEAR OF MISSILES...
WE NO LONGER NEEDED TO LINE UP WITH OUR FOOD RATION COUPONS ...
DETERGENT
SUGAR
RICE
OIL
...THE REST MATTERED LITTLE.
AND THEN, THERE WASN'T ANY MORE OPPOSITION. THE PROTESTERS HAD BEEN EXECUTED.
OR HAD FLED THE COUNTRY ANY WAY POSSIBLE.
THE REGIME HAD ABSOLUTE POWER ...
... AND MOST PEOPLE, IN SEARCH OF A CLOUD OF HAPPINESS, HAD FORGOTTEN THEIR POLITICAL CONSCIENCE.

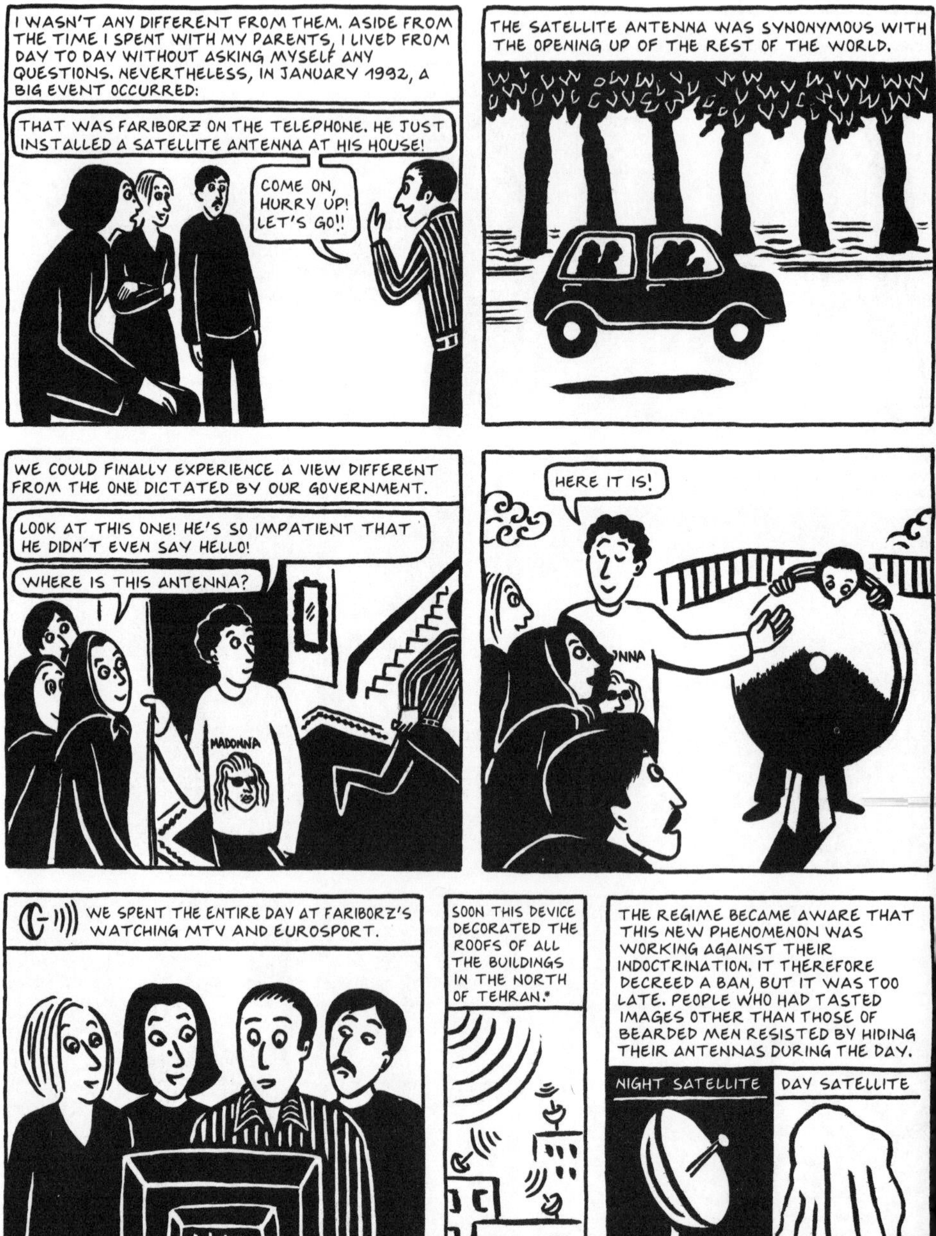
I WASN'T ANY DIFFERENT FROM THEM. ASIDE FROM THE TIME I SPENT WITH MY PARENTS, I LIVED FROM DAY TO DAY WITHOUT ASKING MYSELF ANY QUESTIONS. NEVERTHELESS, IN JANUARY 1992, A BIG EVENT OCCURRED:
THAT WAS FARIBORZ ON THE TELEPHONE. HE JUST INSTALLED A SATELLITE ANTENNA AT HIS HOUSE!
COME ON, HURRY UP! LET'S GO!!
THE SATELLITE ANTENNA WAS SYNONYMOUS WITH THE OPENING UP OF THE REST OF THE WORLD.
WE COULD FINALLY EXPERIENCE A VIEW DIFFERENT FROM THE ONE DICTATED BY OUR GOVERNMENT.
LOOK AT THIS ONE! HE'S SO IMPATIENT THAT HE DIDN'T EVEN SAY HELLO!
WHERE IS THIS ANTENNA?
MADONNA
HERE IT IS!
NNA
WE SPENT THE ENTIRE DAY AT FARIBORZ'S WATCHING MTV AND EUROSPORT.
BY THE END OF THE EVENING, OUR MINDS WERE MUCH BROADER!
SOON THIS DEVICE DECORATED THE ROOFS OF ALL THE BUILDINGS IN THE NORTH OF TEHRAN.*
THE REGIME BECAME AWARE THAT THIS NEW PHENOMENON WAS WORKING AGAINST THEIR INDOCTRINATION. IT THEREFORE DECREED A BAN, BUT IT WAS TOO LATE. PEOPLE WHO HAD TASTED IMAGES OTHER THAN THOSE OF BEARDED MEN RESISTED BY HIDING THEIR ANTENNAS DURING THE DAY.
NIGHT SATELLITE
DAY SATELLITE

*THE CHIC NEIGHBORHOODS

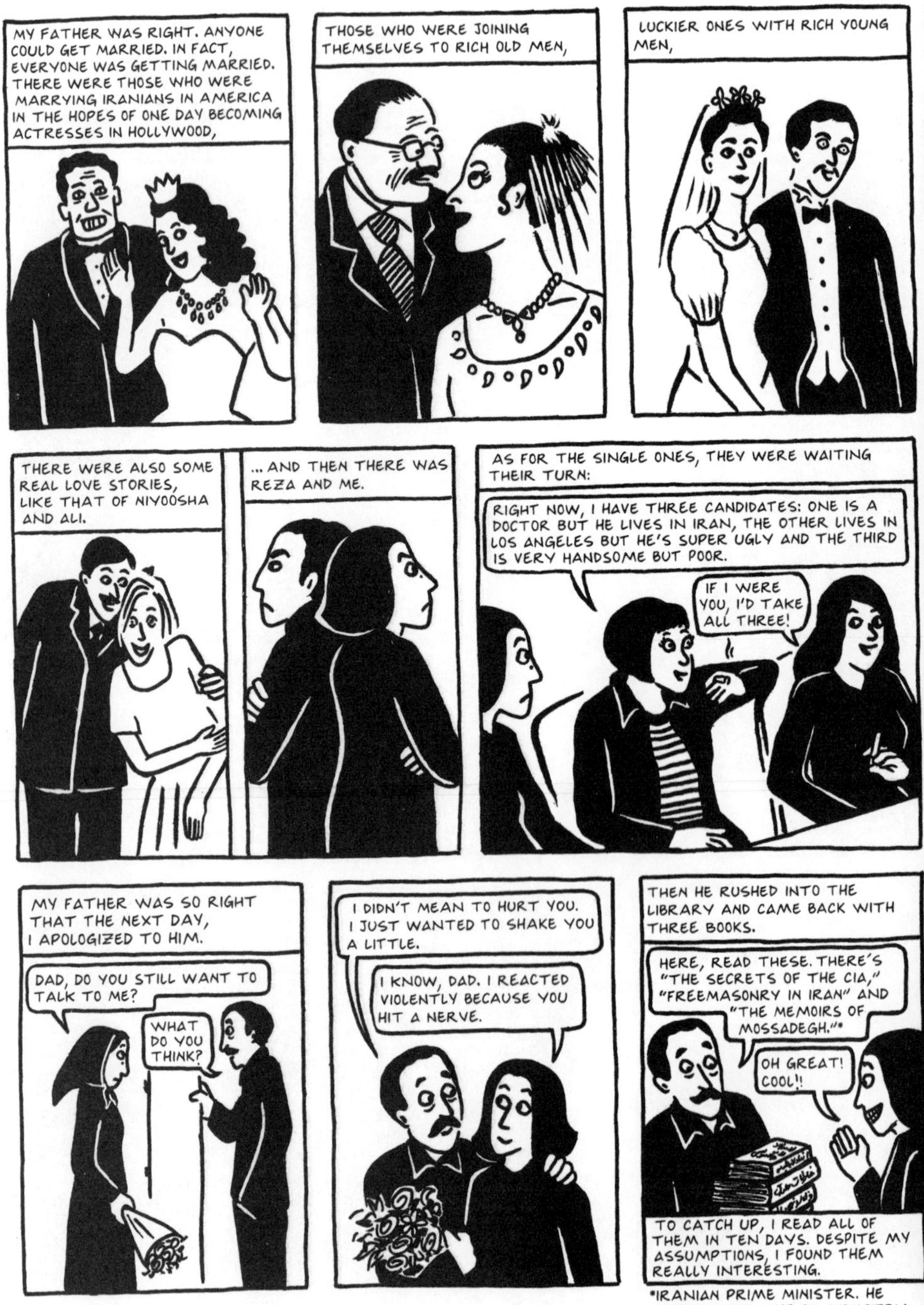
MY FATHER WAS RIGHT. ANYONE COULD GET MARRIED. IN FACT, EVERYONE WAS GETTING MARRIED. THERE WERE THOSE WHO WERE MARRYING IRANIANS IN AMERICA IN THE HOPES OF ONE DAY BECOMING ACTRESSES IN HOLLYWOOD,
THOSE WHO WERE JOINING THEMSELVES TO RICH OLD MEN,
LUCKIER ONES WITH RICH YOUNG MEN,
THERE WERE ALSO SOME REAL LOVE STORIES, LIKE THAT OF NIYOOSHA AND ALI.
... AND THEN THERE WAS REZA AND ME.
AS FOR THE SINGLE ONES, THEY WERE WAITING THEIR TURN:
RIGHT NOW, I HAVE THREE CANDIDATES: ONE IS A DOCTOR BUT HE LIVES IN IRAN, THE OTHER LIVES IN LOS ANGELES BUT HE'S SUPER UGLY AND THE THIRD IS VERY HANDSOME BUT POOR.
IF I WERE YOU, I'D TAKE ALL THREE!
MY FATHER WAS SO RIGHT THAT THE NEXT DAY, I APOLOGIZED TO HIM.
DAD, DO YOU STILL WANT TO TALK TO ME?
WHAT DO YOU THINK?
I DIDN'T MEAN TO HURT YOU. I JUST WANTED TO SHAKE YOU A LITTLE.
I KNOW, DAD. I REACTED VIOLENTLY BECAUSE YOU HIT A NERVE.
THEN HE RUSHED INTO THE LIBRARY AND CAME BACK WITH THREE BOOKS.
HERE, READ THESE. THERE'S "THE SECRETS OF THE CIA," "FREEMASONRY IN IRAN" AND "THE MEMOIRS OF MOSSADEGH."*
OH GREAT! COOL!!
TO CATCH UP, I READ ALL OF THEM IN TEN DAYS. DESPITE MY ASSUMPTIONS, I FOUND THEM REALLY INTERESTING.

*IRANIAN PRIME MINISTER. HE NATIONALIZED THE OIL INDUSTRY IN 1951.

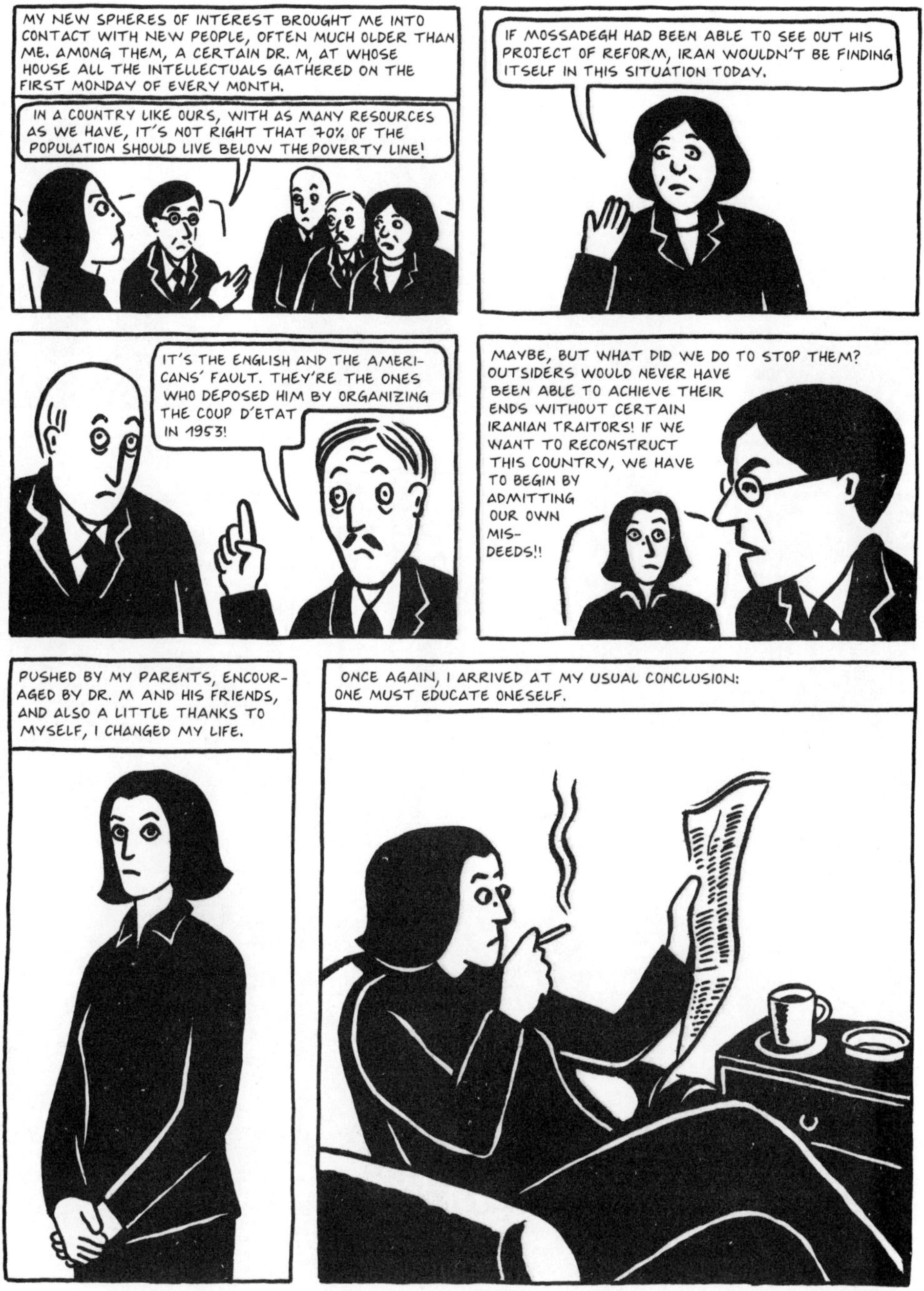
MY NEW SPHERES OF INTEREST BROUGHT ME INTO CONTACT WITH NEW PEOPLE, OFTEN MUCH OLDER THAN ME. AMONG THEM, A CERTAIN DR. M, AT WHOSE HOUSE ALL THE INTELLECTUALS GATHERED ON THE FIRST MONDAY OF EVERY MONTH.
IN A COUNTRY LIKE OURS, WITH AS MANY RESOURCES AS WE HAVE, IT'S NOT RIGHT THAT 70% OF THE POPULATION SHOULD LIVE BELOW THE POVERTY LINE!
IF MOSSADEGH HAD BEEN ABLE TO SEE OUT HIS PROJECT OF REFORM, IRAN WOULDN'T BE FINDING ITSELF IN THIS SITUATION TODAY.
IT'S THE ENGLISH AND THE AMERICANS' FAULT. THEY'RE THE ONES WHO DEPOSED HIM BY ORGANIZING THE COUP D'ETAT IN 1953!
MAYBE, BUT WHAT DID WE DO TO STOP THEM? OUTSIDERS WOULD NEVER HAVE BEEN ABLE TO ACHIEVE THEIR ENDS WITHOUT CERTAIN IRANIAN TRAITORS! IF WE WANT TO RECONSTRUCT THIS COUNTRY, WE HAVE TO BEGIN BY ADMITTING OUR OWN MISDEEDS!!
PUSHED BY MY PARENTS, ENCOURAGED BY DR. M AND HIS FRIENDS, AND ALSO A LITTLE THANKS TO MYSELF, I CHANGED MY LIFE.
ONCE AGAIN, I ARRIVED AT MY USUAL CONCLUSION: ONE MUST EDUCATE ONESELF.

THE END

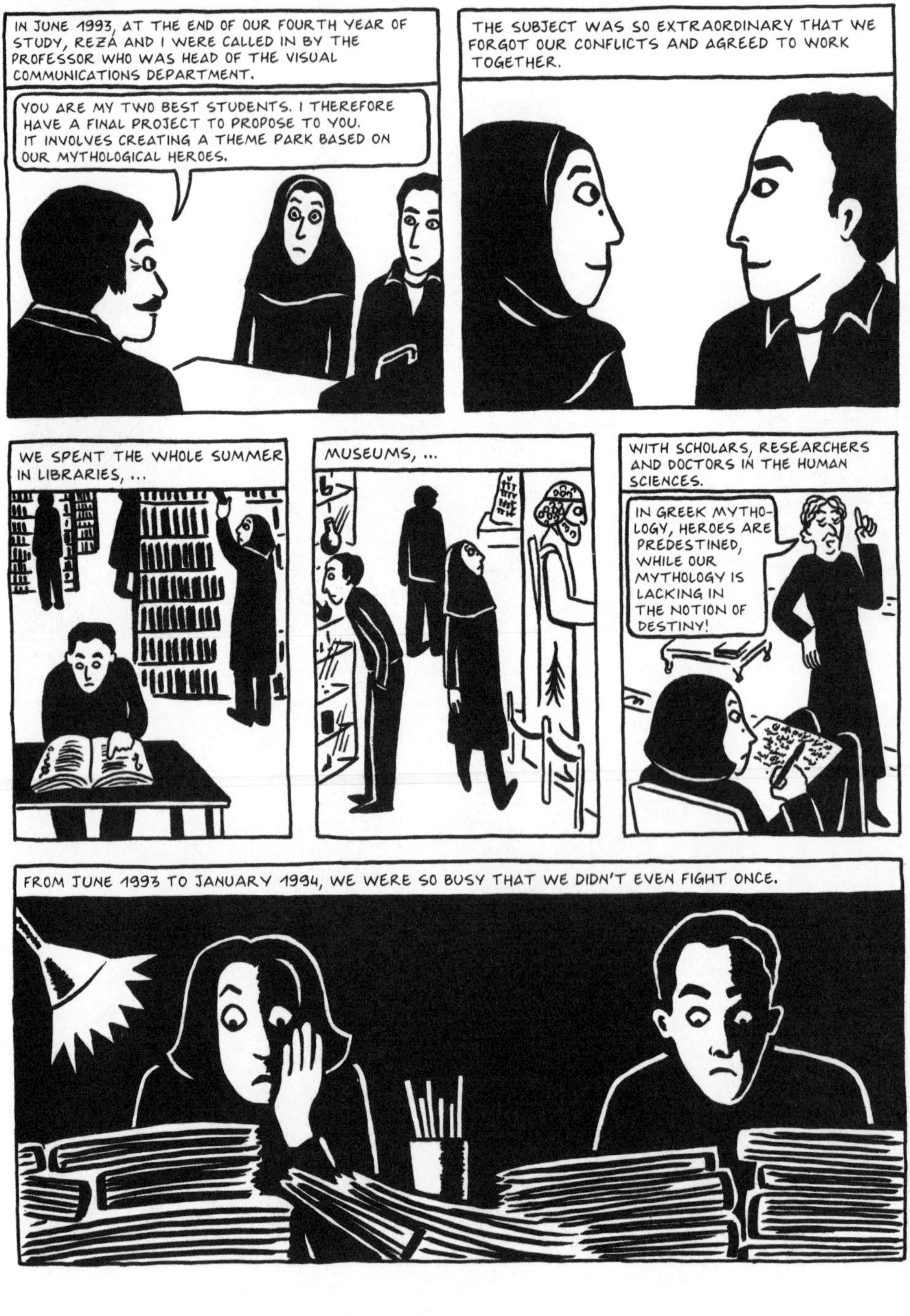
IN JUNE 1993, AT THE END OF OUR FOURTH YEAR OF STUDY, REZA AND I WERE CALLED IN BY THE PROFESSOR WHO WAS HEAD OF THE VISUAL COMMUNICATIONS DEPARTMENT.
YOU ARE MY TWO BEST STUDENTS. I THEREFORE HAVE A FINAL PROJECT TO PROPOSE TO YOU. IT INVOLVES CREATING A THEME PARK BASED ON OUR MYTHOLOGICAL HEROES.
THE SUBJECT WAS SO EXTRAORDINARY THAT WE FORGOT OUR CONFLICTS AND AGREED TO WORK TOGETHER.
WE SPENT THE WHOLE SUMMER IN LIBRARIES, ...
MUSEUMS, ...
WITH SCHOLARS, RESEARCHERS AND DOCTORS IN THE HUMAN SCIENCES.
IN GREEK MYTHOLOGY, HEROES ARE PREDESTINED, WHILE OUR MYTHOLOGY IS LACKING IN THE NOTION OF DESTINY!
FROM JUNE 1993 TO JANUARY 1994, WE WERE SO BUSY THAT WE DIDN'T EVEN FIGHT ONCE.

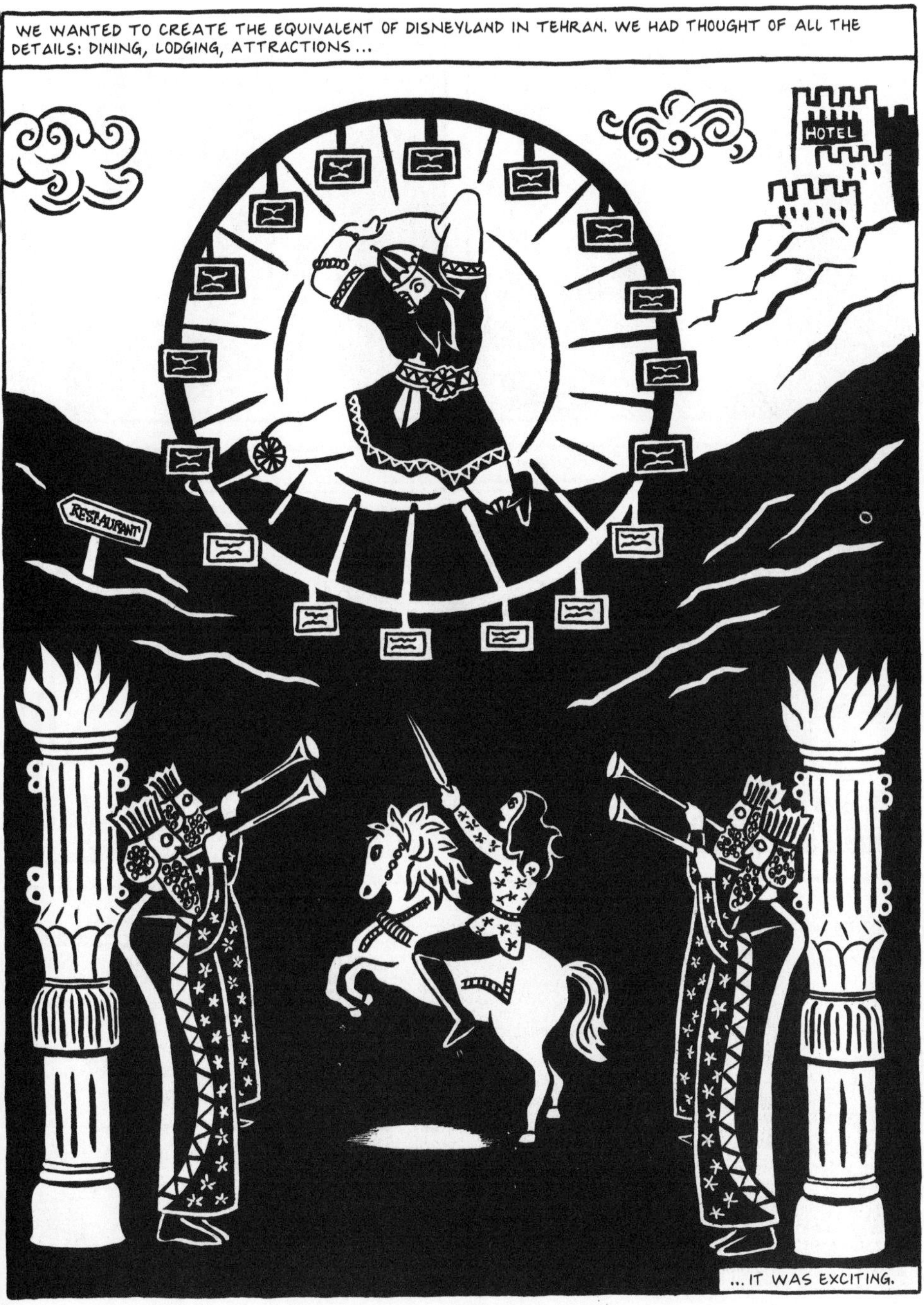
WE WANTED TO CREATE THE EQUIVALENT OF DISNEYLAND IN TEHRAN. WE HAD THOUGHT OF ALL THE DETAILS: DINING, LODGING, ATTRACTIONS...
HOTEL
RESTAURANT
...IT WAS EXCITING.

177

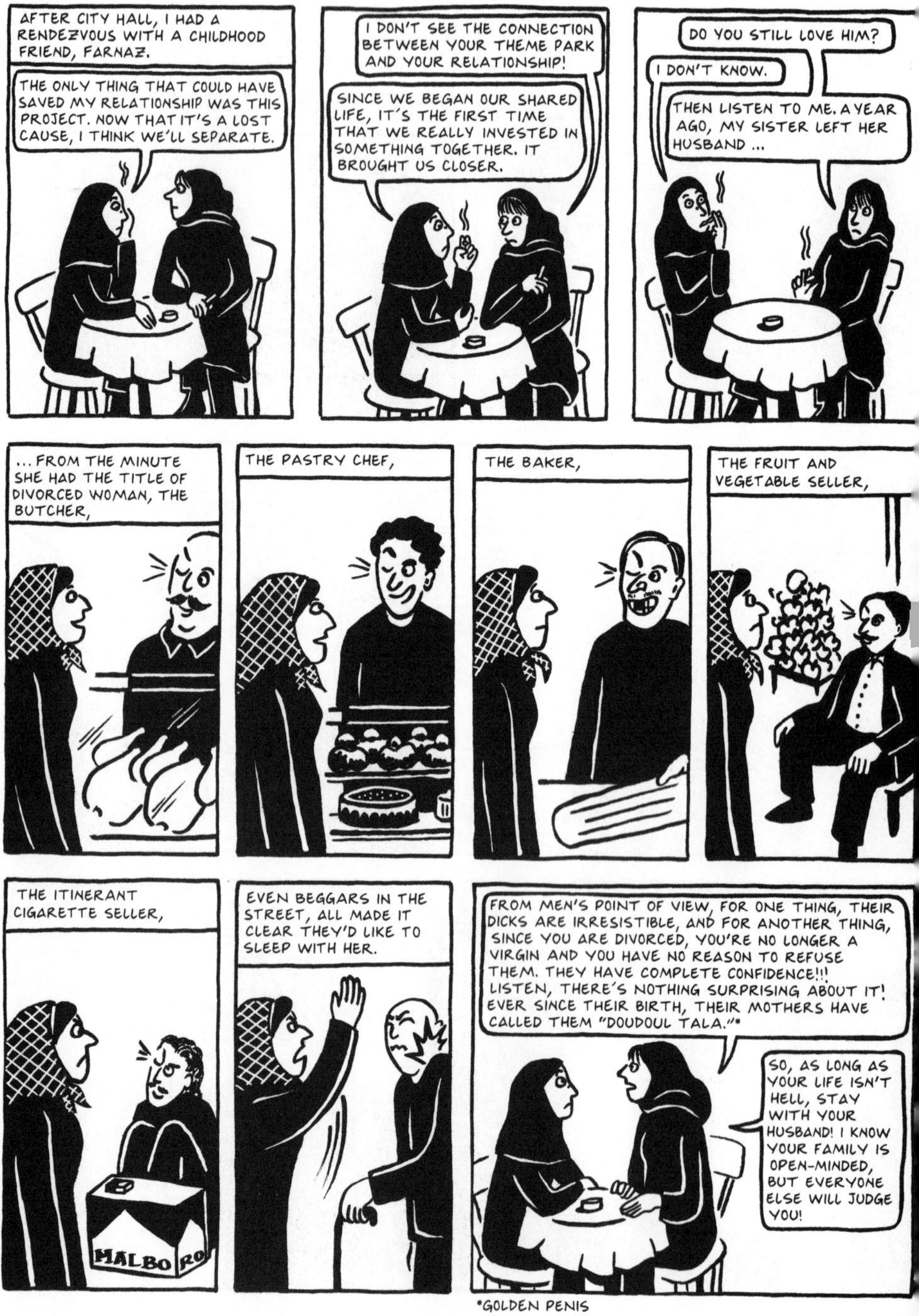
AFTER CITY HALL, I HAD A RENDEZVOUS WITH A CHILDHOOD FRIEND, FARNAZ.
THE ONLY THING THAT COULD HAVE SAVED MY RELATIONSHIP WAS THIS PROJECT. NOW THAT IT'S A LOST CAUSE, I THINK WE'LL SEPARATE.
I DON'T SEE THE CONNECTION BETWEEN YOUR THEME PARK AND YOUR RELATIONSHIP!
SINCE WE BEGAN OUR SHARED LIFE, IT'S THE FIRST TIME THAT WE REALLY INVESTED IN SOMETHING TOGETHER. IT BROUGHT US CLOSER.
DO YOU STILL LOVE HIM?
I DON'T KNOW.
THEN LISTEN TO ME. A YEAR AGO, MY SISTER LEFT HER HUSBAND ...
... FROM THE MINUTE SHE HAD THE TITLE OF DIVORCED WOMAN, THE BUTCHER,
THE PASTRY CHEF,
THE BAKER,
THE FRUIT AND VEGETABLE SELLER,
THE ITINERANT CIGARETTE SELLER,
MALBO RO
EVEN BEGGARS IN THE STREET, ALL MADE IT CLEAR THEY'D LIKE TO SLEEP WITH HER.
FROM MEN'S POINT OF VIEW, FOR ONE THING, THEIR DICKS ARE IRRESISTIBLE, AND FOR ANOTHER THING, SINCE YOU ARE DIVORCED, YOU'RE NO LONGER A VIRGIN AND YOU HAVE NO REASON TO REFUSE THEM. THEY HAVE COMPLETE CONFIDENCE!!! LISTEN, THERE'S NOTHING SURPRISING ABOUT IT! EVER SINCE THEIR BIRTH, THEIR MOTHERS HAVE CALLED THEM "DOUDOUL TALA."*
SO, AS LONG AS YOUR LIFE ISN'T HELL, STAY WITH YOUR HUSBAND! I KNOW YOUR FAMILY IS OPEN-MINDED, BUT EVERYONE ELSE WILL JUDGE YOU!

*GOLDEN PENIS

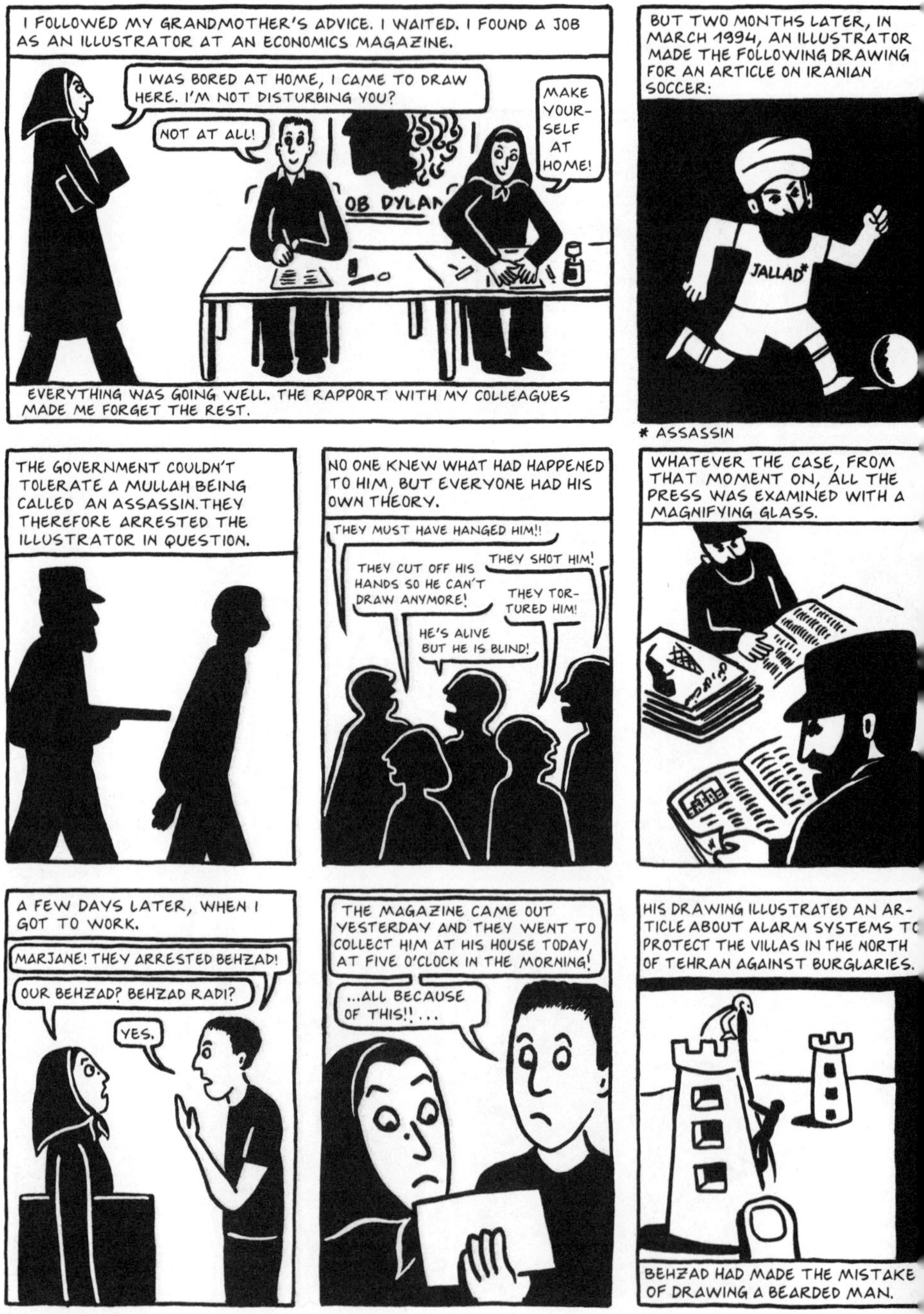

I FOLLOWED MY GRANDMOTHER'S ADVICE. I WAITED. I FOUND A JOB AS AN ILLUSTRATOR AT AN ECONOMICS MAGAZINE.
I WAS BORED AT HOME, I CAME TO DRAW HERE. I'M NOT DISTURBING YOU?
NOT AT ALL!
MAKE YOUR-SELF AT HOME!
OB DYLA
EVERYTHING WAS GOING WELL. THE RAPPORT WITH MY COLLEAGUES MADE ME FORGET THE REST.
BUT TWO MONTHS LATER, IN MARCH 1994, AN ILLUSTRATOR MADE THE FOLLOWING DRAWING FOR AN ARTICLE ON IRANIAN SOCCER:
JALLAD*
* ASSASSIN
THE GOVERNMENT COULDN'T TOLERATE A MULLAH BEING CALLED AN ASSASSIN. THEY THEREFORE ARRESTED THE ILLUSTRATOR IN QUESTION.
NO ONE KNEW WHAT HAD HAPPENED TO HIM, BUT EVERYONE HAD HIS OWN THEORY.
THEY MUST HAVE HANGED HIM!!
THEY CUT OFF HIS HANDS SO HE CAN'T DRAW ANYMORE!
THEY SHOT HIM!
THEY TOR-TURED HIM!
HE'S ALIVE BUT HE IS BLIND!
WHATEVER THE CASE, FROM THAT MOMENT ON, ALL THE PRESS WAS EXAMINED WITH A MAGNIFYING GLASS.
A FEW DAYS LATER, WHEN I GOT TO WORK.
MARJANE! THEY ARRESTED BEHZAD!
OUR BEHZAD? BEHZAD RADI?
YES.
THE MAGAZINE CAME OUT YESTERDAY AND THEY WENT TO COLLECT HIM AT HIS HOUSE TODAY, AT FIVE O'CLOCK IN THE MORNING!
...ALL BECAUSE OF THIS!! ...
HIS DRAWING ILLUSTRATED AN AR-TICLE ABOUT ALARM SYSTEMS T PROTECT THE VILLAS IN THE NORTH OF TEHRAN AGAINST BURGLARIES.
BEHZAD HAD MADE THE MISTAKE OF DRAWING A BEARDED MAN.

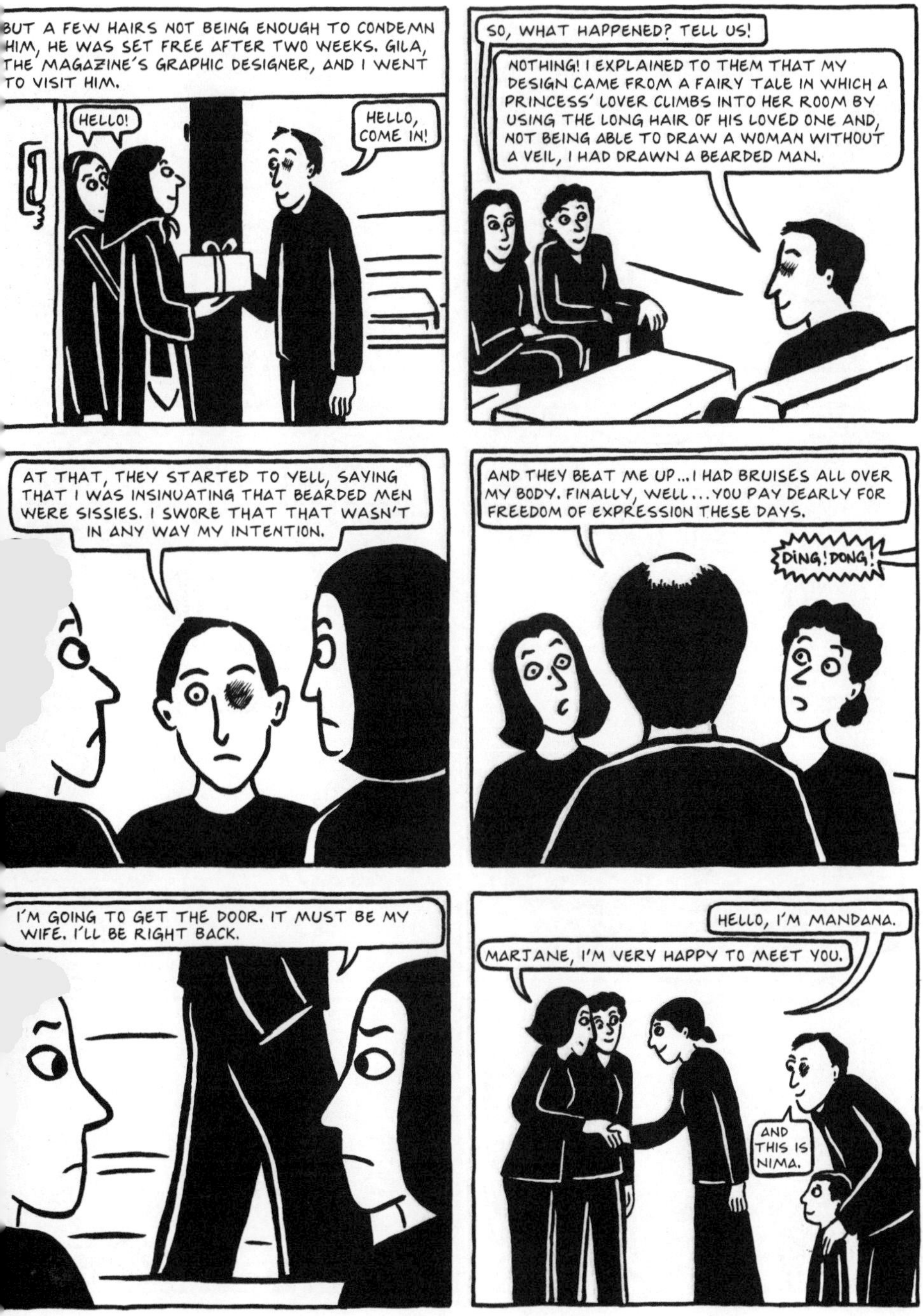
BUT A FEW HAIRS NOT BEING ENOUGH TO CONDEMN HIM, HE WAS SET FREE AFTER TWO WEEKS. GILA, THE MAGAZINE'S GRAPHIC DESIGNER, AND I WENT TO VISIT HIM.
HELLO!
HELLO, COME IN!
SO, WHAT HAPPENED? TELL US!
NOTHING! I EXPLAINED TO THEM THAT MY DESIGN CAME FROM A FAIRY TALE IN WHICH A PRINCESS' LOVER CLIMBS INTO HER ROOM BY USING THE LONG HAIR OF HIS LOVED ONE AND, NOT BEING ABLE TO DRAW A WOMAN WITHOUT A VEIL, I HAD DRAWN A BEARDED MAN.
AT THAT, THEY STARTED TO YELL, SAYING THAT I WAS INSINUATING THAT BEARDED MEN WERE SISSIES. I SWORE THAT THAT WASN'T IN ANY WAY MY INTENTION.
AND THEY BEAT ME UP... I HAD BRUISES ALL OVER MY BODY. FINALLY, WELL... YOU PAY DEARLY FOR FREEDOM OF EXPRESSION THESE DAYS.
DING! DONG!
I'M GOING TO GET THE DOOR. IT MUST BE MY WIFE. I'LL BE RIGHT BACK.
HELLO, I'M MANDANA.
MARJANE, I'M VERY HAPPY TO MEET YOU.
AND THIS IS NIMA.

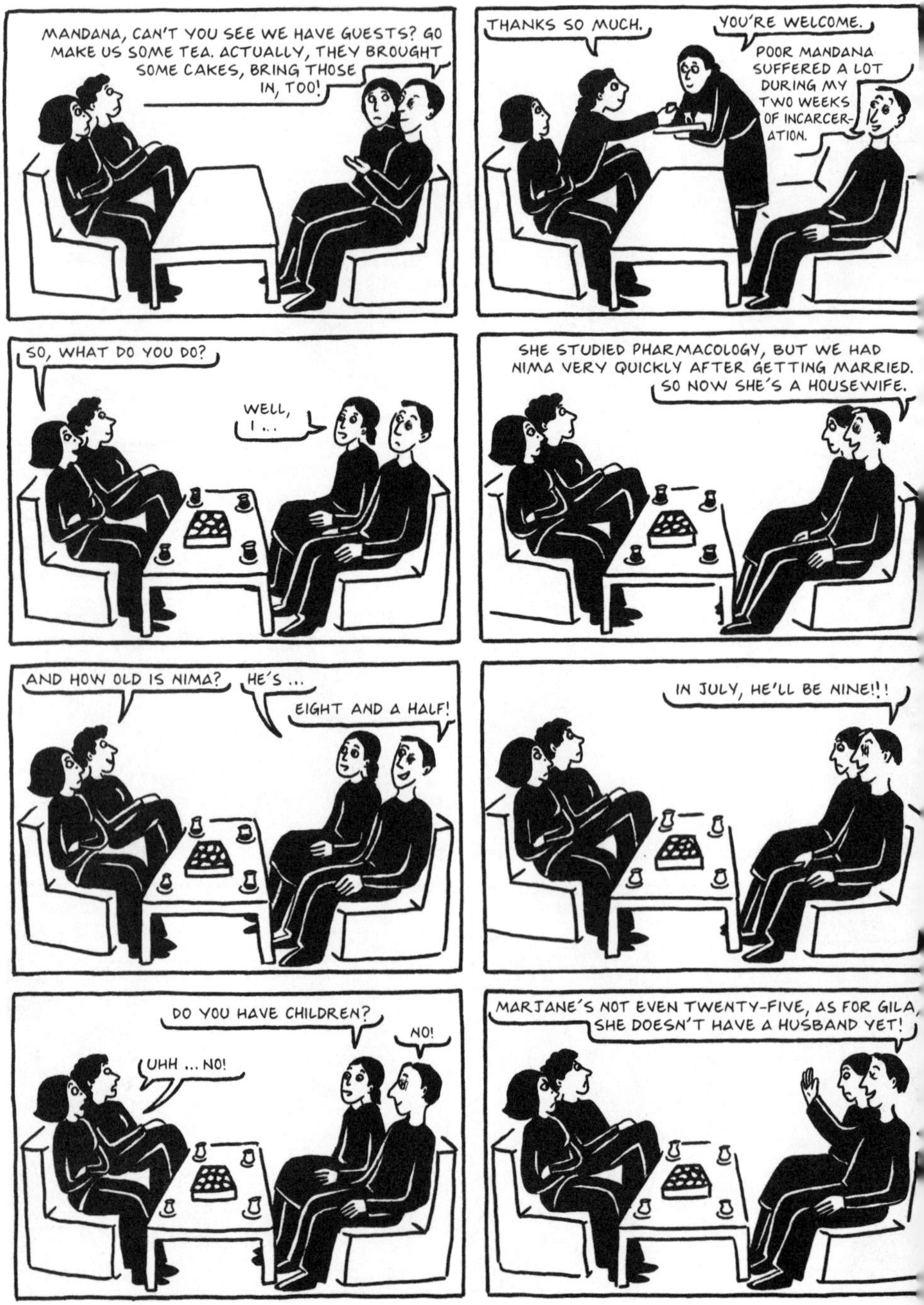

MANDANA, CAN'T YOU SEE WE HAVE GUESTS? GO MAKE US SOME TEA. ACTUALLY, THEY BROUGHT SOME CAKES, BRING THOSE IN, TOO!
THANKS SO MUCH.
YOU'RE WELCOME.
POOR MANDANA SUFFERED A LOT DURING MY TWO WEEKS OF INCARCERATION.
SO, WHAT DO YOU DO?
WELL, I ...
SHE STUDIED PHARMACOLOGY, BUT WE HAD NIMA VERY QUICKLY AFTER GETTING MARRIED. SO NOW SHE'S A HOUSEWIFE.
AND HOW OLD IS NIMA?
HE'S ...
EIGHT AND A HALF!
IN JULY, HE'LL BE NINE!!!
DO YOU HAVE CHILDREN?
UHH ... NO!
NO!
MARJANE'S NOT EVEN TWENTY-FIVE, AS FOR GILA, SHE DOESN'T HAVE A HUSBAND YET!

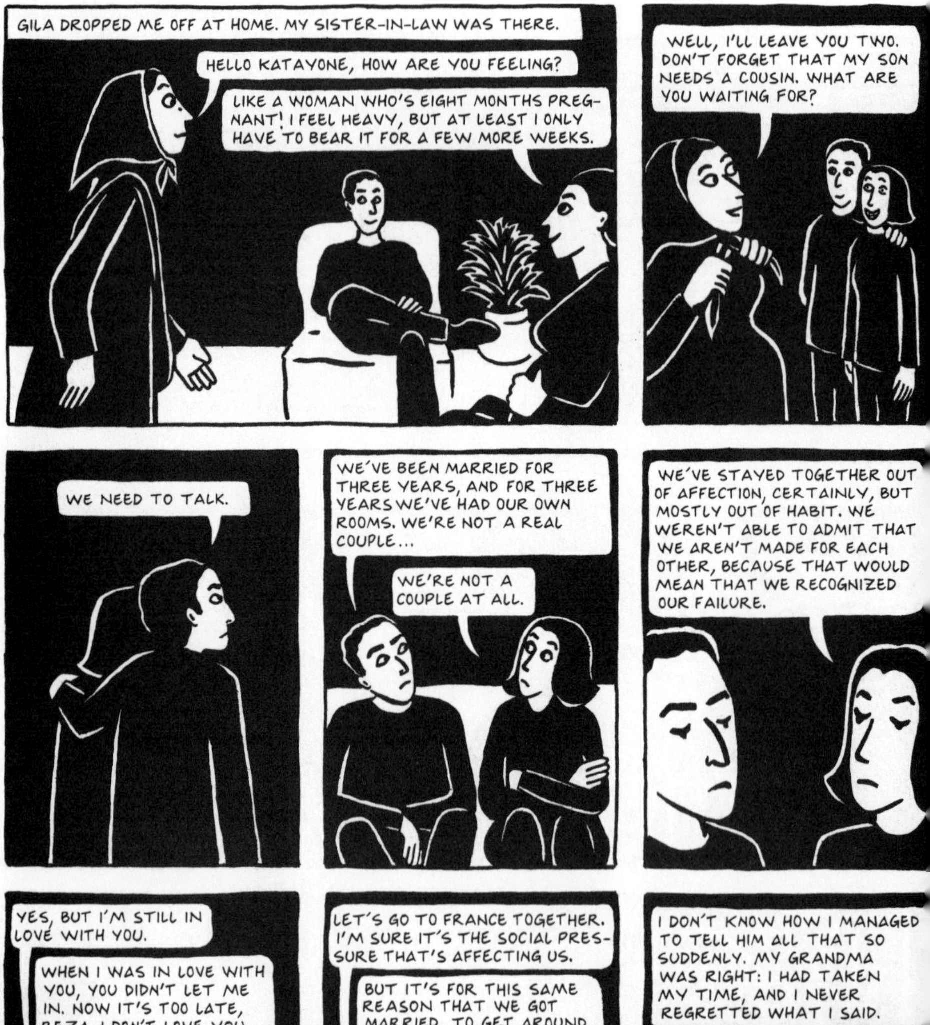
GILA DROPPED ME OFF AT HOME. MY SISTER-IN-LAW WAS THERE.
HELLO KATAYONE, HOW ARE YOU FEELING?
LIKE A WOMAN WHO'S EIGHT MONTHS PREGNANT! I FEEL HEAVY, BUT AT LEAST I ONLY HAVE TO BEAR IT FOR A FEW MORE WEEKS.
WELL, I'LL LEAVE YOU TWO. DON'T FORGET THAT MY SON NEEDS A COUSIN. WHAT ARE YOU WAITING FOR?
WE NEED TO TALK.
WE'VE BEEN MARRIED FOR THREE YEARS, AND FOR THREE YEARS WE'VE HAD OUR OWN ROOMS. WE'RE NOT A REAL COUPLE...
WE'RE NOT A COUPLE AT ALL.
WE'VE STAYED TOGETHER OUT OF AFFECTION, CERTAINLY, BUT MOSTLY OUT OF HABIT. WE WEREN'T ABLE TO ADMIT THAT WE AREN'T MADE FOR EACH OTHER, BECAUSE THAT WOULD MEAN THAT WE RECOGNIZED OUR FAILURE.
YES, BUT I'M STILL IN LOVE WITH YOU.
WHEN I WAS IN LOVE WITH YOU, YOU DIDN'T LET ME IN. NOW IT'S TOO LATE, REZA. I DON'T LOVE YOU ANYMORE.
LET'S GO TO FRANCE TOGETHER. I'M SURE IT'S THE SOCIAL PRESSURE THAT'S AFFECTING US.
BUT IT'S FOR THIS SAME REASON THAT WE GOT MARRIED, TO GET AROUND THE SOCIAL PRESSURE. OUR LOVE HAS BEEN DEAD FOR A LONG TIME! THERE'S NO POINT IN TRYING AGAIN. IT'S A WASTE OF TIME.
I DON'T KNOW HOW I MANAGED TO TELL HIM ALL THAT SO SUDDENLY. MY GRANDMA WAS RIGHT: I HAD TAKEN MY TIME, AND I NEVER REGRETTED WHAT I SAID.

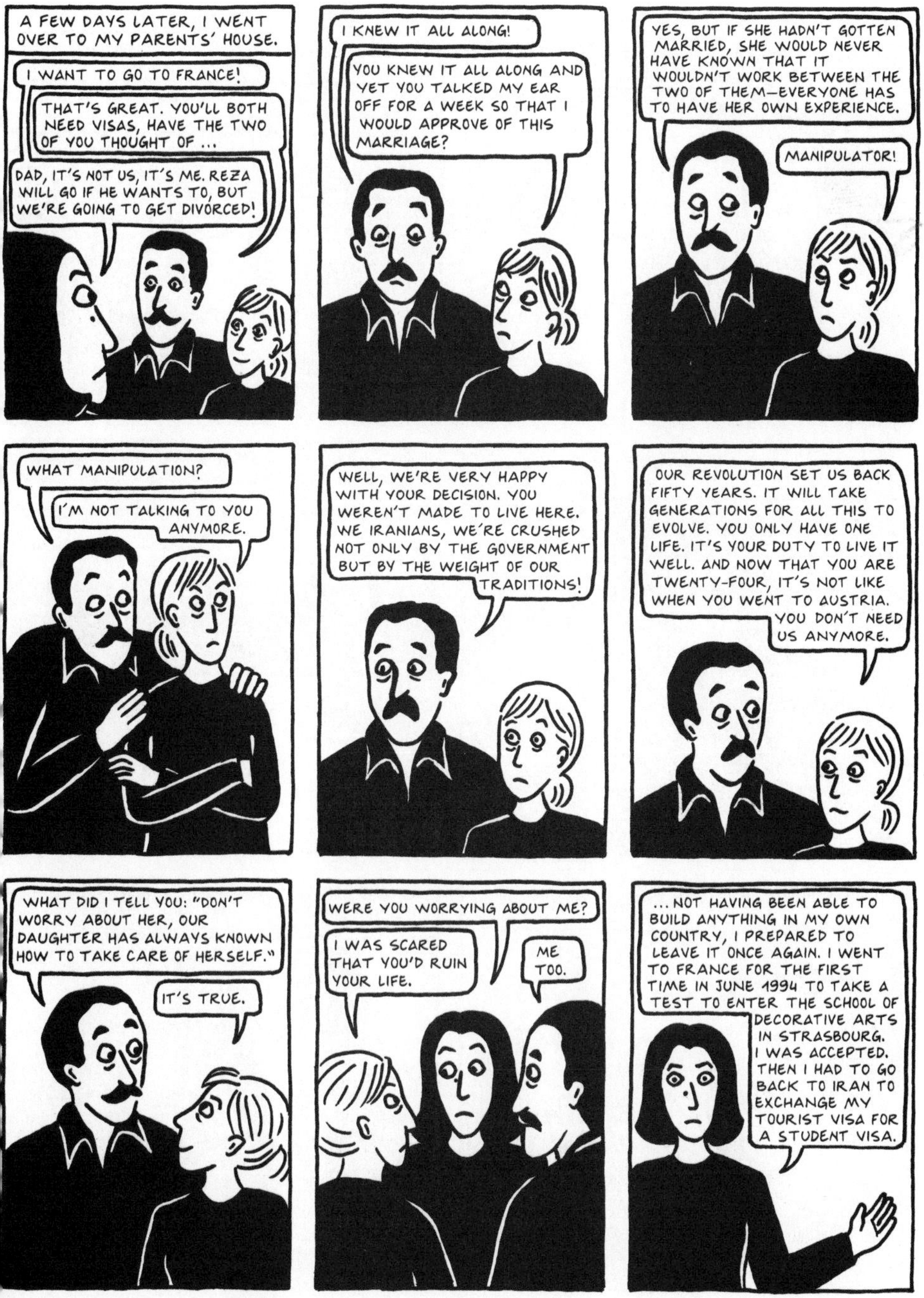
A FEW DAYS LATER, I WENT OVER TO MY PARENTS' HOUSE.
I WANT TO GO TO FRANCE!
THAT'S GREAT. YOU'LL BOTH NEED VISAS, HAVE THE TWO OF YOU THOUGHT OF ...
DAD, IT'S NOT US, IT'S ME. REZA WILL GO IF HE WANTS TO, BUT WE'RE GOING TO GET DIVORCED!
I KNEW IT ALL ALONG!
YOU KNEW IT ALL ALONG AND YET YOU TALKED MY EAR OFF FOR A WEEK SO THAT I WOULD APPROVE OF THIS MARRIAGE?
YES, BUT IF SHE HADN'T GOTTEN MARRIED, SHE WOULD NEVER HAVE KNOWN THAT IT WOULDN'T WORK BETWEEN THE TWO OF THEM—EVERYONE HAS TO HAVE HER OWN EXPERIENCE.
MANIPULATOR!
WHAT MANIPULATION?
I'M NOT TALKING TO YOU ANYMORE.
WELL, WE'RE VERY HAPPY WITH YOUR DECISION. YOU WEREN'T MADE TO LIVE HERE. WE IRANIANS, WE'RE CRUSHED NOT ONLY BY THE GOVERNMENT BUT BY THE WEIGHT OF OUR TRADITIONS!
OUR REVOLUTION SET US BACK FIFTY YEARS. IT WILL TAKE GENERATIONS FOR ALL THIS TO EVOLVE. YOU ONLY HAVE ONE LIFE. IT'S YOUR DUTY TO LIVE IT WELL. AND NOW THAT YOU ARE TWENTY-FOUR, IT'S NOT LIKE WHEN YOU WENT TO AUSTRIA. YOU DON'T NEED US ANYMORE.
WHAT DID I TELL YOU: "DON'T WORRY ABOUT HER, OUR DAUGHTER HAS ALWAYS KNOWN HOW TO TAKE CARE OF HERSELF."
IT'S TRUE.
WERE YOU WORRYING ABOUT ME?
I WAS SCARED THAT YOU'D RUIN YOUR LIFE.
ME TOO.
... NOT HAVING BEEN ABLE TO BUILD ANYTHING IN MY OWN COUNTRY, I PREPARED TO LEAVE IT ONCE AGAIN. I WENT TO FRANCE FOR THE FIRST TIME IN JUNE 1994 TO TAKE A TEST TO ENTER THE SCHOOL OF DECORATIVE ARTS IN STRASBOURG. I WAS ACCEPTED. THEN I HAD TO GO BACK TO IRAN TO EXCHANGE MY TOURIST VISA FOR A STUDENT VISA.

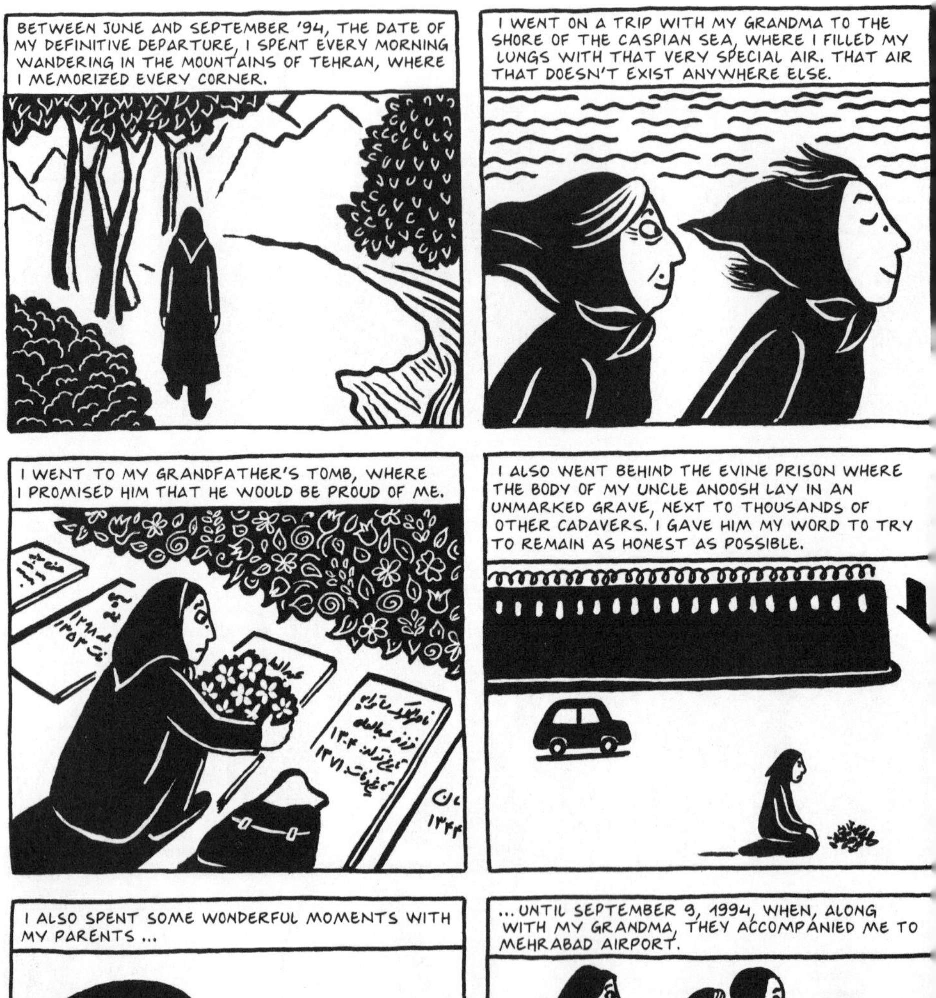
BETWEEN JUNE AND SEPTEMBER '94, THE DATE OF MY DEFINITIVE DEPARTURE, I SPENT EVERY MORNING WANDERING IN THE MOUNTAINS OF TEHRAN, WHERE I MEMORIZED EVERY CORNER.
I WENT ON A TRIP WITH MY GRANDMA TO THE SHORE OF THE CASPIAN SEA, WHERE I FILLED MY LUNGS WITH THAT VERY SPECIAL AIR. THAT AIR THAT DOESN'T EXIST ANYWHERE ELSE.
I WENT TO MY GRANDFATHER'S TOMB, WHERE I PROMISED HIM THAT HE WOULD BE PROUD OF ME.
I ALSO WENT BEHIND THE EVINE PRISON WHERE THE BODY OF MY UNCLE ANOOSH LAY IN AN UNMARKED GRAVE, NEXT TO THOUSANDS OF OTHER CADAVERS. I GAVE HIM MY WORD TO TRY TO REMAIN AS HONEST AS POSSIBLE.
I ALSO SPENT SOME WONDERFUL MOMENTS WITH MY PARENTS ...
... UNTIL SEPTEMBER 9, 1994, WHEN, ALONG WITH MY GRANDMA, THEY ACCOMPANIED ME TO MEHRABAD AIRPORT.

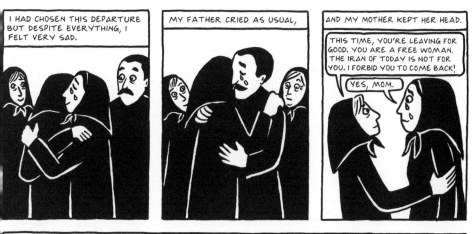

I HAD CHOSEN THIS DEPARTURE BUT DESPITE EVERYTHING, I FELT VERY SAD.

MY FATHER CRIED AS USUAL,

AND MY MOTHER KEPT HER HEAD.

THIS TIME, YOU'RE LEAVING FOR GOOD. YOU ARE A FREE WOMAN. THE IRAN OF TODAY IS NOT FOR YOU. I FORBID YOU TO COME BACK!

YES, MOM.

THE GOODBYES WERE MUCH LESS PAINFUL THAN TEN YEARS BEFORE WHEN I EMBARKED FOR AUSTRIA: THERE WAS NO LONGER A WAR, I WAS NO LONGER A CHILD, MY MOTHER DIDN'T FAINT AND MY GRANDMA WAS THERE, HAPPILY...

... HAPPILY, BECAUSE SINCE THE NIGHT OF SEPTEMBER 9, 1994, I ONLY SAW HER AGAIN ONCE, DURING THE IRANIAN NEW YEAR IN MARCH 1995. SHE DIED JANUARY 4, 1996 ... FREEDOM HAD A PRICE ...

CREDIT
Lettering: Céline Merrien

THANKS TO
Emile Bravo
Amber Hoover
Jean-Christophe Menu
Céline Merrien
Anjali Singh